New Urbanism and American Planning:
The Conflict of Cultures

Planning, History and the Environment Series

Published titles

New Urbanism and American Planning: The Conflict of Cultures

Emily Talen

Routledge
Taylor & Francis Group

NEW YORK AND LONDON

First published 2005 by Routledge,
270 Madison Avenue, New York, NY 10016

Simultaneously published in the UK
by Routledge
2 Park Square, Milton Park, Abingdon,
Oxfordshire OX14 4RN

Routledge is an imprint of the Taylor & Francis Group, an informa business

Reprinted 2006

This book was commissioned and edited by Alexandrine Press, Oxford

British Library Cataloguing in Publication Data
A catalogue record for this book is available from the British Library

Library of Congress Cataloging in Publication Data
Talen, Emily, 1958-
New urbanism and American planning : the conflict of cultures / Emily Talen.
    p. cm. – (Planning, history, and environment series)
Summary: "Presents the history of American planners' quest for good cities
and shows how New Urbanism is a culmination of ideas that have been evolving
since the nineteenth century. Identifies four approaches to city-making:
incrementalism, plan-making, planned communities, and regionalism. Shows how
these cultures connect, overlap, and conflict"–Provided by publisher.
Includes bibliographical references and index.
ISBN 0-415-70132-5 (hb : alk. paper) – ISBN 0-415-70133-3 (pb : alk. paper)
1. City planning--United States–History. 2. Cities and towns--United
States--History. I. Title. II. Series: Planning, history, and the
environment series.
HT167.T35 2005
307.1'216'0973--dc22
2005009165

ISBN 10: 0–415–70132–5 (Hbk)
ISBN 10: 0–415–70133–3 (Pbk)

ISBN 13: 978–0–415–70132–7 (Hbk)
ISBN 13: 978–0–415–70133–4 (Pbk)

Contents

For Gerald and Emma Talen
Who know a good place when they see one

Foreword

Within the field of American planning history this is a very unusual book. The most common texts are primarily descriptive *tours d'horizon* ranging from the insightful *The Making of Urban America* by John Reps and Jonathan Barnett's *The Elusive City* to the many desiccated quasi-official compilations. There are also a few critical engagements of certain specific subjects like Keller Easterling's *Organization Space*. But none has yet attempted a unifying theory for the spectacle that regularly oscillates between rigid technocratic protocols and spineless pandering to the market. Emily Talen's book does.

This is also an unlikely book. It is authored by a member of the *haute-académie* who dares to break cardinal (if unstated) rules. In the teeth of a discourse that has dedicated half a century to the destruction of all authority and the privileging of diversity, Emily Talen dares to propose a comprehensive theory. Furthermore, within an ethos of pessimistic abdication to vast and unpredictable forces, the hypothesis is positivistic and entirely free of irony. And to top it all the conclusion supports the ascendancy of the new urbanism – the devil incarnate of academic discourse. This is truly beyond the pale. Surely this book must be one of those proliferating fundamentalist tracts.

Hardly so. Emily Talen is cognizant of the current academic trends, but she is also immersed in the realities of planning and has studied the actual practice of the new urbanism. How refreshing it is to enter into conversation with someone who knows what is really going on, so that we can get on with the pursuit of what is to be done. How different this is from the 'debate', which seldom rises above the wilful misunderstanding of the new urbanism and hazy, lazy, assumptions about the alternative of suburban sprawl.

The courage to draw conclusions unrestricted by ideology has resulted in an explanation for an unexpected phenomenon: how is it that the new urbanism has succeeded against all odds in dominating the discourse of planning? And, to a growing extent, how is it that new urbanism is forming the nucleus around which disparate forces gather – forces that do not agree that an institutionalized artistic *avant garde* is the only critical position relative to the problems of culture, society and environment?

From the daily manoeuvring within the dissipated American reality arises the intellectual roughness that Robert Beauregard has identified as a singular asset of the new urbanism. By tracing the tensions within urbanism that evolved within this context and are writ large across a century, Emily Talen has been able to resolve, with the retroactive clarity of a mystery novel, the contradictory threads of American planning.

The tensions are many and they are fundamental. The new urbanism is both highly theoretical and deeply immersed in practice, such that the general principles of the Congress for the New Urbanism's (CNU) Charter are circumstantially adjusted through the process of the *charrette*. There are the contradictory prerogatives of art or technique; codes versus everyday urbanism; imposed order versus organidevelopment; private profit and public good; and the recent fruitful quarrel with environmentalism that is the showdown between Eden and the New Jerusalem. The new urbanism is energized by these tensions and immunized by them. Only those who can sustain complexity can long remain new urbanists; others revert to the easy comforts of permanent uncertainties.

It is not the individual new urbanist who adeptly entertains these contradictions but the collective, for the new urbanism is a movement. This generation of work does not belong to individuals – from Le Corbusier to Hillier, with their resolved theories – but rather to an enormously diversified expertise organized by the shared nemesis to suburban sprawl, what Emily Talen calls 'anti-urbanism'.

Another source of new urbanist strength is the discovery that it is possible to do something about the problem. The new urbanism operates to reform the reality, not by expressing the situation through critique or art. That is the difference between the CNU and the other comprehensive urban theory, that proposed by the Office for Metropolitan Architecture (OMA). There is nevertheless much overlap, as Ellen Dunham Jones has written in *Harvard Design Magazine*, because both are interested in the same urban degeneracy. OMA and its excellent research arm, the Harvard School of Design, are, in fact, very useful to all of us. What is to be done with what is learned is where the movements differ.

As Alex Krieger has said, 'You cannot debate a new urbanist, because whenever a good idea is proposed, they will appropriate it'. So be it. New urbanists assimilate what works best in the long run. It is a deeply American pragmatism that is at the heart of Emily Talen's thesis. It is possible that the new urbanists may be the first generation of post-war planners to not fail in thoroughly changing the inevitable outcome of modernism.

Andrés Duany

Acknowledgements

I owe intellectual debts to Jim Kunstler and Andrés Duany. They are to New Urbanism what Lewis Mumford and Raymond Unwin were to an earlier generation of urbanists and planners. Whatever they lack in political correctness they more than make up for by being extraordinarily wise on the subject of urbanism.

Two people who helped me sort through some important theoretical issues in the beginning were Thomas Dozeman, a theologian, who introduced me to the writings of Mary Douglas, and Frederick Turner, a cultural theorist, who enlightened me about the problem of the 'order-disorder dualism'.

I especially want to thank my many New Urbanist compatriots. They are an amazing group, and I have learned a tremendous amount by participating in their rigorous discussions (mostly by way of the 'advanced seminar' listserve known as 'pro-urb'). I have been educated in particular by, and would like to give special acknowledgement to, Lucy Rowland, David Brain, Philip Bess, John Massengale, Sandy Sorlien (thanks for the photos, too, Sandy), Ann Daigle, Diane Dorney, Douglas Duany, Peter Swift, Patrick Pinnell, Payton Chung, Laura Hall, Stefanos Polyzoides, Rob Steuteville, Phil Langdon, Michael Mehaffy, Tom Low, Bill Spikowski, Laurence Aurbach, and Lee Sobel.

Academic friends who have enlightened me on topics included in this book are Ellen Dunham-Jones, Dan Solomon, Patrick Condon, Chuck Bohl, Ernesto Arias and Cliff Ellis. Phyllis Bleiweis, Robert Davis, and all the folks at the Seaside Institute need special thanks for caring about the intellectual advancement of New Urbanism.

I am indebted to colleagues who took the time to comment on earlier drafts, especially Randall Arendt, Doug Kelbaugh, Robert Fishman, and Alex Krieger.

I am grateful to my colleagues in the Society for American City and Regional Planning History (SACRPH, pronounced 'sack-riff'), especially Chris Silver, Bruce Stephenson, Eric Sandweiss, Mervyn Miller and Larry Gerckens. Anyone interested in the past or future of New Urbanism and American planning should immediately become a member of this worthy organization (http://www.urban.uiuc.edu/sacrph/).

John Reps, the pre-eminent planning historian, deserves a special thanks for making available on-line a wealth of writings from the annals of American planning history, and I used them liberally (http://www.library.cornell.edu/Reps/DOCS/). In the same pre-eminent camp, I am indebted to Peter Hall for writing *Cities of Tomorrow*, a work I have come to rely on.

Students at the University of Illinois who have helped me along the way are Genevieve Borich, David Sidney, Todd Bjerkaas, Jason Brody and Zachary Borders.

Ann Rudkin, my editor, has been terrific.

At the University of Illinois Library, Priscilla Yu and Emily Jedlick were always supportive as I searched through the archives of the City Planning and Landscape Architecture library. They forgave me of many library fines. At the Illinois History Survey, James Cornelius was particularly helpful.

The research was supported by grants from the University of Illinois' Research Board, and the John Nolen Research Fund at Cornell University.

Finally and most importantly, thanks to the world's greatest Flemish family, the Anselins: Luc, Emma, Lucie and Thomas.

Emily Talen
Champaign, IL
May 2005

Chapter One

Introduction: Defining American Urbanism

The recent movement known as 'New Urbanism' is attempting to reconcile competing ideas about urbanism that have been evolving in America for over a century. New Urbanism, an urban reform movement that gained prominence in the 1990s, seeks to promote qualities that urban reformers have always sought: vital, beautiful, just, environmentally benign human settlements. The significance of New Urbanism is that it is a combination of these past efforts: the culmination of a long, multi-faceted attempt to define what urbanism in America should be. This revelation only comes to light in view of the history that preceded it.

This book puts New Urbanism in historical context and assesses it from that perspective. Analytically, my goal is to expose the validity of New Urbanism's attempt to combine multiple traditions that, though inter-related, often comprise opposing ideals: the quest for urban diversity within a system of order, control that does not impinge freedom, an appreciation of smallness and fine-grained complexity that can coexist with civic prominence, a comprehensive perspective that does not ignore detail. Amidst the apparent complicatedness, history shows that divergences boil down to a few fundamental debates that get repeated over and over again. This means that American urbanism has endured a habitual crisis of definition. The question now is whether New Urbanists have seized upon the only logical, necessarily multi-dimensional definition of what urbanism in American can be.

My method is to summarize the connections and conflicts between four different approaches to urbanism in America. I call these approaches urbanist 'cultures' – a term I apply unconventionally – and use them to trace the multi-dimensional history of ideas about how to build urban places in America.[1] There are obvious inter-dependencies, but at the same time, these cultures have struggled to connect with each other. This has led to a fragmented sense of what urbanism in America is, namely, a lack of connection among proposals that could be fashioned in a more mutually supportive way, and a poor conceptualization of the multi-dimensionality of urbanism.[2]

What has gradually evolved in the American experience are different approaches to creating good urbanism in America. Some have focused on small-scale, incremental urban improvement, like the provision of neighbourhood parks and playgrounds. Some have had larger-scale visions, drawing up grand plans and advocating for new systems of transportation and arrangements of land use. Others have looked outside the existing city, focusing on how to build the optimal, new human habitat. And some have emphasized that urbanism should be primarily about how the human settlement relates to 'nature'. Multiple meanings of urbanism have, for over a century, been forming in the minds of American planners, architects, sociologists, and others who have endeavoured to define in specific terms what urbanism in America is or should be.

Each of these approaches can be seen to have its own predictable and recurrent cultural biases. Further, the inability to integrate these cultures better has impeded our progress for reform and created a situation of stalemate in which efforts to stem the tide of anti-urbanism in the form of sprawl and urban degeneration remain painfully slow. At the same time, the recurrence and overlap of ideals is one reason why New Urbanism has had such a strong appeal.

Urbanism in American society generally has an ambiguous meaning. Urbanism may simply be defined as life in the big city, or more pejoratively, as the antithesis of nature. There is often a line drawn in the sand of the American consciousness – places are either urban, meaning downtown, or they are sub-urban or rural, meaning less than urban. Yet urbanism defined as big city life is a narrow definition that is not particularly helpful for rectifying the problems of American settlement, either for locations within the existing city or for new developments outside of it. Understanding the American take on urbanism involves much more than density calculations or the square footage of concrete.

New Urbanists have used many of these ideas in their attempt to consolidate a more complete and nuanced definition of American urbanism. Their definition tries to establish a framework for settlement, an integrated, inclusive way of thinking about urbanism. They have recognized that urbanism is not a certain threshold of compactness, a measure of density, or a condition of economic intensity. They have also learned that this makes the attempt to define it much more difficult.

My definition of American urbanism is simply this: it is the vision and the quest to achieve the best possible human settlement in America, operating within the context of certain established principles. To bring these ideals together within one framework – as the New Urbanists are attempting – it is important to recognize that there are essential principles that are recurrent and embedded in the historical

American consciousness. In other words, while urbanism in America involves multiple concepts, it is not 'anything under the Sun'. There is a recurrent normative content, and the interrelated history of ideas about what the best possible human settlement in America should be reveals this. As this book will demonstrate, these recurrent principles consist of, for example, diversity, equity, community, connectivity, and the importance of civic and public space.

Figure 1.1. What is more 'urban'? Contrasting perspectives on what can be used to define American urbanism. Left: downtown Houston, TX (*Source*: Landslides Aerial Photography). Right: Chatham Village, Pittsburgh, PA (*Source*: Clarence Stein, *Toward New Towns for America*, 1957).

Converse principles also exist – separation, segregation, planning by monolithic elements like express highways, and the neglect of equity, place, and the public realm. I bluntly label these 'anti-urbanism', and make a case for this interpretation in Chapter 2. Establishing this difference is necessary because a multi-faceted conception of urbanism cannot coalesce successfully unless it adheres to some basis of commonality. This does not necessarily eliminate conflict, but it does allow the possibility for seemingly conflicting ideas about good human settlement to be drawn together within the same framework. The concepts of urbanism that I review in this book are therefore considered as part of something larger, each forming their contributory part of a broader definition.

But there is a problem in that our current conceptualization of urbanism in America does not take this multi-dimensionality into account. The common critique that 'New Urbanism is simply New Sub-Urbanism' is symptomatic of this problem, and has a history to it. Lewis Mumford and his regional planning colleagues in the 1920s were horrified at the metropolitan 'drift' (outward expansion) being proposed for New York City, but their alternative – the decentralization of population into self-sufficient garden cities – was often mistaken for suburban land subdivisions and landscape gardening. Mumford thought anyone who mistook their proposals for mere suburbs had to be 'deaf and blind' since his organization, the Regional Planning Association of America (RPAA), was proposing complete settlements, not single-use collections of single-family houses (Schaffer, 1988, p. 179). Still, the RPAA was always at great pains to make the distinction – exactly as New Urbanists are today.

By tracing the multiple historical concepts to which New Urbanism is linked, I am hoping to create a more complete and detailed view of American urbanism. This is important because the failure to nuance what is meant by urbanism in an American context has created a dichotomy that may be detrimental to the goal of establishing a better pattern of settlement. There are divisions between those who would focus only on the existing city, or only on urban containment, versus those content to focus on creating new externally situated settlements. Where overlap and complementarity (i.e., synergies) exist, they are not always exploited. If urbanists – primarily planners and architects – are constantly arguing among themselves about the true and legitimate definition of urbanism in America, they undercut the synergies that could be capitalized on. These are precisely the synergies the New Urbanists have attempted to rally. But to accept their strategy requires a much more sophisticated idea about what urbanism is supposed to be.

This is not about justifying suburbia. Nor is it about insisting that suburbs, no matter what their form, be included as essential parts of the city, as some have done (see, for example, Sudjic, 1992). On the contrary, this book is about discerning how urbanism in America is translated from different perspectives. It is about articulating a multi-dimensional view of American settlement that rises to the level of urbanism in a variety of contexts. That level can, in my view, exist in locations outside of downtown cores – meaning suburban locations. Since, in the 1920s, America was already growing twice as fast in the suburbs as in the central cities, this is hardly a radical idea.

There are tactical reasons for taking this approach: most Americans live in suburbs and in single-family homes. Suburbs account for an enormous amount of what we consider to be 'urbanized area' in the U.S., making their ambiguous relationship with the notion of 'urbanism' all the more disjointed. Suburbs are part of the evolution of American urbanism, and that means that many of them can be seen as an inchoate form of urbanism. And some suburbs were composed of the essential elements of urbanity from the start – diversity, connectedness, a public realm. It makes sense, therefore, to pay particular attention to those suburbs that have something positive to offer in our quest to define what urbanity is, despite the fact that they have been labelled sub-urban. It seems reasonable then to develop a definitional language of urbanism that fits the suburban context and that may help them evolve in a way that is more positive.

I attempt to get at this by focusing in particular on what city planners and urban activists have come up with over the past century. In the shadow of repeated disappointment with our physical situation – a commonly despoiled landscape –Americans have continuously laboured to find the 'right' way of American settlement. We have been looking for an approach to building our urban places in a variety of contexts and scales – streets, neighbourhoods, towns, villages, suburbs, cities, regions, and, despite our meagre success at building according to plan, this quest to define American urbanism has never diminished. It is this fact – the persistence of an American teleology when it comes to urbanism – that translates the endeavour of making urbanist proposals from mere utopian dreaming into something more substantial.

This history of urbanism, which functions as a history of New Urbanism, reveals that there are multiple viewpoints, romanticist and rationalist approaches, different ideas about control and freedom, about order and chaos, about optimal levels of urban intensity. There are debates about the relationship between town and country, between two-dimensional (maps and plans) and three-dimensional (buildings and streetscapes) contexts, between empirical and theoretical insights, between the role of the expert and the place of public participation.

My analysis of American urbanism incorporates the existing character of cities and city life, but I am focusing primarily on what we aspire toward. It is a distinction between understanding why urbanists propose what they do and how they go about getting it, versus understanding only the latter. My view of urbanism, as in cultural theory, is that both understandings are needed (Thompson, Ellis and Wildavsky, 1990). We need to know why preferences are formed as well as how and whether goals are achieved because this gives a more complete picture. It is also essential for understanding urbanism, since the quest to build the 'best' human settlement is often more about aspiration than accomplishment.

Thus, I am particularly interested in what we think urbanism in America should be as opposed to attempting to measure only what we have achieved, important as that question is. This is nothing more complicated than the quest to make good cities, and to do so with specific ideas about ends and purposes. But it is not an analysis of lost dreams or utopianism. Countless ideas and plans remain unrealized, but that does not mean they are inconsequential – even seemingly abstract theories generated by intellectuals can have tremendous impact on actual practice, for example in the way Emil Durkheim's theories became a basis for urban renewal (Schaffer, 1988, p. 233). The impact of ideas about urbanism may be appropriately measured by the degree to which they continue to inspire and effect city planning. Because ideas are not formed in a vacuum but rather within a political context, they are on some level a reflection of what Americans think about their forms of settlement. Admittedly, this does not necessarily mean they are based on public consensus: the degree to which urbanist ideals are based on direct citizen input varies widely. The point is that a history of what we aspire towards should not be viewed as somehow existing apart from reality.[3]

I think a more concerted effort to define American urbanism is justified given the rather loose way in which the term has been used in the U.S., and given the fact that there is no official definition of it in any case. It is a term that can legitimately be seen as being fluid, not only because it describes a variable state of being, but also because the multiple traditions impacted upon it are so strong. Neither is it useful to get lost in various technical meanings and usages of the term urbanism. This is exactly what happened at the first meeting of the Congrès Internationaux d'Architecture Moderne (International Congresses of Modern Architecture), known as CIAM, in 1928, where some thought the word incomprehensible and wanted to use instead 'City and Regional Planning' (Mumford, 2000, p. 25).

Accordingly, self-proclaimed 'urbanists', from the Communist 'urbanists' of the 1930s to the 'New Urbanists' of the 1990s, have been critiqued for not living up to the requirements of the term, however that was defined. Starting with a more inclusive sense of the term, we can at least start with the notion that 'urban' is related to 'city', and that the idea of a city was not originally based on anything more specific than a community of citizens living together in a settlement.[4]

Four Urbanist Cultures

In seeking a better definition of American urbanism, a key question is why these common principles – for example, diversity, community, accessibility, connectivity, social equity, civic space – have not coalesced into a more united front when it comes to employing the principles of urbanism. One way to get at this is to explore how these enduring, overlapping or potentially complementary principles have fared under different planning regimes. What happens when they are approached in different ways, under different constraints and legalities, with different levels of political commitment, different methodological insights, different participation rules, different notions of fairness? What happens under different implementation realities and measures of success and failure?

My survey of the past one hundred or more years of urbanist ideals reveals four separate strains that I call incrementalism, plan-making, planned communities, and regionalism. These are the four 'cultures' of American urbanism, four approaches to city-making, constituting four sets of debates, critiques, counter-critiques, successes and failures. Each has built up its own culture, in a sense, with its own set of cultural biases. Each culture has its own unique story to tell, its own contribution to make to the story of American urbanism.

The four strains, or cultures, vary in their level of intensity and sense of order (explained more fully in Chapter 2). Concisely, incrementalism is about grass roots and incremental change; plan-making is about using plans to achieve good urbanism; planned communities focus on complete settlements; and regionalism looks at the city in its natural, regional context. Their differences are substantive and procedural, and they are sometimes empiricist and sometimes rationalist.[5] They differ in their relationship to existing urban intensity and notions of order, but ultimately, American urbanism depends upon all of these dimensions and perspectives, varying as they do in their level of specificity, scale and approach.

In my analysis of these four cultures, I look for the essence of their principles – the underlying causes of their approval or disdain. Each strain has vehement supporters and vehement opponents, and I am most interested in trying to understand the underlying dimensions of these views. Many times, it is the instance where they veer away from urbanistic thinking that forms the basis of their critique. I conceive of the struggles surrounding these four cultures as important for revealing what American urbanism is trying to be.

I see it as somewhat tragic that most ideas about how to build a better settlement in America – how to help the inner city, stop sprawl, save the environment, manage traffic, support schools, and all the other myriad issues related to city building – are so recurrent. There is a need for a wider recognition that ideas for improving the American city came from somewhere, and that they have been similarly critiqued and debated many times before. Freedom, control, diversity, order, plurality, community – none of these are new to the American city-making debate. It is important to realize their tenacity at irresolution, and get to work on the essential task of finding more creative ways forward. We may decide that it is necessary to reframe the debate, or that the debate itself is a necessary part of city-making, or even that there is no resolution for a given issue. Perhaps every generation will need to revisit the same issues and debate them each time in their own way. But at a minimum, we should be engaging in these debates in full knowledge of how they were framed, resolved or unresolved in the past. Such an effort is bound to produce a more enlightened discourse.

Multi-Dimensionality

In city planning history, the attempt to fashion an interconnected set of ideas, joined together to create a coherent basis for American urbanism, goes against the usual view, described by Jencks, that approaches to urbanism are more reminiscent of the 'wandering drunk' than a 'cumulative tradition'. The question I raise is whether aspects of several different approaches can in fact be forged together to create a multi-dimensional project that is the essence of American urbanism, now organized as New Urbanism. It requires the ability to look at divergent ideas and, rather than seeing commonality merely on the basis of 'agitated, sometimes apocalyptic, pursuit of new solutions', seeing a more deeply rooted, substantive form of agreement (Jencks, 1987, p. 301). What this might be based on is what I have set out to discover.

The question to address is whether a coexistence of perspectives is a necessary condition of American urbanism. We can find interconnections, which would seem to help the case for multi-dimensionality. But running throughout the intertwined threads comprising American urbanism, there is a corresponding set of threads that weaken, or perhaps simply obscure the linkages. A clear example is needed to ground this analogy. One connecting thread is the idea of the neighbourhood. The concept of a localized, village-like, self-contained unit is pervasive and is present as a response to the industrial city from the beginning. John Ruskin had his version, and later William Drummond and Clarence Perry articulated it in American terms. The pervasiveness of the idea is understandable. The neighbourhood unit is service-oriented, socially-supportive, and attentive to human need. The problem is that, almost simultaneously, it came to be associated with something more sinister – the eradication of the existing city and the social diversity it contained. Ruskin's programme called for total destruction and replacement wherever cities were less than works of art, while Perry advocated 'scientific slum rehabilitation' (Perry, 1939, p. 129). In any case, the seeming thread of the neighbourhood model of human settlement is shadowed by a tension of associated urban destruction that makes its linkage and lineage less than straight forward.

This attempt to combine proposals will elicit a recurrent criticism – that it is invalid to squeeze out only the positive and reject the negative of a given proposal. The question becomes: what is intrinsic to each element being sought or rejected, that requires that it be packaged together with other specific elements? After all, almost all planning is, in fact, an amalgamation. The City Beautiful movement itself, as Peterson (1976) has argued, was a culmination of the combined forces of municipal art, civic improvement and outdoor art. Lewis Mumford forged a synthesis between Dewey's pragmatism and Santayana's aesthetic idealism which would provide 'the best of both worlds' in science and humanism (Thomas, 1994, p. 284). When these ideas were then merged with Geddes' ideas about regionalism, the resulting amalgamated planning project of the Regional Planning Association of America became one of the most important planning schools of thought this country has ever seen.

For the most part, academics seem particularly uncomfortable with the idea of combining proposals. There is the argument that the attempt to forge a hybrid, amalgamated project is necessarily ambiguous (Beauregard, 2002). Peter Hall's synthetic history of the profession, *Cities of Tomorrow*, weaves a story of planning mishap resulting from the 'monstrous perversion of history' (Hall, 2002, p. 3.). In Hall's view, misinterpretation and naiveté in the planning profession are born of the combining of ideals across time and place.

It is not difficult to find examples of concepts forged together that, when combined, produced amalgamated disasters. The merger of garden cities and the City Beautiful into what Jacobs called the 'Garden City Beautiful' produced notoriously unappealing places. Other critics hone in on the idea that the amalgamated planning project is necessarily inauthentic, and therefore invalid. In this context, some see the New Urbanist brand of 'revivalism' as disturbing because it attempts to revive an urbanism, such as Nolen's, that was itself revivalist to begin with (Easterling, 1999). A revival of a revival can only be viewed as disingenuous.

Thus it is sometimes said that America lacks an authentic urbanism, and because of this American urbanist ideals never seem to gain much stature. According to some observers, America has been raiding other cultures and historical contexts for its city-building approach, and this is why the results have not been very pleasing. American urbanism is viewed as being mostly a matter of inauthenticity when it comes to urbanism – 'a long history of diverse and hybrid models' as if purity of form were a necessary condition of urbanism (Easterling, 1999, p. 157). In a not very ingenious way, the argument goes, Americans have been getting by with forging together pieces of urbanism to create cities that are too sub-urban to classify as truly urban.

But there is a different interpretation of American urbanism. It states that American urbanism is simply more complex than other versions, in part because the whole idea of America is that it is – or is meant to be – a pluralist society. It makes sense, then, that urbanism in America must be defined by more than one stream. And because of its multi-dimensionality, it has been caught in a long, convoluted process of trying to define itself. What has often looked like ambiguity in city-making could be seen instead as an attempt to define and structure urbanism in more than one way.

New Urbanism has tried to formulate a definition of urbanism that is multi-dimensional, expresses commonality of thought while being sensitive to different contexts and scales, and is a combination of related ideas that work together to define what urbanism is and what it is not. The experience of the New Urbanist movement over the past 10 years with trying to make this work has revealed two interesting things. First, the multi-dimensional approach to American urbanism is exceedingly difficult to pull off. It is met with resistance because, by attempting to merge ideas accustomed to opposing each other, there is a reaction that labels the attempt inauthentic and watered down. Second, in the resistance to multi-dimensional approaches, there is a tendency to single out one particular strain as superior in all contexts. One aspect will be, in a sense, forced into predominance.

One of the most enduring examples of this is the seemingly intractable division between the existing city and its peripheral extension. Urbanist culture that I characterize as having high urban 'intensity' insists that existing cities everywhere be reformed and resettled. A second, potentially complementary, view is about looking in currently non-urban places for pockets of potential urbanism. This latter view not only involves looking for urbanism in currently 'unspoiled' places, but it means that the whole spectrum of human settlement types must be considered. One practical question coming out of this division is whether it is possible to embrace both the planned community, positioned externally, and the existing city, with its concomitant urban problems, simultaneously. Proponents of the peripheral planned community – like Lewis Mumford and Ebenezer Howard – believed the existing city would fail. Proponents of the existing city – Jane Jacobs and William Whyte – believed that the planned community was anti-urban. This is an essential contrast that has plagued both sides, evidenced by the fact that American settlement falls woefully short of either perspective's main objective – a revitalized core or a clustered and coherently settled region.

In breaking down these divisions, my hope is that we will begin to acknowledge that each cultural stream has made a contribution to the definition of American urbanism. I cast a wide net over the various proposals that have been put forth over the past century. Small-scale urban improvers, the incrementalists, offered us the idea of using grass roots community activism and principles of diversity and complex order to change the urban environment incrementally. City Beautiful era plan-makers focused our attention on civic design, on the design and massing of buildings relative to streets, and on the relation of three-dimensional to two-dimensional patterns. City Efficient era plan-makers pulled together a wide range of subjects, traversing large-scale comprehensive plans as easily as they did tree selection and bridge engineering. They gave us the ability to be generalists, to discuss multiple currents of city plan-making in an integrative fashion. Planned community advocates contributed the ability to think holistically about city form and to envision alternative, idealized societies. Regionalists showed us how to fit it all together into a much larger, environmentally responsive framework.

In the end, American urbanism may be a composition that requires something from all of these cultures. It may need small-scale incrementalism, larger scale civic improvement, planned communities, and regionalism. My thesis is that, while these four cultures have evolved in separate ways over the past century, there should be recognition not only of their mutual legitimacy, but of their mutual dependence.

Historical Framework

Historic connections are easily drawn throughout history in part because the urban predicaments of the early and late twentieth century have strong similarities. Both eras are marked by change, disorder, and conflicting sentiments. Henry Adams wrote in 1900 that he was 'wholly a stranger' in his own country, and that 'Neither I, nor anyone else, understands it'. Charles Eliot Norton spoke of his age in the early twentieth century as 'degenerate and unlovely' because of the urban degradation he saw around him.[6] These are wholly familiar sentiments towards American places now. And in both ages, the internal conflicts and turmoil of the age created an interventionist strategy that embraced change and promoted optimism among some segments of the population. At either end of the century, there were some who criticized a *status quo* based on commercial interests, and thought optimistically about a new future course.

At the beginning of the twentieth century, urbanists reacted to the extreme crowding in cities, the solution to which was 'to encourage the diffusion of business, industry and population'. Now, urbanists are motivated by the perversities of decentralization, not centralization, but they nevertheless share an identical goal, the quest to procure the best possible human settlement forms. Garden cities, the self-contained, compact, community-oriented settlements proposed by Ebenezer Howard a century ago, were intended 'to make traffic less intensive and movement more comfortable', goals that, despite the changed circumstances, are not inconsistent with urbanist principles today (Lewis, 1916, pp. 318–319).

The historical framework I use is mostly focused on the twentieth century, but the attempt to define American urbanism in fact began earlier. The earliest reform proposals coincided with the start of the Industrial Revolution. When industrialization started to take hold in earnest in the U.S. between 1840 and 1850, the impact on cities was profound. Americans saw firsthand how the arrival of industrial technology (most importantly railroads) and simultaneous improvement in agricultural productivity, set in motion a new sort of urban pattern that required a new type of proactive response. That pattern was intensely congested. Given the fact that productive capacity and urban growth were inextricably tied, this was inevitable. What was clear at mid-nineteenth century was that the symbiotic forces of technological change and industrial expansion were producing a new kind of city. Urban geographers call this period the era of the 'transitional city' (Knox, 1991, p. 9), and it was this transition that instigated a whole new occupation of urbanistic reform.

Thus the American century of urbanization – the nineteenth century, in which the urban population expanded at three times the rate of the national population for each decade between 1820 and 1860 – was logically the period during which the culture of city reform was launched (Schultz, 1989, p. xv). Subsequent proposals were many and varied: utopian communities, civic improvement, municipal art, garden cities, the City Beautiful, the City Efficient, regionalism. Visionaries and writers, religious leaders, philanthropists, politicians, industrialists, architects, and urban dwellers met city growth and change with new ideas and physical proposals for how the human environment could be improved. Some were utopian and es-capist, some were incremental, and some expressed grandeur. Some were religiously motivated and many sought social and moral redemption. Many were never built.

But all were united in a belief that human enterprise could rise up and challenge the shape and pattern of the city, an urban form that was being moulded by forces and interests external to, or at odds with, basic human needs.

Much has been written about the perverse motivations involved in the quest for urban improvement. What started as a preoccupation of zealots and social utopians in the earliest decades of the nineteenth century, became by the later decades, a condition of the growing culture of professionalism – the need for 'experts' to solve problems.[7] Much has been made of the domination by business elites, capitalists, or even an inwardly-focused voting public (Fairbanks, 1996). We have been shown how the motivations to heal the dying city can be characterized in what Charles Jencks calls 'eschatological and hysterical' terms, punctuated by 'overtones of the hospital and operating theatre' (Jencks, 1987, p. 300). In other words, there was an intense preoccupation with sterilizing, opening up, and sorting urban places in ways that would supposedly make them more innocuous.

This supports the common perception that Americans disdain cities. The view is that Americans, still under the spell of Jeffersonian agrarianism, equate urbanity with immorality. Jefferson's view that cities are 'pestilential to the morals, the health and the liberties of men', and constitute 'a malignant social form . . . a cancer or a tumor' has been used repeatedly to expound upon this view and diagnose the sad state of contemporary American landscapes (White and White, 1962, pp. 17, 218; Kunstler, 1996). In large part the disdain is tied into the endless pursuit of the American Dream, and classic studies of suburbia like Kenneth Jackson's *Crabgrass Frontier* (1985) and Robert Fishman's *Bourgeois Utopias* (1987) have investigated both the causes and effects of this enduring quest.

Some scholars, notably Fishman, argue that American anti-urbanism is a 'persistent misunderstanding', and that in fact 'in no other society since the European Middle Ages have cities played such a formative role in creating the national economy and culture' (Fishman, 2000, p. 6). What should be recognized is that there is a rift between what ordinary citizens thought about cities, and the bulk of writing about cities from the American intelligentsia. There were plenty of boosters, orators, ministers and common folk who spoke passionately for cities. To a great extent the fear and anxiety of anti-urbanism was born of the American intellectual, not the common urban dweller (White and White, 1962).

The anti-urban ethos cultivated by America's great intellects – Jefferson, Emerson, Thoreau, Hawthorne, Melville, Poe, James – had to be overcome by progressive era reformers. In writings like *The City: The Hope of Democracy* by Frederic C. Howe (1905) the optimism that the progressives held for cities was made known. As a leading progressive era political reformer, Howe was fundamentally an urbanist, proclaiming urban life to be a condition of the 'great epochs of civilization', through which came 'education, culture, and a love of the fine arts' (Howe, 1905; Howe,

1915, p. 1). This was an enthusiasm for cities caught up in boosterism and rivalry, but it was pro-urban all the same.

The notion that urban reformers had nefarious motivations is particularly challenging to refute since so much of urban reform is rooted in nineteenth-century upper middle-class culture. The whole act of trying to create a better settlement form can easily be reduced to something that is merely reflective of the contradictions of Western capitalist democracies. Ever looming is the fact that ideas about urban improvement were, and continue to be, about fashioning a reasonable human habitat under the forces of capitalism. This was the motivation from the start, and the first ideas were formed under capitalist effect: intense industrialization and social polarization. Yet there was recognition that the processes of industrialization and the rapid growth of urbanization combined to put tremendous pressure on city form in a way that ignored human need and social justice. There was a perception that the industrial city was based on an unjust social structure, and that a new social order would require a new form of city.[8]

The various phases of capitalism, along with the governmental responses to them, have often been viewed as having detrimental effects on city pattern and form. Disorganized capitalism, organized capitalism and now global capitalism have all wreaked havoc on cities that were supposed to be made for people, but instead seemed only about stoking the fires of production and consumption. Through each phase, city makers have had mixed effectiveness at countering the destructive tendencies. Yet there has been no let-up to the task of formulating a response. Consistently, a different reality is envisioned, one that is not content to let the forces of capitalism be the sole determinant of human settlement form.

Thus the real problem for American urbanism is not about identifying what its lineage is but, instead, how to keep it nurtured and growing in the face of cynicism and extreme doubt about the abilities of planners as urbanists to make a positive difference. When Jane Jacobs spoke of 'Garden City nonsense', planners seemed not to argue, presumably because they had already abandoned the project (Jacobs, 1961, p. 289). And yet what is important about models of good urbanism is that they require nurturing and adaptation. Unfortunately, rather than attending to them, we have instead numerous examples of fallen principles – the failing of an ideal in the course of its implementation. What happened to garden cities in the course of their implementation is one of the clearest examples. Unwin and Parker detested the idea of a single home centred in the middle of 'its own little plot' (Creese, 1992, p. 190), but the eventual filtering down of garden city design was in fact largely a matter of houses on their own little plots. Herein lies what may be the mother load of planning conflict: how to hold on to principles while at the same time remaining flexible and open to refinement. One could argue that the failure to negotiate this balance properly is what lies at the heart of our failure to define American urbanism.

Scope, Organization and Sources

It is important to make clear what the scope of the book is, and what is clearly beyond its scope. My focus is on the physical form of the built environment and the ideas that support those forms. Largely excluded is theory about the urban planning process. I do not discuss organizational theories, the nature of rationality, communicative practice, 'power-knowledge' or Foucauldian discourse analysis, social learning, or any of the other theories about what planners do and why, how knowledge and action are related, or the place of planning in society more generally. In short, this book does not directly engage planning theories for and about planners. This is not to say that such theories are unimportant. It is only an acknowledgement that this book has a different kind of focus – the physical side of urbanism. It is a history of ideas that could, perhaps one day, provide grist for the theoretical mill.[9]

The book is divided into three parts. Part 1 sets the framework for the historical lineage. Using some insights from anthropology, a framework for connecting urbanist 'cultures' as a basis for defining American urbanism is presented. This is followed by a delineation of how urbanism can be distinguished from anti-urbanism. This distinction forms an important basis for the subsequent analysis in Part 2, where each urbanist culture is dissected to discern what aspects tend to promote urbanism (which I call 'connections') and what aspects do not (which I call 'conflicts'). This assessment is conducted through the lens of a set of principles about urbanism, as defined in Chapter 2.

Part 2 comprises the main historical analysis. Chapters 4 and 5 discuss urbanist ideas for existing urban areas, and Chapters 6 and 7 discuss urbanism as it is approached in the planned community and region. Thus Part 2 explores, first, two cultures that have been primarily concerned with rectifying what currently exists, and second, two approaches to new development, where the existing city is only of secondary concern and the primary task of the urbanist is focused on the development of new settlements and systems of settlements.

Part 3 serves to condense, summarize and clarify the significance of the historical lineage. It first presents an analysis of the successes and failures in each of the four planning cultures, identifying the commonalities and particularities of success and failure. A concluding chapter offers a final perspective on the historically-rooted definition of American urbanism.

Sources for this book are eclectic. I use the writings of the primary authors discussed, particularly Raymond Unwin, Patrick Geddes, John Nolen, Lewis Mumford, Jane Addams, Nelson Lewis, Thomas Adams, Jane Jacobs, and others who were involved in some way in one or more of the planning cultures I discuss. In addition to these writings, I use magazine and journal articles associated with the planning and architecture professions, particularly those before World War II.

In addition to these primary sources, I rely extensively on secondary sources: published accounts and analyses of planning and urbanist activity. There are many excellent planning histories, and many of these I have used liberally. Since this book is a synthesis of how others have defined American urbanism and what it should be, other authors' interpretations of urbanism comprise a critical part of my analysis.

Notes

1. The word culture is not used in a political or social sense, but more broadly as simply the ideals, behaviour, and approach associated with a particular group.
2. I am equating 'America' with the United States, excluding, for convenience, the more inclusive meaning of America as both North American and South American cultures.
3. Here I agree with William H. Wilson, who made a similar point in a critique of planning and urban histories (Wilson, 1994).
4. *Urban* comes from the Roman name *Urbanus* which meant 'city dweller' in Latin (it was also the name of eight popes). The word *urban* is dated to 1619, but its use remained rare until 1830, corresponding with the rise of the industrial city. Since *urbanus* means 'of or pertaining to a city or city life', there is a close association with the word city, which originally meant any settlement, regardless of size. *City* comes from the Latin *civitatem* (nom. *civitas*) meaning 'citizenship, community of citizens'. The Latin word for *city* was *urbs*, but a resident was *civis*. When Rome lost its prestige as the ultimate *urbs*, *civitas* came to replace *urbs* (http://www.etymonline.com/).
5. See Lang (2000) for the distinctions between two types of paradigms (substantive and procedural) and two philosophical traditions (empiricism and rationalism).
6. Cited in Chambers, 1992, p. 49.
7. Bledstein, 1976, cited in Spain, 2001, p. 27.
8. See Fishman's study (1977) of the urban theories of Le Corbusier, Frank Lloyd Wright and Ebenezer Howard.
9. See Friedmann (1998) for an excellent concise summary of planning theory.

Chapter Two

Framework:
Four Urbanist Cultures

My definition of American urbanism is based on forging together ideas taken from four different urbanist approaches or 'cultures', as I prefer to call them. These essentially come out of the profession of city planning, and thus there is a great deal of overlap between 'planning' and 'urbanism' in the discussion that follows (and throughout the book). This chapter lays out the rationale for categorizing planning, i.e., urbanism, in these terms. The historically-based assessment of American urbanism is made by tracing the four cultures – incrementalism, plan-making, planned communities, and regionalism – over the course of roughly the past 100 years, but with a particular focus on the early twentieth century. The main task is to sort out what is or is not contributory to a definition of American urbanism, what the commonality consists of, and how it can be combined into something that can be used to define it more purposefully.

As I have argued, to get to a more complex definition of urbanism, ideas that have occurred in different times and places, under different political, social and economic circumstances, and that fall into a range of subject matters and methods will have to be compared and contrasted. This task has parallels to the work of cultural anthropologists who seek to discover and interpret different human cultures and explain the differences found. The basic task of uncovering the history and development of human cultures thus parallels the task of understanding the history and development of a particular human endeavour – in this case the building of human settlements.

Despite the strong and sometimes obvious overlaps among the four different planning cultures, their distinctiveness can be clarified along two dimensions – I call these intensity and order. The first dimension is more significant. It divides the lineage of American urbanism into two main traditions: those ideas, principles and implementation strategies aimed at the existing city, and those aimed at creating new ones. Both groups are focused on cities and urbanism, and this is the common denominator that connects them. But there is a key distinction. One approach to reforming urbanism is about working through givens, the other is about forging new realities. This difference affects a range of other issues. For example, how an urban reformer works through the problem of relating the 'urban' to the 'rural' will be significantly shaped by whether the problem is conceptualized through existing forms and patterns, or whether it is possible to envision an entirely new design. In practical terms, one is seeking ways to interject the country into the town, the other is seeking ways to interject the town into the country.

Another effect concerns the difference between having to contend with existing social and political realities, and being able to start fresh, with no existing political or social interests to mollify. Relph (1987, p. 154) argues that two distinct types of modern planning are divided between the 'technical and apolitical' act of planning on the 'unpeopled countryside', and the 'politically saturated activity' of planning at the city centre. This distinction may become somewhat blurred where environmental activism constrains development at the fringe.

Within these two main traditions of contending with established urbanism or starting anew on a greenfield site, there is another discernible dimension. The response to urban problems varies according to the level of its normative sense of order. At one end of the spectrum, urbanism will focus on the creation of very specific plans and designs that can be said to be highly ordered. The solutions will be physically distinct and most often expressed as master plans of various types. At the other end, the focus will be less about making normative plans and will involve instead a range of other types of interventions. These may entail small incremental changes, or they may be expressed as a set of political and economic reforms. Physical change is still the primary subject, but it will tend to be either small-scale or process oriented as opposed to large scale and tied to a physical blueprint.

These two dimensions create four inter-related but distinct cultures. This makes possible a range of urbanisms – big city to small town, small scale to large scale – implemented through a variety of approaches ranging from code revision to regional planning. Often, scale will determine approach, but this is not always the case. There has been a desire to create good urbanism in all cases, even in the context of small, new developments. For example, Ebenezer Howard was trying to create something urban in the context of a small city; his view was that a real city was no larger than a town (see Fishman, 1977). The fact that this has been highly problematic in the American context only underscores the need for multiple approaches in the nurturing of urbanism: finding ways to enhance existing urban places in decline; finding ways to inject urbanism in areas of new development; and using multiple strategies to accomplish both goals.

The four planning cultures vary in their level of internal homogeneity, some constituting a broader range of hybrid ways of thinking about urbanism. Some may coalesce into a particular planning paradigm, such as in the case of the Regional Planning Association of America formalized by Stein, Mumford, MacKaye and others. Other cultures are more loosely connected, as in the case of incrementalism, which, by its very nature, has never had any formal organization. In any case, an important point is that each planning culture is in some way related to every other culture, ranging from strong to weak association.

As with any typological categorization, there are downsides. To begin with, some ideas are not easily categorized. There is a danger in attempting to 'force' a particular idea about urbanism into a particular planning culture. Predictably, this has been a criticism of other attempts at cultural typology building (Asad, 1979; Boholm, 1996). But the idea here is to understand a particular idea or approach in relation to a larger, historically based framework. The typology can always be taken apart. I am not trying to prove whether the typology exists but rather use the typology as a tool for making relevant associations. Thus what matters is not the typology itself but the relationships within it. It should be seen as a structure through which to view the rotating constellations of ideas about urbanism in America.

There are other typologies in urbanism. For example, the New Urbanists divide urbanism into regional, neighbourhood, and block levels. This apparently reflects an initial division among early New Urbanist organizers in which one group felt that the primary principle of organization for urbanism was the region; another group felt it was the neighbourhood unit; and another was focused on small-scale elements of urbanism (Moule, 2002). The other main New Urbanist typology, the 'transect', specifies a range of human habitats that vary according to their level and intensity of urban character, a continuum that ranges from rural to urban. Conceptualizing this range of environments is the basis for organizing components of the built world (Duany, 2002).

There are similarities between these typologies and the one I use, although mine is geared specifically to organizing historical lineages. The exploration of historical precedents is about finding similarities in underlying concepts and ideas, which is somewhat different from trying to organize a set of proscribed solutions. In any event, the historical record of ideas about urbanism is complex enough to require a typology to help make the lineage and its internal associations more accessible.

The typology of four planning cultures can be summarized as follows:

Urbanism tied to the existing city:

1. Incrementalism – concern for existing urban settlements in a way that is necessarily

small scale, incremental, and preservationist, originating with the settlement house and municipal arts movements, and reflected in the writings of Camillo Sitte, and later William Whyte, Jane Jacobs and Christopher Alexander.

2. Urban plan-making – concern with the existing city, but rather than small-scale, grass roots, incremental change, a focus on the larger and more comprehensive endeavour of plan-making – urban improvement guided by a physical plan – associated with metropolitanism; includes the City Beautiful and its close cousin, the City Efficient. Associated with Burnham, Nolen, Adams, and Robert Moses.

Urbanism that focuses on new development:

3. Planned communities – utopian and quasi-utopian ideas about the proper place of cities in the region, the correct functioning of society within urban areas, and the formation of new towns, villages, or neighbourhoods according to specific principles. Associated with Howard, Unwin, and Parker, and the American planners Nolen, Stein and Wright.

4. Regionalism – human settlement in its natural regional context, originating in the writings of geographers in the French tradition (Reclus, Kropotkin and Proudhon), evolving through the work of Geddes, MacKaye and Mumford, influenced by the approach of Olmsted, and continuing through Ian McHarg.

These four cultures represent distinct schools of thought in the history of ideas about American urbanism. Using these categories, it is possible to develop a lineage for American urbanism that blends and contrasts the varying contents and methods employed. Each is present, in various ways and to varying degrees, in the history of urban reform, first as a response to the industrial city, and later, as a response to the global, postmodern one. Each is associated with particular people, events and places, and each has shown some degree of success in effectuating change.

But they do not include every response to urban problems. My analysis focuses on the first several decades of the twentieth century (although nineteenth-century events are also included). Ideas about urbanism that flourished in the mid-twentieth century are de-emphasized for reasons that are explained in Chapter 2. This is not to say that there were not ideas important to our understanding of American urbanism being developed at that time. Some connections do exist, but they are overwhelmed by an anti-urbanist ideology that represents more of an antithesis than a source.

Within the field of city planning, explorations of planning 'culture' are varied. The idea of culture in planning has generally been used to differentiate planning from other professional practices, as in Krueckeberg's *Introduction to Planning*

History in the United States (1983). In this view, planning as a specialized culture is usually discussed as being rooted in mid-nineteenth-century landscape planning and officially sanctioned in 1909, the pivotal year of two major events, Burnham's Plan of Chicago and the first National Conference on City Planning. There have been explorations of the political culture of planning in a particular region (Abbott, Howe and Adler, 1994), whereby the relationship between professional planners and citizens is uncovered. There have been attempts to uncover a single planning culture that defines what it is the profession does, a kind of soul-searching of planning practitioners (Krueckeberg, 1983). Krumholz (2001) defines a 'new planning culture' based on its institutional practices, and its embracement of politics, scientific management, short-range outcomes, and participatory planning.

While these views of planning culture will come in to play, my use of the term will be defined more anthropologically than politically or professionally. That is, I use the idea of culture to explicate the different ways in which the planning and design of cities is conceptualized – how it is thought of and interpreted, and the meaning it holds. This is tied to the physical qualities of urbanism, not the procedural or political aspects of the planning activity alone. Urbanist culture can be defined as the bundle of ideas, strategies, perspectives, and values associated with different ways in which the act of planning human settlement – cities of various forms – is approached. Politics is only one part of that culture.

My use of the term 'culture' is therefore broad, which introduces at least one liability. It has not gone unnoticed that the term 'culture' is overused, prompting Jacques Barzun in his book *Dawn to Decadence* (2000) to view it as having devolved into 'absolute absurdity'. But the overuse of the term may simply reflect the need to fill an explanatory gap. As cultural anthropologist Mary Douglas states: 'Something vital [is] missing from the picture of the real live individual; that something is culture' (Douglas, 1978, p. 5). In this same spirit I use the idea of culture to attempt to understand the spirit of American urbanism. The basic postulation is that ideas about urbanism, as expressed in different planning or urbanist cultures, have tended to self-organize into groups, and four can be identified. These four cultures have interesting similarities to groups found in other cultural contexts, in the sense that they exhibit analogous cultural biases.

Grid/Group Theory

There are many ways to construct cultural typologies. One useful theory, which I use here to help differentiate urbanist cultures, is known as 'Grid/Group', developed by the well-known cultural anthropologist Mary Douglas. The use of this approach, applied to a planning context, is more metaphorical than literal. It has been applied in a range of other fields, however, and can be adapted to apply to city planning and urban reform, i.e., urbanism. Relevant applications include interpretations of environmentalism (Douglas and Wildavsky, 1982; Grendstad and Selle, 1997; Johnson, 1987; Rayner, 1991); educational systems (Bernstein, 1971–1973); analyses of risk (Dake, 1991); rational choice theory (Douglas and Ney, 1998); the abolitionists during the American Civil War (Ellis and Wildavsky, 1990); public administration (Hood, 1996); work cultures (Mars, 1982; Mars and Nicod, 1984); technology and social choice (Schwarz and Thompson, 1990); high-technology and regional development (Caulkins, 1995, 1997); the analytical perspectives of geologists (Rudwick, 1982); and religious communities (Atkins, 1991).

Grid/Group theory, which is also referred to as a method, was devised by Mary Douglas during the 1970s, and its conceptual structure is shown in figure 2.1. Mary Douglas and her associates used the Grid/Group method as a systematic basis for defining types of social environments. These environments are understood in terms of two types of societal controls: (a) externally imposed rules – the 'grid' dimension; and (b) bounded social groups – the 'group' dimension. The grid dimension captures the concept of power in society, whereas group indicates status and the boundaries that exist between the society and outsiders (Kemper and Collins, 1990). The grid dimension defines the rules that guide individual behaviour, 'leaving minimum scope for personal choice, providing instead a set of railway lines with remote-

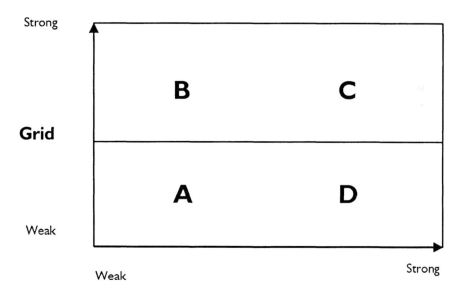

Figure 2.1. 'Four types of social environment', postulated by Mary Douglas in *Cultural Bias*, 1978.

control of points of interaction' (Douglas, 1978, p. 16). Group, on the other hand, is used to define a social setting, determined by the degree to which an individual associates with groups of varying kinds. Such groups have a way of controlling the individual, or making claims on their behaviour.

A primary concern in cultural anthropology has been simultaneously to conceive of the individual in a social setting and the culture of which the individual is a part. Thus grid and group are social constructs, describing the relationship between individual actions and social environments. Interestingly, grid and group are analogous to groups and networks, the two fundamental patterns of relationships in mathematics (Thompson, Ellis and Wildavsky, 1990).

One of the more common uses of Grid/Group has been to analyze political cultures (Caulkins, 1999). Weak grid/weak group[1] (cell A in figure 2.1) is individualistic, describing an entrepreneurial network of free exchange. Moving 'up grid' to the strong grid/weak group quadrant (cell B), the political culture is characterized as being constrained by exterior social forces but lacking the 'security' of a strong social group. The strong grid/strong group cell (cell C) is described as 'the classical Weberian bureaucracy with a clear organizational hierarchy and rule-constrained rational action' (Caulkins, 1999, p. 111). The final quadrant, low grid/high group is characterized as egalitarian, where there is concern with moral purity, group solidarity, and social differentiation is not condoned.

There have been other interpretations. Thompson, Ellis and Wildavsky (1990) gave each quadrant of the Grip/Group typology a 'flesh-and-blood' vignette in their book *Cultural Theory*. Cell A they ascribed to a self-made manufacturer, relatively free from control but exerting control on others. Cell B they analogized as the 'ununionized weaver', the 'fatalist', subject to binding prescriptions. Cell C is equated with 'hierarchy' and the 'high-caste Hindu villager', subject to group control as well as 'the demands of socially imposed roles'. Finally, cell D is the egalitarian 'communard', who rejects ranked relationships and instead values protection from the outside world of inequality.

In addition to defining types of social environments, the Grid/Group types are used to define differences in cosmologies. This is not a causal model – i.e., where social environment is seen as cause and cosmology as effect – but is rather an associational model. Certain Grid/Group structures appear to be associated with certain cosmological beliefs. The degree to which these associational generalities can be made constitutes the value of the Grid/Group framework.

Using the four social contexts as constraints, Douglas identified elements of cosmology 'not circularly implied in the definition of social context' but instead associated with a distinctive 'cosmological bias'. Different types of explanations and justifications about the structure of nature and the universe are derived within each social context. These cosmological derivatives consist of, for example, ideas about nature, space, and time, but also everyday routines like gardening and cookery. Ideas about society, human nature, death, and personal relations were also explored in terms of how they vary with changes in Grid/Group dimensions.

Grid/Group theory conceives of both the social individual and the larger culture in which that individual behaves, and thus is an attempt to come up with an adequate conception of the individual in a social context. In their book *Cultural Theory*, Thompson, Ellis and Wildavsky (1990) use Grid/Group theory to show that 'although nations and neighborhoods, tribes and races, have their distinctive sets of values, beliefs, and habits, their basic convictions about life are reducible to only a few cultural biases' (p. 5). At the same time, in this effort to define culture, there is an effort to reject ready-made cultural constructs, or the 'fixed set of logical pigeon holes for retrieving embedded memories' (Douglas, 1978, p. 6). The aim instead is to seek a conceptualization of how culture is negotiated, transacted, and, above all, what the limits to those negotiations and transactions are.

From Grid/Group to Urbanist Culture

It is possible to think of the problem of situating ideas about urbanism, tying them to a particular framework, as being a matter of differentiating across two dimensions in a manner not unlike Grid/Group. A redefinition of grid and group is required but many of the underlying mechanisms have strong parallels. It is also possible to investigate the belief structures associated with each cell in the Grid/Group system. Cosmologies pertain in the case of urbanism not to religion, but to views about nature, society and the individual; that is, the relationship between nature and the city; the effect of the built environment on society; and the role of the individual in the planning of cities, specifically ideas about the legitimacy and desired approach of public participation.

It is as if the four groups of ideas presented above are analogous to cultures, each with its own identifiable cultural biases which can be defined simply as shared values and beliefs. Where Douglas attempts to account for the social context in which actions take place, I am attempting to account for the normative and environmental context in which ideas about urbanism take place. Rather than conceiving of this context in social terms, as a framework for either permitting or constraining individual behaviour, the context is seen in terms of different levels of intensity of existing urbanism. These levels are relevant to the conscious attempt to alter human settlements, because intensity permits or constrains, so to speak, various urbanist ideas. In this process, cultural biases are identified – arrays of beliefs that are related to each other. All of this is directed towards facilitating the ability to make comparisons.

There is an interesting analogy between what the cultural anthropologist tries to do and the attempt to find a lineage for American urbanism. Douglas states 'instead of worrying about definitions of witchcraft or ancestor cults I am now looking for combinations of beliefs in all the possible social contexts in which the individual has to operate – all the possible social contexts here being limited and clarified by the grid-group axes' (Douglas, 1978, p. 15). This is precisely the project at hand, attempting to find 'combinations of beliefs' that are culturally distinct, but that together make up a combination of concepts and ideas about urbanism in America.

With adaptation, I believe this kind of structuring is appropriate to the analysis of urbanist cultures. By analogy, the group dimension represents how ideas are 'controlled' by a normative, ordered framework, by specific views about how cities ought to develop in response to physical plans that control their order. This control can be weak, in the case of incrementalist and regionalist cultures, or it can be strong, in the case of urban plan-making and planned community cultures. In terms of the grid dimension, the externally imposed rules that it entails can be seen, analogously, as levels of existing urban intensity that form the basis of planning intervention. The intensity can be high, in which the object of concern is the pre-existing city, or low, in which urbanist ideas are applied to an unencumbered, undeveloped site.

My urbanist analogy of Grid/Group, shown in figure 2.2, can be summarized as 'high to low urban intensity/high to low sense of order', which I will abbreviate as 'intensity/order'. By intensity, I am referring to the urban environment with which the planner or urbanist has to work, and this can range from existing to non-existing, from urban core to rural hinterland. This is the primary basis of division in the urbanist typology used in this study. Intensity is positioned along the vertical axis, and amounts to conceptualizing urbanism from the viewpoint of the existing city or from the viewpoint of being external to it. Along the horizontal axis is the second dimension, the degree to which the intervention is expressed as a normative, ordered plan. 'Order' differentiates the range of planning ideas that have high vs. low levels of order or concern for normative structure expressed in the form of concrete, physical plans for cities.

The 'Grid' Dimension: High to Low Intensity

I equate grid – essentially a set of rules – with intensity: the physical context of the existing urban environment. This intensity is conceived on the basis of whether the urban fabric is more, vs. less, pre-existent. Note that where the city is less pre-existent, the natural or rural environment can be seen as constraining. But the main distinction is about the 'rules' from the built landscape, the existence of the materiality of the city. These rules can be interpreted in different ways, and it is this interpretation that becomes part of the grid dimension. Intensity is not

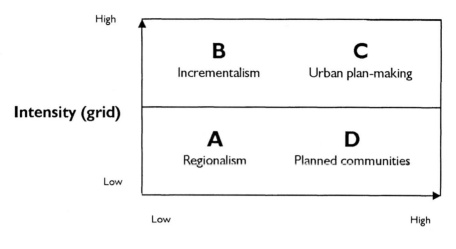

Figure 2.2. Four types of urbanist cultures. Adapted from Douglas,1978.

only the physical reality of the urban condition, but the planner's knowledge of it, incorporation of it, and deference to it. It is the planner's involvement with this materiality, and the way in which the physical context of urban intensity is used, that provides the 'grid' dimension of urbanist culture.

In the grid dimension, the task for cultural anthropologists is to identify how much an individual person is 'classified' by external constraints. If there is strong social classification, the individual is insulated. If there is reduced insulation, there is a correspondingly higher attainment of individual freedom in the form of autonomy and self-expression. The analogy with urbanism is that engagement with the existing urban context means strong urban 'classification' and 'insulation'. Freedom and autonomy to produce and plan for new forms is constrained.

It is important to keep in mind that the grid dimension in urbanism is rooted in urban physical experience. It concerns the tangible, bricks and mortar aspects of the existing environment, the physical elements that define the qualities of place. This separates these elements from social and economic phenomena, such as the exchange of money, traffic flows, the clustering of social groups, crime, poverty, wealth and income, etc. While these processes have complex cause and effect relationships with the physical environment, the difference is that the structure and arrangement of the physical environment is not their foremost defining characteristic. Whatever physical manifestations are involved constitute a sub-level definition.

If urban intensity is low – indicating a correspondingly high rural context – then urbanism may be treated in relative abstraction, where knowledge of the existing, surrounding urban situation is not seen as constraining. This does not preclude the importance of urban precedent, but it does mean that the project of urbanism will not be primarily focused on altering existing urban places. This tends to produce a focus on natural context, perhaps even the integration of 'city' as a monolithic concept within the domain of nature. The primary context is the natural or rural environment and the positioning of cities within it.

In contrast, cultures of high urban intensity must contend with both the form and structure of the existing built environment. Form involves the shape, condition and character of material forms, whereas structure deals with the spatial/locational organization of elements. Thus there will be a consideration of pattern, of the geographic structure of a city or section of the city. That this is not a constraint in low intensity environments is a significant difference in cultural orientation.

In high urban intensity, planning culture springs from an intimate knowledge of the existing urban situation, and urbanist proposals make use of this knowledge. High intensity is not anti-nature, but its concern is more about fitting into, rectifying, or otherwise making adjustments to its primary domain which is urban, not rural. This emphasis is associated with certain values like preservation, infill, congestion remediation, and economic development, whereas low urban intensity may be more about the proper relation between humans and the natural environment.

The 'Group' Dimension: High to Low Order

While grid has to do with the existing urban intensity of engagement, group has more to do with approach. Group, as it is used here, can be defined as the degree to which normative structure is expressed as urban order and, consequently, plan-making. In anthropology 'group' is a setting, but in urbanism, this setting can be defined as an established set of normative principles that find expression in idealized plans for physical arrangement. Such plans are more or less about the ordered positioning of built forms. In a low group (i.e., low order) sense, there are few 'group' memberships to control; control is coming from somewhere other than the normative, ordered plan-making of cities. In a high group (i.e., high order), there is strong 'membership', which corresponds to an allegiance to normative plans that embody some degree of pre-conceived physical urban order.

By analogy, just as a person's position in the group is defined as 'how much of the individual's life is absorbed in and sustained by group membership' (Douglas, 1978, p. 16), so ideas about urbanism will be 'absorbed in and sustained by' the degree to which specific, normative principles about urban order are adhered to. In effect, the normative principles for guiding urban form act as a set of social mores. At the high order extreme, plans are ideological and tend to look static.

In this dimension, the ordered, normative setting – the degree to which certain established ideals will provide boundaries for urbanist ideas or not – will be strong or weak in terms of articulation. In terms of plan-making for urbanism, it will either be less fixed and relative, or more fixed and absolute. Since all urbanist ideas generally have some normative component, the difference along this dimension pertains to the degree to which the normative idea involves order expressed in a physical plan. That is, a plan symbolizes the degree of faith in the normative project of changing the city in tangible terms. It also means that urbanism is predetermined – the 'happy accidents' that result from individualized efforts are not given full licence (quoted in Relph, 1987, p. 143). This has been pejoratively termed the planning 'blueprint' approach.

In the 'high order' extreme, there is a sense that order of a particular type must be imposed or at least that it is possible to define it. This order is harmonious, and coincides with the belief in an objective sense of truth and beauty. Harmonious order is both physical and social, with the former often having an impact on the latter. At the other end of the spectrum, however, the use of order in putting forth a specific plan is less pronounced or even weak. Correspondingly, in the weak or low order context, design plays a less direct role. There is a focus on individual action or other behaviours that exist outside of specific designs and spatial plans. Often there is a concomitant emphasis on social welfare over social order. There may be more of a focus on discovery than design, less concern with harmonious notions of order in the classical sense, and a greater possibility of supporting subjective notions of beauty.

Different ideas about order have different implications for how the existing environment is treated. The stronger the sense of order, the greater the likelihood that existing elements will be viewed as alterable. Strong order contexts are likely to be less sensitive to existing environments, or, they are likely to prefer starting from scratch, on a clean slate, so to speak. In an existing urban context, this means the City Beautiful approach, while at the more rural end (low intensity), this means planned communities and new towns like garden cities.

The dichotomy between the two tendencies in the order (group) dimension in physical planning can be traced over the course of planning history in the last 100 years. The left side of figure 2.2 characterizes a physical planning that works incrementally or through a process, and is less about implementing a set vision of the physical future and more about shaping the city in small steps or by changing its underlying dynamic. The right side of figure 2.2 is exemplified by the City Beautiful and what Kostof (1991) calls Grand Manner planning, and attempts to implement a largely complete picture of urban improvement. The key difference between the two is in how order is treated. Urbanism on the right side of figure 2.2 is concerned with the implementation of a visionary order that is unified, while order on the left side evolves organically through a series of incremental actions.

Low order treats order as something implicit, evolving out of a management or regulatory framework, not a preconfigured plan for development.

This dichotomy in urbanism – whether the implementation of normative ideals involves the creation of a plan or whether it involves specifying a process through which ideas are to be actualized – will be a recurrent theme throughout this book. It is positioned here as a difference in underlying cultural perspective but relates in general to different perspectives about urbanism. It parallels what Broadbent (1990) posits as the two essential ways of thinking about the city, one empiricist and one rationalist. The empiricism of Bacon, Locke, Berkeley and Hume is about building ideas through processes of induction, where what is known about the world is gained by sensory experience. The Rationalist position of Descartes, on the other hand, is one of universal truths reached through logical reasoning, and tends to involve the application of pure, abstracted geometries (Broadbent, 1990). According to Broadbent, some urban designers are more empiricist in approach, such as Lynch, Alexander, and Rowe and Koetter in their book *Collage City* (1978). Others are clearly rationalist, such as Aldo Rossi, Le Corbusier, and Bofill. It is possible for the ideas to mix and merge, and there are examples of urban planners changing from a rationalist to an empiricist orientation (Broadbent gives as examples the plans of Rob and Leon Krier), but the distinction between sensory experience and rational abstraction is pervasive.

Regionalism

The first quadrant, square A (bottom left of figure 2.2) – weak intensity/low order – is labelled 'Regionalism' and its importance to the development of American urbanism is the subject of Chapter 7. Interestingly, the cultural anthropologist views this social context as individualistic, where, at the same time, 'nature is idealized as good and simple' (Douglas, 1978, p. 24). Here the analogy with urbanism crosses bounds to allow a literal use, for it is precisely the veneration of nature, in contrast to a conditional appreciation of urbanity, that, at least historically, drives this cultural perspective. Further, the 'free exchange' within society and the view that 'risk is opportunity' correlates with the regionalist view of an unconstrained association with nature and what was often, at least initially, an anarchist political orientation.

In this grid cell is the regionalism of Geddes, MacKaye and McHarg that has evolved into the dominant environmentalist strain in planning. It is even possible to place Frederick Law Olmsted and his idea of the 'immutable city' in this cultural context. The criteria for inclusion is that, first, there is less involvement with the internal complexities of existing cities relative to other urbanist proposals; and second, that the perspective from which the idea about human settlement is formulated is coming from outside the city, from nature rather than from within the urban environment. What matters is the natural regional context of urban development, and accordingly, the internal arrangement of the city often receives less attention.

Another interesting parallel is that, in this cell, the individual's success is measured by 'the size of the following the person can command' (Thompson, Ellis and Wildavsky, 1990, p. 7). The individual is relatively free from control, but is at the same time readily willing to exert control of others. One analogy is thus that, in regionalist culture, urbanism is a matter of being positioned (controlled) by the larger region. The region is not to be controlled by urban or governmental fiat, but by its intrinsic need. Ideally, urbanism is subjected to the needs of the region.

As with the evolutionary processes that have taken place within the other cultures, there has been a definite, even profound, transformation within this culture. The result has been a significant divergence between the regionalism of Patrick Geddes and members of the Regional Planning Association of America, and the regionalism of contemporary urbanists such as Peter Calthorpe. Where the former was anarchistic and applied to wholesale regions regardless of metropolitan boundaries, the more recent version is essentially metropolitan in scale and decidedly not anarchistic. While the former was a 'back to the land' movement inspired by Thoreau, the latter is more about efficient government and the management of natural resources.

In political cultures, the tendency of this quadrant is to blame 'incompetence' for problems and failings. The anarchist roots of this cultural strain certainly point to a parallel emphasis on the incompetence of existing governments. Later articulations (contemporary regionalism) likewise stress the incompetence of the existing government structure, with its wasteful overlapping of government services, unfair resource distribution, and inefficient delivery of services. There are strong ties between this way of thinking and the 'blame the system' orientation of the planned community culture described below, which is not surprising given that both strains originated from anarchist roots.

Incrementalism

The second grid cell, square B (top left of diagram) – weak order/high urban intensity – is labelled 'Incrementalism' (incidentally, the term used here is unrelated to that by Charles Lindblom (1959)). In cultural anthropology, the social context of this cultural type is dominated by 'insulation'. The individual is constrained by the classifications of the social system. The cell has also been described as 'fatalistic', where individual autonomy is restricted, but fatalists 'are excluded from membership in the group responsible for making the decisions that rule their life' (Thompson, Ellis and Wildavsky, 1990, p. 7). This makes the environment unpredictable, difficult to grasp mentally, and requires the need for personal survival skills.

Translating this to the planning context, the 'constraints' are those encountered in the existing urban environment. Since this is a low order culture, there is a tendency to work with whatever is given rather than attempting to procure a clean slate through some form of pre-conceived, and more radical, alteration. This culture thrives on working with and within the existing city. Within this high urban intensity context, in which plan-making is not emphasized, the existing city plays a strong role in prescribing urbanist ideals. The notion of being excluded from 'membership' from the main decision-making group explains the grass roots, bottom-up, incremental nature of their approach to urbanism.

Again there is a useful analogy between urbanism and political culture in regard to who or what is 'blamed' for cultural problems and deficiencies. In political cultures, there is a tendency to blame 'fate' (Schwarz and Thompson, 1990). This means that the locus of control is external to the culture, and there is little for which the group itself or individuals within the group feel they can be blamed. The analogy with urbanism is that cities are taken, so to speak, for what they are. In the spirit of 'self-organizing complexity', incrementalism is a product of multitudinous decisions and incremental processes guided by emergent properties that are seen to occur naturally. In this context, there is no room for master-minded planning schemes that attempt more complete forms of control. Such an attempt would be foolhardy, since natural processes (guided, analogously, by nothing more than 'fate') are responsible for the emergent city. In fact, to interrupt these processes is to disrupt the organized complexity that is emerging. It was in this vein that Jane Jacobs launched her attack on the planning schemes of both the garden city advocates and the modernist planners – the right side of the group dimension.

There is an interesting evolution that took place within this culture. I will make the case that the incrementalist cultural type is one that links both the earliest efforts to improve the city in small-scale ways, such as through the settlement house and municipal arts movements, the later ideas of Jane Jacobs, Christopher Alexander and, most recently, the 'Everyday Urbanism' of postmodern planning culture (Chase, Crawford and Kaliski, 1999). This evolution has changed its internal orientation, but nevertheless the common denominator of existing context, high urban intensity, incremental change, de-emphasis on plan-making and order, and self-determination of urban values are all perspectives that link these urbanist approaches together.

Urban Plan-making

I call the top right of figure 2.2, Square C – strong order/high urban intensity –

'Urban Plan-making'. In this category, planning is both strongly contextualized and ordered and, also, there is a strong sense of normative idealism. Places of high urban intensity are the main arenas in which approaches to urbanism are formulated, and attention to the existing city is therefore paramount. There is relatively less focus on the need to present an externally situated master planned community, although the links between this culture and planned communities is strong.

The grid cell has been labelled 'hierarchy' by cultural theorists. There are strong group boundaries and prescribed modes of conduct, and individuals are subject to control from the group as well as on the basis of socially-prescribed roles. In this context, it is interesting to think about the plan-making of Daniel Burnham and Robert Moses as being similar to how the exercise of authority in this cell is justified. Control and hierarchy are needed because 'different roles for different people enable people to live together more harmoniously than alternative arrangements' (Thompson, Ellis and Wildavsky, 1990, p. 6). This is a case of collective manipulation, of an environment in which everything is regulated in order to fit into its proper place, and in which rules are maintained in order to maintain this collectivity.

High intensity/high order can be seen as a case in which the materiality of cities combines with ordered design to create a strong vision for future development. Imaging plays a critical role. This image is usually in the form of graphics and plans, and this is generally recognized as being one of its greatest assets as well as one of its greatest liabilities. What is exploited is the aesthetic vision of the city and what this image can wield for furthering urban reform.

In a political analysis, this quadrant is characterized by top-down decision-making and bureaucratic control. When things go wrong, there is a tendency to 'blame deviants' who stray from the established norms. In urbanism, the external constraints and ascribed roles are analogous to a strong normative, top-down planning approach that does not leave room for individual behaviours and deviations from the norm. Nor is there much chance of electing to participate in the planning scheme being imposed, since the planning directives are given 'from above'.

This cell characterizes the type of planning that, like the other 'high group' dimension, planned communities, has a strong notion about what the right form of urbanism is – specifically, what the future city should look like. The difference, of course, is that good city form is not begun with a clean slate, as a new town on the outskirts of the city, for example, but as manipulation and refinement of the existing urban context. This necessitates a somewhat more forceful approach, since the prospects for altering what is existing often require leviathan efforts even when compared to building new towns.

In terms of internal evolution, here I will explore the short-lived but influential City Beautiful movement and its subsequent transformation into the City Efficient. Both traditions involved a strong emphasis on order, normative plan-making and imaging. Both traditions are strongly a part of American urbanism and while both have been widely criticized, there is also a recognition that strong urban visions and plans have a better-than-average chance of bringing about real change.

Planned Communities

I call the fourth grid cell, square D (bottom right of figure 2.2) – strong order/low urban intensity – 'Planned Communities'. Here the planning culture is 'constrained' by a strong sense of order based on normative principle. In ideal situations, from the perspective of this planning culture, ideas about urbanism will be derived solely from these normative views about order, and not from individualized incremental conceptions of the good city. These normative principles can be rationally or empirically derived.

The cell is equated with 'egalitarianism', because the principle of organization at work in this culture is equality. There are problems that arise from the notion of ruling without authority, such as how to retain membership and how to resolve internal conflict. There is a lack of role differentiation because of the low position on the grid dimension – the rules that relate one person to another. The basis of this society, and here the analogy with the idealism of the planned community holds, is one in which all are equal. This also tends to signify the necessity of cutting off (as the planned community sometimes does) from the outside world: 'egalitarian collectivity cuts itself off from the nasty, predatory, and inegalitarian outside world by a "wall of virtue" that protects those on the inside' (Thompson, Ellis and Wildavsky, 1990, p. 9).

The relationship with the existing urban context is weak, which means either that the ideal of nature is given ultimate authority over and above existing urban intensity, or that both nature and existing urban context are generally unobserved. In the most extreme case, the existing city is ignored, or even disdained, while the role of nature and its integration within the city is seen as paramount.

This then is the planning culture that posits the remaking of human settlements from scratch, using strong ideas about order. New city plans are constructed in more or less total form, prompting the criticism about over-reliance on blueprints and ordered visions (Jacobs, 1961). These are the new towns, garden cities and suburbs and other planned developments that literally begin with a clean slate, *tabula rasa*. There are no pre-existing conditions that would dictate how land must be divided and developed, although there are a number of recurring parameters and historical precedent can be strong.

Here planning culture can arrange urbanism as it pleases, manipulating its elements on new sites. This is different from the bottom left quadrant (regionalism), with its weaker sense of order, because there the normative idea of urbanism is subordinated to questions of natural contextuality. When dealing with human cultures in anthropological research, there is a tendency for the low grid/high group to produce 'ill-will and frustration' internally, but in the context of urbanist ideals, there is only the tendency to conceive of total community structures. This amounts to complete towns, the bounded framework of the garden city, or other holistic notions of the planned community.

In Grid/Group analyses of political culture, this quadrant has the characteristic of blaming 'the system' for failures, such as the inability to achieve goals (Schwarz and Thompson, 1990). The analogy with urbanism is that the tendency for the Planned Communities culture to posit the establishment of complete developments is often correlated with a perception that the existing urban 'system' can only fail to accomplish planning goals. There is thus a certain 'escapist' orientation. The system being blamed is not only political and social, but also encompasses the existing city that can not be rectified internally. This prompts the need for alternative systems, in the form of new planned communities and towns.

There has been a definite progression within this planning culture. It begins with the earliest ideas about industrial-era planned environments or company towns, such as those postulated by Fourier, Owen and Pullman. It includes the early residential suburbs planned by Olmsted, moves through Ebenezer Howard and the articulations of the garden city concept by Unwin, transforms into the Greenbelt towns of the New Deal era, and finally emerges, radically altered from the earlier conceptions, as planned suburban communities in the post World War II era.

Inter-relationships

The main ideas within each of these four planning cultures, embodying four conceptions of urbanism that vary along two dimensions, have been explained so far only in broad terms. Each culture consists of a set of ideas that form a particular orientation toward urbanism. The remaining task is to develop these cultures more explicitly and thoroughly, and link them to a more complete definition of American urbanism.

Between the cultures, there are a number of interesting relationships that can be analyzed. One of the more important dynamics is that the relationships between cultures vary. Figure 2.3 attempts to show this graphically. The heavy line separating the top and bottom half represents the fact that the division along the intensity dimension is stronger than the division between weak and strong order. This also means that the horizontal relationships – between the two cultures in the top half and the two cultures in the bottom half – is stronger and more fluid. Diagonal relationships are also present, and their strength has varied, one stronger than the other.

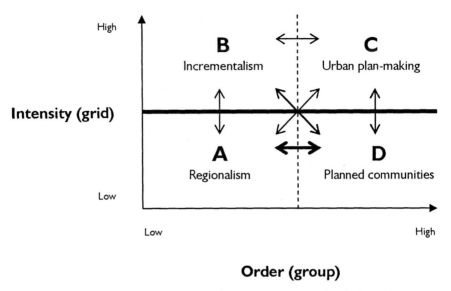

Figure 2.3. Four types of urbanist cultures and representative strengths of relationships.

It will be an important task in this study to understand how these relationships have changed over time. The interaction between the regionalist and planned community approaches, for example, was especially connected during an earlier time, but has changed and somewhat lessened more recently. The relation between regionalism and urban plan-making was once strained, but is now less so. Regionalism and incrementalism have always been at odds, and continue to be so in many cases. All of these relations, whether complementary or contrasting, will be discussed throughout the book. In fact it is these relations that provide the basis for postulating a multidimensional definition of urbanism in America.

Two overall observations can be made about these inter-relationships. The first is that these cultures, which had different starting points but by the turn of the nineteenth century were concurrent, were initially very much overlapping and inter-connected. There have always been differences in orientation, and the distinctions were always present, but the relationships were more complimentary and even inter-dependent. For example, there were originally strong connections between the incrementalists and the planned community advocates, or between the urban plan-makers and the proponents of planned communities, and the divisions between the card carrying members of each group were fluid. Many planners worked within more than one cultural domain simultaneously.

The second observation is that through the course of the twentieth century, these cultures have evolved (some would say mutated) into different and diverse projects. The planning ideas included within each cultural type have transformed themselves in such a way that the tensions both within and between cultures have become more pronounced. But the tensions are not always two-way – incrementalists may have developed a disdain for urban plan-making, and regionalists may loathe the work of the incrementalists for its nurturing of the large metropolis, but these animosities have not necessarily always been returned. Or they may ignore each other, as is the case with incrementalists giving little attention to the regionalist perspective. Mostly, through the transformations within each culture, the differences between them have become more rather than less pronounced over time.

With these trends in mind, American urbanism can be interpreted as a project that needs to reconcile these cultures in such a way that the best parts of each are brought together, while still retaining their individual integrity. It can even be postulated, as I already have, that urbanism in America seems to get its vitality through the process of attempting to resolve the tensions that exist within and between urbanist cultures. It is thus feasible to try to capitalize on potential mergers and points of interaction among different planning cultures, although where this constitutes too much compromise there is a danger of contributing to urban failure. The process is different from the 'pragmatic compromise' of the American planning tradition that Fishman (2000, p. 17) referred to. Urbanism in America as I am approaching it is more about utilizing multiple perspectives and strategies, while at the same time attempting to guard against a reconciliation that waters down initial principles.

This strategy of merger without compromise sounds appealing, but it is also full of difficulties. Mostly, these stem from the fact that the historically rooted ideals of urbanism in different forms are often the same ideals that have turned out to be the seeds of perverse urban patterns. The first and foremost difficulty has been how to work out the relationship between the country and the city, the rural and the urban, that began in earnest in the nineteenth century. The result was what Schuyler calls a 'new urban landscape' in which the commercial city was repudiated and opened up, the city became regarded as anti-middle class, the suburban home strengthened as a place of family values and domestic refuge, and finally, space and land use became differentiated (Schuyler, 1986). Whether this new landscape was the result of a failure to work out appropriately the combination of, or relationships between, cultures of urbanism is something this book attempts to shed light on.

An important task will be to identify within each grid cell the events, main ideas, and key historical figures that define its main purposes. Each planning culture forms the conceptual glue that binds together the associated individuals, events, projects, plans and writings. As already indicated, some individuals straddle more than one culture. Such multi-dimensional thinking characterizes figures like Lewis Mumford, Charles Mulford Robinson, and even Frederick Law Olmsted, Jr. Others, like Jane Jacobs, are more embedded in one particular culture, and refuse to yield in any other cultural direction. In any case, the four cultures should mainly be viewed as sets of ideas that coalesce around a main theme. This is analogous in cultural anthropology to 'polythetic classification', where classes consist of combinations of characteristics, and ideas have only to show that a majority of their features belong to a particular class (Douglas, 1978, p. 15). Divisions between cultures do not have to be sharp, although in many cases they can be.

Note

1. Note that the labels 'weak' and 'strong' are sometimes replaced with 'low' and 'high' in describing the grid cells.

Chapter Three

Principles:
Urbanism vs. Anti-Urbanism

This book is about formulating a more complex definition of American urbanism based on ideas embedded in different planning or urbanist 'cultures' that have been proposed for over a century. But this assumes that there is some working definition of urbanism to begin with. It rests on an initial conceptualization of urbanism from which to judge whether ideas about human settlement contribute to urbanism or not.

Thus the analysis of urbanist cultures presented in this book relies on a particular, underlying set of normative ideas about the nature and meaning of urbanism. This is not meant to be formulaic. What I outline in this chapter are simply the broad outlines, the flavour of what urbanism, in the most general of terms, means in America. Urbanism cannot be divorced from social conditions, but the focus here is on the physical settings that sustain these conditions.

In a nutshell, urbanism is defined here as human settlement that is guided by principles of diversity, connectivity, mix, equity, and the importance of public space. Diversity is the linchpin. As one urbanist put it, 'the simple truth is that the combinations of mixtures of activities, not separate uses, are the key to successful urban places' (Montgomery, 1998, p. 98). For Jane Jacobs, diversity was 'by far' the most important condition of a healthy urban place. She also recognized that diversity is not only a social condition, but translates to physical forms and patterns that maintain human interactions – relationships and patterns of relationships. In the context of sustaining diversity, urbanistic ideals are likely to consider place, form and the materiality and substance of settlement on a human scale. These considerations will vary by level of intensity and size of place.

The antithesis of urbanism can also be defined. The tendency toward separation, segregation, planning by monolithic elements like express highways, and the neglect of equity, place, the public realm, historical structure and the human scale of urban form are all symptomatic of the opposite trend, which could be called 'anti-urbanism'. All of these principles, both urbanist and anti-urbanist, are a matter of degrees, vary in terms of their negative effect, and can and do overlap, both geographically and temporally. On the other hand, urbanism and anti-urbanism are not entirely subjective and relative – they are distinguishable concepts.

Against the principles upon which urbanism is conceptualized, the four planning cultures can be seen to fail on certain criteria and succeed on others. The same can be said of modernist urbanism, which is discussed in this chapter as the near embodiment of anti-urbanism. While it is recognized that everything about urbanism and its ideals is a matter of degree, modernist urbanism failed so completely, as Jane Jacobs and many others readily recognized, that its deleterious mark on American places can now be held up as an exemplar of anti-urbanism.

The principles of urbanism are not new or particularly controversial. That urbanism ideally rests on diversity (social, economic, physical), connectivity (appropriate integration of elements, as well as the concept of permeability), public space (opportunities for interaction), and equity (in terms of access to meaningful goods, services, facilities), and implies a variety of strategies necessary to make those principles work successfully, is widely acknowledged. Allan Jacobs and Donald Appleyard, for example, wrote a widely cited manifesto in which they argued that 'an urban fabric for an urban life' required the integration of activities, an emphasis on public place, and diversity. To these elements they added space enclosure and minimum density level, which is consistent but goes further than the defining parameters I use here. Other articulations have included the criteria of density (although without any given threshold), public space, variety, memory, and 'the stranger' (Jacobs and Appleyard, 1987; see also Larco, 2003).

Anti-urbanism and its fostering of separation, inequity, and various conditions that impede the principles of diversity, connectivity and equity, is the flip-side of this definition. It is easy to identify in the American pattern of settlement, particularly since it was stated so explicitly as an ideology in the twentieth century under the leadership of modernist architects and planners. But now, without this guiding ideological purpose, anti-urbanism has become a by-product of global realities. One of the key challenges of urbanism is therefore to find ways to forge a coherent relationship between globalized economic structure and the principles of diversity, mix, connectivity and equity. One way to do that is to recognize that urbanism is not simply a matter of efficiency and making globalized capital networks flow smoothly to maximize profit. It is also about individual spirit and collective good, a point made repeatedly and cogently by Lewis Mumford.

Diversity and the other related tenets of urbanism are not primarily an aesthetic concern. This is a contentious issue. Although aesthetics play a role, Melvin Webber declared in 1963 that he was 'flatly rejecting the contention that there is an overriding universal spatial or physical aesthetic of urban form' (Webber, 1963, p. 52). To the degree that certain aesthetics are associated with urban forms that are diverse and connected vs. those that are not, this seems too strong a statement. Aesthetics in urbanism does not pertain to symbolic communication in the postmodern sense, but it can be interconnected to the proper functioning of urban places in terms of human need and behaviour. In any case, design in the environment is 'the bearer of the cultural value system of a community' and as such cannot really be completely detached from a discussion of urbanism (Lyndon and Halprin, 1989, p. 62).

There are no scientific proofs or moral laws backing up my claims about what urbanism is and is not. Rather, the broad parameters that define urbanism are grounded in recurrent empirical conditions, and by an historically-rooted understanding of the American settlement experience. The criteria are derived from outcomes, consequences and knowledge of what works, not in terms of universal truths, cosmology, or overarching world views, but as reliable, self-evident notions that, except in very specific cases, are necessary in order for urbanism to succeed. They are, in short, the cultural practices for making good cities, towns and other forms of human habitation as experienced in American history. They are also backed up by a great deal of writing about cities, and thus are not, as broadly articulated here, particularly contentious. In fact they have come to dominate the main ideas of urbanism in the early twenty-first century, under the familiar headings of smart growth, sustainable development, and New Urbanism. They are accepted ideas that nevertheless need to be explained well.[1]

As I work through the connections and conflicts within and between urbanist cultures, the underlying perspective about what will work or not work in the continued project of articulating and promoting American urbanism will become clearer. This viewpoint rests on a very basic idea: that the distinction between urbanism and anti-urbanism can be used to assess the positive and negative aspects of each planning culture. In other words, all four planning cultures are at their best when they are adhering to the main principles of urbanism, and they are at their worst when they veer away from it. Where the definition of urbanism gets complicated is in terms of process and extent: how to make urbanism happen and to whom and where it applies.

Throughout the evaluation, the criteria I use – diversity, equity, mix, connectivity, public space – serve to define the telos of the American planning cultures reviewed. The 'sketched historical and utopian urban form ideas' in a 'teleological format' have constituted a major part of the effort to mould American urbanism (Hill, 1993, p. 53). Having an end and purpose in mind – an Aristotelian final cause – gives some assurance that the diverse ideas will effectively interrelate. Note that this does not mean consensus, but rather coherence. Note too that it contrasts with the view that equates planning with process itself. Instead, contested terrains, moral discourses, collective self-empowerment and other labels for the crucial role of public participation in planning are deemed an essential part of the expression of urbanism (see Friedmann, 1989).

The two dominant principles or criteria that are most often used to define good urbanism – diversity, or principles about mix and interconnection, and equity, or principles that in a spatial sense are about location and distance – can be found throughout the discourse on urbanism over the past century and longer. The debate is over specific articulation of these principles. A socially diverse environment can be physically non-diverse, or a homogeneous population can occupy a physically diverse urban place. Further, economic diversity can exist within places of physical monotony. There is no one answer. It is possible to say, however, that social, economic and physical diversity that effectively co-exist, and that therefore most likely exist within some underlying system of order (which may or may not be recognizable), are a condition of urbanism. Jane Jacobs had such a definition, and she called it 'organized complexity'.

Equity, unlike diversity, is much more an ideal in urbanism than something that has ever been achieved. Yet, there are settlement conditions that can be said to either help or hinder equity. In talking about urbanism, social equity is largely a matter of spatial equity, meaning that goods, services, facilities and other amenities and physical qualities of life are within physical reach of everyone, no matter what their social status, and no matter what their mobility constraints.

What makes the implementation of urbanist principles like diversity and equity challenging is that, in the U.S., such principles will need to be applied in a variety of contexts. In an idealized sense, it is necessary therefore to take basic notions like diversity, connectivity and equity and make them work successfully, on the ground, over time, for a diverse society. Where there is separation and inequity, or where there are impediments to diversity and equity, there may be elements of a failed urbanism.

Each principle, in order to be implemented successfully, tends to imply other notions about urbanism. Diversity implies the need for integration, and equity implies the requirement for accessibility. Integration means that urban elements are inter-related socially, economically and physically. Accessibility and integration imply the need for fine grain and permeability, and for things like small, dispersed facilities. They imply the need to consider pedestrian orientation in addition to other transportation modes. They engender considerations of three-dimensional form as factors in the quality of place and experience. They imply the need for citizen input and the importance of the communal and public realms. They necessitate civic space and collective movement in the form of public transit.

Most urbanists will say that good urbanism depends on a certain denseness of social and economic relations. But density does not tell the whole story. Urbanism is the complex interplay between form and process, between structure and function, between social and economic systems and the supporting infrastructure these require. Diversity means that separation of urbanism into components, like land use categories, or miles of highways, or square footage of office space, or park acreage per capita – all of these abstracted calculations lead to, as Mumford termed it, the 'anti-city' (Mumford, 1968, p. 128). Jane Jacobs had the same argument in *Death and Life*, berating planners for treating the city as a series of calculations and measurable abstractions that rendered it a problem of 'disorganized complexity' and made planners falsely believe that they could effectively manipulate its individualized components (Jacobs, 1961). The real task of urbanism is to maximize interaction, promote interchange at all levels, stimulate both social and economic contact, and look for ways to promote diversity wherever feasible. That is the essence of urbanism.

But the physical articulation of these principles is not agreed upon. The principle of diversity of urban form is especially susceptible to an interpretation so broad that it becomes meaningless. In one recent interpretation, for example, urbanism was defined on the basis of indeterminacy, where the legitimate need to incorporate the ability for urbanism to adapt was said to be a matter of equating 'discontinuities and inconsistencies' with 'life-affirming opportunities' (Durack, 2001). This kind of definition, which lacks a clear idea about what diversity in urbanism requires, may just as readily condone haphazard growth and chaotic urban form. It can entail, on the one hand, an elevation of the importance of the 'mythic aspect of the ordinary and ugly' (Kelbaugh, 2002, p. 287), and on the other, a promotion of the view that strip malls merely represent a new, as yet under appreciated, aesthetic ideal (Kolb, 2000). In architecture, mass consumer culture or the speed of an automobile can become fetishized. All of these views are the extreme of urbanist relativism, akin to a philosophy that separates facts from values, regards all human nature as relative, and believes that virtues cannot be identified or ranked. Many architects believe urbanism is simply a matter of using architecture to help deal with, and perhaps work through, existing anxieties.

The urbanistic ideals explored in this book are about concerted, often planned efforts to engender or revitalize urbanism, not the appreciation of what exists irregardless of the level of urbanism involved. This is based on the assertion that concepts like diversity and equity are not completely ambiguous. For example, equity as a quality of urbanism means that, ideally, all residents of a place have equal access to the good things and equal distance from the bad. Equity as an element of urbanism is about geographic access and the locational distribution of elements and people. When this very basic idea is translated to physical principles of urbanism, it means that where people live must be equitably proximal to what people need, irregardless of income and wealth, age, gender, race, or other socioeconomic conditions. This means that pedestrians must have access to the good things cities can provide – like public facilities and services – to the same degree that car-owners do, since equity conditioned on car ownership is not truly equitable. This condition of urbanism has significant implications, not dissimilar to the implications of diversity.

But even where there is general acceptance of principles like diversity and equity, there is disagreement about whether such goals should be treated as matters of physical planning. Some question whether urbanism can be affected by manipulating elements of form, or whether such an approach merely superficially treats the symptoms of deeper problems. If economic and social systems are the root cause of bad urbanism, should not these be the target of any urbanistic goals, rather than improved physical designs? Should not good urbanism start with building the local jobs base, for example, reconnecting local economic networks, and empowering small-scale, independent improvement efforts?[2] This same underlying critique has been expressed in multiple ways for the past 150 years in proposals for improving the industrial and post-industrial city. It was the argument against urban design efforts at the very start: Friedrich Engels thought of proposals for ideal cities as folly unless the underlying capitalist system could be overthrown. Contemporary observers view proposals for changing the physical landscape as misrepresentative and therefore negligent of 'dominant and oppressed cultures, power and powerlessness' (Ellin, 1996, p. 157). Expressed another way, proposals for new urban landscapes may simply be expressions of market fragmentation. Such proposals are therefore 'reflecting and reinforcing the broader fragmentation and polarization of urban space' (Knox, 1991, p. 203).

At a minimum, urbanists have to consider the fact that physical and economic realities are interlocking. For example, the way in which a dendritic street system of arterials supports a strip mall is based on the latter's requirement for a certain number of daily drive-bys, thus necessitating a collector system that is often viewed as harmful to urbanism overall. The question is, do we adjust our view of urbanism according to dominant forces, or assume that changes will be made in support of our urbanistic goals at some future point? These questions constitute a major division in urban planning, forming two different perspectives on urbanism. The debate has created an essential divergence in every planning culture. What it relates to is the perception that fostering good urbanism based on the ideal of social equity in a capitalist system is a contradiction, since the engine of economic growth will always dominate any pretences of social concern.

In this book, I use a definition of urbanism that considers physical goals as both ends and means, that acknowledges the fact that underlying social and economic systems must be considered in tandem with physical objectives, but that physical urbanistic goals are also vehicles of change. Building housing without jobs can undermine urbanism, but at the same time, the importance of the physical framework as a means of accomplishing a more effective integration of work and residence should also be acknowledged. There is little doubt that specific perspectives on social, political and economic relationships go hand-in-hand with specific physical outcomes. This means that recurrent principles of urbanism imply certain viewpoints about social and economic systems. For example, elevation of the importance of civic society goes hand in hand with paying greater attention to cultural infrastructure. A compact, pedestrian-scale, diverse community that emphasizes connectivity, access, and civic space rests on a social vision of shared, or communal, civic responsibility. By contrast, and as discussed below, the anti-urbanism of the modernist city is based on a social vision that is bureaucratically run from the top down, focused not on collectivism but on mass production and efficiency (Luccarelli, 1995, especially pp. 205–208). The modernist attempt to rationalize and make efficient the complexities of social and cultural life resulted in what many consider a cold, sterile urbanism.

The difference manifests itself in other ways. It can be seen as a contrast between the historically-rooted vision of what cities and urban places are supposed to be like, and the more recent view that we should find ways to make do with the urban forms that the marketplace or technology has given us. In this sense, the lines between urbanism and anti-urbanism have become blurred. Scepticism about normative views of urbanism translate into the idea that we should not necessarily despair about miles of asphalt in the form of highways and parking garages, but instead should look for ways to interpret these elements as interesting cultural phenomena, something to be studied and incorporated in new personal visions by forward thinking designers. All that is needed is the right equipment for a more broad-minded type of interpretation. In the book *The 100 Mile City* (Sudjic, 1992), for example, almost anything constitutes urbanism – a cluster of big box retailers on the highway, or an airline terminal. Furthermore, if we turn our backs on this 'new form', we are being both 'condescending and self-defeating' (Sudjic, 1992, p. 297). The individuality of experience found in the Las Vegas commercial strip, scrutinized in Venturi, Scott Brown and Izenour's *Learning from Las Vegas* (1972), and more recently celebrated in *Everyday Urbanism* (Chase, Crawford and Kaliski, 1999), offer similar perspectives.

Division revolves around the problematic concept of 'order'. Order in urbanism has to be reconciled with diversity, and this has been a key sticking point in attempting to define urbanism. Diversity in all forms – social, economic, cultural, but also in terms of physical components – is essential for urbanism, but there are requirements for order as well. Some argue that order is required in order to identify the 'collective' aspects of urbanism, i.e., order is what conveys its public purpose. It allows us to grasp a shared construct, a collective expression that counterbalances the individualism of diversity. Order supports the ability for diverse urban elements to relate to each other in some way.

A key contribution to understanding the complex relationship between diversity and order was made by Jane Jacobs, who argued that order is not the opposite of diversity. Her solution was more akin to the idea of imposing a few basic rules to guide a process, rather than the imposition of a pre-conceived plan put in place by one person or group. The same idea was behind Christopher Alexander's influential 1965 essay 'A City is Not a Tree' in which he argued against 'trading the humanity and richness of the living city for a conceptual simplicity which benefits only designers, planners, administrators and developers'. Separation, compartmentalization, and 'the dissociation of internal elements' were signs of the 'coming destruction' of urbanism.

But the incremental, complexity-generating processes promoted by urbanists like Jacobs and Alexander have to be weighed against the fact that specific design visions – in their ordered coherency, in the strength and conviction of their vision, in their 'clarity of standards' – have tended to have the greatest and most immediate impact on urban reform.[3] Such reform is often criticized as being anti-urbanist, but there are also urbanist successes. In the end, the general consensus that accommodating difference and diversity is a basis for urbanism may mean that there is a need to find a material expression for it that rests on some, however nuanced and subordinated, sense of order. The investigation of urbanism in this book leaves open the possibility that there are legitimate ways of nurturing diversity that involve pre-conceived designs and coerced urban forms.

Despite these means of balancing order and diversity, order continues to be equated with the attempt to deny social conflict and control the unexpected. This is why M. Christine Boyer (1983, p. 7) critiqued planning as preoccupied with 'disciplinary order and ceremonial harmony', whereby humans are organized, but alienated. Planners and architects with a normative vision are routinely criticized as being imposers and stiflers who are threatened by the unknown and the uncontrolled. It is a critique legitimately rooted in the fact that almost all ideas about the spatial planning of cities have been linked to some form of social planning and reform (Kostof, 1991). The transparency of social intent has differed – more overt in Haussmann's grand planning, perhaps less authoritarian in the planning of neighbourhood facilities – but the issue of social manipulation has always been a source of disapproval.

When the quest for diversity is brought under the aegis of urban planning, there is a fundamental conflict that surfaces. The question that critics pose is this: how can diversity, which is the byproduct of many individuals working in myriad, individual ways to constantly alter urbanism, be conceived of on a level that is not individually-scaled, but is the product of one planner's or one group of planners' decisions? This was the theme explored by Jane Jacobs (1961), Christopher Alexander (1979), Richard Sennett (1990), and countless other sceptics of the viability of the urban planning profession. Urban planners, in defence, argue that the 'freedom' of the random, chaotic, unregulated urbanism of individual choice creates an inhumane, sometimes anti-urban settlement form. This argument was made most cogently by Lewis Mumford.

In short, some urbanists find it impossible and politically untenable to support pre-determined definitions and parameters about urbanism – 'we are too adventurous, inquisitive, egoistic and competitive to be a harmonious society of artists by consensus' said Jacobs (1961, p. 374). Yet, there is a counter-recognition that maintaining integrity, liveability, and place requires intervention. In light of these competing renditions, perhaps the best strategy for defining urbanism is to offer a definition that is multi-dimensional, not uni-dimensional. It should be inclusive and not overly self-confident, but at the same time it should not be about accommodating all patterns and forms of human settlement. The question is, on what basis is this distinction justified, and how are ideals like diversity and equity translated into a specific language of urban form? The multiplicity of answers, within a framework of clear principles about urbanism, constitutes the main content of this book.

Anti-urbanism

If good urbanism is about diversity, equity, mix, interconnectivity and the ability to make those principles work successfully, what is the nature of anti-urbanism, and where does it originate? One way to summarize this is to look for ideas that seem to work against the basic principles, and, in the American context, there are some formidable forces that can be analyzed. These will be discussed in the remainder of this chapter.

As already argued, distinguishing between urbanism and anti-urbanism is not about density or even level of intensity. Louis Wirth (1938) argued in 'Urbanism as a way of life' that large, dense cities produced the greatest heterogeneity. This may be true, but diversity can be found at other scales too. The measure of a town, as Witold Rybczynski (1995) analyzed it, is not dependent on physical size or population level. Ebenezer Howard held that all the elements of a 'city' could be contained, at least theoretically, in a place the size of a town. And Spiro Kostof (1991) pointed out that urban places, to be cities, did not need to be of a particular population. Ancient settlements could be limited to a population of less than 5,000 inhabitants and still be considered 'urban'.

This justification for a more inclusive definition is not just about a broadened consideration of urban intensity levels and scales. It is also about the idea that rural areas support urbanism by controlling, bounding or in some other way helping to define human settlement. This is why the view that urbanism should be bounded in some way and distinguished from rural environments and nature has been a recurrent theme in urbanistic thought and pervades every planning culture. In fact the desire to form 'a coherent and lasting relationship with nature' is a basic connection between even the most apparently divergent approaches (Fishman, 2000, p. 82).

Yet this has historically been a major source of puzzlement, and the inability to work out the difference between urban and rural domains has a long, tortured past in the annals of American urbanism. Part of the confusion has to do with how suburban development is to be reconciled with urbanism. Suburban development is routinely regarded as 'anti-urban' despite the fact that it has, throughout history, been viewed as an integral and necessary component of dense cities. Thomas Sharp, speaking about the problem in Europe, identified the essential issue in 1932 as one of 'debased' town development: 'Rural influences neutralize the town. Urban influences neutralize the country. In a few years all will be neutrality' (Sharp, 1932, p. 11). Now, the inappropriate mixing of the rural and the urban is one of the key concepts being used to define sprawl (Duany, 2002). The unsuitable mixing of urban and rural realms, not the rural itself, is thus one way to define anti-urbanism.

The more pervasive characterization of anti-urbanism in America concerns the principles of separation and segregation. While each of the urbanist cultures reviewed in this book can be said to contribute partially to anti-urbanism (separation, inequity), the cultures I focus on are distinguished precisely because they are *essentially* aimed at defining urbanism in a way that upholds the basic principles defined above. Again, some of the cultures have been more successful at upholding certain principles than others. The important question still to be discussed is: what should be made of the normative ideals that seem to be about the opposite, that were intended to create a type of settlement that, based on the criteria for urbanism identified above, can only be described as 'anti-urbanist'? While the anti-urbanism discussed in the remainder of this chapter is connected in many ways to all other planning cultures, and many would see the models described below as extensions of ideals already well established, they can nevertheless be readily separated out as approaches to human settlement that were so counter to an urbanism of diversity, connectedness and equity, that they stand apart as object lessons of what anti-urbanism is.

Two sets of ideas stand out in particular as exemplifying anti-urbanism in the American context: post World War II suburbanization, generally in the form of large-scale residential development; and modernist concepts of urbanism promoted through planners and architects associated with the Congrès Internationaux

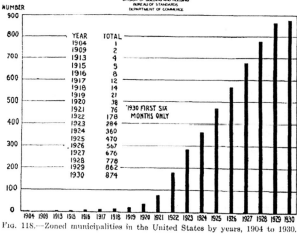

ZONED MUNICIPALITIES IN THE UNITED STATES
BY YEARS, 1904 – 1930*

DIVISION OF BUILDING AND HOUSING
BUREAU OF STANDARDS
DEPARTMENT OF COMMERCE

YEAR	TOTAL
1904	1
1909	2
1913	4
1915	5
1916	8
1917	12
1918	14
1919	21
1920	38
1921	76
1922	178
1923	284
1924	360
1925	470
1926	567
1927	676
1928	778
1929	862
1930	874

*1930 FIRST SIX MONTHS ONLY

FIG. 118.—Zoned municipalities in the United States by years, 1904 to 1930.

Figure 3.1. The phenomenal growth of zoning, mostly by single-use categories. From a textbook on planning published in 1931. (*Source*: Karl B. Lohmann, *Principles of City Planning*, 1931)

d'Architecture Moderne (CIAM). Both of these anti-urban phenomena have been discussed at length in numerous texts. Here, I review them in order to illuminate the essential differences between urbanism and anti-urbanism in America. I will spend more time on the issue of modernist urbanism not because it had a greater effect, but because its position as being anti-urbanist is more complicated.

In the case of suburban extension, the anti-urban tendencies vary in degree. In Chapter 6, I present the case that some aspects of the planned community, often a primary means of extension, form an important dimension of American urbanism. But where the planned community ideal leans too heavily on separation, white middle-class escape, and an exclusively residential focus, all of which constitute segregation and inequity, the link between the planned community and American urbanism becomes difficult. Such communities become more a case of anti-urbanism than urbanism.

Levittown is the quintessential example of residential development in the form of a planned community that was clearly built on the idea of spatial separation of land use and population. But there are examples where the planned community was built more urbanistically, that is, with ideas about diversity, equity, and the creation of more inclusive communities rather than isolated residential enclaves. Then there are examples of planned communities that seem to fall somewhere in between, such as the 'decentralized industrial growth poles' created by industries in the Los Angeles area, described by Greg Hise as examples of 'peripheral urbanism' (Hise, 1996). Here were discrete communities with a workplace-residence link, complete with neighbourhood centres and other daily life needs. They were not commuters suburbs. To the extent that they did in fact offer a full range of services and were intended to be socially and economically diverse, it is possible to discuss their urbanistic contributions.

Aside from these exceptions, postwar suburbanization is generally regarded as the antithesis of urbanism since it was based on principles of separation, segregation and inequity. And it was nurtured for years by planning organizations, the federal government, and powerful groups like the National Association of Home Builders, a topic explored in Marc Weiss' *The Rise of the Community Builders: The American Real Estate Industry and Urban Land Planning* (1987). That study showed how development was not simply unfettered sprawl, but was orderly, controlled, and designed. The community builders helped put in place the deed restrictions, zoning, subdivision regulations, and other land development controls that engendered the segregated pattern of postwar suburbanization. Although not all developments had the same level of anti-urbanism, the ubiquitous, large tract of single-family housing was an obvious example of separation. It usually also connoted inequity by excluding housing for lower-income groups and failing to provide services that were not automobile-dependent. What Ada Louise Huxtable called 'slurbs' became an embodiment of homogeneity and conformity (quoted in Shaffer, 1988, p. 275).

It is this anti-urbanism that has now come to epitomize much of the American pattern of development, a general attitude about settlement that began in the early part of the twentieth century and was fully in place by 1940. As Weiss makes clear,

Figure 3.2. Growth by subdividers and lotsellers, the predominant American pattern of growth. (*Source*: Landslides Aerial Photography)

the attitude grew out of the need for greater market control. This has always been the main pre-occupation of community building, and the main reason why it is often viewed as an exercise in anti-urbanism. This is especially true since many community building enterprises were (and are) geared to upper-income groups, catering to their need for residential exclusion.

Weiss points out that, because of their support for public planning, the community builders were not typical subdividers, but were a 'minority breed' (Weiss, 1987, p. 5). Mere subdividers or lot sellers actually created instability in the marketplace, and the community builders sought to undermine them. But the residential exclusiveness of the community builders, together with the efficiency of the lot subdividers, created a situation conducive to the subsequent postwar production of sprawl. The promotion of large-scale residential land subdivision, coupled with supporting federal policy, automobile dependence, increasing affluence, and racial tension, supported the rapid deployment of a settlement model that ran counter to the key tenets of urbanism.

At the same time that these forces were disrupting urbanism peripherally, a second category, generally referred to as 'modernist urbanism', was creating a different type of disruption. Whereas postwar suburbanization, whether guided by the community builders or not, was about peripheral, low-density, residential extension, modernist urbanism covered all aspects of urbanization – from downtown redevelopment to suburban shopping malls, to expressways that traversed the entire system. Unlike postwar suburbanization, modernist urbanism had a conceptually powerful, well-reasoned and well-articulated ideological basis. The mindset of the community builders was also articulated and publicized, but its physical vision was less ideological.

If we define urbanism on the basis of diversity, equity, and the related principles discussed above, then modernist urbanism would seem to epitomize the opposite. This is not a particularly controversial statement, as the modernist city is often derided on the basis of being anti-urban (see Boyer, 1983, p. 283). But it is important to stress at the outset that there are grey areas. While the most obvious source of anti-urbanism is the doctrine of the Functional City promulgated by the Modern Movement in architecture (discussed below), there are many ideas associated with the movement that are not so easily categorized as being urbanist or anti-urbanist.

We can look at two examples in which the principles of urbanism are not clear-cut, and where the dispute over implementation issues is ongoing. First is the debate over traffic separation. The question is whether the separation of pedestrian and automotive space is essential and non-detrimental, or whether it is deemed simply another type of separation that is antithetical to urbanism. Many planners throughout the past century have advocated separate systems. Lewis Mumford, Clarence Stein, Henry Wright and others believed that pedestrian routes and facilities like cafés and schools were being ruined by the noise and fumes of wheeled vehicles, thus making separation imperative. A counter-argument, from Jane Jacobs to the New Urbanists, has insisted that separation does more harm than good, and that there are other ways of mitigating the mix of traffic and people.

A second, related example has to do with the issue of whether hierarchical plans can accommodate the complexity of urbanism. Lewis Mumford wrote in the essay 'Social Complexity and Urban Design' about the problem of hierarchical circulation, whereby expressways undertake the 'impossible task of canalizing into a few arteries what must be circulated through a far more complex system of arteries, veins and capillaries' (Mumford, 1968, p. 161). What was needed to alleviate the mistake of 'monotransportation' was to make 'the fullest use of the whole system'. Related to this, Christopher Alexander later advocated a 'semi-lattice' urban network to replace the hierarchic structure of a tree endorsed by functionalist planning in his essay 'A City is Not a Tree' (Alexander, 1965). But there is another side to the issue. Some urbanists call for both hierarchical and non-hierarchical structures, based on the idea that some spatial differentiation is needed. They do not advocate a centralized, rigid hierarchical order, but they do argue that hierarchy that is multi-scaled and promotes connectivity need not be dismissed altogether. It may be a matter of accommodating both hierarchy and network, separation from traffic sometimes and integration in other instances, and knowing how the two can be combined. Often it is a matter of not allowing one interpretation to dominate absolutely, whereby an imbalance is created. This, many would say, was the downfall of the modernist city.

If there is a need for balance and flexibility in interpreting the requirements of urbanism, that is something the ideology of modernist urbanism did not permit. Modernism itself is rooted in the Renaissance and the Enlightenment, in which classical learning was rediscovered and rational order and reason formed the basis of social understanding and change. As a cultural phenomenon, modernism was more a matter of breaking with European realism in about the mid-nineteenth century, whereby the passiveness of 'reflectionist aesthetics' was rejected in favour of something more socially transformative (Pinkney, 1993). Modernism in the context of architecture and urbanism has an even more specific definition, associated with ideas formed in reaction to the industrial city, and, by the 1920s, ideas in which the 'dead hand of tradition' was firmly rejected in favour of technological innovation, formalism, universalism and functionalism. These were rationalist paradigms, combining what was believed to be progressive social organization with Platonic geometric shapes (Lang, 2000, p. 85).

The start of the modern period in urbanism is sometimes linked to Tony Garnier and his Cité Industrielle, displayed in Paris in 1904 and unique because it embraced the basic principles of mass production and industrial efficiency and applied them

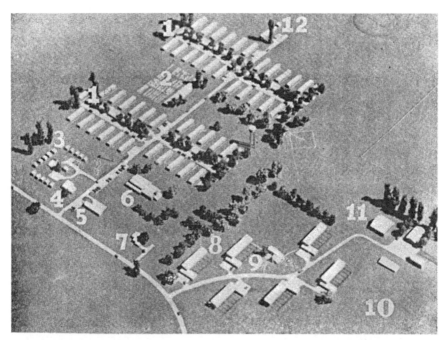

Figure 3.3. 'Rural Urbanism' according to CIAM, showing functional arrangement of land use. Included are row shelters (1); apartments (6); a central utility building (2); and 'homemaking and laundry building' (9). (*Source:* Jose Luis Sert, *Can Our Cities Survive?*, 1944a)

to city form. The plan boldly rejected past historical styles and offered a 'machine-age community' of hydro-electric plants, aerodromes, and highways, all strictly segregated according to function (LeGates and Stout, 1998, p. xxxi). It also separated the building from the street and the pedestrian from vehicular traffic, signalling the beginning of a century of free interpretation of urban form.

Modernist ideas about urbanism that reached full flowering by the 1950s and that exerted a powerful effect on urban form are widely familiar. These are: the separation of land uses, the accommodation of the automobile in the form of high-speed highways, the rejection of the street and street life, the treatment of buildings as isolated objects in space rather than as part of the larger interconnected urban fabric, the reliance on two dimensional plans that ignored the three dimensional aspects of urban form, the encouragement of unformed space, the rejection of traditional elements like squares and plazas, the demolition of large areas of the city to make unfettered places for new built forms, and the creation of enclosed malls and sunken plazas. These ideas and others were part of an ideology about urbanity, generated by planners and architects, that was already in evidence in the 1920s. As such, they were not ideas that came by default: they were part of a proactive programme of reform. And although these principles were ideologically driven, they were not always well explained. For example, the rejection of the street was considered self-evident by many Modernist architects, but no specific justification was given (Mumford, 2000, p. 56).

The ideas have been referred to as the Functionalist Movement (Trancik, 1986), but were essentially the main tenets of the organized group, CIAM. As Eric Mumford recounts in his detailed study, *The CIAM Discourse on Urbanism, 1928–1960* (2000), the CIAM definition of urbanism was essentially a continuation of longstanding ideas that had taken hold by the 1920s – that is, the focus on efficiency in city-building, the strong belief in the ability of technology to solve social problems, and the reliance on the master planner/expert to accomplish a better world. As Jane Jacobs analyzed things, Le Corbusier's Radiant City came directly out of Howard's Garden City, the former was simply adapted to much higher densities. Garden city advocates and regionalists who were later aghast at Le Corbusier's brutal towers in a park were only getting what they deserved, Jacobs contended, which was essentially a more intense interpretation of the city for the automobile. Super-highways, super-blocks and pedestrian separation had all been advocated prior to CIAM. Garden city advocates had to admit that they had already severed the building line from the street line in the early decades of the twentieth century. And the demolition of large sections of cities – so-called 'slum clearance' – was already an established part of urban planning in the 1930s. CIAM clearly strengthened the general approach, but it cannot be said to have solely created it.

What is striking about the history of CIAM is how much its rhetoric sounded like the common sense principles of virtually every other urbanist culture – principles that, on an abstract level, are not difficult to agree with, even now. They advocated the equitable distribution of wealth, utopian, future-oriented plan-making, affordable housing, efficiency in production methods, collectivism, and the need to situate places of work within reasonable distance of places of residence. A set of resolutions crafted in 1933 at the 'Functional City' CIAM event consisted of such statements as 'the city should assure individual liberty and the benefits of collective action,' that 'all urban arrangements should be based on the human scale', and that 'urbanism should determine the relationships between places . . . according to the rhythm of everyday activity of the inhabitants' (Mumford, 2000, p. 87). Siegried Giedion stated unequivocally that what was most important to CIAM was 'planning from a human point of view' (Giedion quoted in Sert, 1944*a*, p. xi). Later, in a reaction against functionalism, CIAM's Team X architects stressed notions like 'human association' and 'cluster' to claim an urbanism more responsive to human need (Mumford, 2000, p. 7). In a broader sense, we can even connect Le Corbusier's insistence on density as the prerequisite of economic, social and cultural vitality, with Wirth's insistence on social heterogeneity as a basis of urbanism. On the surface, it would seem to be fitting of a basic, urbanistic approach to settlement.

But CIAM associated architects, among many others not associated but nevertheless subscribing to the same modernist approach to urbanism, parted company with traditional urbanism by embracing entirely new ways of thinking about cities. Traditional and historically referenced urban forms were not allowed to be part of the new modern city. In fact the new ideology, abstracted and 'free', was superior because of its newness. Without constraints, ideas could be taken to their extreme conclusion. Abstracted principles could be elevated to approach what the philosopher Alfred North Whitehead called 'the fallacy of misplaced concreteness'.[4] When this happened, the complexity that was the original source of the abstraction became undervalued.

Principles were abstracted, traditional methods of place-making were rejected, and architects, working under a newly found freedom of expression, were individually given much credit for the ability to change society. Le Corbusier's belief that the mass production strategies advocated by Henry Ford and Frederick Winslow Taylor were 'natural' and therefore 'above politics' (Mumford, 2000, p. 20)

J. L. Sert, 1944.

Figure 3.4. Human scale in city planning according to modernist planner Jose Luis Sert. From a 1944 book edited by Paul Zucker. (*Source*: Thomas A. Reiner, *The Place of the Ideal Community in Urban Planning* 1963)

☐ 160 acres   1''=4 mi.

▬▭

1/2 mi. 0   1 mi.

is indicative of the kind of city-building approach that was in fact antithetical to the more humanistic thinking of planners like Geddes and Unwin. The latter group sought individual liberation through collective enterprise, something CIAM also claimed concern for, but which CIAM arrived at through a completely different urban logic. That logic was about arranging and combining the material elements of urbanism as if they were abstract, geometric shapes.

The force with which these ideas took hold is explained by the existence of multiple intersecting currents that crossed paths in the mid part of the twentieth century. Le Corbusier is said to have had an impact because he combined two dominant ideas – the bureaucratized, standardized, machine-made environment, and the natural, open space environment to offset it (Mumford, 1968, p. 118). On the other hand, modern architecture is also blamed for causing the split between planning and architecture. The exhibition of modern architecture organized in 1932 by Philip Johnson and Henry-Russell Hitchcock for the Museum of Modern Art expressed the importance of formal style over social function, leaving planning and architecture with no common language (Boyer, 1983, p. 303).

In short, the CIAM movement gave expression to an anti-urbanism that went far beyond anything that had been put forward before, and crafted a supporting language that replaced all prior conceptions. The focus on collectivism, the merger of art and science, and the ability of architecture and urbanism to create social cohesion were not new or uniquely co-opted by CIAM members. But CIAM transformed these concepts in a way that was so abstract and so removed from history, local condition, and pedestrian scale that it became a fundamentally different project. The denial of history was not only expedient (which indeed it was), but it was seen as a positive way to gain insight into a newly emerging urban reality. The result was another manner of separation, a loss of connection with time.

Some observers have pointed out that modernism was not completely ahistorical, and that there was always a subculture in CIAM where tradition and history remained more prominent. They point to the fact that Siegfried Giedion liked to lecture on ancient Greek architecture and urban form (Ellin, 1996, p. 303). However, the appreciation stopped short of any materially translated connection. Whatever the intellectual appraisal of history, the urban structures and forms created under modernist ideology lacked referent. Architecture was to be 'of its time'.

Under an ideology that suppressed past forms, Catherine Bauer proclaimed things like 'we must first get rid of all our preconceptions as to what a building *should* look like: for the new conditions . . . determine entirely new forms' (Bauer, 1934, p. 218). In a similar vein, Le Corbusier had famously recommended the destruction of Paris and then Manhattan as mere accretions of the past that must now make way for modern forms (New York had also, incidentally, been slated for demolition by Ruskin and Frank Lloyd Wright, among others). In its place was a proposal for the complete reorganization of urban life. The highly ideological system of abstracted rules about urbanism had little connection to local or regional culture, material, or building types. Individual expression in urbanism, other than by the architects themselves, was condemned. Le Corbusier interpreted walls of individually formed houses as a 'grotesquely jagged silhouette of gables, attics, and zinc chimneys' (Le Corbusier in Mumford, 2000, p. 56). This left little room for historical continuity. As Kenneth Frampton notes, the problem with CIAM was not necessarily its conflicted ideology, but that 'there was ultimately no ground left upon which to continue any kind of rational discourse' (Frampton, 2000, p. xv).

Maintaining historical connection did not have to mean imitation and sentimentality but CIAM members seemed not to recognize this. The difficulty, for the modernists, was that people generally did not share their appreciation of a-historical form. Some admired its rational purity, but architectural bleakness was rarely beloved outside the architectural *avant garde*. Some people may have been awed by the vision of skyscraper downtowns laced with highways – the type immortalized in Norman Bel Geddes's 'Futurama' at the 1939 World's Fair – but CIAM's need to reject what they regarded as bourgeois forms and styles from the past ultimately produced places that disenfranchised the average urban dweller. It was a detached set of propositions that ultimately produced a grim urban reality.

While almost all urbanist cultures have been concerned with efficiency, technological solution, and social purpose, CIAM members pushed the notion of functionalism to an ideological extreme. The efficiency principle began to exclude other considerations and merged with stripped down design to reinforce the idea that maximizing open space (light and air) and minimizing construction costs, was a perfectly worthy way to build cities. The Functional City became a uni-dimensional cure for urban ills, all by way of scientific principle devoted to furthering the common good.

Jane Jacobs thought other urbanist proposals like garden cities and the City Beautiful were similar. Yet there were key differences. Notions of human behaviour, scale, context, urban form, treatment of space, circulation – elements of urbanism came together in fundamentally different ways under modernist urbanism. One example of this difference can be seen in Le Corbusier's approach to the building of high rises. The very high densities he promoted, surrounded by open green spaces and highways, and inserted in the urban core by way of radical 'surgery' (as in Plan Voisin), was an exercise in abstraction and detachment, with little regard for concepts like appropriateness and context that were deemed much more important, or perhaps inescapable, in other, previous visions of an improved urbanism. Garden city dogma included a reappraisal of dense urban conditions and corridor streets, but it was not a complete rejection nor a reconstituted urban vocabulary. The new, radicalized language of modernist city form can be seen vividly in Ludwig

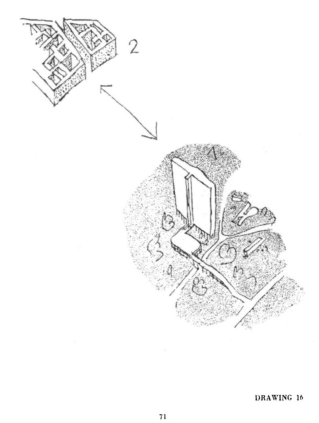

Figure 3.5. One of Corbusier's concise drawings, showing how roads 'teeming with a confusion of vehicles and pedestrians' can be transformed in a 'Vertical Garden-City'. (*Source*: Le Corbusier, *Concerning Town Planning*, 1948, © 2004 Artists Rights Society (ARS), New York/ ADAGP, Paris/FLC)

DRAWING 16

71

Hilberseimer's 1927 counter-proposal to Le Corbusier's Ville Contemporaine, 'Scheme of a High-Rise City' in which virtually all functions are combined in one block-long building. The detached, abstracted scheme was well suited to a highly organized mass society, but unlikely to be embraced by urbanists of the garden city or City Beautiful variety (Banik-Schweitzer, 1999, p. 68).

The problem was not with density, but with the devaluing of context. Andres Duany has commented that 'high density housing offers an inferior lifestyle only if it is without urbanism as its setting'.[5] Thus, what comes across in the modernist love for the high-rise 'solution' is an aversion to diversity. Gropius thought of high rises as the only real means for counteracting the congestion that resulted from low-rise buildings. It was believed that the coverage of land by row-houses and detached or attached two-storey buildings would disintegrate the city, creating its very antithesis (Martin and March, 1952). The high-rise would eliminate ground-level overcrowding, exactly what Gropius was after. But social diversity, as Jacobs and many others later argued, could not be effectively locked up in high-rise buildings and contained, and doing so denied human complexity. It needed, among other things, to be externally connected.

On some level, large-scale plans for urbanism are related to each other simply by virtue of their involving massive land acquisition, creative financing, and the need for cooperation between public and private entities. There are connections by way of communal land ownership or the acquisition of large, centrally located parcels for redevelopment, and possibly, the transferring of profits from the developer to the community. It is on this basis that Ebenezer Howard and H.P. Berlage have been linked to CIAM and Le Corbusier (Mumford, 2000). Via the principle of cost saving through large scale development, the modernist Catherine Bauer is linked to the garden city architect Raymond Unwin (Birch, 1980a). Here again, however, there are wide differences in urbanistic outcome, despite the similarity of certain processes. The fact that Howard advocated a community of 30,000 while Le Corbusier's was 3,000,000 gives some indication of the variation in concern for place, form and context. Frank Lloyd Wright's Broadacre City can be compared to Ebenezer Howard's vision of garden cities on the basis of self liberation (Hall, 2002, pp. 279–281), but the physical articulation of form and the collective experience it was to invoke are not comparable. And Berlage's street oriented perimeter blocks at Amsterdam Zuid had the social mark of uniformity, but they were four-storey, traditional row housing blocks that defined space in the same way as the corridor street. They were superblocks with internal green spaces, but there was no functional separation, rejection of the street, or centralized density. They still retained traditional concepts of place-making, and this is what made these and other projects significantly dissimilar from most CIAM proposals.

The conceptions of urbanism being espoused by urban planners in the U.S., either in the form of plans for existing cities or as new, self-contained planned communities, rarely lost sight of a specific outcome. Planners were increasingly concerned with process, but they did not initially reject the material subject matter, the physical, detailed, conditions of urban form in the way that CIAM proponents did quite early on. This is especially true of City Beautiful era planners, and later, planned community advocates. But in Le Corbusier's 1928 Ville Radieuse, urbanism had become open-ended, fixed but strangely detached, and concerned more with process. The statement on the title page of *La Ville Radieuse* by Le Corbusier that 'plans are the rational and poetic monument set up in the midst of contingencies' gives an indication of the level of abstraction that was transforming this new conceptualization of urbanism into something very different from that of Burnham, Geddes, and Unwin (cited in Mumford, 2000, p. 49).

The level of abstraction that CIAM was promoting comes through clearly in their manifesto, *Can Our Cities Survive? An ABC of Urban Problems, Their Analyses, Their Solutions: Based on the Proposals Formulated by CIAM*, written by Jose Luis Sert, published in 1944, and containing the statement of principles known as the Athens Charter. Meant for the mass American public, the polemic of the functional city was strongly argued in the text, but its presentation was fairly detached. Details of urban form, planning and design are lacking, perhaps as a way of ensuring that the mistakes of past urbanism – with its 'parade' of mere aesthetics – would not be repeated. As Joseph Hudnut argued in the preface, city design in places like Paris had 'a basis no firmer than a logic of form and a reward no deeper than an aesthetic experience'. The antidote was a city planning that was based on 'those processes by which material things are shaped and assembled for civic use' (Sert, 1944a, p. iv).

Can Our Cities Survive? is a revealing look into the mindset of the modernist approach to city-making. The solutions to the problem of the congested city are not only explicitly laid out, but they expose an approach that has been so widely discredited by the past 50 years of experience that, with hindsight, the proposals seem almost absurd. But there was nothing light-hearted about the advice, on page 62, that 'Modern building technics should be employed in constructing high, widely spaced apartment blocks whenever the necessity of housing high densities of population exists'. This was because 'only such a disposition can liberate the necessary land surface for recreation purposes, community services, and parking places, and provide dwellings with light, sun, air, and view'.

What we know now is that this is an anti-urbanist statement of separation and detachment. In fact, most of the proposals of the Athens Charter, have, at their root, separation. This makes them appear simplistic and utterly denying of the intricacies of urbanism. An example of how diversity is purposefully thwarted is in the call to have dwellings grouped in neighbourhood units so that 'the number of points of departure' could be reduced as much as possible. 'Express highways' would be used to connect destinations and origins in the urban system. In this arrangement, people were viewed like robots moving between points on a map, with highways serving as 'channels' to move the population to and from 'districts' as fast as possible. With highways serving as the fastest means of connecting two points, 'the evacuation of great masses of the population in the business district' could be easily accomplished.

The separation endemic to the functional city also squelched social diversity. In this it prefigured the monocultural, single-class housing separation of suburban sprawl that CIAM architects outwardly condemned. The CIAM manifestation of this principle was overt. In Le Corbusier's *La Ville Contemporaine*, for example, class was highly differentiated. The social structure that the city reflected was one of segregation by occupation, where one's job dictated one's dwelling type (Hall, 2002, p. 225). In Chandigarh, the new capital of the Punjab designed by Le Corbusier, such differentiation was built in.

Perhaps most importantly, what is missing from modernist urbanism is the notion of place-making, or what Lewis Mumford called 'social and civic character' (Mumford, 1968, p. 119). It could not really be any other way. All goals and principles were based on scientific, 'rational' decision-making devoid of recognition of the importance of culture and symbolism, and as if progress were a matter of geometric order. The narrow focus on speed and efficiency caused an inability to appreciate past urban forms, since traditional urbanism was unlikely to have been motivated by such modern considerations. A focus on utilitarian needs meant not only separation but a rejection of amenity and aesthetics. Planning in the 'grand manner', for example, was rejected because, although likely to 'achieve magnificence', it failed to function 'structurally in the life and movement of the city' (Mumford, 1968, p. 180).

Because of the focus on utility, modernist city design produced sterile places of institutionalized quality. It is a general rule in city-making that, as Boyer put it, 'functional and rational precision exude a cold and sober aesthetic' (Boyer, 1983, p. 282). The initial rhetoric coming from CIAM might have sounded right, but the translation of principles into city building was recognized as highly problematic. CIAM members liked to talk, for example, about 'The Human Scale in City Planning' (Sert, 1944b), but Lewis Mumford pointed out that 'there is nothing wrong with these buildings except that, humanly speaking, they stink' (Mumford, 1968, p. 184). It was as if the rise of the 'Orgman', the 1950s sociological conception of the anonymous, mobile urban man, was now finding an architectural parallel (see Jencks, 1987). It was an architectural expression of the relationship between abstractness and capitalism. Since capitalism seems incapable of grasping the substance and materiality of life (Kracauer, 1975), experiencing the city mechanically would seem the perfect method of capitalist expansion. What it meant was that there was no attention given to context, to the spaces between buildings, to the perspective of residents as they moved through the built environment, to the city's experiential qualities. Presumably, these were unimportant to CIAM members, or at least such considerations were subordinated to matters of efficiency, speed, and rationalized separation.

There was a separateness, too, in the way cities related to nature. It was as if urbanity needed to get out of the way to allow more of nature to come in. Ironically, what started as perhaps a logical need for green space wound up being a criticism of traditional urban forms as 'urban and stony', as if the quality of being 'urban' was something pejorative and in need of replacement by something greener (Mumford, 2000, p. 56). Concrete and steel would make this happen – it would allow people to live more compactly and therefore open up larger areas of green. But the modernist city related to nature in a very different way from, for example, the garden city. The modernist city abstracted nature. Nature became another statistical category to be rationalized and controlled. The complexity and diversity of nature, as in urbanism, was something to be overcome.

Figure 3.6. How 'Dwelling areas reclaim their right to occupy the best sites', according to CIAM. (*Source*: Jose Luis Sert, *Can Our Cities Survive?*, 1944*a*)

The idea of opening up the city to let in light and air led to wholesale clearance. 'Slums can not be remodelled,' Sert proclaimed unequivocally (Sert, 1944*a*, p. 24), and therefore 'the only remedy for this condition is the demolition of the infected houses'. And there was an insistence that the areas slated for a 'clearance programme' be large and inclusive, not minimized. That the cleared out area should be large enough was mandated by the need for 'a new urban scale' including 'new street patterns for modern traffic requirements' (Sert, 1944*a*, p. 36). What was to replace them was their antithesis, and dwellings that did not therefore consist of high rises set in large green areas (towers in a park) were berated in Sert's book. The point was illustrated with a number of examples of 'dwelling blocks' that had clearly got it wrong because they lacked the necessary space around them, and because of their incorrect insistence on 'perpetuation of traditional street patterns' (Sert, 1944*a*, p. 37).

CIAM proposed to quarantine the new housing developments it used to replace the slums. Rehousing projects were to control the environs of sites 'so that these environs might not again in the future have a deleterious influence upon the newly constructed area' (Sert, 1944*a*, p. 36). Here was another manifestation of separation in urban form – cordoned off neighbourhoods protected from outside encroachment. It was the urban translation of the doctrine of 'separate but equal'. It also gave such projects a case of what Stern and Massengale call 'projectitis' – the tendency to cut off connections to surrounding neighbourhoods because of 'artificial programmatic requirements' (Stern and Massengale, 1981, p. 48). The emphasis on accommodating housing need while simultaneously increasing open space invariably meant that buildings had to become monumental. Even worse, in combination with the stripped down 'International Style', and the decontextualized and purified aesthetics of the Bauhaus, the principle of the high-rise set in green space eventually translated into high-rise slab housing projects that were nothing less than disastrous. While CIAM members had no direct involvement in this translation, they can be cited for making such housing projects appear the only logical, rational choice (Mumford, 2000).

The isolated building, free floating in space, a megastructure in a superblock, also contributed to anti-urbanism by promoting separation and by suppressing diversity. Freestanding and competing 'towers' vied for attention while contributing nothing to the integration of space. The phenomenon of the isolated building and the building line separated from the street line was not limited to housing, of course. It became a symptom of all types of downtown redevelopment plans. Cultural centres of major U.S. cities often exhibited the basic form of isolated building set in open space, part of a master planned project. The difference between these types of schemes and the City Beautiful were significant if viewed in terms of the rules of traditional urban form, street and block arrangement, and the relationship between building and street. Plan-makers in the grand manner would have been concerned that their open spaces should not become lifeless since their primary concern was the civic realm. But the modernist isolation of buildings resulted, as Oscar Newman pointed out, in disregard for the functional use of space surrounding buildings. Modernist planners did not seem to understand the crucial difference between visual open space and habitable open space, and thus became like sculptors working in an unencumbered sculpture garden (Newman, 1972).

Many see this conception, pushed in widely disseminated books like Siegfried Giedion's *Space, Time and Architecture* (1941), as a damaging over-reliance on the architect's individualized notion of space. It thrived particularly well in the commercial American city where the individual building could be aggrandized even if it lacked civic, cultural, or religious significance. Modernist ideology supported the view that buildings did not have to be subordinated to the urban fabric as a whole. This often resulted in ambiguity. Because of the failure to appreciate the importance of context and the need to create connectedness between buildings, buildings became ensconced in vast expanses of asphalt, useless plazas, and other forms of what Trancik calls 'lost space' (Trancik, 1986).

Another consequence of the isolated building was the tendency to locate buildings in non-standardized ways, creating a chaotic urban fabric that has now become a defining characteristic of sprawl. Rather than a gradual increase in intensity of land use from periphery to centre, the Corbusian system translated into a haphazard urbanization of rural lands. Now, at least in part a result of this thinking, the American urban pattern plunges abruptly from edge city high rise to single-use residential development, creating a non-hierarchical city that, instead of an organized system of greater or lesser intensity, or any method of spatial differentiation, is extended using 'easily reproducible units pulled from the box of urban tinkertoys' (Abbott, 1993, p. 138). Other authors have likened the result to a train wreck (Duany, Plater-Zyberk and Speck, 2000).

The process advocated by CIAM for land subdivision almost guaranteed this non-hierarchical arrangement. The modernists repeatedly emphasized the need to do away with small lots, with what they saw as 'a chaotic maze of land fragments' that needed to be replaced by a single, consolidated land unit. This was how housing was rationalized – not only by new technologies (cement slab, glass), but by an enlarged scale of development. CIAM architects were not the only

Figure 3.7. Sert's manifesto boasted 'the great possibilities that are being developed in modern highways' and included this one from Long Island as a 'good example'. (*Source*: Jose Luis Sert, *Can Our Cities Survive?*, 1944a)

group to accept this new unit of urbanism. Catherine Bauer, the housing advocate and fan of Walter Gropius, agitated for the 'complete neighbourhood' as the unit of planning, financing, construction, design, and administration (Bauer, 1934). The neighbourhood planner Clarence Perry also adopted a modernist scheme in his low-cost treatments, resulting in bleak high-rises set in generous open spaces and described in his book as 'blight resisting' (Perry, 1939). Ultimately, the monolithic planning scale not only fostered building placement that separated and decontextualized the urban fabric, it almost guaranteed the elimination of diversity. Fifty years later, one of the key methods for generating urban diversity is generally acknowledged to be through the mechanism of small lot development.

In fact, variety was not something viewed as positive. Small scale diversity was something to be avoided because it meant the loss of control and uniformity. Property limits and streets simply got in the way of large scale rehousing projects. This is why Unwin never became a modernist, and why Howard and Unwin would have hated collective living that stressed uniformity of style. Their interpretation of collectivity did not have to do with sameness.

Again, it is this division between the traditional elements of urban form – street, block, square – and the CIAM conceptualization of form as high rise building set in green space that reveals a stark contrast in approach. The modernist rejection of figural space may have seemed reasonable on the surface: to free up more open, green space and let in more light and air, one could build at higher and higher densities and therefore occupy smaller and smaller land area. This could produce the 'biologically important advantages' that Le Corbusier thought so important (cited in Mumford 2000, p. 38). It is also reflected in the fact that consideration of the third-dimension was limited to height, since 'it is in admitting the element of height that efficacious provisions can be made for traffic needs and for the creation of open spaces for recreation or other purposes' (Sert, 1944a, p. 150). But, as Eric Mumford points out, this was a 'fateful formulation' used to justify 'vast numbers of high-rise slab projects built over the last seventy years around the world' (Mumford, 2000, p. 38).

The organization of the urban environment in terms of the essential categories (functions) of dwelling, work, transportation and recreation was a key aspect of anti-urbanism. Separation of uses was, in general, a modernist idea, and Tony Garnier's separation of living and working areas was one of the earliest articulations. Functionalism became virtually synonymous with separation. Jacobs referred to it as 'sorting', and thought it destroyed cities. In the U.S., the proliferation of zoning by functional use category was well underway by the 1920s and was reinforced in the 1929 *Regional Plan for New York and its Environs*. Later, the 'Functional City', CIAM's best known theoretical approach, constituted the theme of its 1933 Congress. Using statistics to project the amount of land needed for a particular use, numerous plans were created that looked interesting on paper, but excluded consideration of contextual, figural space.

For an urbanist like Lewis Mumford, the proposal to organize cities according to separate functions was immediately suspect. In a letter rejecting Sert's invitation to write a foreword to the CIAM manifesto, *Can Our Cities Survive?*, Mumford asks, 'what of the political, educational, and cultural functions of the city: what of the part played by the disposition and plan of the buildings concerned with these functions in the whole evolution of the city design' (quoted in Mumford, 2000, p. 133). Obviously, Mumford was not buying the view espoused by CIAM that modernization in the form of speed and other technological improvement was making the functional city inevitable. What he saw was a negation of the complex weave of urbanism into rationalized, disaggregated, functionally 'pure' and therefore controllable categories.

Movement systems were to be vertically separated. Automobile traffic was to be accommodated usually above all else, a way of thinking that had significant repercussions in the post World War II era, continuing through to today. It was an ideology that viewed the speed and flow of traffic as worthy phenomena in their own right. Already in the 1920s, architects aligned with CIAM, like the Rotterdam group Opbouw, were proclaiming that traffic should be the 'foundation of town-planning design' (Mumford, 2000, p. 22). This should be compared to Raymond Unwin, who earlier wrote that the less area given over to traffic, the better (Kostof, 1991).

The focus on designing for cars, speed and unimpeded flow was simply a narrow conceptualization of settlement that discounted the complexity of cities and human behaviour. It caused CIAM to get some basic truths about urbanism wrong. For example, Sert's treatise proclaims that 'the insufficient width of streets

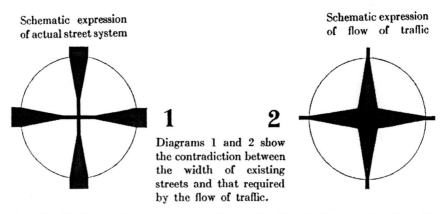

Schematic expression
of actual street system

Schematic expression
of flow of traffic

1   **2**

Diagrams 1 and 2 show
the contradiction between
the width of existing
streets and that required
by the flow of traffic.

Figure 3.8. The diagram, Sert wrote, suggests 'the gravity of the situation' . . . 'where the traffic is greatest, the streets are narrowest'. (*Source*: Jose Luis Sert, *Can Our Cities Survive?*, 1944a)

causes congestion' and that 'distances between cross-streets are too short' (Sert, 1944a, pp. 170, 174). There was dismay at the fact that the 'absence of parking space' means that 'the city motorist can no longer drive up to the place where he wishes to go'. Such statements signify a gross misinterpretation of urbanism by failing to address the interrelationships that sustain it – between, for example, land use and transportation.

The failure of the functionalist city and its procurement of separation was recognized by CIAM's own membership. Team X, the British architectural group led by Alison and Peter Smithson, criticized the functionalist approach toward the end of CIAM's organizational life in the early 1950s. They recognized that the separation that CIAM fostered was untenable, giving way to an inorganic form of urbanism. What the Smithsons retained, however, was the rejection of traditional urban form. The Smithsons analyzed neighbourhood life with its discernible 'hierarchy of associational elements' expressed in such traditional forms as house, street, district and city, but then they emphasized that they wanted only to reinterpret the 'idea', not the forms. Their 'task' was 'to find new equivalents for these forms of association in our new non-demonstrative society' (Smithson, 1982, p. 7). Streets and squares could not be used because 'the social reality they presented no longer exists'. Instead, 'streets-in-the-air', as proposed in Team X's Golden Lane competition project of 1952, were a new, more up-to-date expression of the hierarchy of association, now 'woven into a modulated continuum representing the true complexity of human association'. This was to replace the functional hierarchy of the Athens Charter.

But it was still another form of abstraction, another system of separation, another rejection of historical context and the traditional forms and patterns of urbanism. Almost all of the schemes of CIAM – isolated and monumental buildings, functional categories of land use, functional grids, streets in the air and separated circulation systems – shared these qualities. And unfortunately, many translated into city building principles with unquestioned authority in the decades following World War II. In fact, much of what happened to modern cities was prefigured by Le Corbusier's 'little sketches and terse statements' (Barnett, 2003, p. 28). In part it was due to the tremendous clarity and order of the vision of a mechanized, segregated and highly rationalized city, all presented in a 'monomaniacal' diagram showing the relationship between the height of buildings, the spaces between them, and the angle of the sun (Solomon, 2003, p. 173). And it lent itself well to the bureaucracy of planning. Where the vision could not be implemented via project planning, it could be translated into a zoning code to 'reflect, if only a little, the dream' (Jacobs, 1961, p. 23).

The legacy of modernist urbanism, functionalism and CIAM is an anti-urbanism of isolated buildings set in parking lots and along highways, of separated forms of

Figure 3.9. The modernist traffic solution was to provide 'unimpeded flow of traffic'. According to Sert, such solutions, like the one above for Stockholm, 'do not in any way interfere with what may be of interest in the architecture of this historic district'. (*Source*: Jose Luis Sert, *Can Our Cities Survive?*, 1944*a*)

housing and land use, of an inequitable pattern of access, and of a downgrading of public space to utilitarian rather than civic concern. It was a well-organized polemic. The manifesto *Can Our Cities Survive?* was widely disseminated, not only to important federal agencies like the National Resources Planning Board and the Federal Housing Administration, but also to educational institutions (like Harvard's Design School) as a textbook. Robert Moses and other powerful city planners at mid-century were responsible for implementing these ideas on a large scale. The first 'tower in the park' project in the U.S. was in New York in 1940 (Parkchester), which housed 42,000 people in fifty-one high rises. Soon after, New York built Stuyvesant Town, which housed 24,000 in thirty-five, 13-storey structures. These projects and many others – virtually every city in the Northeast and Chicago had numerous examples – quickly became the sole expression of public housing. In 1951, Pruitt-Igoe Homes in St. Louis would be heralded by *Architectural Forum* as the 'best high apartment building of 1951' (Mumford, 1995).

Already by the late 1950s, however, the ill-effects of CIAM's approach to urbanism were becoming the subject of popular criticism. Jane Jacobs was the most forceful, and her critique is still unmatched. But there were many others. There was recognition of the need to return to, as Christopher Tunnard wrote in 1953, in *The City of Man*, a place of 'memory, hope and visual pleasure' (Tunnard, 1953, p. 384). There were calls for 'contextuality' and the appreciation of the vernacular, and proclamations of the death of the Modern Movement with its 'blueprint for placelessness' and 'centralized corporate decision-making' (Ley, 1987). Rowe and Koetter's *Collage City* was an effective critique of modern architecture and urbanism, which they viewed as 'too contradictory, too confused and too feebly unsophisticated to allow for any but the most minor productive results' (Rowe and Koetter, 1978). Christian Norberg-Schultz (1990) lamented the loss of traditional urban structure and its associated meaning. Aldo Rossi assembled building typologies and forms as a kind of counter response to CIAM ideology (Rossi, 1984). Trying to re-establish the 'experience of place' became the cause of regionalism, historicism, townscape, and the legibility of Kevin Lynch.[6] From the planner's side, the response was to reject master planning in favour of advocacy planning, beefing up the techniques of public participation in direct counter-response to the expert-driven urbanism of CIAM. Ecologists and social scientists also weighed in with strong critiques of the Modern Movement in architecture. The ecologists based theirs on the failure to understand place and natural ecology, and the social scientists for attempting the social engineering of humankind.

However, despite these rejections and counter offensives, modernist ideas about city-making have become so thoroughly a part of the entrenched system of settlement that turning the tide on the CIAM approach to urbanism has still not been accomplished. And as post World War II productive capacity expressed itself in phenomenal material growth diverted to the suburbs, there was no viable model other than the modernist city ready to re-direct it. The International Style of architecture associated with CIAM has been overthrown, but the method of urbanism has proven more tenacious. No doubt this is because modernist urbanism offered an easier, cheaper method of reconstruction, particularly following World War II. From zoning and subdivision regulation to financing and engineering standards – all of these dimensions of city building fed off of CIAM's intrinsic separation and inequity much more readily than any notions of planning for diversity and equity. In post-CIAM urbanism, functionalism stayed on as a bureaucratic organizing device (zoning) now stripped of its underlying, untenable ideology. This was retained even when the new, postmodern ideal of breaking down divisions came to the fore. In the midst of a postmodern collapse of distinctions between fact and value, city and suburb, academic disciplines, and a range of other dualisms (Ellin, 1996), functionalism as an administrative reality of urbanism thrived.

Obviously, CIAM cannot be held responsible for all failure in American urbanism. It is no doubt the case that, as Eric Mumford argues, 'CIAM became a foil, the producer of an anti-urban urbanism that had met its symbolic fate with the demolition of the Pruitt-Igoe housing project in St. Louis in 1975' (Mumford, 2000, p. 269). And, although the Athens Charter is now recognized as 'an anti-idea of the city' (Huet, 1984), it was never intended to contribute to sprawl. CIAM architects strongly decried sprawl for its lack of collective context, a critique that is now echoed in the arguments used by New Urbanists. The model of a skyscraper downtown linked by highway to commuter suburb, all with a strong racial and class bias, was not something proposed by CIAM. But it was the legitimation of separation on a variety of fronts that made its way from CIAM to general urban planning practice, a trickle down of theories about rationalized planning that helped generate an anti-urbanism of sprawl.

Notes

1. David Brain, personal communication, August 2003.
2. These arguments have been made by Michael Pyatok (2002).
3. See, for example, Altshuler's discussion of the intercity freeway (Altshuler, 1983, p. 227).
4. Personal communication, Michael Mehaffy, 2002
5. Andres Duany, Pro-Urbanism listserve, August 22, 2003.
6. Although now, history of place has been segmented into nodes, landmarks, and other artifacts that can be fit into the reordered, functional city. See Jencks (1987); see also Boyer (1983).

Chapter Four

Incrementalism:
Beauty, Redemption, Conservation and Complexity

I call the first planning culture *incrementalism*: a suite of ideas that focuses on small scale, incremental improvements to the existing city intended to happen 'organically' and from the bottom up. This culture is the most internally diverse. As I will argue, different types can be identified, focusing alternatively on beauty, social redemption, conservation, or complexity. But in all facets, incrementalist culture views the existing city as ameliorable. Unlike other types of urban reformers, for example Ebenezer Howard, Le Corbusier and Frank Lloyd Wright, incrementalist reformers do not take as their starting point the need for a fundamental overthrow of the physical structure of the metropolis. Where at first this may have been born out of the inherent inability to make larger scale change, later incrementalists would not have advocated such change at all.

Incrementalist culture has tended to vacillate between 'romanticist' aestheticism and universalist idealism. Early on, its romantic inclinations veered toward universalisms and objective truths, particularly since early incrementalists operated during the Gilded Age and the American Renaissance of art and architecture.[1] By the mid twentieth century, however, the incrementalist approach had been picked up on by those who disdained universalisms, especially as they were being applied to the inner city in the form of urban renewal. Now, any discussion from the incrementalist camp of the need to improve the 'urban condition', uses concepts like 'repair' and 'revitalize' only with great caution.

The incrementalist approach now reigns at the forefront of American urbanism. For one thing, it is politically popular. In the American context, it could be interpreted as the Jeffersonian style of localism and self-government applied to

Figure 4.1. Hull-House buildings on South Halsted Street, Chicago, 1920s. (*Source*: Wallace Kirkland Papers (JAMC neg. 152), Jane Addams' Memorial Collection, The University Library, University of Illinois at Chicago)

urban places rather than the rural hinterland. This is appealing because the 'many changes by many hands' method of urban improvement has the potential to create a rich urban vitality and complexity.

This chapter traces the task of urban repair via small scale incremental change as it has evolved over the past century. The methods and specific areas of concern are diverse. There have been civic improvement groups, municipal arts societies, settlement house workers, neighbourhood guilds, and a whole range of individuals and groups trying to make cities more viable and healthy. What binds these individuals, and their associated ideas and activities, is that they never attempted to disassociate from the existing city. Their concern was to improve the city in a non-totalizing, non-plan-making, non-aggregate kind of way. *City* is used here in the broad sense of Louis Wirth (1938) who, in 'Urbanism as a way of life' defined the city as 'a relatively large, dense and permanent settlement of socially heterogeneous individuals'. But this is an inclusive conceptualization, and activities in any city that are focused on its improvement are included (despite the higher visibility of such activities in larger cities like New York and Chicago).

Incrementalists are focused on the urban interior: the inhabitants, the institutions, the physical structure, and the activities that occur in its various spaces. There are no big plans here, no attempts to radically alter the nature of cities. Neither does this culture include developments extraneous to the existing city like garden cities and garden suburbs, since the objective is not to escape the city's harsh realities but to transform them in small ways. This implies an optimism about the city. The incrementalist sees the potential for urban improvement and focuses on ways to make changes that are immediately achievable. This optimism was endemic in the Progressive Era, the period during which many of the incrementalist activities discussed here took place. This strain of urbanist culture is activated, in many cases, by a citizenry devoted to neighbourhood-level change that could have a direct impact on the everyday life of urban residents.

The radical surgery of the kind advocated by Daniel H. Burnham would not fit the mindset of a culture deeply engaged with the intricacies and eccentricities of urban life. The incrementalist is engaged in trench warfare. Their determination to improve the existing city implies an acceptance of the raw implications of urban life, among them congestion and a concomitant rise in social problems. Later incrementalists like William Whyte and Jane Jacobs who emerged in the 1950s, would extend this to include an appreciation of urban concentration for its own sake, and view it as a source of goodness.

There is an eclectic quality about incrementalists. Benjamin Marsh, a prominent early city reformer, was a Fabian socialist who advocated settlement houses, organized art exhibitions, and especially liked the German approach to city building. J. Horace McFarland, a leader of the civic improvement movement who later travelled the country extolling the virtues of city planning and zoning, was also the founder of the American Rose Society and instrumental in the establishment of the National Park Service. Jane Addams was an arts activist who, in addition to founding the famous settlement house in Chicago, championed the artistic abilities of the immigrant poor, agitated for trash collection in the inner city, and later went on to win the Nobel Peace Prize.

Incrementalists are pluralists who see urban diversity as an asset in a way that is more explicit than other cultures. In this they can draw support from the human agency side of political theory. They would agree that the shape of the city is moulded by larger economic and political forces, but they would also stress the role that individuals have in shaping city form. They might determine that elites hold too much power as shapers of the city, but this would only make them work harder, given their belief that individual forces can be rallied to enact change. Changes are necessarily small and incremental, but this, as Jacobs later argued, produces vitality. The downside is that the power of individual human agency can result in fragmentation. Rosen's study of the rebuilding of cities after major fires during the late nineteenth and early twentieth centuries suggests that power was not only fragmentary, but so complex in its distribution that it thwarted urban recovery (Rosen, 1986).

Another problem for the incrementalists is that certain social inequities may warrant – in fact, require – a more rapid and fundamental response. While the approach of the incrementalists has to be gauged against the inequities of the social structure at the time, changes advocated by nineteenth-century incrementalists may appear too tentative. As Fishman points out, many of the proposed solutions to the problem of urban slums were little better than the *status quo* (Fishman, 1977). Still, the degree to which incrementalists were willing to enmesh themselves deeply within the urban situation makes their efforts seem exemplary, even by more recent standards.

Because of this direct involvement, incrementalists produced plenty of ideas about how to make life better for city dwellers. Most often, these ideas were not constituted in the form of *plans*. In incrementalist culture, cities are taken, so to speak, for what they are. There is an understanding – more explicit with the later incrementalists – that cities are a product of a complex array of people and individual decision-making. The master-minded plan-making of Burnham, the comprehensive plan-making of John Nolen, or the new town plan-making of garden city advocates, does not fit this understanding.

Of course, ideas in urbanist history often overlap more than one type of planning culture. For example, small scale planning ideas, such as how to arrange a building on a lot in order to maximize sun exposure, may be a topic of interest in all planning cultures. What makes it incrementalist, as I am interpreting it, is how far a proposed change is meant to go. The answer to this question can be a source of disagreement. For example, Andrew J. Thomas, an architect working during the 1920s on garden city apartment design, was criticized by members of the Regional Planning Association of America for not going far enough because his focus on improving garden apartment design was devoid of a concern for larger-scale community planning and regionalism. It was interpreted by the regionalists as only an improved variation of the speculative city-building approach. Yet it was possible, according to Lewis Mumford, for architects who thought in regionalist terms, like Clarence Stein and Henry Wright, to escape his 'limitations' by considering factors well beyond site design (Lubove, 1963, p. 55).

I will review the varieties of incrementalism under three headings, using the terms beauty, redemption, and the combined topic, conservation and complexity. I will argue that each integrated with the other, each transformed over time into something different, and each can be linked to urbanism now in different ways. Importantly, each variety began before a time when there was such a thing as a professional 'planner', and city plans were a relative novelty. But they nevertheless constitute a critical part of the historical lineage of urbanism in America.

It would be overstepping the bounds to say that the different strains of incrementalism are the product of a universal love of cities. In reality, the motivations for urban engagement were very different. The redeemers were motivated by the conditions of poor urban dwellers, especially new immigrants, but this was not the main focus of civic improvers. For them, the driving force was a concern for urban beautification and the amelioration of industrial ugliness. For the conservationist, the motivation was often simply to save small-scale urbanism from the bulldozer. Complexity advocates were most interested in maintaining diversity.

The three strains of beauty, redemption and conservation and complexity all emerged in the second half of the nineteenth century, a time of explosive urban growth. This was also a time in which a new conceptualization of urbanism in America was being formulated. The new outlook for cities was one in which, as historian Carl Smith's study of Chicago revealed, 'reality, city and disorder became closely related, if not interchangeable' (Smith, 1995, p. 8). Disorder, in fact, came to be regarded as 'normal'. It is this orientation that set the stage for the initial development of incrementalist culture.

Beauty

America, during the second half of the nineteenth century, was urbanizing rapidly. From 1870 to 1900, the urban population roughly tripled, from about 10 million to 30 million urban dwellers. If the first era of American history was frontier expansion, the second era, according to Frederick Jackson Turner (1961), was taking place in the nation's metropolises. Turner used the word 'revolution' to describe the changes, and this does not seem exaggerated. One particularly chaotic venue of the 'second industrial revolution' in the later nineteenth century was Chicago, which increased in population sixty-fold between 1850 and 1900. There 'the combination of sudden titanic growth out of a virtually nonexistent past combined to make Chicago seem a place hostile to traditional ideas of order and stability' (Smith, 1995, p. 5). Chicago's fire of 1871, the Haymarket bomb explosion of 1886 and the Pullman riots of 1894 stand as metaphors for the urban disarray that flourished. The response of significance in the history of American urbanism was to promote beauty in urban areas via what was known as municipal art and civic improvement.

The unruliness of cities was furthered by centripetal and centrifugal effects resulting from new transportation systems that allowed both dispersal around cities and congestion at the core. But the planning responses were weak. From colonial times to the late nineteenth century, American planning focused primarily on the width and arrangement of streets and the distribution of open spaces (Reps, 1965). By the mid-nineteenth century there were only inklings of city planning activity. These were initially focused, out of necessity, on urban infrastructure investment, sometimes referred to as the 'scientific efficiency' mode of pre-planning activity (Krueckeberg, 1983, p. 3). These included efforts to improve drinking water, control contagious disease, and improve sewerage systems in cities. There was also concern for improving the housing conditions of the urban poor, and the first tenement house laws were enacted in the 1860s and 1870s. All of these early efforts were aimed at ensuring a minimum standard of public health and safety.

Early parks planning can perhaps be seen as the bridge that closed the gap between a concern for health and basic living conditions and the legitimation of a concern for beauty. Frederick Law Olmsted, Sr. is important in this transition, the quintessential urban reformer, who, as a landscape designer, interconnected urban health and beauty. The provision of parks for urban dwellers came to be seen as a legitimate municipal concern not only because it alleviated congestion and had other healthful effects, but because it provided the urban dweller with a much needed exposure to something beautiful. Olmsted and Vaux's Central Park in New York City, constructed between 1858 and 1876, embodied exactly these ideals. The 'townsite consciousness' of Olmsted's work made important contributions to the science of planning for good drainage and considerations of light and air, but at the same time, his was a project of beautification.

The helter-skelter of unregulated municipal expansion motivated early urban beautifiers, who generally worked at a much more modest scale than Olmsted. Urban beautification was about incremental and relatively feasible ideas that would, it was thought, make cities better places. Like the later City Beautiful movement, the urban beautifiers were not particularly in tune with the social and economic implications of their efforts, although a more forgiving view would be that they elevated beauty as the primary means through which social and economic goals could be accomplished. Scott postulated that 'Americans needed something more soul-satisfying than trunk sewers, elevated railways, and metropolitan water supply systems to stimulate their local pride and induce them to continue the work of providing the utilitarian essentials of urban growth' (Scott, 1969, p. 45). Thus the legions of municipal artists and civic improvement clubs that proliferated during the late nineteenth century were not primarily focused on utility, although there was always an effort to find a link between beauty and utility for obvious reasons. Their project was largely aestheticism.

The concern for beauty as a small scale, incremental project preceded the City Beautiful era, the latter generally dated from 1899 to 1909. The City Beautiful had already peaked in 1902 with the release of the MacMillan Commission's Plan of Washington, but beautification efforts had been underway for at least three decades before that. Thomas Adams, writing in 1936, stated that the World's Columbian Exposition of 1893 represented a culmination of effort in the preceding 20 years in the improvement of cities along sanitary and aesthetic lines. Thus it is important to emphasize that improvement efforts preceded not only the World's Fair, but also the monumental plans of the MacMillan Commission and especially Burnham's 1909

Plan of Chicago. Charles Mulford Robinson, a leading proponent of the municipal arts movement and later the City Beautiful, wrote that it would be false 'to say that the world's fair created the subsequent aesthetic effort in municipal life' (Robinson, 1899, p. 171). He acknowledged that the fair 'immensely strengthened, quickened and encouraged' the work of the municipal arts movement, but his main point was that there was a lot of artistic endeavour going on beforehand. Robinson, of course, was largely responsible for the eventual coalescing of these groups into the City Beautiful era through his widely-read publications on civic art.

According to Peterson there were three of these City Beautiful antecedents, together constituting its 'forgotten origins and lost meanings' (Peterson, 1976, p. 53). All of them were small-scale and incrementalist in orientation: municipal art, civic improvement, and outdoor art. They all revealed a concern for civic spirit, beauty, artfulness, order, and cleanliness. The solution to urban disorder was not abandonment or constructing anew, but rather beautifying the existing in a multitude of discrete ways. It revealed an intimacy with urbanism that pre-dates Jane Jacobs by almost a century.

The municipal arts movement was focused on small-scale adornment and decorative art – stained-glass and murals in public buildings, sculpture and fountains in public places like parks. It officially began in New York during the 1890s when the Municipal Art Society of New York was founded by Richard M. Hunt, who personally witnessed the transformation of Paris at the hands of Haussmann. The neoclassical architecture of H.H. Richardson, Stanford White and Charles McKim in the decades before were strong precursors. McKim had a particularly important effect on the movement when he pushed for sculpture and murals to adorn the Boston Public Library, bringing together painter, sculptor and architect to produce a supreme example of civic adornment (Peterson, 1976). Essentially, the movement was devoted to getting municipal government involved in art patronage. Backed by municipal art commissions, promoters sought artistic influx in all city domains. Although they pushed as well for street tree plantings, smoke ordinances, and billboard eradication, their main legacy was a call for the installation of art wherever possible. Charles Mulford Robinson, a main proponent, wrote: 'If drinking fountains, for man or beast, band stands, or lavatories have the conspicuousness in site of a public statue, their artistic character should be scrutinized as rigidly. Utility should not excuse ugliness' (Robinson, 1901, p. 212).

The municipal art movement sought to improve the city's appearance through what Peterson called 'activated urbanity' (Peterson, 1976, p. 44) rather than any specific ideology. This urbanity was affirming rather than obliterating. Proponents admired European cities and especially Paris, but they did not condone Haussmann's approach of slum eradication, nor did they dismiss the value of diversity. It had been recognized at least as early as 1854 that the street should be valued as a container of the 'diversities of human conditions' (Chapin, 1854). The lesson of these urban 'diversities', Chapin preached, is 'that out of them come some of the noblest instances of character and of achievement' (Chapin, 1854, p. 21). In fact, Charles Mulford Robinson, an incrementalist who later became an urban plan-maker, saw the potential of urban diversity in the latter nineteenth century and labelled parts of the inner city 'picturesque'. By this he meant that the complexity of multiple immigrant residential environments, juxtaposed in a way that celebrated rather than homogenized the city, was to be preserved, not eradicated. Robinson expressed his desire for greater articulation of the diversity of peoples – i.e., immigrants – living in American cities, lamenting that 'Russians and Italians live in the same sort of houses, of a style that is foreign to both, starving their own natural yearnings and depriving the city of beauty. All national characteristics are crushed to one monotonous level of architectural utility, until a part of the city that might be most attractive and interesting becomes the dullest of all' (Robinson, 1901, p. 211).

Beautification efforts were not about producing a 'White City'. Municipal artists sought the 'judicious use of color' as a way to enliven the street (cited in Peterson, 1976, p. 45). Many proponents wanted municipal art to be colourful in the sense of being indigenous. Art must appeal to the great masses of the public, wrote Frederick S. Lamb in 1897. It must 'tell the story of the human heart', whereby 'the daily struggle of the individual is felt and recorded' (Lamb, 1897, p. 683).

Municipal art proponents did, however, desire order and cleanliness. Its members detested crassness, banality, litter, billboards, and pushed for, and got, designed plaza entryways, triumphal arches, monuments in public squares, embellishments on bridges, and planned groupings of public buildings. These were

Figure 4.2. Civic improvement groups adorned the city by adding small public improvements, like fountains, gazebos and statues. These photographs were both taken in 1900. Left is Montgomery, AL; right is Oakland, CA. (*Source*: Cynthia Read-Miller, *Main Street, U.S.A. in Early Photographs*, 1988)

adjustments. They wanted civic buildings and places adorned, but they were not interested in creating entirely new urban cores. A Chicago art historian of the period explained that the essential task was to 'take every element of ugliness one by one, and try to root it out' (Peterson, 1976, p. 45). Existing urbanity offered something for the municipal artist to work with, a conception fundamentally different than the Grand Manner plans of European capitals.

A second category of incrementalism (having to do with beauty) is referred to as civic improvement.[2] It was broader than the first. It characterized the multitude of organizations that wanted cleanliness, order and beauty in cities and sought to inspire others to want the same. Its lineage is usually traced to Andrew Jackson Downing (Peterson, 1976; Wilson, 1989). In 1849 in an essay entitled 'On the Improvement of Country Villages', Downing exhorted the gospel of village improvement, emphasizing especially the planting of trees. In a subsequent publication by Downing's devotee, Nathaniel Hillyer Egleston, *Villages and Village Life: Hints for Their Improvement* (1878), there is a specific call for collective organizing, and Stockbridge, Massachusetts is credited with being the first community to create a formal organization in 1853, the Laurel Hill Association. From there the movement spread, especially in New England, and by the 1890s hundreds of mostly women-led village improvement societies had been formed throughout the country, predominantly in small and medium-sized cities.

National magazines such as *The American City* reported on the village improvement phenomenon, but the movement was given particular impetus when, in 1899, the Springfield, Ohio based publisher of *Home and Flowers* magazine began publicizing village improvement efforts around the country (Peterson, 1976). A subsequent convention in Springfield in 1900 led to the creation of the National League of Improvement Associations. At its second convention, the League was renamed the American League for Civic Improvement. The group adopted the civic spirit of the Progressive Era, moving from its ruralized village ethos towards a more reformatory urban orientation. At this time, too, it aligned itself with the Chautauqua movement, a society that sought to 'awaken in all genuine souls a fresh enthusiasm in true living, and bring rich and poor, learned and unlearned, into neighborship' (Vincent, 1886, p.2).This was indicative of the progressive civic-minded reform spirit taking hold.

Whether officially members of the League or not, the concerns of the improvement societies were eclectic. One of the organizers of the movement, Jesse Good, wrote 'No task is too great for these associations to undertake. They will direct the digging of anything from a sewer to a flower bed' (Peterson, 1976, p. 48). Like the municipal arts movement, civic improvers wanted to do something about urban degradation on a block-by-block, lot-by-lot basis – providing rubbish boxes, ornamental lamp posts and street trees, and agitating for litter clean-up, noise and

Figure 4.3. Hundreds of organizations like the Andover Village Improvement Society were formed in the latter half of the nineteenth century. (*Source*: Andover Village Improvement Society, Andover, MA)

smoke abatement, and the beautification of vacant property. A women's town improvement organization in Westport, Connecticut laid 2,000 feet of sidewalk; an association in Roseville, California planted date palms to line the entrance to a train station (Beard, 1915). There was a strong sense of collective responsibility for the condition of cities.

An integral part of civic improvement is what Daphne Spain, in *How Women Saved the City*, refers to as the 'Voluntary Vernacular' (Spain, 2001). Between the Civil War and World War I, women's groups founded hundreds of places to help the immigrant poor and women 'adrift' cope with urban life. In the process, they created a network of neighbourhood level improvements. Their motivation originated with domestic ideals and moral redemption (discussed below), but the effect was 'municipal housekeeping' – the effort to keep the city looking as neat, clean and orderly as the home. This provided newcomers with a recognizable community pattern, helping them to become socially established, but at the same time producing a tangible physical effect.

In 1904 the American League for Civic Improvement (ALCI) merged with the American Park and Outdoor Art Association (APOAA) to form the American Civic Association (ACA). The latter group was headed by Horace McFarland, an inclusive man whom Wilson (1989) called 'a firm feminist' – a wise position since so many civic interest groups were comprised of activist women. Unfortunately, since women lacked the professional credentials to become official members of the ACA

(Birch, 1994, p. 479), there was a certain reliance on the good-natured openness of their male colleagues.

The APOAA, the third antecedent of the City Beautiful identified by Peterson (1976), had many of the same motivations as the civic improvement groups, committing itself to billboard removal and litter abatement in addition to its focus on landscaping improvement and forest preservation. By 1903, the organization was so broadly conceived that it included the same efforts to arrest urban ugliness as those with which the members of the ALCI were involved.

In 1906, Robinson reported that there were some 2,400 improvement societies in the U.S., apparently swelled by a grand civic awakening in which Americans were seeking, as the president of the ACA stated in 1904, 'to give us here on earth in our urban habitations conditions at least approximating those of the beautiful wild into which our forefathers came a few generations ago' (Scott, 1969, p. 67). But what had started after the Civil War as a movement devoted to small scale urban improvement was, at the turn of the century, evolving into something bigger in scale. Charles Mulford Robinson, who referred to himself as a 'city improver' played a major role. He organized the interconnected ideals of the three strains of municipal art, civic improvement and outdoor art and became a spokesman for their coalescence into the City Beautiful (Peterson, 1976). Robinson was therefore simultaneously a promoter of small civic improvements, independent of larger and grander plan-making, and a proponent of its transformation into the City Beautiful. In his second major work, *Modern Civic Art* (Robinson, 1903), his theme was in fact the need to organize small scale improvements into a harmonious general plan.

The transformation was one of acquiring larger and more comprehensive visions of urban improvement. Even before the turn of the century, village improvement groups were joining forces with park and boulevard systems planning, yielding a new, more majestic notion of civic beauty (Wilson, 1989). In the City Beautiful, the interest in beauty, which had been the common denominator of municipal art, civic improvement, and outdoor art, became more single-minded, moving way beyond the more modest spirit of incremental change involving multiple actors that had characterized the earlier reform efforts. There was a transformation then from the 'activated urbanity' of hundreds of small groups to the contrived urbanity of a few visionaries, with significantly different implications. Small-scale changes to the everyday world of urban residents were not only increasingly seen as insufficient, but largely impossible to accomplish by a small improvement group.

Organized, small-scale beautification efforts lessened after World War I, and the American Civic Association changed into something completely different. In 1935 it merged with the National Conference on City Planning to form the American Planning and Civic Association. This entity joined forces with a number of other groups along the way, forming, eventually, the National Urban Coalition.

The National Urban Coalition is essentially an inner-city advocacy group, whose official purpose as 'an urban laboratory for education, economic development, and leadership programs whose recipients include persons of color' (National Urban Coalition, 1999) would be barely recognizable to the civic improvement predecessors of a century ago.

Redemption

Another branch of incrementalism, less secular than the beautifiers, was focused on social redemption. The redeemers were particularly interested in strengthening local communities, the 'parochial' world that exists between private and public realms (Lofland, 1998). The efforts of settlement house workers and a myriad of other groups sometimes referred to as the 'City Social' were involved not only in personal redemption, but in helping the conditions of urban neighbourhoods in tangible ways as a path to redemption (Wirka, 1996). Thus physical improvement of neighbourhoods was fundamental to their task, using tactical methods including public protest to bring about physical change.

To be sure, urban redeemers were fully encamped in the social work tradition. Their ideology was the social gospel – poverty as a public rather than a personal failing (Mills, 1959), and they invoked domestic as well as religious rhetoric down the 'path to civic usefulness' (Scott, 1991, p. 146). Settlement houses, parks, playgrounds, and community centers were all 'movements' with direct ties to the idea of social reform through improvements in social organization. The playground movement, an ideological endeavour aimed at the proper socialization of youth, has been described as 'militantly environmentalist' (Wilson, 1989) in the sense that the environment was to be the primary agent of social reform.[3]

The majority of urban redeemers were composed of woman's volunteer organizations – the 'voluntary vernacular' in pursuit of 'redemptive places' (Spain, 2001). The redeemers expressed a fundamentally different view of urbanity than that expressed by other reform movements of the period, namely the City Beautiful. The redemptive urbanists saw the diversity of urban life and attempted to make it more liveable. Therefore, the 'inspired scene painting, static and splendid' of the Columbian Exposition of 1893 (Miller, 2000) was unrelated to the goals of the redeemers. Spain uses a fabric analogy to characterize the difference between the redeemers and the promoters of the White City: 'While Daniel Burnham was busy trying to create cities from whole new cloth, women volunteers were strengthening the existing urban fabric by focusing not on commerce and large public spaces, but on daily life and the neighborhood' (Spain, 2001, p. 60). The difference was immediately recognizable. Frederick Douglass, a black leader, chastised organizers of the Exposition for failing to acknowledge the contributions and plight of the urban poor in the way that Hull House was actively doing.

One important function of these redemptive efforts was the statistical documentation and publicizing of urban blight that reflected a belief in the importance of the physical aspects of cities. Earlier systematic surveys of urban life centred on sanitary conditions. The incrementalists expanded this to document social conditions and physical context: Jacob Riis' account of immigrant neighbourhoods in *How the Other Half Lives* (1890), W.E.B. Dubois' exposure of racial prejudice and urban conditions in *The Philadelpia Negro* (1899); Robert Woods' account of neighbourhood poverty in *The City Wilderness* (1898); and the writings of Jane Addams and her settlement house colleagues gave powerful testimonies of the conditions in Chicago:

Little idea can be given of the filthy and rotten tenements, the dingy courts and tumble-down sheds, the foul stables and dilapidated outhouses, the broken sewer-pipes, the piles of garbage fairly alive with diseased odors, and of the numbers of children filling every nook, working and playing in every room, eating and sleeping in every window-sill, pouring in and out of every door, and seeming literally to pave every scrap of 'yard'. (Holbhook, 1895, p. 5)

Intellectuals of the time attached great importance to acquiring deep knowledge and understanding of all aspects of the urban environment. The field research of sociologists in Chicago is particularly well known, where Robert Park, a key figure, worked in the 1920s in a manner not unlike that of an urban reporter (Lindner, 1996). But prior to the methods of the Chicago School, urban reformers developed innovative ways of recording the details of their subject, the physical city. W.E.B. Dubois, in his 1899 study of the Philadelphia black community, urged that 'a complete study must not confine itself to the group, but must specially notice the environment', by which he meant all details relating to both the physical and social aspects of urban living. Frederic C. Howe reflected the sentiment, stating that a concern for personal redemption only was 'like a business man who neglects his factory in the perfection of a system of bookkeeping', and that the failure 'to appreciate that the city is a physical thing involves costs which the future cannot repair'. Here was one of the most famous Progressive Era political reformers pushing the idea that 'The basis of the city, like the basis of all life, is physical', and that human happiness 'is intimately bound up with the material side of the city' (Howe, 1912).

Jane Addams' work in Hull House is perhaps the best example of the importance attached to the physical urban environment and the need to know it intimately. Hull House was a thirteen building complex located in a poor neighbourhood on the westside of Chicago. *Hull-House Maps and Papers*, a collaborative work that included the efforts of Florence Kelley, was an example of the quantitative social survey work that was beginning to take hold at the time – a mini version of Charles'

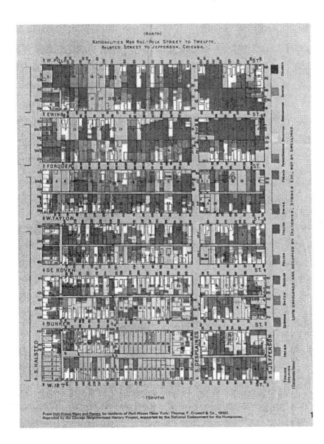

Figure 4.4. Nationalities Map No. 1 – Polk Street to Twelfth, Halsted Street to Jefferson, Chicago, IL. (*Source*: Jane Addams Hull-House Museum, University of Illinois at Chicago)

Booth's famous survey work in London (Booth, 1902–1903). It was a meticulous exposure of every facet of urban living. Detailed, parcel-by-parcel surveys had been accomplished as early as 1864 (Peterson, 1976), but those efforts were generally not concerned with both the condition of the building and characteristics of the occupants. The Hull-House maps accomplished both. For a one-third square mile area of dense urban intensity, the survey includes the dimensions of every room in every dwelling, details on light, air, and ventilation, and even the location of washing hung to dry. Addams viewed the detailed maps and surveys as valuable not as sociological work, but 'because they are immediate, and the result of long acquaintance' (Addams, 1895).

Accompanying this knowledge of physical conditions was a strong sense, on the part of Jane Addams and others in the redemptive stream of urbanism, of moral decline. In America, the response to urban squalor ranged from direct religious intervention and the legislation of morality through laws like Prohibition (enacted as the Eighteenth Amendment in 1919), to a focus on simply improving the environment of poor, mostly immigrant, neighbourhoods. The latter approach

Figure 4.5. 'The Playground', an essential part of early twentieth-century social reform. (*Source*: Graham Taylor, *Chicago Commons: A Social Center for Civic Co-operation*, 1904)

to redemption has been branded environmental determinism, whereby the moral righteousness of urban reformers was to be given tangible effect. Frederick Law Olmsted's parks were a well-known part of this redemptive effort. His moralisms, and the ability of landscape design to achieve them, are legendary.

But Olmsted's ideas were fundamentally different in approach to those of the redeemers. The redemptive strain of incrementalism was directly engaged with urban intensity, not in escaping from it in the manner of a picturesque garden. It was a form of engagement that can be traced more specifically to the settlement house movement that emerged in the mid-nineteenth century when John Ruskin, Arnold Toynbee and other activists urged university students in England to settle in poor areas. The first settlement house, Toynbee Hall, established in East London in 1885, was founded by Canon Samuel Barnett as a way of fulfilling 'a primal ideal' that 'University men' should take up residence in the poorest slums 'for the sake of influencing the people there toward better local government and a wider social and intellectual life' (Addams, 1895, p. 1). By 1889 twenty settlements had been established in America, and by 1910, there were 400. While 40 per cent of these were located in Boston, Chicago and New York, most small cities had at least one settlement by 1910 (Davis, 1967).

The settlement house movement and its brand of reform was morally heavy-handed, but its deep interest in physical urban conditions gives it a role in the lineage of American urbanism. Its approach was specifically influenced by the idea that the city is an organism, composed of interdependent parts – neighbourhoods – that work together to produce a viable urban whole. One implication was that the physical presence of reformers in urban neighbourhoods was deemed essential. Although some settlement houses were institutionally sponsored, Addams declared that the idea of residence 'must always remain an essential factor' (Addams, 1895, p.1). This was part of the organic conception, in which, wrote a contemporary, settlement houses should be seen as 'the organic life of society crying out against inorganic conditions' (Boyer, 1983, p. 25).

What this was emphasizing was the interconnectedness of urban life at all levels – the requirement for social mixing and social diversity. That urban redeemers recognized this as essential is significant. Jane Addams comprehended it when she stated that she no longer thought it radical to say that the salvation of East London depended upon the destruction of West London (Addams and Woods, et al., 1893, p. 26). At the level of the individual, the value of interrelatedness drove not only the idea of social mixing, but the notion that human lives are mutually supporting. Lillian Wald, an early settlement house activist in New York City, put it directly: 'the vision which long since proclaimed the interdependence and the kinship of mankind was farsighted and is true' (Feld, 1997).

Urban organicism was a late nineteenth century response to the disorganization of industrial, rapidly urbanizing cities (Melvin, 1987), a view coexistent with redemptive strategies like settlement houses. The intellectual underpinnings are traced to Herbert Spencer, the Victorian era philosopher and Social Darwinist who promoted an organic conception of society.[4] In Spencer's view, the more society became separated into specialized functions, the greater the interdependence among its parts. This view offered a way of coping with urban complexity: an organic whole of interconnected groups instead of a loose, unconnected disarray of unattached individuals was a much more fathomable way of addressing the problems of the city. Jane Addams, Mary Simkhovitch (a major leader in the settlement house movement who co-founded Greenwhich House with Jacob Riis), leaders of the community centres movement – all were working under the theoretical assumptions of organicism.

Within an organic frame of reference, the redeemers focused on providing basic services that could constitute a network of *places*. Their legacy can be narrowly interpreted as the physical manifestation of moralistic ideals, but the effects – parks, playgrounds, baths, facilities at the neighbourhood level – were valuable irregardless of the religious or moral objectives. And there were other approaches. Activism by redeemers was focused not only on neighbourhood improvements, but also on blocking developments regarded as threatening. In 1903, a group of settlement house workers in New York was able to block an effort by New York's mayor to allow the building of schools in public parks, a practice they saw as a zero sum game (Davis, 1983). Such strategies played an important role in shaping the fabric of American cities (Spain, 2001).

Some associations renovated buildings in poor neighbourhoods as a way of establishing residency there. For example, the College Settlement Association renovated a building for its headquarters on the Lower East Side of Manhattan. The Association's founder, Vida Scudder, who described herself as a 'revolutionary socialist' saw this as an urban manifestation of heaven comprised of 'valiant spirits, happiest of modern men and women, on pilgrimage to the Holy City of social peace' (Scudder, 1912). In Cleveland, Philadelphia, Atlanta, Boston and many other cities, similar efforts were underway by organizations like the YWCA, the Salvation Army, and the National Association of Colored Women (Spain, 2001).

If one can get past the moralisms, the ability to plan for neighbourhood needs – before there was such a thing as 'neighbourhood planning' – is not dissimilar to current quests to bring residents and needed services into closer alignment. The redeemers were building incrementally, working towards better functioning urban neighbourhoods in very pragmatic ways. Hull House was exemplary; its emphasis on neighbourhood service provision demonstrated a genuine commitment to urbanism. It established a series of firsts in the city: the first public baths, first public playground, first public gymnasium, first small theatre, first public kitchen, first group work school, first painting loan programme, first free art exhibit, first fresh air school, and first public swimming pool. Here was a social service organization using the physical form of the urban neighbourhood as its catalyst for change. Provision of neighbourhood public facilities was the physical articulation of community-building. Jacob Riis, 'the most useful citizen of New York' according to Theodore Roosevelt, worked along similar lines, agitating for public installations of baths and playgrounds to help the same neighbourhoods he photographed (Alland, 1972).

Urban reformers during the Progressive Era understood the importance of what we would today call 'mixed use' for the simple reason that the integration of uses, if done right, meant the equitable distribution of resources. Social justice was defined on the basis of spatial access. Jane Addams complained that basic facilities like libraries, galleries and other 'semi-public conveniences for social life' were 'blocks away' from workers' housing (Addams and Woods, et al., 1893, p. 2). Benjamin Marsh, who straddles both the small scale efforts of the settlement house workers and the later activities of the urban plan-makers, made an explicit proposal for mixed use. At an exhibition of the Committee on Congestion of Population in 1907, he proposed the need for working class housing in which workers could walk to work and neighbourhood facilities. The idea of mixing uses was thus proposed as a way of relieving congestion. Mary Simkhovitch was equally aware that facilities and services made urban neighbourhoods viable and, where suburbs lacked these services, she was against the proposal to suburbanize urban populations as a way of relieving congestion (Sies and Silver, 1996). Simkhovitch (1949, pp. 90, 98) wrote that the neighbourhood as a focus on urban life was appealing because of its potential to be a 'manageable microcosm'.

Sociologists also fuelled the focus on neighbourhood. Charles Horton Cooley (1902), inspired by the German sociologist Ferdinand Toennies who thought the condition of society in cities deplorable, promoted the importance of the face-to-face local community. Settlement house workers took the social integration aspects of this doctrine to heart, as did the related community centre movement. But they did so by giving the concept physical expression, i.e., by attaching importance to the provision of a local meeting place that would help give neighbourhood community life structure (Mumford, 1968). Edward Ward, who originated the community centre concept in 1907 in Rochester, New York, was particularly committed to the idea of using neighbourhood schools for multiple community functions (Ward, 1915), an idea also advocated by Jacob Riis. Clarence Perry, regarded as the key articulator of the neighbourhood unit concept,[5] placed similar stock in the supportive role played by centralized neighbourhood facilities.

Finally, social redeemers did not discount the importance of art and beauty in urban places. They had the idea that beauty was an important quality of everyday living that must be constituted in all neighbourhoods, particularly impoverished ones. Jacob Riis also believed in art as a positive influence, and Greenwich House was an outlet for neighbourhood music and handicrafts. Jane Addams was a firm believer in promoting high arts for immigrants of all ages, and at Hull House young children performed Shakespeare and Molière. A protégé of the Hull House music school was Benny Goodman, who took clarinet lessons there in the 1920s.

This interest in art meant that the redeemers had strong similarities to civic improvers and municipal arts supporters. The redeemers' perspective on art had two important qualities, both of which were in keeping with their overall approach to neighbourhood improvement. First, art was to be 'of the people' rather than imposed from above. A strong case was made for the importance of vernacular art in the Ellen Gates Starr article 'Art and Labor', published in 1895 in *Hull-House Maps and Papers*: 'Let us admit that art must be of the people if it is to be at all . . . no man can execute artistically what another man plans'. There was a related interest in reviving craftsmanship. In 1900, the Hull House Labor Museum opened to showcase the craftsmanship of neighbourhood immigrants. The connection to Ruskin and Morris is direct, but Addams' goal was to inspire children to appreciate their parent's artistic talent (Jane Addams' Hull House Museum, 2002). Another aspect of the redeemers' experience with art and beauty in the urban environment was that, like the civic improvers, there was a recognition of the importance of variety. Mary Simkhovitch (1949, p. 110) wrote that one of the 'defects' of public housing was that it did not have enough variety of architectural design. Starr (1895) admonished against the 'dismal experience of life barren of beauty and variety'.

The work of the social redeemers began to fade when municipal government started to assume responsibility for many of the functions they provided. Kindergartens, public health centres, community centres, parks, and playgrounds were all facilities whose locationally strategic provision defined the incrementalist agenda early on. Their necessity is now widely recognized, if not always provided with the same fervour, or sense of collective spirit. A feminist view is that male authority came to dominate the redemptive efforts that were initially run by women, and the activities of the smaller groups were pushed backstage (Spain, 2001).

Conservation and Complexity

There is a third 'stream' of incrementalist culture that can be used to define American urbanism. These are the efforts aimed specifically at conservation and the retention of urban complexity. As with all incrementalist culture, there is an appreciation of the small-scale, intricate nature of city life, but this stream focuses on these qualities explicitly and sometimes exclusively. There is much in common with the beautifiers and the redeemers, particularly in the appreciation for the vernacular. Later, a more sophisticated articulation of these principles emerged as the 'organized complexity' of Jane Jacobs and the pattern language of Christopher Alexander.

The lineage of this aspect of incrementalist culture began in Europe in the mid-nineteenth century. At the time, a great deal of demolition was occurring in the old city centres. It was not limited to the Haussmannization of Paris – many medieval cores were subjected to a radical opening up in order to accommodate expansion of the industrial complex, alleviate congestion, and link central cores to surrounding fringe development. The opposition to this, a 'cultural, social and historicizing' defence of old towns, coalesced first around the preservation of significant buildings, and later moved to the issue of contextualism. The shift was motivated by the treatment of older buildings, or where important buildings were preserved, the radical alteration of their setting. Significant buildings would be 'disencumbered', isolated and stripped clean of surrounding historical context (Kostof, 1991).

Camillo Sitte was one of the most widely read and influential architects to lament the loss of historical accretion. His 1889 book, *City-Building According to Artistic Principles*, was a defence of the aestheticism of picturesque old towns, and for this

Sitte is regarded as the quintessential romanticist in city planning (Ley, 1987). But he was not narrowly focused on only organic, medieval patterns. His importance in the urbanist lineage lies in the degree to which he fostered an appreciation of complex, diverse urban forms as opposed to the geometric regularizing being advocated in large European cities and their extensions. He understood the social implications of this, as he was especially critical of the disappearance of the 'scenes of public life' (Sitte, 1965, 1889, p.2). The complexity of which he made his readers aware was about land uses, buildings and their contexts, and the spaces that cities contain. He advocated the *Gesamtkunstwerk*, an intermingled rather than functionally dispersed city (Krier, 1982). Thus he was against the segregation of uses into zones and promoted instead 'the science of relationships' (Kostof, 1991). The design component of this integration was focused on the need for enclosed space and the articulation of public squares as if they were outdoor rooms.

Sitte, who has been compared to William Morris (Peets, 1927), defended 'the small incident, the twisted street, the rounded corner, the little planted oasis unexpectedly come upon' (Kostof, 1991, p. 84), reflecting an interest in promoting incremental, small-scale change as opposed to radical readjustment. Here was both an appreciation of complexity and a promotion of conservation. There were others who, like Sitte, were reacting to radical urban change in the form of regularization. The mayor of Brussels, Charles Buls, invoked the authority of Sitte and in his 1893 book *L'Esthetique des Villes* (*The Design of Cities*) wrote that old streets please because of their 'beautiful disorder'. Kostof (1991, p. 84) reports that even by 1909 in Paris the Prefect of the Seine was talking about the dangers of too much regularity, and the need to avoid the American habit of grid regularity. For France, this extended to a change in urban renewal policy for the medinas in the African colonies, previously subjected to ruthless 'modernization'.

Conservation was not only about an appreciation of earlier urban forms, with their complexity, enclosed spaces, and interrelatedness. It was also about the maintenance of cultural identity, and this aspect was promoted by such famously anti-big metropolis intellectuals as Lewis Mumford and Patrick Geddes. Both spoke disparagingly about cities, Geddes stating that 'any metropolis . . . stunts the mind, warps it to a viewpoint of fancied superiority over the provinces' (Boardman, 1944, p. 241). Yet they could appreciate that there was a cultural benefit to urban complexity. What they were against was improvement that was mechanical and uniform. With an appreciation of the complexity and diversity of old towns, Geddes devoted great energy to the preservation of traditional cities. His renewal plan for Balrampur in India (1917) is illustrative. The plan called for leaving the city alone and allowing citizens to express their individuality (Kostof, 1991). There was a sensitivity to urban places that mirrored Sitte and contrasted strongly with Haussmann.

Figure 4.6. The type of urban environment Jacobs appreciated, and Mumford disdained. Mumford's caption on this photograph, from his book *The Culture of Cities*, discusses the plight of the 'sustaining proletariat' in service to the rich. (*Source*: Lewis Mumford, *The Culture of Cities*, 1938)

In the U.S., where there was no medina or medieval town centre to rally behind, the appreciation of urbanistic complexity came in the form of an appreciation of the cosmopolitanism of U.S. cities. This was a different brand of support from the beautifiers and redeemers. It entailed an even more overt understanding of the advantages of ethnic and cultural diversity than the redeemers demonstrated. Thus New York was admired for the 'restless innovativeness that seemed to leap forth from every corner'. A journalist writing in 1907 described New York as 'a collection of cities' in which many nationalities met with 'flattering acceptance' (Lees, 1984, p. 90).

It is true that an appreciation of complexity in urbanism was overshadowed by a counter response that, by the 1920s, pushed for garden cities, greenbelt towns, and neighbourhood units. The famous 1929 *Regional Plan for New York and its Environs* was decidedly not a celebration of urbanistic qualities in the way of beautifiers and redeemers. Admiration of urban conservation and complexity diminished, not coincidentally, as massive suburbanization began to affect the urban core in noticeable ways. At the same time, there was conceptual support for these anti-urban views from the sociologists of the 1920s and 1930s, who were obsessed with the idea of the impersonal city. By 1951, sociologists like C. Wright Mills were writing papers like 'The Modern City: Anomic, Impersonal, Meaningless' (Mills, 1951). Although this work is rooted in the much earlier writings of Durkheim and Toennies, it resonated in a particular way with the post World War II assault on urban complexity.

But a counter response to this conception emerged almost simultaneously. Already in the 1940s, some were arguing that planned communities were sterile. Garden cities, some believed, lacked the very qualities that urbanists were attempting to preserve. Preservationists were aware of the need to conserve the residential areas of central cities as early as the 1920s (Silver, 1991), a strategy that countered the decentralization efforts of garden city advocates. The 1947 book *Communitas* by Percival and Paul Goodman explicitly called for a renewed appreciation of urbanism in the sense of conservation and complexity. The architect/philosopher team called for urban preservation, celebration of diverse urban neighbourhoods, and an appreciation of earlier city form of the kind Sitte admired.

Magazine articles that appeared in the 1950s picked up on the theme that planners failed to understand cities and their complexity. Writing in *Architectural Forum* and *Fortune*, contributors like William Whyte and Jane Jacobs loudly protested the decline of the metropolis. Charles Abrams (1952) objected to decreases in density, writing in 1952 that Unwin's proposal for twelve units to the acre was tyrannical and, in some locations, 'downright nonsense'. Not everyone was advocating modernist towers; many of these attacks were essentially in support of urban complexity in the sense of traditional urban form. Whyte's (1958a) edited volume, *The Exploding Metropolis*, was, he said, 'a book by people who like cities' – places that were centripetal, naturally concentrated, and well-liked because of it. These post World War II incrementalists were now promoting urbanism as a counter response to sprawl, and William Whyte's (1958b) article 'Urban Sprawl' made this connection vociferously.

Jane Jacobs was less focused on the problem of sprawl, but her defence of cities was (and is) unparalleled. Her writing brought a new level of sophistication about what makes cities work, and what makes them good places to live in. Her contemporary, Robert Moses, thought city living could be made attractive for the middle class if it contained suitable recreational opportunities and if their automobile-dependency could be accommodated (Wilson, 1983). Such an approach had nothing to do with urban vitality, and Jacobs thought Moses could not have been further afield. What was needed instead was a celebration of urbanity itself. This was different from earlier incrementalists only in the degree to which complexity and concentration were explicitly admired. Jacobs' admiration extended previous incrementalist thinking, which had been more utilitarian, into an appreciation of the natural underlying order of urban complexity.

Jacobs' critique in *Death and Life of Great American Cities* is so well known that it is not necessary to review it here. But it is possible to sort out the concepts that tie into other tenets of incrementalism. Her disdain for the destruction of established communities is the most basic link. Instead of garden cities or the cities-within-cities of modernist high rises set in parks, Jacobs celebrated the diverse, fine-grained city with its multiple integrated uses. Such uses, if fine-grained, were mutually supportive. She was in favour of high urban densities, that employed the right idea about how cities function; that is, those with mixed uses, short blocks, aged buildings, and a sufficient level of concentration.

It is important to recognize that the value of concentration was recognized well before Jane Jacobs and William Whyte. Charles Mulford Robinson had stated that the density of population in tenement districts was not necessarily an indication of overcrowding if the buildings were 'safe and commodious' themselves (Robinson, 1903, p. 258). Benjamin Marsh, in his 1909 treatise *An Introduction to City Planning* stated that 'a careful distinction must [be] made between congestion of population and concentration of population . . . Concentration of population is a normal social condition, congestion of population is a pathological condition' (Marsh, 1909, pp. 16–17). Marsh knew that concentration, which he attributed to humankind's natural 'gregariousness' was important for the viability of cultural amenities, good schools, and other social and economic functions.

Jacobs' prescriptions tie into a particular view about 'the kind of problem a city is'. As far as understanding the nature of cities, modernists, according to Jacobs, lacked this understanding. Neither Le Corbusier's towers in the park nor Eliel Saarinen's 'organic decentralization' constituted the right approach. Their mistake was in treating the city as if it were a two-dimensional problem of simplicity rather than treating each issue as a multi-sided, complex problem of 'organized complexity'. Such problems are made up of factors that interrelate simultaneously. This invoked Jacobs' particular notion of the organic city where, not unlike the redeemers, cities are conceived as an interrelated set of variables organized in subtly interconnected ways. Cities, as heterogeneous settlements, can not be treated as relationships between two variables, like the ratio of open space to population. This was something that other urbanists had recognized earlier. Charles Mulford Robinson complained in 1903 that population density and park distribution 'all counted for more than a mere ratio' (Wilson, 1989, p. 74).

Like Robert Park and other Chicago School sociologists, incrementalists noticed that, as in natural ecologies, human life is enriched when interdependencies become more complex. This theme was also picked up earlier than Jacobs by Eliel Saarinen, the Finnish architect (and father of Eero), whose architectural philosophy was based on ideas that integrated art, nature, and science. But Saarinen's philosophy also demonstrates how the organic conception can run counter to an appreciation of complex interdependencies and veer instead towards an urban policy that promotes radical urban 'surgery'. In Saarinen's view of organicism, explained in 1943 in *The City*, bad cells in the hearts of cities caused slums to spread in the same way that cancerous tissues caused biological organisms to disintegrate. Harland Bartholomew, one of the country's earliest and most successful professional planners, was making proposals in 1932 for eradication of slums and their replacement with neighbourhood units built on superblocks using an identical, 'organic' logic.

The difference between these proposals and those of urbanists like Jacobs is that the latter group focused on small-scale, incremental change. Using tactics of 'emphasis and suggestion' (Jacobs, 1961, p. 377), the goal of planners, Jacobs states, should be to help people make order out of the chaos around them. Small changes that accomplish this would include the provision of visual interruptions in long city streets, or the placing of limits on the maximum street frontage permitted for a single building. Tactics for illuminating an underlying order in a way that promotes a more vital and intense city can be relatively small. Jacobs wrote, 'emphasis on bits and pieces is of the essence: this is what a city is, bits and pieces that supplement each other and support each other'.

Again it is possible to surmise that the earlier incrementalists had a similar appreciation and understanding of organized complexity on some level. In a manner similar to Jacobs, the actions of Charles Mulford Robinson and Jane Addams can even be thought of as methods of clarifying and illuminating underlying systems of order, Robinson through well placed art objects and Addams through well placed settlement houses. And their methods were consistent with the 'bits and pieces' approach of Jacobs. All relied on small-scale incremental change to accomplish their objectives.

There is also a connection between older and more recent incrementalism in regard to conservation. Sitte and Geddes deplored the destruction of small scale urban diversity and its replacement with wide boulevards, large public monuments, and other vestiges of the grand manner of planning. More recent incrementalists deplore the building of 'cities-within-cities,' and self-contained, in-town projects are regarded as bulwarks that stand, as one architect put it, 'against the very diversity that [they] capitalize on'. What is being objected to, in either era, is the disregard for urban complexity in favour of the clean slate necessary for large urban projects. This could only result in the 'ersatz' city.[6]

It was also recognized early on that zoning militates against diversity. Sitte was one of the first to see the negative affects of zoning and, like Jane Jacobs and William Whyte, was against zoning by use and the segregation of the urban realm into classes. An appreciation for the interconnectedness of urban life meant that virtually anything that produced separation in the city was regarded as unhealthy. Early incrementalists had translated this to mean that middle and upper-middle

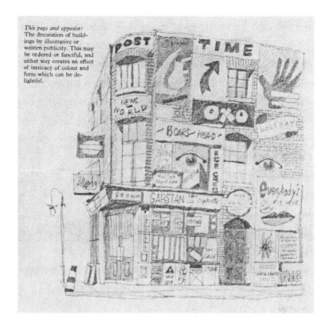

Figure 4.7. The celebration of urban diversity. This drawing is from Gordon Cullen's *The Concise Townscape*, 1961, p. 153 and includes an appreciation of building decoration that 'creates an effect of intricacy of colour and form which can be delightful'.

class residents must live among the immigrant poor in settlement houses. To later incrementalists, who were more focused on the principles of physical design, this meant that different parts of the city should not be segregated by use. Elbert Peets, the architectural critic admired by Jacobs, had this in mind when he criticized the planning of Washington, D.C. for segregating government buildings from the rest of the city (Spreiregen, 1968).

Christopher Alexander carries the same message – a healthy urban place is to be composed of interrelated patterns that support each other. His organicism is about both structure and process. Structurally, there is an appreciation of 'wholeness' that exists on multiple scales. Like early and later incrementalists, there is a sense that if there is an organic coherence to the 'whole' (i.e., the city), then the parts that make up the whole will also have coherence, and vice versa. Such reasoning does not in this case lead to the need to root out 'bad' cells, as in Saarinen's approach. Alexander's method is more process oriented. Cities should be formed through an iterative process that is implemented at multiple scales, and in this way, the desirable properties of cities can be allowed to emerge. Thus it is the underlying processes of city-making that need to change and, unless there are changes in the way buildings are 'conceived and funded and regulated and constructed . . . one is not actually changing anything at all' (Alexander quoted in Grabow, 1983, p. 140).

For Alexander, optimal principles of city pattern are arrived at through empirical observation. After all, observers can readily identify spaces in the city that are 'alive' or 'dead'. Their quality will depend on their interconnectedness, or the way in which the various patterns existing on multiple levels in any given space interrelate. Here there is an obvious connection to the townscape movement and its emphasis on urban experience. Townscape consists of a human vocabulary for urbanism consisting of textures, sights and sounds. Through the writings contained in the *Architectural Review* and the work of Gordon Cullen, there emerged a new appreciation of the emotional impact of cities, through phenomena like closure, reflection, undulation and mystery. The city was a dramatic event having to do with the art of relationship, and the urbanist could not rely on sterile technical solutions to achieve good places (Cullen, 1961).

Jacobs, Alexander and Cullen are connected by way of their promotion of a synthetic understanding of places. Their understanding of urbanism hinged on the idea that urban change can not be made in isolation, but must be cognizant of how it interlocks with other patterns. Alexander worked this out in detail. His 'pattern language' is formulated as a network, to be used as a structured language that allows individual freedom to emerge (Alexander *et al.*, 1977). This is important because it emphasizes that organic wholeness can not be implemented in one master-planned project, but must be developed sequentially.

The most current trajectories of the conservation and complexity stream of incrementalism are following along two paths. The first involves the celebration of urban pluralities without any accompanying agenda for urban design even in the rudimentary way Jane Jacobs laid out. This line is more difficult to connect to the earlier incrementalists. Missing are both the standards of beauty explicit in the efforts of the urban beautifiers, and the socially integrative goals of the social redeemers. The phenomenon can be loosely termed 'everyday urbanism', based on a recent book of the same title (Chase, Crawford, and Kaliski, 1999), but its roots are earlier. Cultural analysts have attempted to see the beauty of the vernacular

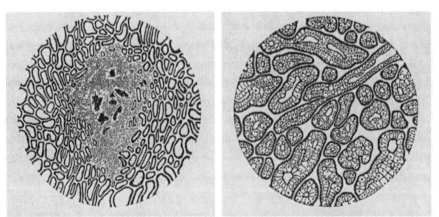

Figure 4.8. The healthy organic city. According to Eliel Saarinen in 1943, 'slum growth' was like the diseased cell tissue on the left, while the healthy cell tissue, on the right, was more like 'community planning'. (*Source*: Eliel Saarinen, *The City: Its Growth, Its Decay, Its Future*, 1943)

in myriad ways, from Venturi *et al.*'s appreciation of Las Vegas (1977), Jackson's interpretations of ordinary landscapes (1984), Dolores Hayden's celebration of American diversity through an appreciation of the vernacular urban landscape in *Power of Place* (1997), to Rem Koolhaas's more extreme statements about celebrating the 'Nietzschean frivolity' of urbanism (Koolhass, 1997). What this new group of incrementalists question is the ability of self-proclaimed improvers to determine what the goals of good urbanism should be. There is an indignant questioning of 'Whose Culture? Whose City?' in the attempt to beautify and improve, since such improvements are believed to be driven by middle-class and/or commercial interests bent on sanitizing urban space (Zukin, 1995). Early incrementalists, particularly the urban beautifiers, would have found such objections somewhat irrelevant.

In everyday urbanism, what is of value in urban places is much more open-ended than before, and largely dependent on local custom and preference. Everyday urbanism reflects on the urban vernacular, where vendors, improvisation, bricolage, and the use of commonplace objects like 'doggie drinking fountains' make everyday urban worlds something to celebrate (Chase, Crawford and Kaliski, 1999). For their part, the role of the urbanist is to work to accommodate the 'endless process of adjustment' in the urban realm, finding ways to 'manoeuvre' within an open-ended, indeterminate approach to city improvement (Durack, 2001). It could be argued that this is not dissimilar to the incremental approach of all earlier urbanists, who also found some inspiration in the diversity, multiplicity and contrasts of urbanism.

The second path taken up by the most recent incrementalists is very different from the first. Inspired by the work of Jacobs and Alexander in particular, some have focused on how the idea of urban complexity can be articulated with even greater – that is, mathematical – specificity. This group has seized upon the idea of chaos and how it might be implicated in the search for a complex, vital urbanism. For example, Salingaros has developed a 'mathematical theory of the urban web' which attempts to work through the connective principles of complexity and apply them to cities (Salingaros, 1998). Urban settings can be viewed as nodes of human activities and maximizing the connections between nodes viewed as the basis of a successful urban setting. This can be worked out mathematically, implying that good urbanism may not be subjective. It amounts to a mathematical justification for the otherwise known fact that most people prefer 'the disorder of an overcrowded Athenian agora to the clinical orderliness of the broad boulevards of Brasilia' (Brendan Gill, quoted in LaFarge, 2000, p. 269).

But there is more at work here than mathematical formulae. Cultural theorists working in the 'radical centre' – a philosophy that considers the objective basis of beauty and values – may also be supportive. Frederick Turner has pursued the idea that freedom does not have to mean 'random'. Turner (1997) writes, 'It was only in the desperation measures of the existentialists, faced with the logical positivist universe of their times, that freedom came to be identified with 'gratuitous acts' or motiveless whims'. He counters with a repudiation of the 'dualism of order and disorder', accomplished by looking to new kinds of order like chaos. This supports latter-day incrementalists seeking to understand the mathematical basis of good urbanism.

The reduction of a cultural phenomenon like a city into a mathematical algorithm can be seen as alienating. Relatedly, some have argued that the rules of good urbanism are similarly not that complex (Jacobs, 2002), such that the idea of finding an emergent order in cities may have only an academic fascination. Worse, it may downplay human intuition and judgment. On the other hand, new approaches may be necessary under contemporary constraints that make it increasingly more difficult to evolve connectivity and urban complexity – the hallmarks of urbanism – intuitively.

Connections

Beauty, redemption, conservation and complexity can be viewed together as similar attempts to find and structure the goodness of cities from the bottom up. There is an underlying structure to be imposed, but it requires many hands to implement. This can only be accomplished if there exists a respect and appreciation for dense urban places. Jane Jacobs is often credited with postulating a credible justification for cities, but turn of the century incrementalists were similarly committed. Robinson (1901, p. 291) talked about how Americans loved their cities, not about defecting to the countryside or suburbia. Where city and nature converged, he was content that a project like a harbour 'be made richly urban'. The respect for urbanism showed through in the attention to every city detail: street paving and cleaning, the exact positioning of street trees, the function and placing of sculpture, the need for colour.

Incrementalists embodied a defence of cities – the big, messy, cities often disdained by regional planners, modernists, progressives, and garden city advocates. Essays like Frank Lloyd Wright's *The Disappearing City* (1932) or Clarence Stein's 'Dinosaur Cities' (1925), constituting rejections of the large metropolis and its replacement with a lower-intensity urbanism, stand as antitheses to the pragmatism of urban incrementalism. Early incrementalists disdained the injustices of the industrial city, but the view that 'we shall solve the City problem by leaving the City', as Wright famously proposed, would have been antithetical to their notion of urban reform. For the incrementalists, the city was something to be taken seriously, requiring an engagement with the existing urban environment that was highly localized. Incrementalist culture focuses pragmatically on working with the resources at hand. Practically speaking, this means that incrementalists are not likely to require or even condone huge expenditures of capital to support singular projects devoted to the business establishment.

The trajectory of incrementalism can be traced as follows: first, an implicit phase – small-scale urban beautification and civic improvement, and social change through physical neighbourhood improvement. Second, an explicit phase – greater recognition of the need to foster urban complexity and diversity, leading to the development of more sophisticated tools to implement these conditions. In the latter phase the qualities of urbanity may either have been stripped of any pre-conception of goodness or badness, or expressed normatively as mathematical principles. Everyday urbanism is as equally distanced from grand utopian visions as the previous incrementalist strains, but the goal is essentially limited to exposure. On the other hand, complexity theory applied to urbanism demands specific, normative application.

The goals of incrementalism have shifted from being implicit, then needing exact formulation, and now, in the most recent incrementalist phase, to being neither obvious nor subject to rulemaking of the type Whyte, Jacobs and Alexander were implying. For some incrementalists, the use of networked languages and even ideas about organized complexity are too limiting of individual expression, and may be culturally stifling. A love of urbanism does not mean that the city should be made to behave in certain ways. Thus the transformation from civic improvement to everyday urbanism has left out the normative structure that all earlier incrementalists would have found necessary, and which some later urbanists have tried to structure. Jane Addams and Patrick Geddes would no doubt applaud the appreciation of vernacular art and the emphasis on visceral understanding that is a strong part of everyday urbanism. But they would be less likely to interpret *any* vernacular space as potentially artistic. In short, they would have applied a stronger set of normative standards.

One interesting linkage is that recent incrementalists, with their justification of complexity and vitality, provide a theoretical structure for the seemingly haphazard approach to urban improvement of earlier times. There were, in the work of the beautifiers and redeemers, the thousands of individual actions that somewhat unpredictably created great urbanism in many places. The gradual, collective city building process that Jacobs and others spoke of so approvingly was already dispersed, by necessity, in the multiple actions of beautifiers and redeemers that existed outside the realm of centralized city government.

The early and later incrementalists seem, at first glance, miles apart in their level of understanding of the complexities of urbanism. But there may be an implicit connection. Early incrementalists, not needing an explicit theory of urban complexity and emergence, focused their energies instead on capitalizing on it – integrating income classes, celebrating urban diversity, and promoting the development of amenities and services in poor neighbourhoods. Later incrementalists, faced with the disintegration of synthetic pattern and a lack of intuitive knowledge of the value of organized complexity, had to focus energy on getting the pattern re-established. For example, Alexander proposed his network system of pattern language, and showed how it could be used to reconnect the urban fabric. His system is necessarily more sophisticated than that which early incrementalists would have employed, but the effects are not different. The patterns call for such things as: neighbourhoods, greater accessibility between home and workplace, adequate distribution of facilities, celebration of the colourfulness of urbanism, the importance of public space, the need for street cafés and corner groceries. Beautifiers and redeemers would have found these goals obvious.

An ongoing issue for incrementalist culture is the degree to which cities can or should be differentiated. Some differentiation is present in all manifestations of incrementalism. For settlement house workers, the neighbourhood was to be a basis of social support, but it was also a means for organizing service provision. But such differentiation only 'works' if it is organic. This was accomplished because settlement houses, public baths, playgrounds and community centres served to make the neighbourhood a whole that was interconnected to the larger city. Later incrementalists shared this view, although they were more explicit in their rejection of the idea of a 'self-contained' neighbourhood. Jacobs (1961) viewed the idea of a self-contained neighbourhood with an 'artificial village life' as 'silly and destructive'. Neighbourhoods were about city – especially street – life, consisting of informal networks and social relations, not discrete units, a position famously stated by Alexander in 'A City is not a Tree' (1965). Earlier incrementalists were also able to see the importance of the street-level neighbourhood and how it plays an important part in the life of the city as a whole. They were likely to see this as a way of coping with a newly constituted city in which the old conceptualization of an undifferentiated urban whole became irrelevant. Later incrementalists liked organicism because it made practical sense. If neighbourhoods were complementary and interdependent, it would be possible to focus simultaneously on the local and larger urban environment.

Containment is antithetical to the incrementalist notion of organicism. Jacobs based her promotion of neighbourhood on organic ideology, but rejected outright the idea of self-containment. In fact there are now few urbanists who would take the unrealistic view that it is possible to conduct all of life's activities within one self-contained neighbourhood, given the reality of globalized systems of production and consumption. Yet the critical importance of proximity – between home and workplace, school, store, and all other daily life needs – remains. Now, a century after Charles Mulford Robinson and Jane Addams, the science of urban relationships and the ability of neighbourhood to sustain healthy proximities is still an explicit part of the urbanist agenda.

Incrementalists also recognize the need for institutions and spaces that can support social functions. Lewis Mumford's summation could have been stated by any early urban improver or social redeemer: 'the spotting and inter-relationship of schools, libraries, theaters, and community centers is the first task in defining the urban neighborhood and laying down the outlines of an integrated city' (Mumford, 1937, p. 94). He decried the mechanical order of modernist approaches to city building because they failed to respond appropriately to the social purpose of cities, which was to provide an outlet for sociability. Here is urban complexity expressed as social function, which Mumford expressed as 'social theater', Jane Jacobs as 'street ballet', and Whyte the 'urban stage'. Improvements to the city should humanize and democratize the city so that the theatre can function. For Mumford and Whyte especially, the way to do this was to make the physical environment of the city socially coherent, a goal not dissimilar to that of Jacob Riis and Jane Addams.

The implications have become more complicated, since there is now the issue of gentrification to contend with. Even incremental improvements will have the collective effect of raising property values, taxes and rent. Early incrementalists like Sitte, Buls, and Geddes were unconcerned. Beautifiers and redeemers welcomed middle and upper class involvement in inner-city improvement. William Whyte did not agree that gentrification was a problem. He argued that it is the deterioration of neighbourhoods, not investment in them that hurts the poor (Whyte, 1988). In any event, simply promoting an urban appreciation of the kind stimulated by Jane Jacobs can trigger a back to the city movement, and Jacobs was critiqued early on for stimulating, however inadvertently, the replacement of the corner grocery store with 'Bonjour, Croissant' (Muschamp, 1983).

Yet the motivation of the incrementalist approach was not about economic gain. Besides an insistence on tangible outcomes driven by a sense of civic responsibility, there has always been a sense that the act of 'doing' itself has benefits. Building, planting, and physically improving were beneficial not only because these tasks could directly involve many people, but because they could bring diverse groups together, united in a common, active purpose. In 1895, one village improvement leader wrote about the improvement society's ability to act as 'solvent' for the 'animosities of politics and religion' through its method of collective participation. This was believed to have had an impact as well on class integration: 'A society engaging all classes instead of one or two is bound to be more immediately successful than one that includes only one class or 'set' (Northrup, 1895, p. 104).

A focus on civic responsibility and citizen involvement in procuring community improvement would be known today as grass-roots, bottom-up planning. Improvers and redeemers especially emphasized these requirements. This was one reason why the beautification organizations flourished during the Progressive Era – the small-scale nature of their projects generated vitality. Peterson (1976, p. 54) writes, 'A comely park, a clean street, a dignified city hall: these and dozens of other practical goals kept local organizations active and larger dreams alive'. This same grass-roots activity is what later incrementalists sought, hoping for an urban vitality based on thousands of independently made choices.

The civic-mindedness of these actions has waned, however. One writer in 1887 asked, 'Thousands of men have been found ready and willing to die for the United States . . . Where are the men who would die for Brooklyn, or Chicago, or San Francisco?' (Municipal Patriotism, 1887). Municipal patriotism has since been diluted to a more realistic call for manageable civic projects, concerned with the most basic of neighbourhood level needs. Earlier urbanists would have thought these goals modest and tentative, with the main difference having to do with the balance between utility and aesthetics. The urban beautifiers viewed the city as an aesthetic object (Wilson, 1989). The belief in the ability of beauty, in and of itself, to evoke feelings of civic pride or at least awareness is still recognized, but the terms have been significantly toned down. There is still a belief in the force of aesthetic expression, but the early urbanists had the advantage of greater solidarity when it came to the task of recognizing what beauty, in fact, was. There seemed to be mutual agreement between improvers and the public, and thus not as much effort was expended on trying to ascertain what the public's interest in matters of aesthetics was.

Another dimension of this concerns Lynchian imageability concepts. Incrementalits of all generations have shown interest in legibility – making clear definitions of urban form, and admonishing against blurred distinctions between city and country. Robinson stated that the fault of most cities was 'the lack of definiteness in the impression they make as one approaches them' (Boyer, 1983, p. 51; Robinson, 1903, p. 39). He spoke about the need for recognition of the city threshold, and that the contrast between city and country should not be obscured. This is certainly a theme among later incrementalists, who have always detested the blurred lines of sprawl. Jane Jacobs observed that cities and surrounding countryside could get along well, but only if we stopped 'sentimentalizing' nature in the form of suburbs.

Legibility is also related to appreciating the fine-grained qualities of cities, as well as the individuality of place. Uniqueness is found in their detailing. This connects such seemingly divergent approaches as municipal arts and everyday urbanism, since small scale 'beautification' is about recognizing the importance of the unique qualities of individual places. Related to this is a recognition of the experiential qualities of places, for example the way in which Whyte investigated the details of what makes places viable as public settings or not. Prescriptions were often the same: buildings flush to the sidewalk, stores along the frontage, windows on the street, and an absolute disdain for blank walls (Whyte, 1988). This is not dissimilar to the municipal arts activists, civic improvers, and social redeemers who were hoping to increase attentiveness to urban places.

This attentiveness requires a tolerance for diversity. As a social goal, diversity has been both implicit and explicit in incrementalism. The redeemers promoted diversity by advocating for, in today's terminology, neighbourhoods of 'mixed income housing'. The whole premise of the settlement house movement, for example, was to entice middle and upper middle class individuals to live in close proximity to working class and immigrant groups, thereby facilitating diversity. This can be interpreted as patronizing and manipulative, but it should be born in mind that the men and women of Hull House were supposed to learn from, not just provide for, poor immigrants.

The incrementalists were concerned with integration along multiple dimensions: the redeemers wanted to integrate the poor, the civic improvers wanted to integrate amenities like parks and playgrounds, and the conservationists and complexity theorists saw urbanism as the science of relationships and interconnections. Good urbanism was largely about creating spatial patterns that maximized connectivity. Incrementalists approach this by seeking the kind of urban environment that results from many changes by many hands. This is one reason why medieval cities were admired. Ruskin and Morris, who were particularly influential with early incrementalists like Sitte and Geddes, were interested in the medieval city's dense urban fabric and the way that cities developed slowly over time, through many individual and thus human scaled adjustments. This is promoted by incrementalists now by insisting on development using small lots, or by promoting the work of multiple designers for one development.[7]

This way of thinking is shared by the other urbanist cultures, all of whom, by definition, had some recognition of the need to accentuate linkages, connections, integration, and think as a generalist rather than a specialist. Raymond Unwin, the quintessential planner of communities, took this very seriously, and it defined his work. He was constantly devising geometric formulations, measuring spatial patterns, looking for 'interlocking details' and complicated relationships that could be the basis of an organic form of community (Creese, 1967). Unwin's genius has been defined by Creese as 'the interchangeability of the instruments of his philosophy' ranging from regional plans to textile patterns (Creese, p. 23). And of course, beyond spatial patterning, interconnection also had a strong social dimension. Elements like porches and balconies, used to observe and therefore engage in communal activity, were one device for interconnecting social groups.

Incrementalists are united in their adherence to practical empiricism, or the idea that the improvement of the city should be understood in terms of precedent, of observing what works and understanding what does not. In turn, reliance on precedent required tolerance for flexibility. Sitte, the great admirer of urban informality, was willing to use gridirons in his plans, if the context warranted it. The landscape architect Elbert Peets (1927) referred to this as 'inconsistencies' in Sitte's thinking. But incrementalists would see this as a necessity of adaptation, a condition of incrementalist culture that had to be accommodated. Even Jane Addams' view of settlements was pliable. She stated, 'The one thing to be dreaded in the Settlement is that it lose its flexibility, its power of quick adaptation' (Addams, 1893, p. 126).

There is a connection here to Pragmatism, the American school of philosophy developed in the late nineteenth century and associated with William James and John Dewey. Its emphasis on the usefulness and practicality of ideas and policies, its stressing of action and experience over principles and doctrines, made it particularly suited for incrementalists who tested the validity of their ideas based on how well they worked. For Jane Addams, ideas needed to have practical value, and for this she was admired by James and Dewey. William James told her: 'you are not like the rest of us, who seek the truth and try to express it. You *inhabit* reality' (Lasch, 1965).

This is why incrementalists place great importance on having intimate, that is, first-hand, knowledge of their subject. For Jacobs, knowledge was accumulated by walking the streets of New York City. The city played the role of great educator, and in this Lewis Mumford, Jacobs' foremost critic, strongly agreed. Municipal artists and the social redeemers also knew their subject well. The redeemers were advanced empiricists, making great use of social surveying and mapping techniques then coming into vogue. They placed particular importance on the role of images,[8] and Jacob Riis' well-known photographs of urban conditions exemplified the approach.

These methods were not about the cold hard gathering of facts. It was instead the cultivation of a visceral understanding based on the idea, to use Jane Addams' phrase, that 'the best teacher of life is life itself' (Addams and Woods *et al.*, 1893, p. 26). Patrick Geddes, the great surveyor, made maps that were not just maps, but 'romantic visions' (Geddes, 1915, p. xiii). His surveys were aimed at discovering the 'collective soul' of a city (Geddes, 1915, p. xxx). Camillo Sitte, an empiricist to the core, based his prescriptions on nothing more than direct observation of spaces that he experienced, and that he thought worked well. He knew that public squares should have an enclosed character because he observed the positive social effect first hand. Incrementalists recognize that it is the lack of direct experience and observation that has lead to the two-dimensional planned arrangements that look good on paper but do not produce good urbanism.

For social scientists, the visceral nature of the incrementalist approach is suspect, and Jacobs has been criticized for weak empirical methods.[9] Part of this critique is that the empirical observations of Addams, Whyte, Jacobs, Alexander, and other urbanists allowed their related feelings, intuitions and experiences a certain legitimacy. Some would call this a practical, common sense quality; others would call it bias. They gathered evidence by direct observation, and were fully prepared to let it drive their normative prescriptions.

Conflicts

Despite the similarity of approach, early and later incrementalists experienced widely different urban realities. Earlier incrementalists tended to ignore peripheral urban development (except to the extent that some settlement house proponents were also involved in planned communities), but by the mid-twentieth century, the surrounding metropolis had to be confronted. The contrasting images between urban core and suburban sprawl left later incrementalists with perhaps a greater sense of appreciation for the city itself. The early incrementalists did not have to contend with sprawl and its effects, and, had little conception of the destructive effects of which decentralized planning was capable. The approach on the part of early incrementalists was thus less about adoration of the core and more about survival. This explains why an avid incrementalist like the settlement house proponent Dame Henrietta Barnett – obviously willing to deal with the city on its own terms – became involved in, simultaneously, the development of a garden suburb outside of London. For her part, there was no incongruity.

Changes in urban form resulted in changes in strategy. For example, the need to increase block permeability in order to promote pedestrian activity was not an issue for early incrementalists because this condition of urban form had not been lost – early incrementalists were working at a time before the theory of the impermeable superblock had been implemented on a large scale. But now, in some cities, damage has been so fundamental that improvements that might have been the staples of urban beautifiers, like brick sidewalks, bollards, banners, benches and trash cans, may have negligible effect (Duany, Plater-Zyberk and Speck, 2000).

The impact of commercialism was also experienced differently. For the later incrementalists, it was government that played a strong role in the commercial take-over of the city, not, as in Addams' time, the government's lack of control. Reflecting these changes, the inchoate institutionalization of planning moved from housing reform to public entrepreneurship, a change that initiated the split between housers and planners, but later and more significantly in the split between housing advocates like Catherine Bauer and urban redevelopers like Edmund Bacon (Bauman, 1983). The involvement of official planners by the time of Jane Jacobs revealed in very stark terms what the participation of government in the 'regulation' of commercialism translated to.

The most fundamental point of conflict within the incrementalist culture is how far incrementalists are willing to go in terms of defining, controlling, and planning the internal form of the city. History reveals the existence of two incrementalist camps: those that focus on aestheticism and social redemption, stemming from the earliest efforts at urban improvement, and those of the later variety, focused on a simple, less invasive recognition of the value of urban complexity. This is in some ways a reflection of the enduring conflict between universalist rationalism and localist romanticism that pervades twentieth century American thought, a division that incrementalism – despite its common denominator of small-scale, grass-roots activity – has not escaped.

In incrementalist culture, the conflict emerges as a difference in the degree to which incremental changes can or should be guided by an imposed principle. How the bits and pieces of urban change are defined is the basis of conflicting interpretation. The question is, to what degree can urban improvements, no matter how small and incremental, be planned for? At one end of the spectrum, the earliest incrementalists – the civic improvement associations, for example – were willing to be more demonstrative in their quest to improve city life. Later incrementalists have a more libertarian view of civic improvement. It is essentially a matter of conflicting ideas about freedom. Jacob Riis thought of the tenement slum as the antithesis of freedom: 'Life, liberty, pursuit of happiness? Wind! says the slum' (Riis, 1901). Given the ensuing experience with 'slum eradication', later incrementalists might be less inclined to interpret freedom in this way.

Early incrementalists sought government control over private development. Many later incrementalists have advocated for freedom from control, a strategy that exposes them to criticism from the left. Fishman (1977) compares Jacobs' critique of large-scale planning to the ideas of Joseph de Maistre and other counter-Enlightenment theorists from the early nineteenth century who opposed the French and American revolutions, and who thought the writing of a constitution for government was too complex a task for the human mind. Jacobs is sometimes aligned with anti-government ideology, and conservatives like William F. Buckley, Jr and Steven Hayward have latched on to Jacobs' views as part of the 'pedigree of conservative urban thought' (Hayward, 2000).

Jacobs (1961, p. 391) expressed 'great wonder' at the intricate order of cities. It was an order derived not from government control, but from 'the freedom of countless numbers of people to make and carry out countless plans'. Richard Sennett, in, *The Uses of Disorder* promoted an urban social life that is 'disordered' and 'unstable', because it causes residents to become more directly involved with the mitigation of neighbourhood problems (Sennett, 1970, p. 144). In the absence of land use laws, Sennett reasoned, residents would not rely on government or plans to solve problems, but would take it upon themselves to effect change. To some extent, this view appears unrealistic in light of Rosen's study in which shared neighbourhood power was largely negative (Rosen, 1986). Individuals and small groups – not business elites – thwarted each other's attempts at urban improvement.

Somewhat ironically, this free approach was the main one available to the early incrementalists. The post-Civil War generation did not have the option of implementing sweeping reforms because the existing conception of the public interest was still very limited. In matters of urban improvement, apart from utilities, most municipal governments did not become involved in a significant way until the 1920s. There is now the option of favouring limits on government intervention, but it can be debated whether early incrementalists should have expected limits on government to produce organically the services neighbourhood residents required.

The case of playgrounds can be used to illustrate the difference between improvement via control versus improvement through relaxation of control. Improvers and redeemers both sought control, although for different reasons. Redeemers wanted safe, clean places for children to play. Civic improvers supported the playground movement generally, but they also wanted some consideration of urban beauty. Robinson (1901, p. 185) stated: 'until the playground has beauty, the good deed falls short of the perfection it ought to have'. For the social redeemers, playgrounds were a necessary provision for the cramped poor; for the civic improvers, playgrounds could teach children a valuable lesson in civic aesthetics.

More recent incrementalists would have a difficult time with either of these justifications. Alexander and Jacobs thought playgrounds too contrived. Jacobs (1961, p. 85) saw playground development as an attempt to 'incarcerate incidental play', and, according to Alexander (1965, p. 14), 'Few self-respecting children will even play in a playground'. The reasoning behind this is that playgrounds are seen as isolated from the rest of the urban system. They constitute segregation that later incrementalists find hard to tolerate because disassociation even at this fine a scale leads ultimately to the destruction of the city. If systems of activity – whether for children or for the elderly – do not overlap, there will be anarchy and sterility. Later incrementalists have thus become more concerned with the underlying processes that will generate connectivity and complexity, for example, as opposed to basic service provision as a static goal.

One hundred years ago, the idea of purposefully fostering greater amounts of complexity and purposefully avoiding planned elements like playgrounds using the argument that they are too disruptive of urban connectedness would have seemed a strange way to put things. Instead, early incrementalists would have been looking for social connectedness through a variety of strategies. Like the later incrementalists, early incrementalists abhorred segregated places. They disliked the idea of creating, in the modern city, separate venues for youth, such as dance halls, on the grounds that they not only segregated young from old, but they required an unnatural surveillance. What they saw, however, was that if the city did not provide places for organized play – public places where all members of society congregate – then the population would be forced to find segregated venues. Jane Addams was aware of the implications. She wrote that if the city fails in its civic duty to provide public venues for play, 'then we, the middle aged, grow quite distracted and resort to all sorts of restrictive measures' (Addams, 1909, p. 2). She regretted the loss of the village green as a venue for youthful frivolity because there 'all of the older people of the village participated. Chaperonage was not then a social duty but natural and inevitable'. This statement could have been written by a modern day incrementalist. The idea of natural chaperonage is not far removed from Jacobs' idea of 'eyes on the street'.

But the difference is in how to go about procuring the public realm. There will always be some obligation for public funding in urban places, but how far this should be taken is debatable. Again, this is a question of how the concept of 'freedom' is regarded. Jane Addams thought that the city should be obligated to provide organized places. To assume otherwise, she wrote, assumes 'that the city itself has no obligation in the matter, an assumption upon which the modern city turns over to commercialism practically all the provisions for public recreation'. As Mumford characterized it, 'the hit-and-miss distribution of the present city' is simply not effective (Mumford, 1968, p. 197). But bad design, endorsed by government, changed the receptiveness of later incrementalists to the need for organized, government-sponsored places for play. At the same time, the implications of congestion had changed. Jacobs was able to romanticize city streets as the ultimate playground for children, 'teaming with life and adventure', because it contrasted with the sterility of the modernist plaza (Jacobs, 1961, p. 85). But Jacob Riis and other incrementalists disdained streets as places where children were *forced* to play. Playground provision was thus not a matter of separation, but of resource equity.

The control versus freedom issue is reflected too in the conflict between keeping the city clean and ordered, and the messy diversity tolerated if not sanctioned by later incrementalists. To the extent that dirt is disorder, an anthropological observation explored by Mary Douglas (1966), the search for cleanliness can be interpreted as an attempt to find boundaries and order within a chaotic social structure. But, as Spain (2001) points out, women's groups in the municipal housekeeping movement were trying to establish order where there was none in existence. They were trying to establish a meaningful pattern of urban places, one that could help urban newcomers cope with urban disorder. This is a different project from the attempt to reorder an existing structure. Cleansed disorder may not be too far removed from organized complexity, except that cleanliness was associated more closely with the notion of civic pride. 'As a man is judged by his linen, a city is judged by its streets' wrote Charles Mulford Robinson (1899, p. 175).

There is a similar duality with the idea of beauty, which Jacobs finds only in organized complexity, but which early incrementalists of the municipal arts stream would have defined more objectively. Here again Mumford picks up the basic tension, pointing out with sarcasm that Jacobs was apparently never hurt by 'ugliness, sordor, confusion' (Mumford, 1968, p. 197), and that, requiring only a 'haphazard mixture' of urban activities, found no further basis for beauty. This position he called 'esthetic philistinism with a vengeance'. Later groups, such as everyday urbanists, would simply question whose idea of beauty and art was to be implemented. Robinson, writing in 1901, stated that the appearance of municipal improvements must be approved by 'an artistic authority' (Robinson, 1901, p. 35). Now, urbanists wonder who the 'authority' is, and how such an authority is selected.

The early incrementalists did not find the question that difficult. They had an eclectic sense of beauty that stressed common preference. It was vernacular in the sense of J.B. Jackson: vernacular space represented shared, common ground (Jackson, 1994). In this way, some of the critiques of beautification efforts which later met City Beautiful proponents, were initially deflected. The opposition to civic improvement and municipal art, i.e., that beautification should not be placed above basic social services fell flat on settlement house workers who believed in both. It was later, during the City Beautiful era, that arguments against civic improvement on the grounds that they elevated beauty above basic needs like street cleaning, became vocal and more convincing.

A well-known critique along these lines is M. Christine Boyer's *Dreaming the Rational City: The Myth of American City Planning* (1983), which attempts to expose a dark underbelly intrinsic to the 'planning mentality'. Planning's failure, Boyer argues, was that it was essentially a quest for ruralized social order imposed on the assumed unnaturalness of urban disharmony. Boyer equates civic improvements of the 1890s with the 'self-righteous superiority and economic militarism' of American imperialism in Cuba, Puerto Rico, and the Philippines around the same time. Improvements under either heading – beauty or redemption – are exercises in social control, impositions of a façade of ceremonial harmony. Similarly, the surveying work of the urban redeemers is interpreted by Boyer as unhealthy surveillance. The detailed collection of data on the city was used to 'carve up the field of urban disorders' into specialized concerns (Boyer, 1983, p. 32). Whether concerned with worker exploitation or damage to the urban physical environment, the critique is based on a perception that these concerns essentially involved 'fear of the urban crowd and a belief that the city was an unnatural abode for humanity' (Boyer, 1983, p. 9).

The critique does not apply well to incrementalist planning culture. The early incrementalists would not have thought in terms of expanding the role of government for the purpose of promoting capital productivity, unless this effort could have been translated directly into a better living environment for residents. But, as already discussed, an expanded governmental role was not a particularly viable option for the early incrementalists. Later incrementalists were (and are) likely to be sceptical of state-controlled expansion in urban improvements, preferring instead a bottom-up approach that fosters small, individual activity.

In the end, the problem of whether to view cities as planned versus unplanned, as controlled versus spontaneous, may be somewhat misleading. One is viewed as a product of order and control, while the other is associated with being eventful and responsive, but as Kostof points out, the duality has to be strongly qualified. Even the most seemingly random, meandering path can be the product of order having to do with established conventions and social contracts, 'a string of compromises between individual rights and the common will' (Kostof, 1993, p. 85). One interpretation is that early incrementalists were more focused on planning the 'string of compromises,' while later incrementalists were more focused on appreciating the compromises being made.

What may be emerging now in American urbanism is the idea that it is necessary to accommodate both ways of thinking. Public places, especially playgrounds, must be 'contrived' where alternatives for play are lacking, but in addition, children should be able to play within the interstices of urban complexity. Children need freedom, but it is a freedom they can only get if cities are alive and vibrant. That requires some degree of foresight and control. It requires faith in the legitimacy and ability of a collective response, a faith that Jacobs, for one, seemed to lack. Urbanists must decide whether there is a point to excluding one approach or the other. It is a question of whether the provision of playgrounds, which will be appealing to some and not to others, necessarily limit the ability of children to engage in incidental play. Cannot both a collective response and freedom of exploration coexist?

Another issue for incrementalists to contend with is about the function and legitimacy of the neighbourhood. Although there were two separate neighbourhood traditions in existence between 1880 and 1920, one focusing on social integration and service delivery, the other on homogeneity and protection (Melvin, 1987), the incrementalist use of the concept has generally been about directing urban reform towards small-scale, localist strategy. On this there is less disagreement internally – that is, among the various strains of incrementalist culture. Yet using the neighbourhood as a focus of urban improvement has long been critiqued on the basis of being parochial, segregationist and unrealistic (Schubert, 2000). Since city residents can obtain services and goods anywhere, have fluid, non-proximal social contacts, and view their local environment as being complex and geographically broad, what is the point of using some arbitrarily delimited subunit?

The problematic of the neighbourhood is linked to its historical endorsement of homogeneity. Robert Park (1915) was explicit on this point, writing that local attachment could be used as a basis of control. Isaacs (1948), Banerjee and Baer (1984) and Silver (1985) are a sample of writers who have been particularly critical of the neighbourhood idea, because of its use as a basis of directed social engagement. Clarence Perry was seeking some degree of homogeneity in his neighbourhood unit scheme, using it to prevent 'the miscellaneousness that characterizes most urban neighborhoods' (Perry, 1939, p. 76). This critique does not apply to incrementalist intentions, but it is directed at the unintended effect of urban differentiation. The identification of neighbourhoods and communities throughout incrementalist culture was not directed at maintaining uniformity – in fact class mixing was an important goal of the redeemers – but perverse effects could not always be avoided.

Even if unintended, many are not willing to interpret the activities of the incrementalists as innocently benevolent. Some say that the early incrementalists – the beautifiers, improvers, redeemers, and to some extent conservationists – approached their task with a fervour that was too much about the 'conviction of their own rightness' (Wilson, 1989, p. 41). Even the optimism inherent in the provision of a community or neighbourhood centre can be interpreted as being too much about control. Hull House has been thus critiqued as an example of social and moral coercion. Peter Hall labelled the women-led voluntary movement an 'oddity',' though 'touching' (Hall, 1996, pp. 42–43). But it was much more. The focus on the provision of neighbourhood level services was an early – if not the earliest – affirmation of one of the most basic city planning ideals in existence. Perhaps Addams' critics have been unable to get past the religious underpinning of her program of urban service provision.[10]

Early incrementalists were more aware of the liabilities of their approach than contemporary critics allow. Charles Mulford Robinson reflected on the problem of specialization and used it as a rational for his 1901 treatise:

The specialist, seeing much in little, does not see far. In zeal for pavements one forgets the trees; in zeal for parks the thoroughfare is forgotten. It has seemed well, then, in the great new awakening of enthusiasm and concern for city beauty in a score of directions, at last to grasp them all, to group them logically in a single volume and show the relative positions. (Robinson, 1901, p. x)

This was the first step on the road to the institutionalization of incrementalism, recognized by later incrementalists as a problematic turn of events. Virtually all the incrementalist movements described under 'beauty' and 'redemption' were involved in one way or another with the eventual professionalization of city planning. Yet ironically, this institutionalization was what led to the need to get the complexity of urbanism back. On this basis the ideas of early and later incrementalists diverge, but only in terms of perspective. Early incrementalists had plenty of complexity and wanted order; later incrementalists saw a sterile order and wanted complexity.

But the strategy of Jacobs, to use disorder deliberately as a remedy, lead to another critique. It was argued that the anti-planning of Jacobs does not lead to a healthy 'organized complexity' of urban life, but instead undermines it. Mumford (1968, p. 113) called the approach 'aimless dynamism', an approach that results in confusion as the essence of life, and that writes off 'the accompanying increase in nervous tensions, violence, crime, and health-depleting sedatives, tranquillizers, and atmospheric conditions'. Proponents of 'everyday urbanism' have been similarly critiqued (see, for example, Kelbaugh, 2002).

Notes

1. For a discussion of the American Renaissance of art and architecture between the Civil War and World War I, particularly as it relates to city planning, see Wilson, 1979.
2. This is also Peterson's second antecedent of the City Beautiful (Peterson, 1976).
3. The playground movement was not organized until 1906, with the founding of the Playground Association of America. Its ideology and activities were established well before that time, with the first public playground developed in 1885 in Boston.
4. Spencer is often cited in support of libertarian views. See especially Robert Nozick, 1974.
5. Although he was preceded by William Drummond in 1913; see Johnson, 2002.
6. Catharine Ingraham (1986), writing about a self-contained middle-class project in Chicago.
7. A common strategy in New Urbanist developments
8. Lewis Mumford (1968, p. 114) points out that the word 'idea' comes from the Greek word for 'image'.
9. Herbert J. Gans, email communication.
10. But it was a secular path to salvation. The characterization of Addams as a prissy moral do-gooder grossly mis-characterizes a woman who went on to become an international leader in the peace movement and was the first woman to be awarded the Nobel Peace Prize, in 1931.

Chapter Five

Urban Plan-Making: the City Beautiful and the City Efficient

Urban plan-makers, like the incrementalists, were focused on the existing city. Both cultures responded directly to existing historical precedent, such that any change or plan made to the human landscape was conditioned by pre-existing form and pattern. But the plan-makers were not particularly interested in small-scale, grass-roots, incremental change in the Jeffersonian style of self-determination. They were more Hamiltonian, seeking comprehensive solutions that were necessarily larger in scale. This is the culture of the 'metropolitan idea' (Fishman, 2000, p, 82), of Burnham, Nolen, Adams, and Moses, that was eventually either killed off by latter-day incrementalists, or evolved into something much more policy-driven and removed from the durable, material qualities of cities.

I have labelled this urbanist culture *urban plan-making* – the effort to secure improvements to the existing city by way of a physical plan. While other cultures obviously made use of plans, urban plan-makers used their plans to create urbanism. I will trace two distinct phases: The City Beautiful and the City Efficient. What is significant about their common focus is that plan-making coincides with an increase in the scale and ambition of urban change. A more encompassing reach needed a plan that would allow the city to be taken in all at once, from one vantage point; something Leonardo da Vinci understood when he drew the plan of Imola in 1502.

A basic theme running throughout this history of urban plan-making is the role of order and its legitimacy in procuring good urbanism. In plan-making, the quest for order pervades its main endeavours: the reliance on experts, the tendency towards bigness in plan-making, the notion of social control, and the unfortunate

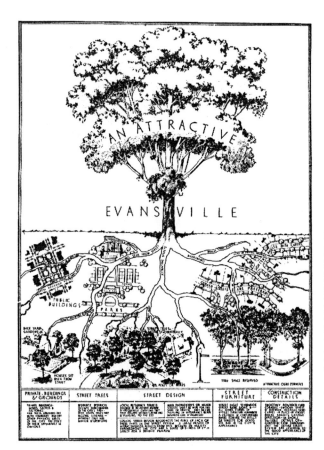

Figure 5.1. The urban plan-makers shifted the focus from small scale incremental change to the making of plans. In this diagram of the Evansville, Indiana Comprehensive Plan, 1922, planning consultant Harland Bartholomew used diagrams to tell the 'planning story'. (*Source*: Eldridge Lovelace, 1992, *Harland Bartholomew: His Contributions to American Urban Planning*)

trend towards separation and segregation in the urban environment that was put in motion under the watch of the plan-makers. The central task in this chapter will be to assess what urban plan-making has to offer for the development of American urbanism, and whether some of its more positive aspects can be weeded out from a culture weighed down by an over enthusiasm for order and control. This should be possible, theoretically, unless there is something inherently flawed about the whole premise of plan-making.

Urban plan-making got off the ground at a time when cities were monocentric, the kind described by sociologists of the period as consisting of a singular downtown core, factory zones, and rings of residential areas (see, for example, Burgess, 1925). Centralization, according to Moody's 1909 *Wacker's Manual*, a treatise written to support the implementation of Burnham's *Plan of Chicago* and revealingly subtitled *Municipal Economy*, was necessary for maximal efficiency. This is, as Fishman writes, 'the American planning tradition at its most confident: that intelligent, imaginative, collective action could genuinely shape cities and regions that met the highest ideals of the nation' (Fishman, 2002, p. 14).

This is not to say that the surrounding metropolitan region was not considered – even L'Enfant's Plan of Washington encompassed 50 square miles around the city centre. But plan-making was distinguished by its focus on what was already there, not on the undeveloped fringe. City Beautiful plan-makers were especially focused on the urban core, and had little interest in 'the agricultural village, the Country Life movement, industrial utopias . . . or the Garden City' (Wilson, 1989, p. 78). Instead of the creation of decentralized arcadian habitats for humans, urban plan-makers created plans for downtown, rail networks to link population to the centre, and, in the later City Efficient era, efficient industrial zones with attached housing for workers. For the earliest plan-makers like Burnham, the development of utopian new towns would have been viewed not only as uninteresting, but too radical. It was not until the rise of the professionalization of planning that many plan-makers of the City Efficient variety became as involved in the creation of new towns and suburbs as they were in the development of plans for existing cities.

The City Beautiful is the chronological centre of the Progressive Era, which dated from 1890 to 1920 (Chambers, 1992). The Era was marked by rapid change, the rise of the metropolis, increased consumption, populism, imperialism, Darwinism, social reform and control, and the rise of the Women's Movement. Through it all there was an intense optimism on the part of Progressive Era reformers. Cities were, in fact, the focus of progressive reform, and plan-making was the method by which reform of the physical city could be achieved. The response to change was intervention. Given the spectacular nature of many City Beautiful plans, it is not surprising that Daniel Burnham, the most celebrated figure of the City Beautiful era, thought of his efforts as the progressive and reformist idealization of environmental intervention.

City Beautiful planners shared not only an ideology, but also a white, middle-class and upper middle-class background. They were also urbanites. At the time, the country was roughly one-half urban – by 1910, 46 per cent of the population lived in cities larger than 2500. Turning the city into something beautiful and by implication virtuous was seen as entirely in step with the reformist focus on cleaning up political corruption, exploitation of labour, and a host of other perceived injustices and immoralities.

In either manifestation of urban plan-making culture, the City Beautiful or the City Efficient, the same tensions that existed in incrementalism can be seen: the conflict between freedom and control, and between localism and universalism. The difference between the City Beautiful and its transformation into the City Efficient presents another version, this time more directly caught up in the wrestle between aestheticism and rationalism. Chapter 4 discussed how, in incrementalist culture, connections and conflicts arose during the point at which its romantic inclinations veered toward universalisms and objective truths. This is also true of urban plan-making, but in a reverse direction. That is, both of the major manifestations of urban plan-making, the City Beautiful and the City Efficient, are essentially modernist Enlightenment projects, and their connections and conflicts grew out of their venture into the romantic, subjective, interpersonal side of aesthetics and city planning. Burnham's ideology has been compared to the Enlightenment figure Giambattista Piranesi (Boyer, 1983), whose urban designs imposed rational order on the city. But at the same time, Burnham is critiqued as the ideologue who was more concerned with art-for-art's sake than rationality (Ellin, 1996).

With its strong normative vision and sense of order, particularly in its first manifestation as the City Beautiful, the main point of conflict in urban plan-making was in the degree to which incrementalist, bottom-up views were permitted and incorporated. In urban plan-making culture the tension between rationality and romanticism played itself out somewhat differently. This was because urban plan-making introduced an aspect of city planning less prominent in incrementalist culture – the explicit idea of physical *order*. A concern for the spatial arrangement of urban elements, the interrelationships they maintain or give rise to, and the patterns they create for urban life, are all ordering concepts embedded in plan-making.

Order in urbanism can be defined as the act of finding a purposeful arrangement of elements. But this is not necessarily about, nor does it imply, a certain *type* of regularity or sequence of things. There is a multitude of forms, from gridded, rectilinear order, to irregular, curvilinear order, for example. The important defining element of relevance here is that it is a disposition of urban elements, and that the arrangement is according to purpose. In short, order in urban plan-making specifies a predetermined, implementable, physical idea about the material condition of cities that went well beyond the strategic placement and preservation of urban facilities.

The City Beautiful

Because of the progressive fervour of the time, the writing of City Beautiful proponents is loaded with rhetoric. This makes its analysis awkward. Wilson, a proponent of the movement, cautions against 'setting too much store' by its polemics. I will focus, as in the other chapters of this book, on trying to understand its underlying ideology, and how its main ideas can either be connected to or contrasted with the trajectory of American urbanism.

Like the early incrementalists, the City Beautiful emerged at a time when cities were struggling with extreme chaos. Historian Harold Evans (2000) argues that there were three reasons cities were in such dire shape by the late nineteenth century. First, they were relatively new to self-government, having been dominated by states with predominantly rural interests. In 1894, the National Municipal League was invented for the explicit purpose of trying to free cities from state control, an indication of their diminished status. Second, there were simply too many new people to contend with. Parts of New York City had 30 per cent more inhabitants per square mile than any area in Dickensian London. Third, both the political machines and the progressive reformers lacked a vision of how things could be changed.

It could be argued that the City Beautiful movement was the physical manifestation of the needed vision for urban reform. The vision had been presented as an incremental, small-scale series of projects in the decades before, but now the watchwords were comprehensiveness and master planning. While muckrakers like Ida M. Tarbell, Upton Sinclair and Lincoln Steffens focused on political corruption and capitalist exploitation, City Beautiful proponents were focused on developing a positive, concrete vision of physical urban reform (Chambers, 1992).

The phenomenon of the City Beautiful era has been dated with some precision, starting in the year 1899 and ending in 1909. Before then, the term had been used to describe the 1893 Chicago World's Fair, and it gained momentum following an Arts and Crafts exhibition published in 1897. But the first use of the term to describe a specific programme of improvement has been traced to Harrisburg, Pennsylvania in late 1900, and use of the 'vivifying phrase' in publications like *Municipal Affairs* gave the term traction. After 1909, the term died out quickly, coinciding with several key events in city planning history – the *Plan of Chicago* and the first National Planning Conference being the most important (Wilson, 1983).

Taking a broader view, the history of thinking in City Beautiful terms extends

Figure 5.2. Court of Honor, World's Columbian Exposition, 1893. Civic adornment on a massive scale. (*Source*: Stanley Applebaum, *The Chicago World's Fair of 1893*, 1980)

much further back. Kostof's review of what he calls planning in the 'Grand Manner' or 'Baroque planning' is part of the City Beautiful lineage (Kostof, 1991). It begins with classical antiquity, where Greek and Roman cities displayed elements which, in late sixteenth century Europe, reappeared as Baroque planning. At that time, elements of the Grand Manner may not have been implemented as a complete system or through a master plan, but instead may have evolved through a series of 'responsive efforts' over several generations (Kostof, 1991, p. 214). In Europe, the city of Florence demonstrated Baroque planning principles when it attempted to straighten streets leading between churches and public buildings. The important change was that the street was now viewed not merely as the space left over between buildings, but as an element to be designed in its own right.

The climatic phase of the Grand Manner occurred in sixteenth-century Europe, paralleling new developments in science and culture in which the view of the world shifted from being static and earth-centred to infinite and sun-centred. This changed conception of space meant that the objects of cities could be altered to produce desired visual effects, like a 'new world of illusion in theater and theatrical spectacle' (Kostof, 1991, p. 215). This change was fundamental to the later development of the City Beautiful.

The American version began with smaller-scale influences, as documented by Peterson (1976), where the three branches of urban beautification presented in Chapter 4 together culminated in the City Beautiful. The culture of urban plan-making is in many ways the logical outgrowth of the activities of the early incrementalists. Organizationally, these efforts – municipal art, civic improvement, outdoor art – coalesced at the turn of the twentieth century into the National Civic Improvement League. Charles Mulford Robinson was instrumental, and he was just as fervent about the City Beautiful as he was earlier about small-scale municipal improvement.

Given the aesthetic connections, this was not inconsistent on Robinson's part. He made the case for the City Beautiful in his second book *Modern Civic Art, or, The City Made Beautiful*, published in 1903 and republished 3 times in the next 15 years. Here was the glorification of the city through art restated in bigger, bolder terms than before, and with a more fervent integration of beauty and utility. It was a Ruskinian notion of beauty. What Robinson (1906a) wanted was a plan that would guide city development according to 'good sense, attractiveness, sanitation, and convenience', goals that he had previously relied on small civic improvement groups to accomplish. He carried the connection to its fullest extreme when he stated 'art lies fundamentally in complete adaptation to function' (Robinson, 1906b). This seems a somewhat desperate measure to try to convince people that concepts like art and beauty have legitimacy, but it is pure Ruskin, who stated: 'what is most adapted to its purpose is most beautiful' (Lang, 1999, p. 20).

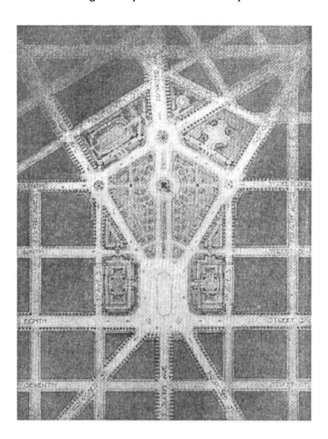

Figure 5.3. Plan of a proposed civic centre in Minneapolis, showing law courts, auditorium, and public library. (Source: John Nolen, *City Planning: A Series of Papers Presenting the Essential Elements of a City Plan*, 1929)

There were two other influences besides small-scale urban improvement efforts: Frederick Law Olmsted, Sr. and the Chicago World's Fair. Wilson discusses both of these influences at length in his authoritative treatise, *The City Beautiful Movement* (1989). Olmsted's contributions were threefold: his emphasis on the planning of entire (comprehensive) park systems rather than individual sites; his conceptualization of parks as restorative and 'a benign instrument of class reconciliation and democratization' (Wilson, 1989, p. 10); and his involvement in establishing private, outside consultancy as a method of solving urban problems.

The relationship between the Chicago World's Fair and the City Beautiful is more complex. Both Thomas Adams and Charles Mulford Robinson had stated that the City Beautiful was the culmination – not the origination – of many years' efforts (Adams estimated two decades' worth) in aesthetic and sanitary improvement. The American spirit of civic improvement, as already discussed, had been in evidence since the Civil War. Thus the effect of the Chicago World's Fair of 1893 (the Columbian Exposition) on the formation of the City Beautiful should not be overstated. According to Wilson (1989, p. 53), any direct connection is 'mostly mistaken'. One reason is that the chronology does not work well – there is a 6 year gap between the Exposition and the City Beautiful's official start. This cannot be attributed solely to the depression of 1893 since plenty of civic improvement activity was seen throughout the 1890s. In any event, it is safe to say that historians and contemporaries like Robinson and Adams agreed that the Exposition had at least some effect on the rapid rise of the City Beautiful in the years after.

Through individuals (F. L. Olmsted), events (the Columbian Exposition), and organizations (nineteenth-century beautification efforts), the City Beautiful emerged. These uniquely American influences must be combined with the much-longer European tradition of Grand Manner planning to complete the lineage of the City Beautiful. On the European side, the connection is through L'Enfant, although 200 years of experience with the European Grand Manner had preceded L'Enfant's Plan of Washington. The revival of L'Enfant's plan through the McMillan Commission in 1902 was a high-point, if not the only *bona fide* interpretation of Baroque planning in the U.S. The mall of Washington, the principal feature of the plan, has been described as 'an element the Sun King himself would have admired' (Scott, 1969, p. 53).

The 1902 McMillan Plan of Washington emphasized the importance of the plan itself. The McMillan Commission was praised by contemporaries exactly for this reason. Architectural critic Montgomery Schuyler thanked the Commission for making the public aware of 'the all-importance to a city of having a plan' (Schuyler, 1902, p. 5). City plans go back to the Harrappan Civilization of 2500 B.C.E. (Morris, 1979), but the American conception of a city plan as a statement of principles was limited at the time. City Beautiful plans went significantly beyond the laying out of streets, towards a bold, comprehensive vision of the future. Daniel Burnham pushed the importance of a plan more than anyone, hammering in the idea at every opportunity that the plan made the parts greater than their sum. For Burnham and other urban plan-makers, this was because the plan allowed the parts to be brought into harmonious relationship (Burnham, 1902).

The McMillan Plan was intended to 'restore, develop, and supplement' (U.S. Senate, 1902) the plan made in 1791 by Major Charles L'Enfant. There were a number of goals. There was a desire to make Washington D.C. as significant culturally as European cities, and for this Burnham and other McMillan Commission members made a tour of Europe in preparation for their work on the plan (see Hines, 1991). There was also a desire to pronounce the ideals of the Republic, including both the European cultural heritage of the Founders and the democratic government they had established. Finally, there was the City Beautiful emphasis on the civic realm, particularly that public space is something to be prized and aggrandized.

Following the publication of the 1902 Plan of Washington, many communities around the country wanted to emulate the beautification principles it espoused. Commissions were established, plans drawn, and referenda submitted for the funding of large and small public works projects. Projects included New York City's 1903 parkway and civic centre plan, Philadelphia's 1907 Fairmont Parkway (now Benjamin Franklin Parkway), Kansas City's park and boulevard system (first proposed by Kessler in 1893), and civic centre plans in Cleveland, Denver, Chicago, Seattle, and San Francisco, among others.

But not all City Beautiful activity was on as large a scale as Washington. Throughout its 10-year lifespan, activities varied from small to grandiose plans for civic centres and entire urban areas. The smaller projects can be viewed as holdovers from the small-scale incrementalist culture already reviewed but, by the early 1900s, thoroughly embedded in the ethos of the City Beautiful. The two thousand civic improvement associations identified by Robinson in 1906 now viewed themselves as part of a larger, organized movement. Even the larger plans had input from many smaller improvement groups and neighbourhood-level interests, a result of the wide dissemination of 'the gospel of municipal improvement and beautification' (Scott, 1969, p. 65) carried out by local media.

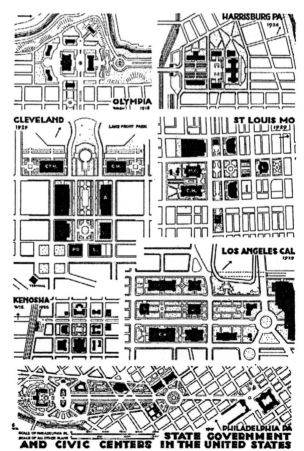

Figure 5.4. State government and civic centers in the U.S. (*Source*: Thomas Adams, *Outline of Town and City Planning: A Review of Past Efforts and Modern Aims*, 1935)

The climatic achievement of the City Beautiful era was the 1909 *Plan of Chicago*, written by Daniel Burnham and Edward Bennett and backed by the Commercial Club of Chicago. The plan embodied all the achievements and all the failings of the era. On the positive side, the plan is heralded for its regional scope, its attention to transportation and circulation systems which were not the usual fare of City Beautiful plan-making, and its planning and preservation of the waterfront as a linear park free of railroads and industry. On the negative side, the plan is disdained for its heavy-handed visual emphasis on classicism and especially the grandiose civic centre that was never implemented. A more sympathetic view ignores the obvious incitement of conformity and control and instead sees Burnham's plan as 'an awesome visual idealization of civic harmony' (Wilson, 1989, p. 282).

Although the quest for civic harmony meant order in its most formal expression, the uniformity of height and style shown in numerous Jules Guerin watercolour renderings in the Chicago Plan were not meant for literal interpretation. They were symbolic. The plan was aimed at public projects, and the imposition of uniform height and style in Chicago's commercial sector would have been infeasible. The buildings served as the 'matrix' for Burnham's proposals where 'individualism was subordinated to the harmony of the greater good' (Wilson, 1989, p. 283). Diversity and discordance were to be subdued in order to make the civic elements stand out.

City Beautiful plan-makers often thought of the existing city as utterly lacking in beauty and used the term 'ugly' often. The head of the Civic Improvement League in Dallas declared in 1902 'in the whole civilized world there is no more slovenly community than Dallas' (cited in Wilson, 1989, p. 257). The remedy for this was a strong emphasis on order and uniformity, and the style selected for that sense of order was Beaux Arts classicism. Classicism was appealing because, historically and symbolically, it expressed grandeur – the monumental version of traditional architectural form perfect for expressing civility. But it was also adaptable. The language of classical orders could be used to create constrained variation. It had the significant advantage of giving even the most mediocre architect a framework to work with, thus helping to ensure higher quality architecture. Working within the requirements of 'proportion, harmony, symmetry, and scale' (Wilson, 1989, p. 79), the City Beautiful was often able to achieve a high architectural standard for public buildings. This tied the aesthetic principles of the City Beautiful to earlier European planning in the Grand Manner, which became a source of disdain. Jacobs (1961, p. 24) labelled it a 'retrogressive imitation Renaissance style'.

The formality was not only architectural. It applied to individual planned elements as well as the city as a whole. There were focal points (formal public squares, monuments, buildings of civic importance), connected by diagonals or straight streets – lines of communication, usually in the form of tree-lined boulevards. Vistas were an important consideration, and monuments or architectural

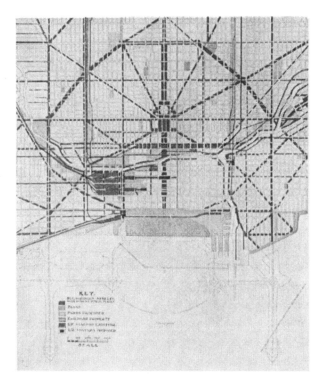

Figure 5.5. The ultimate City Beautiful plan, the 1909 *Plan of Chicago*. This map shows proposed streets and widenings, parks and playgrounds, and railway lines and stations.(*Source*: Daniel H. Burnham and Edward H. Bennett, *Plan of Chicago*, 1909)

markers like obelisks were used as termination points. The spatial order of buildings and streets was highly regularized, with grouped public buildings and radial streets terminating in monumental arrangements. A geometric order was imposed on the finer-grain grid of the existing urban fabric.

City Beautiful aestheticism was also concerned with linking classicism and 'naturalistic constructivism'. Wilson argues that the City Beautiful was in fact more interested in naturalistic landscapes and natural beauty than in classical architecture, noting that urban beautification and scenic preservation (Olmsted's 'Outdoor Art' movement) occurred concurrently with the City Beautiful because of this pervasive interest. But this was not a simple deference to pastoralism. The difference between the Columbian Exposition and Central Park, as Schuyler points out, is that the White City promised to supplant the chaos of the Victorian city, not just offer an escape from it (Schuyler, 2002). City form and landscape design became inseparable. This was seen earlier in the French Baroque tradition where urban design and landscape design shared the same principles of formality (Kostof, 1991), meaning that nature had to be tamed considerably to fit into the urban order. In the American City Beautiful version of the Grand Manner, the tradition of romantic landscape design born of Olmsted was successfully merged with the formal, monumental streets and squares of urban plan-making. Landscaped elements were not separated as remedial anti-city components as Olmsted conceived, but rather 'greened the main city form itself' (Kostof, 1991, p. 228). This is not to say that the social purposes were very different – both saw green spaces and parks as having the ability to cure social malaise and stress. The important point is that landscape became a way to celebrate and embellish the city, not escape from it.

That the American version of the Grand Manner was predominantly limited to the public realm made it different from the European version. In Europe, there were formal residential squares associated with the Baroque tradition. This would have required an extension of the eminent domain that American courts would have been unlikely to uphold. The furthest extension was in the case of Washington, D.C. where, given the importance of the public realm, control stretched beyond boulevards, parks and monuments to include architectural controls on both public and private buildings.

Even limited to public places, the City Beautiful struggled to find a more utilitarian basis for its existence. Beauty and utility were always emphasized simultaneously as interdependent goals. Reformers reasoned that the way to deal with government ineptitude, waste, and a frustration with getting things done was to push the idea of efficiency. Burnham and other architects had already applied such principles, including 'rationalization, standardization, and centralization' to their business practices (Schlereth, 1994, p. 145). This is consistent with the early twentieth-century Nietzschean ideal of merging art and science that appealed to so many architects (see Turner, 1977). In the City Beautiful, it was another example of the combined projects of rationalism and romanticism being worked out in tandem. The aesthetic concern was romantic in the sense that it emphasized art-for-art's sake, but its emphasis on utility and efficiency provided the rationalist counterpoint. During the City Beautiful era, however, practicalities were often overruled by aesthetic concerns, which is one reason the era was short-lived. Overlooked practicalities included the omission of consideration of the automobile in Burnham's *Plan of Chicago*.

More menacingly, the idea of efficiency could be used for social control, based on the thinking that increased efficiency translated into increased wealth and a greater ability to appease the masses. For Theodore Roosevelt, the problem of social disorder could be solved by 'baking a bigger pie', in turn a matter of increasing efficiency and therefore production (Hays, 1995, p. 115). Physically and architecturally, the emphasis on efficiency transferred into some very basic city plan-making ideas. Public functions were to be consolidated into civic centres, centrally located to 'ensure the efficient, economical conduct of the city's business'. This had symbolic and artistic importance, nowhere better expressed than in the Court of Honor of the

World's Fair of 1893, but also was formally expounded in Burnham, Carrere and Brunner's group plan of Cleveland. The idea of grouped public buildings arranged in a civic centre expressed a system of order and unity that would supplement, but be subordinate to, the industrial and commercial core of the city (Wilson, 1989).

Reliance on the expert was another way to increase efficiency. Since government was not only corrupt but highly inefficient, and City Beautiful proponents did not have unlimited resources, efficiency in urban plan-making was critical. One interpretation was to enlist an authority. One contemporary asked, 'what if [City Beautiful] designs conflict artistically?', answering that 'One solution would be the finding of some . . . cooperative body of men, who combine in themselves all the requirements for deciding such questions in an authoritative manner' (*Municipal Journal and Engineer*, 1906). In short, getting the beautiful city accomplished expeditiously required the expert.

Significantly, Robinson moved away from reliance on the citizen activist, the foundation of civic improvement activities, towards a reliance on the 'expert', motivated by 'disgust with the inept, piecemeal, patchwork efforts to stay abreast of urban needs' (Wilson, 1989, p. 83). This can be viewed either as a dangerous giveaway of public power, or as an understandable response to the frustration of trying to enact change. As long as the principles of the City Beautiful were upheld, the judgment of engineers and architects as well as sculptors, artists and landscape designers was to be trusted. It was an arrangement between citizen watchdog and expert plan-maker intended to move through an evolutionary process that must have been inspired by Robinson's study of Darwin. It was fervently optimistic. Robinson believed that the perfection of the city was ultimately possible (Wilson, 1989). Steps toward this perfection involved a series of realizations on the part of the general public – the need for beautiful buildings, interior embellishment, the grouping of public buildings, their organization in a civic centre, and finally, the requirement of expert advice.

Social control is a definite part of this, a subject, as Wilson (1989) acknowledges, 'over which a great deal of ink has been spilled'. Almost all attempts to improve the living conditions of cities before and during the Progressive Era had moral overtones, some more direct than others. This was evident in earlier incrementalist culture. Civic improvement groups interested in such mundane tasks as good pavements, street cleaning, and the provision of trash cans nonetheless saw their function as the promotion of 'a higher public spirit and better social order in the community' (Robinson, 1899, p. 176). But the City Beautiful gave this idea an even more durable expression. Burnham's *Plan of Chicago* has been interpreted as a treatise on physical disorder seen as both cause and effect of the 'deeper spiritual malaise' of the city (Boyer, 1983, p. 272). The imposition of social order was not directly coercive, but, Burnham believed, would naturally follow from the order, symmetry and civic magnificence of the plan, which would represent 'a long step toward cementing together the [city's] heterogeneous elements' (Burnham, 1902, p. 29).

A more forgiving interpretation of the social order aspect of the City Beautiful requires an understanding of its embeddedness in the era more generally, from which it would have been difficult to disassociate. Even Boyer recognizes that, given the long-standing quest to effectuate social control, the 'contradictions and paradoxes' of the *Plan of Chicago* start to make sense. Social and cultural repression was widespread during the Progressive Era. Most attempts at intervention were a matter of trying to force people into the white, Anglo-Saxon version of the norm. Anglo-Saxonism during the time was overtly racist, and some interventions amounted to an affirmation of white superiority (Chambers, 1992).

Control in urban plan-making was evident in more than one way. Burnham and Bennett write in the *Plan of Chicago* that the school playground should not only serve recreational needs, but should be the children's centre, 'to which each child will become attached by those ties of remembrance that are restraining influences throughout life' (Burnham and Bennett, 1909, p. 35). And, in speaking about the importance of yard maintenance in residential areas, they wrote: 'A well-kept grass plot in front of the house induces habits of neatness and comfort within; and cool shade brings people from cellars and dark rooms out into the light, thus contributing to good order and a higher morality' (Burnham and Bennett, 1909, p. 84).

Yet the belief in order and harmony did not mean that the City Beautiful was devoid of local variation, or at least insensitive to it. Wilson argues that City Beautiful planners did not, in fact, disregard local sentiment. This was politically motivated (they needed popular support), and they looked to the existing local context and wishes of neighbourhood residents for input. As a result, 'Embarrassing contretemps among arbiters of public beauty . . . occurred rarely' (Wilson, 1989, p. 79). The appreciation of localisms was more recognizable in America than in Europe, where restrictions on originality were commonplace. Robinson wrote that it would be dangerous to 'Haussmannize' American cities, and frequently made statements supporting the uniqueness of cities : 'Every good [city plan should] retain whatever is worthy in the individuality of the city . . . The idea is not to remodel cities until they conform to a certain pattern – that would be absurd; but accepting them as they are' (Robinson, 1906a, p. 8048). Another City Beautiful proponent, Charles Zueblin, was adamant that the majestic uniformity of Beaux Arts classicism meant no loss of individuality (Zueblin, 1903).

What Zueblin meant was that some underlying system of order was necessary to discern individuality. Wilson argues that the Columbian Exposition, known somewhat deceptively as the 'White City', used uniformity of form and colour as a backdrop to display the equally important component of diversity in form and colour. The Fair celebrated international culture as well as 'a showcase of American urban possibilities'. The colours, lush vegetation, and shear spectacle of diverse peoples and events made for a rich, variegated, festive atmosphere that is impossible to appreciate from black and white photographs (Wilson, 1989, p. 63).

The City Efficient

The City Beautiful movement did not simply vanish, but rather transformed into something else. Out of the City Beautiful, there emerged what is generally referred to as the 'City Efficient', although it is also termed the 'City Functional', or the 'City Scientific' (Scott, 1969). The new sentiment was summed up in 1909 by Cass Gilbert at the annual meeting of the American Institute of Architects. He pleaded for a new conception of what city planning was to be: 'Let us have the city useful, the city practical, the city liveable, the city sensible, the city anything but the City Beautiful' (Wilson, 1989, p. 287).

The difference between the City Beautiful and the City Efficient was not stylistic. The oft-cited tension between the romantic, gothic vernacular planning inspired by Ruskin, Morris and Sitte and the formality of the axes and classical uniformity of Haussmann and Burnham was more an issue of garden city versus Grand Manner plan-making. In the creation of new towns, the tension was resolved by Unwin, Nolen, and other planners of the City Efficient era. But in the creation of plans for existing cities, there was a continuity of stylistic preference, and the focus on classicism continued well into the 1930s under Roosevelt's New Deal projects. Often the criticisms were the same, as both were condemned for proposing solutions mostly acceptable to a 'caste of bankers'(Mumford, 1931). Even the Regional Plan Association (RPA) and its *Regional Plan of New York and its Environs* has been viewed as a 'late chapter' in the City Beautiful movement (Easterling, 1999). The fact that the main motivator behind the Plan of New York was Daniel Burnham's son-in-law, an active proponent of the 1909 *Plan of Chicago*, supports the connection.

The 20-year period following the City Beautiful was an era of plan-making focused on redevelopment of the existing, congested city and the orderly planning of areas immediately surrounding it. Planning was to be scientific, and goals were to be accomplished through the 'prompt and courageous execution of the plan found to be best for all concerned'. The plans consisted of some elements found in the earlier City Beautiful era – street widening, diagonal thoroughfares, rerouting of railways, removal of poles, wires and billboards – and some elements missing from the City Beautiful – rehabilitation of housing and restrictions on the use and occupancy of private property (Scott, 1969, p. 98).

Many of the projects in the 1910s and 1920s look very similar to City Beautiful era plans. A 1917 city planning survey by the American Institute of Architects reported

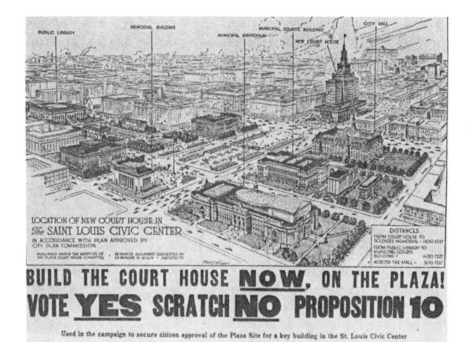

Figure 5.6. City Efficient era plan-making stressed the scientific approach, but its projects looked very similar to City Beautiful era plans. This ad is from a 1923 bond issue in St. Louis. (*Source*: Eldridge Lovelace, *Harland Bartholomew: His Contributions to American Urban Planning*, 1992)

233 cities that had developed 'project plans', and chief among such projects was the familiar civic centre of grouped public buildings. Harland Bartholomew's 1922 Civic Center plan for Wichita, Kansas was typical, and called for a civic centre 'within or next to' the central business district, which would serve the purpose of 'improving the functioning and adding to the beauty of the city's central area' (Lovelace, 1992, p. 52). But the editors of the document distanced themselves by stating that city planning in America had been 'retarded' by the lingering attention to City Beautiful projects, and that all city planning should begin on a foundation of 'economic practicable-ness and good business' (Scott, 1969, p. 167).

The domination of practicality over aesthetics was already started in the 1909 Chicago Plan. Unlike earlier City Beautiful plans, Burnham paid great attention to practical matters like transit and transportation. When he presented the plan at the Town Planning Conference in London in 1910, he downplayed its architectural vision and instead presented his ideas as a 'noble logical diagram' (Manieri-Elia, 1979, p. 109). The essential change was that city planning had become a discipline devoted to the rational functioning of cities, capitalizing on a new found organizational bureaucracy and an increasing preoccupation with the latest technological advances. Concern for aestheticism was enlisted exclusively in support of efficiency and commerce, at least ostensibly.

Supporters of the City Beautiful who were swept up by the call for efficiency found themselves arguing that the City Beautiful had been scientifically based. For example, Robinson traced the beginnings of the City Beautiful to the 1901 Plan of Washington, stating that it was the first effort 'to beautify cities scientifically' (Robinson, 1906a, p. 8046). Burnham continually spoke of the need to merge beauty and utility, and intended to make the city not only 'well-ordered, convenient, and unified', but also 'an efficient instrument' (Burnham and Bennett, 1909, p.1). Walter Moody's promotional *Wacker's Manual of the Plan of Chicago* (1917) considered his task to be 'the scientific promotion of scientific planning' (Schlereth, 1994, p. 71). There was even the supposition of scientific impartiality, as Burnham and Bennett claimed that the *Plan of Chicago* was made by 'disinterested men'. The whole scientific basis of plan-making seemed, at the time, unchallenged, and one study of parks planning in Chicago between 1902 and 1905 showed that social reformers did not see a conflict between the aesthetics of the City Beautiful and the science of parks planning (Draper, 1996).

But despite the claims, it was the lack of, or at least the perceived lack of, both efficiency and concern for social welfare that led to the recasting of the City Beautiful as the City Efficient. Early planners attacked the aesthetic, showy plan-making aspects of the City Beautiful at the first National Planning Conference held in Washington, D.C. in 1909. The conference was organized mostly by social workers and, not surprisingly, included a number of tirades against a manner of planning that was considered to be unprogressive. John Nolen's report 'What is Needed in American City Planning?' answered with a condemning 'Everything', meaning that the manner of course up until that point was seriously deficient.

Yet Nolen's contention that planners must 'frame an ideal of what we wish the city to be, and then work to make it real' links the City Beautiful and the City Efficient as two sides of the same plan-making coin. Here was a rephrased, if toned down, expression of the same thoughts Burnham had during his final days, telling his assistant Edward Bennett of his belief in 'the infinite possibilities of material expression of the spiritual' (Manieri-Elia, 1979). Both Burnham and Nolen, exemplars of their respective movements, were focused on the power of visionary city plan-making.

The prescriptions of the City Efficient plan-makers can be seen as subdued versions of the City Beautiful infused with a new methodology and purpose. Scott (1969, p. 123) describes the transformation as one of 'social impulses' that 'crept into' the City Beautiful. The Boston 1915 plan fitted this bill, and planners worked to include in it the social consciousness that Burnham had missed. But this did not mean that the City Efficient rejected beautification as a goal. There was ample talk about the 'art of city planning,' the 'happy combination of use and beauty', the integration of 'servicableness and charm', and that 'nothing is really finished until it is beautiful' (Nolen, 1909a, p. 1). Discussions of the 'art and science' of city planning were still prominent in the 1930s, for example in Thomas Adams' *Outline of Town and City Planning* (1935).

The difference is a matter of perceived objectives. Whereas the City Beautiful is viewed as using beauty and art for the needs of the corporate establishment, the City Efficient is viewed as using beauty and art for more socially progressive goals. However, the change in social concern in the first few decades of the twentieth century was limited to an increase in regulation, now extended to private development. Burnham was concerned about private speculation, but control over private investment was simply not within reach of City Beautiful era planners. His insistence on uniform building height and other approaches to beautification were all aimed at limiting private enterprise, and he spoke disparagingly of the 'speculative real estate agent' and the 'speculative builder' who exerted themselves to 'make every dollar invested into as many dollars as possible' (Burnham and Bennett, 1909, p. 34). Changing this was not something even Burnham could have accomplished.

Early in the century, divisions over how to balance social goals and private enterprise created a rift between housing reformers and physical planners that became unbridgeable. In 1910, hopes of city planning that included housing reform were put to rest when the National Housing Association was formed by Robert DeForest and Lawrence Veiller. This occurred one year after the formation of the National Conference on City Planning (NCCP). The NCCP became more concerned with professionalism than social reform, and, where the two groups had once shared constituencies, they became more and more divided (Kantor, 1994). The housers' view was that urban plan-makers had become more concerned with social organization than social welfare.

This was a fair criticism. Urban plan-makers were profoundly attracted to the principles of rationalization and the promise of engineering, and they did not hesitate to apply these principles towards people. Thomas Adams (1935, p. 322) wrote about the need for science to 'develop and build up' urbanized social organization, not unlike the 'mechanical processes of industry'. John Dewey promoted the idea of applying science to social issues (Dewey and Tufts, 1908), Oliver Wendell Holmes applied it to law, and planners applied it to urban plan-making. By the 1920s and into the 1930s, planners were in line with the technocracy movement in which engineering was seen as the tool of public policy. They may not have been as extreme as Thorstein Veblen and Howard Scott, who wanted to use technology to promote socialism, yet they did not veer far from George B. Ford's 1913 pronouncement that 'city planning is rapidly becoming as definite a science

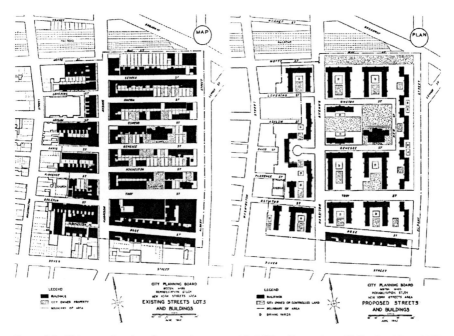

Figure 5.7. This map is taken from a chapter entitled 'The Correction of Mistakes' in a 1943 reissue of *The Planning of the Modern City* by Nelson P. Lewis (first published in 1916). The plan on the left is a proposed layout for a blighted area in Boston by the Boston City Planning Board, 1943. (*Source*: Harold MacLean Lewis, *Planning the Modern City*, 1943)

as pure engineering' (Ford, 1913, p. 551). Missing was the idea that technology, applied to urbanism, could be unsettling and even destructive.

In fact engineers helped to define the City Efficient approach to urbanism. Nelson P. Lewis was an engineer whose 1916 book *The Planning of the Modern City* was based on the idea that 'the fundamental problems of city planning are, and from their very nature must be, engineering problems' (Lewis, 1916, p. 1). City planning was to be a technical problem. On the other hand, Lewis was not without aesthetic sensibilities, and the problems of housing, the distribution of public facilities and services, the protection of public health and other social issues were matters that Lewis believed planning administrators needed to address. Lewis' own conception of urban plan-making included only transportation and street systems, parks and open spaces, and the location of public buildings.

The new ideology coincided with the need to promote a budding profession. Professionalization tended to shift concern towards 'practical humanitarianism as defined by specialists' (Wilson, 1989, p. 286). Under the spell of professionalism, any attempt at mere aestheticism was both hollow and too limiting, and City Efficient plan-makers fashioned instead a notion of beauty based on economic efficiency and social utility. The professionalization of planning was completely consistent with

COMPREHENSIVE
CITY PLAN
CITY OF ROANOKE

Figure 5.8. 'Master plan for a small city' from a 1933 text. The plan provided 'a framework of major traffic streets, parks, etc., within which sound neighborhood development may proceed under the direction of the plan commission with the assurance of economy and public welfare'. (*Source*: Russell Van Nest Black, *Planning for the Small American City*, 1933)

Progressive Era goals. 'Professionals', wrote Charles Beard in 1914, had a role to play as 'counter revolutionaries', that is, as activists working to set right the wrongs created by the industrial revolution.

The professionalization of planning paralleled a rise in organizational activity. The 1909 conference on City Planning was subsequently transformed into an annual event, and by 1915 had hired an executive secretary, Flavel Shurtleff. In 1917, a professional wing of the Conference was formed, the American City Planning Institute. This group had its own publication, *The City Plan*, which in 1925 was changed to *City Planning*, significant because it reflected a shift in emphasis to planning process (Krueckeberg, 1994). From 1920 on there was a substantial increase in government sponsored planning activity, as well as further division of planning into professionals, citizens, and now public administrators (Birch, 1980*b*).

Like the City Beautiful, City Efficient planners had strong ideas about the role of the expert. Nolen liked to quote John Stuart Mill's famous dictum that 'the people should be masters employing servants more skilful than themselves' (Nolen, 1910*b*).

The tone of urban plan-makers was universally paternalistic. Many perceived the reliance on elite-run planning commissions popular at the time as an extension of nineteenth-century patronage. Thomas Adams believed that 'what people will accept is what they can understand' (Adams, 1935, p. 26). He stressed the need for education by two methods, instruction in 'sound principles' and what he liked to call 'object lessons', by which he meant actual construction of planning projects.

At plan-making they were prolific. John Nolen, who began his career as a planner at the midpoint of the City Beautiful era and continued working through the New Deal, produced more than 400 plans between 1904 and 1937, ranging from playground designs to multi-state regional plans (Hancock, 1994). Harland Bartholomew and Associates, one of the first of a new breed of planning professionals, produced 56 plans, or 3 per year, between 1919 and 1935.[1] Mostly these plans would be described today as blueprints for the future physical form of the city framed as zoning maps. It was not until just after World War II that planners began preparing future land use plans of the kind we think of today; up until that time, the 'comprehensive land use plan' was a zoning map (Lovelace, 1992). They also carried the range of subjects treated in city plan-making further than the City Beautiful era planners had done. Nolen's list of planning issues to be addressed for the city of Bridgeport, Connecticut in 1913 gives an indication of the range: 'Congestion of traffic . . . lack of public docks . . . factories scattered throughout the city . . . [need for] a new City Hall . . . Housing . . . Zoning'.[2] Just a decade earlier, Robinson had limited his ideas about the 'city plan' to only two elements, circulation and community facilities.

City Efficient planners fashioned a new conceptualization of 'comprehensive', by which they meant that a plan should include all the physical elements of the city, and that it should encompass the entire future area of urban development. Thomas Adams, one of the leading city planners of the City Efficient era, admonished against planning that focused on 'tinkering' rather than 'replanning of whole cities or towns' (Adams, 1935, p. 27). In contrast to this broadened conception of plan-making, Olmsted, Sr.'s idea of comprehensive had been to plan for discrete areas of the city that were interconnected. Burnham's idea had been to extend the master plan to an entire city. But Olmsted, Jr., like Adams, representing the new City Efficient strategy, expanded the notion to ultimately reject the 'big once-for-all schemes' of Burnham (Peterson, 1996, p. 50) and substitute it with plans of a wider geographic and temporal framework. What this often amounted to was a proposal for smaller projects embedded in a wider framework. Thus there were still plenty of master plans produced, but the day to day operations of planners, under supervision of a lay commission, was to compare development to a comprehensive plan.

One of the most important outcomes of the City Efficient era was an increase in zoning. Spurred by citizens clamouring for protection of residential areas, planners embraced it and, starting in 1918, zoning took the country 'by storm', as one contemporary put it (Kimball, 1922, p. 32). By 1915 a majority of planning activists thought that zoning for the regulation of the height, area and use of land should be included as one element of the comprehensive plan.[3] It escalated after 1922, after the establishment of an Advisory Committee on Zoning in 1921 by the Secretary of Commerce, Herbert Hoover. After widespread adoption of standard zoning and planning enabling acts, by 1926, 400 communities had zoning ordinances. By 1929, this number had almost doubled to 754 communities (Hubbard and Hubbard, 1929, p. 3).

Herbert Hoover embodied the idea of an engineer capable only of seeing urbanism in black and white, failing to understand its human dimension. Hoover 'did not make jokes or admit errors', and was so out of touch with the realities of the Depression that he believed that people had left their jobs to pursue the more profitable one of selling apples (Evans, 2000, p. 236). That he was an engineer who had a hand in popularizing zoning as a technically efficient approach to city building is significant. It epitomizes the attitude of later City Efficient planners towards zoning and the regulatory side of planning, often in virtual isolation of its effects on urban form and beauty.

Zoning was a logical consequence of the increasing externalities of the industrial city. Residential areas – specifically, property values – needed to be stabilized, and industrial zones needed to be efficient, functional, and non-harmful. Thus began the adaptation of German zoning philosophy, and the City Efficient became focused on manipulating spatial relationships for maximum separation and mobility (Scott, 1969). The New York zoning ordinance of 1916 was the first such comprehensive scheme, but the suggestion to separate the city into zones was made earlier. The decentralization and separation theme was prominent at the First National Planning Conference in 1909, where Robert Anderson Pope argued for dispersal of factories to the outskirts and 'wider dispersal of the laboring class' (NCCP, 1909, p. 76). Benjamin Marsh advocated the German model of zoning in his 1909 city planning text, and Kessler's plan for Dallas in 1910 was all about segregating the city into zones, 'each devoted to its own particular purpose', and including the provision of 'ample' thoroughfares (Scott, 1969, p. 124).

Like the incrementalists, the City Efficient plan-makers were especially interested in the city survey. Nolen's collection of materials on cities (now housed at Cornell University's Division of Rare Manuscripts), includes hundreds of index cards of block sizes, ratios of land uses, measured street widths, dimensions of public spaces, and details of urban form that few planners today would concern themselves with. A thorough understanding of the existing city is important, wrote Unwin in 1909, because both the economic success and the preservation of a city's 'individuality of character' depend on it. The survey work of Patrick Geddes was often referred to, although Unwin suggested that the extent of survey work required by Geddes 'may not always be practical'. But, importantly, Geddes' approach extended beyond the surveying of physical elements to include the survey work of 'the sociologist, the historian, and the local antiquary' (Unwin, 1909, p. 141).

The geographic scope of urban plan-makers, whether City Beautiful or City Efficient, was the metropolis, an extent that regionalists of the Geddes-Mumford variety found troubling. The metropolitan plans can be described as 'supraurban schemes' (Wilson, 1983, p. 98), and included Russel V. Black's plan for the Philadelphia region, Harland Bartholomew's Plan for San Francisco, and the Regional Plan Association's *Regional Plan for New York and its Environs*, all of which were conceived during the 1920s. Like the *Plan of Chicago*, these plans were exemplary exercises in plan-making. They focused on transportation circulation, parks and boulevards – the focus of City Beautiful era plans – but extended their focus to include neighbourhoods, housing, and suburban development. In these plans, it was the centrality of the urban realm that caught the planners' attention. The fact that the main critique of the RPA plan, at least from its RPAA rivals, was that it invested too much in an already dominant urban centre is an indication of this.

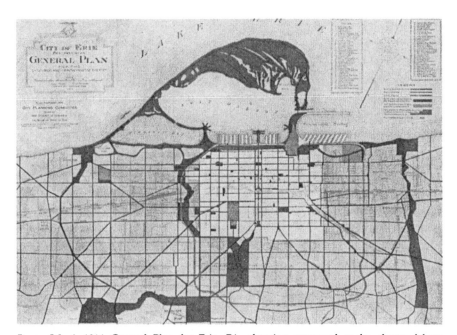

Figure 5.9. A 1914 General Plan for Erie, PA, showing proposed parks, thoroughfares and parkways. (*Source*: George B. Ford, *City Planning Progress in the United States*, 1917. Reproduced with permission from The American Institute of Architects, 1735 New York Ave. NW, Washington, D.C. 2006)

The 1929 Regional Plan of New York represents the quintessential event of the City Efficient variety of urban plan-making. It was attempting to be, as all City Efficient era plans were, a plan that blended the practical and the beautiful – as one reviewer put it, 'the logic of the lawyer, the technique of the artist and engineer, and the idealism of the prophet' (Kantor, 1994, p. 174). Such was the final culmination of the urban plan-making approach to urbanism.

The plan-making approach that City Efficient era planners developed – the physical, comprehensive plan, the smaller master plans, the professionalization of city planning – came under attack in the New Deal era of the 1930s. It was again asserted that the focus on physical planning did not go far enough in addressing social problems (Heskin, 1980). Certainly the content of the plans produced by consultants such as John Nolen and Harland Bartholomew were sometimes deficient in terms of sophisticated social thinking. The plans were often focused on stabilization of property values through zoning, the separation of urban land uses, and the accommodation of the automobile. This is not to say that Nolen and Bartholomew lost influence. Nolen was a consultant on virtually every New Deal planning programme until his death in 1937 (Schaffer, 1988).

Eventually, the blend of planning as art and planning as science that dominated the City Efficient era broke apart. By the 1940s, the definition of planning had come down to 'the comprehensive arrangement of land uses and occupancy and the regulation thereof' (Oppermann, 1946, p. 3). By the end of World War II, planning as science was the dominant mode, and by 1963 planners were warned by Webber that it was time to stop their 'conventional reliance upon personal experience and private intuition' (Webber. 1963, p. 238). Then in 1967 the American Institute of Planners amended its charter and deleted all references to physical planning, a reversal of its previous policy to limit membership to those interested in the physical development of cities.

It must be acknowledged, however, that the loss of the artistic side of planning to the forces of technical and scientific efficiency has always been recognized by some urbanists as harmful. In the early 1940s, Eliel Saarinen argued that practical plan-making was 'dangerous' (Saarinen, 1943, p. 355). In the 1950s, some planners lamented the technical takeover, expressed in editorials like 'The art in city planning' by G. Holmes Perkins, or 'Cities by design' by Christopher Tunnard, both written in 1951. There were articles that recognized that American cities were losing their cultural heritage and were in need of an active preservationist strategy (see Lillibridge, 1949). Books like *The City of Man* (Tunnard, 1953) and *Town Design* (Gibberd, 1953) were, in the 1950s, stressing the importance of three-dimensional civic design and art in American planning. Tunnard's book even included a chapter entitled 'The New Urbanism'.

Connections

The main tenets associated with the City Beautiful have inspired widespread criticism. William H. Wilson attributes this to misunderstanding, and questions each of the following assumptions: 'that centralization does not allow for considerable local autonomy'; 'that bureaucracy and expertise are antithetical to democracy'; 'that social control is of little or no merit'; 'that class control is bad unless it is the working class that is asserting its privileges over those of the others'; and 'that small-scale democracy and neighbourhood control are creatable or preservable values in the era of the metropolis' (Wilson, 1989, p. 86).

The City Efficient has not escaped these same criticisms. Both eras have been deemed too controlling, too much about order, too negligent of social needs, too deferential to the expert, and too focused on blueprint-like plans. The question to be explored now is whether urban plan-making culture can contribute to a definition of American urbanism, and, if this cannot be done in a positive way, what are the lessons learned?

One potential contribution to American urbanism is the linking together of technology and efficiency with beauty and art. Urban plan-makers were intent on merging the two, at least initially, and there is value in the fact that the necessity of a merger was recognized. The lead planner of the Regional Plan of New York, Thomas Adams, expressed the view that the creative force of planning should be given primary importance. Great plan-makers like Patrick Abercrombie thought primarily in design terms and not in terms of the 'paraphernalia of planning' – forecasts, projections, and the evaluation of alternatives (Hall, 1995, p. 229).

For all of the rhetoric about technical efficiency and planning as science, plan-makers, especially after 1909, at least *thought* in holistic terms, or recognized the importance of doing so. Right alongside their obsession with rational planning and the need to be 'modern', some engineer-planners of the day were in fact deeply concerned with the effect of their proposals on the living experience of the urban environment. This can be seen in the 1916 engineering manual by Nelson P. Lewis, who wanted his engineering 'brothers' to know the proper arrangement of public buildings and civic spaces, the details of street design that responded appropriately to building arrangement, and the value of garden cities. In the manual he worries about inharmonious colour, 'hideous bill-boards', streets that are 'gloomy' and lamp-posts and street signs that are 'conspicuously ugly' (Lewis, 1916, p. 220). Such considerations would not be included in today's public engineering documents.

Urban plan-makers also tended to have deep regard for the historical development of cities, although this may not have included vernacular structures. Many contend that the City Beautiful plan-makers carried historicism to excess in their classicist revivalism. City Efficient era plan-makers were intent on using knowledge of the past as a starting point rather than something to be copied. This did not diminish its importance. Thomas Adams' text *Outline of Town and City Planning* (1935) was subtitled 'A Review of Past Efforts and Modern Aims'. More than half of the text is devoted to historical planning, starting with ancient cities. In contrast, the 'bible' of contemporary American planning practice, *The Practice of Local Government Planning*, published by the American Planning Association, completely omitted the section on history from its latest edition (Hoch *et al.*, 2000).

The City Beautiful and its metamorphosis into the City Efficient both stressed order, universal truth, and beauty. Urban plan-makers favoured the 'master plan' to impose this order because it made redevelopment predictable and put the municipal government (or other civic leadership in a quasi-governmental role) in the role of downtown developer. The goal was to put a physical vision in place and then proactively promote that vision. The advantage was that the quality of new development could be predetermined, with the government acting as 'lead booster' for urban regeneration. Many urban plan-makers at the beginning of the twentieth century shared the view that the making of good cities and communities could not be entrusted to private interests that were strictly profit-motivated. The reason is the same then as it is now – private investors could not be expected to consider long term community benefit on their own accord.[4]

In addition to the master plan, zoning codes fulfilled a similar purpose and could go some way towards implementing a specific physical vision of the future city. We have urban plan-making culture to thank for zoning in America, and that attribution is not usually viewed positively. But the use of codes and zoning, in and of themselves, have a place in American urbanism. The question is how far should they go. New types of codes are being promoted as cities 'emerge from a prolonged crisis of confidence' in which they steered clear of articulating an ordered, predictable future. The intent of code reform now is to provide an environment 'for the market to thrive in.' But the debate then and now is over what level this control should extend to. Codes can be all-controlling, or, they can stipulate a few key principles, and, from there, 'let it go' (Jacobs, 2002, p. 139; Duany *et al.*, 2000, pp. 174, 177, 179).

American urbanism by plan-making faces the issue of control in other, less direct ways than codes. Critics contend that whoever is in control of plan design and imagery will have an unfair advantage. Plans, especially flowery, colourful images, can be seen as a form of propaganda that are in themselves a form of control. Design is manipulated by controlling what gets put on the table, the definitions of terms, and the attractiveness of the plans proposed. This can be overcome to the extent that public opinion is allowed a real voice, so that alternative conceptions of what gets put on the table are given equal exposure, but whether or not this actually happens is an open question.

But is there a place for the aesthetic ideology of the City Beautiful in American urbanism? Broadly viewed, the movement can be said to have made creative use of a few, versatile elements to construct a language of form and pattern that allowed, to some degree, both diversity and harmony. A central issue is whether diversity in both an aesthetic and social sense requires an underlying, framing sense of order. The City Beautiful rested on the idea that stylistic variability needed a 'language' to allow the variation to work successfully in an urban context. The value of the classical language of architecture could be seen therefore not as the reapplication of traditional forms, but as the need for new forms of expression to be tempered. This was the thinking of H. P. Berlage, an early twentieth-century Dutch architect who thought of proportion as the guarantor of permanent value in architecture, and who admired the 'system of definite proportions' of Greek architecture (Banham, 1967, p. 142). American urbanism struggles to interpret the difference between innovation as a means to an end and innovation as an end in itself. A century ago, the classical was called upon to create 'a solid, durable, comfortable, beautiful human world' (Krier, 1998, p. 51) where freedom was interpreted through a particular language of architectural form.

Urban plan-makers believed that diversity would only be palatable to people if it existed within a framework that de-emphasized difference. One manifestation of this has to do with accommodating mixed use. Plan-makers during the City Efficient era understood that an objection to a particular use in a given neighbourhood could be more a matter of incompatible design than incompatible use. Adams postulated that people object to buildings without good reason because of 'an ugly type of design' or a perception that an 'untidiness of arrangement' is associated with a particular use. What they were getting at was that, as Adams put it, 'it is the character of the structure in which business is done rather than the business that is offensive' (Adams, 1935, p. 323). This lament is unchanged. Now the importance of consistency in building typology is stressed as an important element in achieving mixed use. The importance of uniformity in non-public and non-civic buildings was not only to allow public and civic buildings to stand out. It was also important in residential architecture because it allowed class distinctions to be minimized.[5]

These are physical reflections of the plan-making view that both individualism and collectivism should be emphasized simultaneously. Collectivist thinking that placed the common good ahead of all else was seen as liberating for the individual. Unwin's philosophy was socialist, but his commitment to organized, communitarian plan-making was for the purpose of protecting individualism. It was not meant to procure conformity (Creese, 1967). This same view – that collectivism and its expression in ordered physical form is ultimately liberating for the individual – is a pervasive thought in contemporary American urbanism. American urbanists find themselves simultaneously embracing the libertarianism of Ayn Rand in the same breath that they express commitment for the cooperative society.[6]

The legitimacy of control in urban plan-making, whether based on master plans, zoning, architectural codes, or some other mechanism, hinges on the issue of appropriateness. The 'doctrine of appropriateness', to coin a phrase, is the idea that many concepts, ideas, and principles in the urban plan-making approach to urbanism are only appropriate for certain times and places, depending fundamentally on context. Architecturally, this means that the principle of proportion in design must be properly treated. In urban plan-making, it means that the nature of the plan and the elements it contains must be considered *vis-à-vis* context. Thus the heroics of the City Beautiful may be deemed appropriate depending on the context to which it is applied. The use of focal points in the form of buildings and formal squares, direct lines of communication in the form of straight streets and diagonals, and design elements like tree-lined boulevards, vista markers, public monuments, and formal squares – all of these components combine to create a language of urban form that can be useful in American urbanism if the adaptation is responsive. Failure to adapt, noted Mumford, is what created the 'brilliantly sterile' urbanism of Le Corbusier and Mies van der Rohe (Mumford, 1968, pp. 162–163).

The doctrine of appropriateness was understood by many City Beautiful and City Efficient plan-makers. Raymond Unwin was particularly strong about it, arguing for the need to consider not whether the formal or the informal is desired,

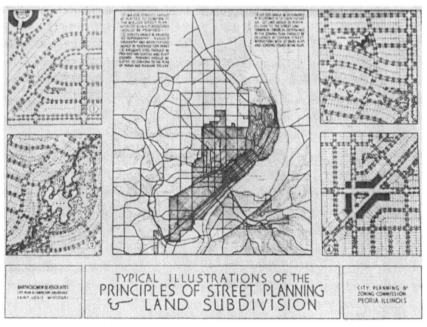

Figure 5.10. Principles of street planning and land subdivision from the 1927 *Plan of Peoria, Illinois*. (*Source*: Eldridge Lovelace, *Harland Bartholomew: His Contributions to American Urban Planning*, 1992)

but whether the 'requirements of the case' and the 'conditions of the site' have been thoroughly weighed (Unwin, 1909, p. 138). One of Unwin's favourite quotes was by the painter Jean-Francois Millet (1814–1875), who wrote: 'The beautiful is that which is in place' (Creese, 1967, p. 40). John Nolen spoke in similar terms, and explicitly defined beauty as 'fitness and appropriateness' (Nolen, 1908, p. 2). The view of Nolen and Unwin was that, just as the love for informality should not be allowed to degrade public convenience, so formal planning should not justify 'riding roughshod' over property lines or the sentiments of residents and property owners (Unwin, 1909, p. 139). This thinking is what prompted Nolen, on numerous occasions, to discuss the differences between the landscape planning of Le Notre and Olmsted to demonstrate that while the underlying principles were always the same, the application of principles was always different.

Nolen also stressed the importance of understanding the place and function of the street before prescribing its specifications. It was the inappropriateness of street design relative to place and function that Nolen disdained, writing in 1908: 'We have curved streets where they should be straight, straight streets where they should be curved, narrow streets where they should be broad, occasionally broad streets where they should be narrow' (Nolen, 1908, p. 7). Writing much later, in the mid-1930s, Thomas Adams tied the doctrine of appropriateness to the essence of the artistic process. He stated, 'As in all art it is not the name of what you do that counts but how you do it in relation to time, place, and surroundings' (Adams, 1935, p. 321).

H.P. Berlage wrote in 1908 of the need for 'Unity in Plurality', that 'all is governed by circumstance and relationship' (Banham, 1967, p. 144). This was perhaps a more sophisticated view of the need for order guided by circumstance, but there is a parallel understanding of it in the American City Beautiful. Wilson (1989) gives a number of examples in which City Beautiful proponents warned of the dangers of stylistic singularity, of the problem with accepting Beaux Arts Classicism in all cases. Charles Mulford Robinson understood the choices, which is why he traversed both the incrementalist and urban plan-making cultures. Having expressed the importance of unique immigrant architecture in his incrementalist phase, by 1903, he advocated stylistic flexibility, arguing in favour of Flemish Gothic over classical architecture.

Linked to the need for appropriateness was at least the intent in urban plan-making to value local tradition. The issue of maintaining the individuality of every city was stated repeatedly as a counter response to the critique that plan-making was prone to rubber stamping. Unwin (1909, p. 146) referred to the individuality of urban character as 'the poetry of its existence'. Nolen (1909a, p. 74) wrote of the need to instil 'love and pride in local traditions and local ideals'. By the time Nolen wrote 'Civic art furnishes the most available means to express these local customs'

(Scott, 1969, p. 98) he had rejected the City Beautiful but nevertheless saw it as a means to accomplish the goal of affirming local aspirations.

Appropriateness in the City Beautiful era was tied to large scale plan-making, whereby smaller elements were positioned relative to the city as a whole. For Burnham, the value of a plan was that it ensured 'that whenever any public or semi-public work shall be undertaken, it will fall into its proper and predetermined place' (Burnham and Bennett, 1909, p. 4). Thus, appropriateness was determined by placement of buildings relative to the urban complex, and smaller scale diversity would have to take place within this larger framework. If American urbanism has the capacity to legitimize this larger urban framework it will be on these terms – that a coherent pattern helps rather than hurts smaller scale diversity by allowing that diversity to be recognizable. But this requires an endorsement of the idea that there is a place in American urbanism for bigness (large in scale, time, and financial commitment), alongside the smallness of incrementalism.

The derision that the City Beautiful was about display, power, theatrics, and 'a total concentration on the monumental and on the superficial' (Hall, 2002, p. 216) seems less relevant where the City Beautiful was able to conform to the doctrine of appropriateness, and, in addition, where it stayed focused on a reverence for the public domain. Plan-makers understood these principles. They saw that the proper siting of an otherwise insignificant building could give it significance, a simple rule realized, at least historically, in American urbanism. The 'tyranny of the straight line' (Kunstler, 2001, p. 30) could also be overcome by using public monuments to create vistas, something plan-makers were attuned to. Even Jane Jacobs was in favour of visual cues in the urban landscape, and her 'visual street interruptions' – dead ends that are not 'final' – are akin to the vista markers of the Grand Manner.[7]

American urbanists must determine whether other Baroque planning principles that no longer hold overt symbolic content can still be used in service to the public realm. The straight street need not be about ceremony and riot control, but can instead be helpful for re-establishing the street as public space. Perhaps the use of drama and theatrical expression in city form could be rescaled so that it does not become too dominating. The issue, as Kostof framed it, is whether American urbanists can 'turn to the rond-points and the Baroque diagonals and even the accursed cermonial axis, reject their symbolism, and find in them something guiltless and eternal'(Kostof, 1991, p. 276). The formal plan of, for example, the New Urbanist town of Seaside – a development that Kostof (1991) labels 'Post-modern Baroque' – exhibits Burnhamesque spatial qualities (axes, tree-lined avenues, vistas with landmarks as terminating markers) that are simply intended to exonerate the public realm.

For American urbanism, what must be determined is the degree to which civic idealism can or should possess moral or ethical potential. Burnham wrote that 'good citizenship is the prime object of good city planning', an insupportable concept if by citizenship is meant blind deference. In the 1909 *Plan of Chicago* he wrote that his social objective was partly to save money: 'haphazard and ill-considered projects invariably result in extravagance and wastefulness' (Burnham and Bennett, 1909, p. 4). A more palatable interpretation of citizenship would be to invoke responsibility and communitarianism, in the sense of Amitai Etzioni (2004). In fact this notion was interpreted by plan-makers as relating to the need to mix social classes in the city. Burnham stated that the prosperity generated by good planning was aimed at 'all of Chicago', largely a matter of class mixing: 'The very beauty that attracts him who has money makes pleasant the life of those among whom he lives, while anchoring him and his wealth to the city' (Burnham and Bennett, 1909, p. 8). This was Burnham's way of endorsing social diversity, and it continues to hold relevance for American urbanism today.

The physical manifestation of civic consciousness was the civic realm, the primary vehicle through which urban plan-makers attempted to promote social welfare. It was a matter of providing places of beauty for all urban residents, regardless of class. Nolen stressed that civic art was capable of being democratic because 'it is not art for art's sake, but art for the people's sake' (Nolen, 1909a, p. 2). Robinson discussed how the beautiful city, complete with a civic centre, strengthened 'the mutual thoughts and feelings and interests' of the citizenry (Robinson, 1903, p.91). The trick is to define this in a way that does not limit it to middle- or upper-class consensus, or to one particular venue. For the 1902 McMillan Plan for Washington D.C., the civic realm was heavily symbolic, where the laying out of the mall was meant to instil a sense of civic awe and, at the same time, strengthen the primacy of the federal government. Naturally, if this were to be the only type of civic space provided, this would contribute to a very narrow conceptualization of urbanism. While there is a place for public space grandeur in American urbanism, the symbolism of well designed and apportioned public space cannot be about domination, control, and manipulation of the public ethos, but about the need to provide a public identity through the provision of suitable settings for collective, i.e., public, activity.

Because of this more realistic role, the goals that can be accomplished via the provision of public space have been significantly downscaled over the past century. There is no longer an emphasis on 'mutual thoughts and feelings', since the ease of deriving a unified public sentiment is long since past. Carefully crafted public realms that could serve as symbolic endorsement of controlling regimes or homogenous social feeling are not supported (at least overtly) by today's plan-makers. Now, a pervasive urbanist ideal is simply to elevate the stature of our collectivity by providing a dignified setting for public engagement.

Emphasis on the public realm has often led to the view that commercialization of the city must be downscaled in its expression. Washington, D.C. was able to exert this kind of control (but not with universal approval). In American urbanism, what seems to have emerged is recognition of a need to limit the expression of private development if such development is done at the expense of the public realm. One New Urbanist text reasoned it this way: 'If every building were to croon at once, nothing could be discerned from the cacophony' (Duany et al., 2000, p. 211). Hegemann and Peets expressed this sentiment artfully in their treatise *The American Vitruvius: An Architects' Handbook of Civic Art* , which expressed the City Beautiful view that 'the well designed individual building in order to be enjoyed fully must be part of an aesthetically living city, not of chaos' (Hegemann and Peets, 1922, p. 1). The book's 1203 illustrations are grouped in order to portray graphically the importance of context and situation rather than the individuality of design. Toning down non-public expression was something urban plan-makers obsessed over. The use of monumental classicism or monumental anything for the celebration of modes of production and market exchange was considered debasing

Adherence to these principles required design leadership. Interestingly, Progressive Era planners did not see a conflict between democracy and the need for experts, and in fact believed that democracy could be enhanced by interactions between ordinary people and experts (Melvin, 1987). Most importantly, the prominence of the expert did not exclude public decision-making. Wilson argues that since City Beautiful programmes depended upon the public referendum, beautification and plan-making were dependent on public approval, not shielded from it. This was exactly the liberal approach of the Progressive Era – political innovation involved 'equalization of political power through the primary, the direct election of public officials, and the initiative, referendum, and recall' (Dal Co, 1979, p. 219). In this atmosphere, it would have been impossible for Burnham to ignore the need for popular support. And he did not particularly like this condition. He complained that publicity 'exposes everything in the United States to open view. Our thoughts are headlined in the Press almost as soon as they are formed in the brain . . .' (Burnham, 1910).

Thus top-down planning was secured from the bottom up, and there are indications that the strategy worked. Robinson attributed increases in street lighting to a public willing to pay for it: 'Public opinion is permitting a more generous use of it than strict necessity demands' (Robinson, 1899, p. 178). And it was not a one-time involvement. Wilson notes that the public had to vote more than once on planning projects, and thus had to approve of what had already been accomplished. In this way 'the relationship between public and expert or citizen board was not authoritarian or undemocratic but reciprocal' (Wilson, 1989, p. 76).

Despite these arguments, the case for the expert has been very difficult to sustain, largely because it is so open to abuse. Urban plan-makers lacked sensitivity to non-expert viewpoints. The view almost universally expressed by City Efficient planners was that the public needed to be educated, that 'object lessons' which demonstrated the concrete application of planning principles were needed, and that if both of these things happened then the public would go along. Nolen, who advocated the establishment of planning commissions to implement plans, insisted repeatedly that the commissions would only be successful in the wake of a 'campaign of education' intended for 'prominent elements of the community' as well as 'the laboring classes and the public at large' (Nolen, undated (c), p. 3). This would work because it was not that the average citizen wanted the wrong things, only that 'the average citizen lacks knowledge of how to attain what he wants' (Adams, 1935, p. 322). There may be some truth to this, but ultimately American urbanism must negotiate a role for experts that does not attempt to negate the legitimacy and importance of layperson views.

Urban plan-makers were a conservative group. While many incrementalists were open to radical (i.e., socialist) change, the urban plan-makers were mostly content to work within the existing system. This was reflected in a political division between plan-makers who stressed regulation and those who stressed 'object lessons'. This had been seen earlier in the division in housing reform between those like Lawrence Veiller and Jacob Riis who stressed regulation, and public housing advocates like Catherine Bauer who wanted direct government involvement in housing construction. This same debate persists today. On the one hand, there are strong promoters of regulatory reform. On the other, there are those who emphasize the need for demonstrable planning success in the form of tangible projects.

Both the early and late twentieth century has been profoundly affected by the challenge of posing collective goals in the face of private consumption. Always there is the difficulty of justifying public expenditure when it is seen as getting in the way of individual gain. In the late nineteenth century, the arrival of inexpensive goods to satisfy the consumption of the middle-class had arrived in the form of the 'five and ten-cent' store (F. W. Woolworth's store opened in 1879) (Chambers, 1992). The opposition to the City Beautiful came from middle- and upper-class citizens who were content with the existing city, and thus felt that the cost of planned intervention was not justified. As long as the consumer was satisfied – as long as goods were distributed, housing was provided, and people could get to their jobs – there was no need for planned intervention (Wilson, 1989). Today's translation of this same dilemma may be, for example, a contented suburban public unwilling to accept changes or controls because living conditions are not bad enough, or have not prevented consumption of inexpensive goods. Sprawl may be an inconvenience, but not always to the extent that either public expenditure or regulatory controls are warranted.

Conflicts

In the previous section I laid out what I considered to be the most positive elements of plan-making culture – what would be viable to retain in an inclusive definition of American urbanism. These included the notion of a sense of order and its role in supporting diversity, the role of plans and experts within certain limits, the ability to merge utility and beauty, and the ability to accentuate the public realm. But there is much to critique in urban plan-making culture.

To begin with, belief in the ability to improve the city through urban plan-making was a highly optimistic enterprise. The strong visual imagery ('no little plans') of the well-ordered city may be seen as simply a necessary component of building public support, but can also be interpreted as something much more perilous. In Kolson's *Big Plans, The Allure and Folly of Urban Design* (2001), the author warns that

Madison.—State Street, One of the Capitol Approaches as It is Today.

Madison.—State Street, as Proposed with Poles and Wires Removed and Dignified Business Buildings Lining the Sidewalks.

Figure 5.11. The regularizing of streets during the era of plan-making. The proposed street leading to the capitol in Madison would be lined with 'dignified business buildings'. (*Source:* George B. Ford, *City Planning Progress in the United States*, 1917)

big plans are 'dangerously efficacious in arousing complicated human passions and expectations that they are unable to fulfil'. In other words, plan-making, even if ultimately limited to a basic statement of aspirations, is not innocuous. Part of the problem with plan-making is the tendency to rely on a formalized type of order. Elbert Peets held the view that Americans had a difficult time relating to this. He lamented the attachment Americans have to informal landscape planning and their disdain for axiality and formal pattern: 'They look at the Lincoln Memorial and see a symbol of a tragic life' (Peets and Spreiregen, 1968, p. 164). Rational and formal art was, Peets said, 'fundamentally irritating to people' because of the irrationality in their own lives, and a failure either to understand it, or attach sentiment to it. This is why, Peets said, visitors to Williamsburg love the disorder of the 'quack-colonial' shopping centre, while the formality of the plan may go unappreciated: 'Freed from any burden of necessity to observe and understand an organized unity, they can freely enjoy the toy-town prettiness and the lush sentimentality' (Peets and Spreiregen, 1968, p. 164).

What Peets was identifying, perhaps, was an early rendition of the postmodern celebration of discord, now extended through the work of modern architects like Rem Koolhaas and Peter Eisenman. Plan-makers would not have allowed these freedoms, and perhaps with current open-endedness of urbanism is somehow linked to the perceived rigidity of earlier urbanist ideals. For example, Burnham's *Plan of Chicago* postulates, referring to road design, that 'bad kinks and sharp turns should not be tolerated' (Burnham and Bennett, 1909, p. 39). This thinking only became stronger in the City Efficient era. Later, Thomas Adams called for easy gradients and curves, separation of pedestrian and vehicular traffic, 6-lane highways, urban arterial links and flyover junctions, all for the purpose of smoother traffic flows (Simpson, 1985).

This all seems like an early rendition of modernist urbanism, and in many ways it was. One of the delegates to the 1909 National Conference on City Planning, landscape architect Robert Anderson Pope, suggested the need for a *Ringstrasse* around existing cities that could attract industry and people out of the central city. Planners seemed unaware of the negative impacts of centrifugal circulation, or at least their image of the city was incomplete (Scott, 1969, p. 99). And at the same time that they were dismissing the impracticality of the City Beautiful, City Efficient planners were ignoring their own era's practical problems. The 1917 publication *City Planning Progress in the United States* failed, as had most City Beautiful documents, to address adequately the impact of mass automobile use, despite the fact that the impact of the Model T was by then 'right under their noses' (Wilson, 1989, p. 284). Great plans were made but failed to anticipate the massive suburbanization about to take place, spurred to a great extent by increasing middle-class mobility. When its effects did become known, the car was seen not only as a great liberator, but as the basis of a new type of urban structure. By the 1930s, when highways were penetrating the city under the leadership of plan-makers like Robert Moses, the new automobile-inspired city form – a system for commuters – was taking shape.

In retrospect, there seems little to extract from City Efficient era plan-making that could be useful for defining American urbanism. They certainly seemed unable to offer something to better the most important city making phenomenon of their day – suburbanization. Mumford's critique of RPA's Plan of New York – that it promoted both congestion at the centre and sprawl at the periphery – identified this failing precisely. Earlier in the decade, Raymond Unwin's warning against focusing transportation facilities at the centre, without considering how to plan for decentralization, was unheeded (Kantor, 1994).

Another problem for urban plan-making culture has been the critique that it ignores social conditions. All urbanist cultures face this criticism in some form simply because they are focused on the physical city, but plan-makers seem particularly susceptible. For the City Beautiful, social concern is said to have amounted to an attempt to control the masses, with little regard for the improvement of social concerns such as poverty and housing. The *Plan of Chicago*, the quintessential City Beautiful plan, is condemned as seeking to procure 'essentially an aristocratic city [for] merchant princes' (Scott, 1969, p. 108), an exercise in 'aesthetic megalomania' (Boyer, 1983, pp. 274–275) devoted to visual rather than humanitarian goals. Some plans may have promoted the inclusion of parks, playgrounds, and neighbourhood centres, but most plans issued during the City Beautiful period excluded housing, and did not make the connection between blight and the regulation of private development. The plans of the City Beautiful era were known to cover up the slums left to fester behind the Beaux Arts façades. The City Efficient era plan-makers had at least a greater expressed interest in housing issues, but they were still condemned for excluding social concerns and seeking, instead, technical solutions to narrowly conceived problems (Simpson, 1985). Tenement-house reformers, who were previously allied, separated from plan-makers when they opted to pursue zoning and land use efficiency.

The tension between aestheticism and social welfare is a continuous problem in American urbanism. That one must not exclude the other is central to successful urbanism, but the experiences of the urban plan-makers lend reality to this idealism. It seems a straightforward task to implore aesthetically minded planners to heed the needs of the poor. But when does this effort lapse into social control, and when do unintended perverse affects begin to appear? Urban plan-makers made it that much harder by overstepping their bounds. It is not unusual to find claims that a beautiful city would lead to better 'moral development'.[8]

Later, a slightly more sophisticated basis of social order was applied via the neighbourhood unit. Through this mechanism, and bolstered by prominent sociologists like C. H. Cooley and R. D. McKenzie, earlier plan-makers had little trouble postulating a proximally-based conception of social relationship. But we can now see the problems that emerge wherever spatial principles rest on assumptions about the localization of social relationships rather than, more simply, daily life needs. This has been a difficult distinction to make, in part because urbanists continue to use the rhetoric, albeit significantly toned down, of the early plan-makers.

The issue is whether the quest for principles of beauty, civic decorum and the neighbourhood unit in terms physically similar to the earlier proposals of the urban plan-makers can now be detached from their earlier underlying motivations, and assigned to different ones. American urbanists can no longer use the 'situational context' argument that Wilson used in defence of the City Beautiful to claim they were required to act according to a reigning, Darwinian viewpoint. Now, any open statement, even if rhetorical, about the ability of design to exert influence on moral or social order would be viewed in negative terms. And it is not even clear whether aesthetic and social/moral goals can be detached from one another, since it is in any case likely to be labelled a subliminal goal, whereby critics must assume hidden intentions.

Still, the 'social control' critique of urbanism lacks proof. This is because claims of social control are self-limiting. If plan-makers held that urban beautification could foster not only moral order but also civic loyalty they would have great difficulty backing up their assertion. Since it is not possible for urban plan-makers to effect a new socially and morally perfected order through physical improvement, any implicit or explicit attempts to do so are somewhat meaningless.

More palatable now would be the recasting of 'civic loyalty' as individual responsibility and environmental stewardship. The concept of pride is now promoted in the context of sustainability but it is not about patriotism or loyalty, nor is it interpreted as Burnham-type coercion. It is, instead, environmental awareness. It was in this spirit that an urban ecologist recently equated the idea of 'cultural sustainability' with the need to promote pride, pleasure, stewardship, and community attentiveness within urban landscapes (Nassauer, 1997). The role of the designer is to allow these ideas of 'pride' to flourish via environmental design, a quest that on some level parallels the intentions of earlier plan-makers.

Thus the rhetoric about pride – either expressed as a collective value in the early part of the twentieth century or as individual environmental stewardship in the latter part – persists. The problem, of course, is that expressions of pride and stewardship are not always innocuous. One example concerns the optimistic response – essentially, pride – plan-makers had towards technology. Urban plan-makers effectively employed technologies like electricity, steel and reinforced concrete to accomplish their goals, and some view this as the main achievement of the era (Fishman, 2000). But another interpretation is that pride and optimism in these technologies seemed to gloss over the inherent conflicts of capitalism as if there were an underlying social harmony just waiting to be awakened through the planner's technological finesse of the physical landscape.

Nolen's quest was to use technology to get closer to nature. It was technology that would allow 'the rapid increase of suburban and country living'. According to Nolen, it was a matter of 'self-preservation', and that 'without the healing of the woods and open spaces . . . our modern city life would soon destroy what is most precious and most indispensable in our manhood and womanhood' (Nolen, 1910a). The answer was to endorse a technological response, whereby 'the automobile, the good road, electricity, the telephone, and the radio' would allow us to achieve 'a more natural, biological life' (MacKaye, 1925, p. 153).

With this as a goal, it was not surprising that Nolen approved of the ideas of Le Corbusier. The affinity was merely a desire on Nolen's part to be efficient and modern, principles that Le Corbusier exemplified. Nolen wrote a review of Le Corbusier's *The City of Tomorrow and its Planning* in which he stated that 'The modern world needs a modern city. It needs something more like what Le Corbusier has proposed' (Nolen, undated, b, p. 9). What Nolen was reacting to favourably was the efficiency of the machine for living in, the way in which Corbusier focused on opening up and widening the urban realm for greater ease of movement. Nolen did caution that the street was more than a 'traffic machine' and 'a sort of factory for producing speed', as Corbusier proposed. But he did not hesitate to throw his support behind Corbusier's call for demolition of 'blight', standardization of commercial buildings, zoning to increase the amount of space required around buildings, and, in general, the need to 'combat' 'habit and convention' that did not move by 'logic and reason'.

Another major source of conflict in urban plan-making is the whole notion of grandeur and monumentalism. 'Mega-projects' in downtown areas like stadia, art museums and even churches are, if they can be considered renditions of the City Beautiful civic center concept, widely discredited in terms of their effects on urbanism. The importance of preservation (Gratz and Mintz, 2000) and Richard Florida's argument that cities must appeal to the artistic needs of the 'creative class' support the view that small, not large, urban enterprise is needed (Florida, 2002). Many planners now believe that indigenous revitalization is more important, not grandiose attractions for tourists like aquariums and enclosed malls. Yet such projects are still being implemented (Altshuler *et al.*, 2003). The $189 million Cathedral of Our Lady of the Angels complex and the recently completed $260 million Walt Disney Concert Hall, both part of a 'Cultural Corridor' in downtown Los Angeles, are symptomatic of the ongoing fascination city leaders have with grandeur.

One problem for American urbanism is that grandeur appeals more to the freeway driver than the pedestrian. Often, large projects leave the surrounding urban fabric empty and sterile. They have a tendency to be extremely disruptive of the existing environment, and are notorious for doing little for the revitalization of small businesses. For these reasons, grandeur in American urbanism, if it is to find a role, will have to respect some rules of urbanism. If there is acceptance of the need for some grandeur, there will also have to be less intrusive alteration of the historic environment, respect for diversity, and attention to urbanism at multiple scales.

The argument has been made that grandeur and order may be necessary for the appreciation of complexity, but not everyone bought into the idea. The attempt to accommodate diversity within an ordered system was already recognized as a fundamental problem of city design in the mid-eighteenth century (Kostof, 1991). Hegemann and Peets (1922, p. 1) hoped for 'willing submission of the less to the greater', but the attempt at uniformity in design has been seen as conflicting with the goals of innovation, diversity and complexity. For this reason, City Beautiful plan-makers were most often criticized for stifling the creative expression of American architecture (Mumford, 1924).

Bigness requires experts, and, as I have already argued, if there is a role for experts in American urbanism now it will have to be unlike previous versions. During the City Beautiful and City Efficient eras, plan-making was highly centralized, supported by powerful, if temporary, bureaucracies, and expertise prevailed against the opinions of non-experts. Despite the benefits discussed earlier, there is little current support for urbanism that is expert-driven, and debate over this has become even more divisive. The issue of the role of the expert has evolved from one of centralized versus non-centralized planning, to one of planning as physically-oriented and visionary versus planning as process-oriented and communicative. The rift was already evident in the 1940s when the National Resources Planning Board, under the influence of sociologist Louis Wirth, embarked on a progressive planning model in which long-term, continuous programming replaced the much-maligned idea of a 'master plan' (Funigiello, 1972). Now, planners are looking for ways to recombine perspectives. In the edited volume *The Profession of City Planning, Changes, Images and Challenges: 1950–2000* (Rodwin and Sanyal, 2000) a sizable majority of the 35 papers touch in some way upon the separation, but possible convergence, of planning as physical urban design versus planning as process.

It is easy to see why the idea of an expert-derived master plan is looked at sceptically, and why planning subsequently discarded 'the strategy of public persuasion' (Fishman, 2000, p. 5). Some planners point to the urban redevelopment era of the 1960s, after which architecture and planning were blamed for the disastrous effects. Both professions had helped to implement the failed modernist concepts of slum clearance, superblocks, inner-city expressways, and a host of other redevelopment disasters made famous by critics like Jacobs (1961). Rybczynski (2000) notes that both professions subsequently withdrew from the field. Architecture stopped talking about social goals and returned to its function as master builder, 'exchanging the role of environmental designer for that of fashion maven'. Planning, having no 'sheltered field of professional activity' to retreat to, recast itself as a profession of negotiators and land-use regulators. As with everything else about American urbanism, the solution to the conundrum of the expert lies in our ability to extract the good from the bad – using what is beneficial and fair, and avoiding what is not.

If it is possible to get past the problem of expert-driven plan-making, the next question is whether there is legitimacy to the representation of civic harmony, given tangible expression in a civic centre, uniform building style, or other elements of the Grand Manner. The simple critique is that grandeur is about suppression of dissent. Architectural expression of civic unity seemed symbolically to undermine the right of disagreement in the political process. Similarly, the insistence on Beaux Arts classicism had a way of intensifying the opinion that the City Beautiful was more interested in façades than underlying causes in satisfying business interests rather than social needs.

Perhaps the urban plan-makers could have made a better attempt to incorporate the issue of appropriateness. I have argued that they did recognize and appreciate it, but perhaps they did not balance it out correctly. Lack of attention to appropriateness meant that City Beautiful plan-making went too far in some cases, an overextension of the 'dimensions and ratios' of plan-making. The concentration of the civic centre was too concentrated, the use of diagonals too ceremonial, the straight street too long, the uniformity of style too uniform. Burnham's statement

Figure 5.12. Lewis Mumford labelled the New York Public Library (built 1898–1911) an 'inept design' because it forfeited the 'Benedictine luxuries' of 'light, air, space, and silence'. (*Source*: Lewis Mumford, *The Culture of Cities*, 1938)

that there is 'true glory in mere length' (Burnham and Bennett, 1909, p. 89), and that 'the highest type of beauty can only be assured by the use of one sort of architecture' are indicative of an extremism that could not be sustained.

The inability to gauge appropriateness has other implications besides 'the wrong thing in the wrong place'. One is the failure to preserve and appreciate the existing urban, 'informal' fabric. The dozens of civic centre projects that were proposed in the first decade of the nineteenth century were simultaneously beautification and slum clearance projects (Scott, 1969). The strategy extended to the urban renewal of Robert Moses in New York, Edmund Bacon in Philadelphia, and Charles Blessing in Detroit. Underlying this type of radical transformation of the existing city was an ambitious ideology that viewed radical urban change as necessary for multiple social and economic reasons. Any sense of appropriateness could be overridden by the pursuit of crowd control, the need to speed up communication, or the symbolic display of governmental power (Kostof, 1991).

The unwanted symbolic content is difficult to divest. There is an ongoing distrust of the Grand Manner because of the association with imperialism and fascism, a critique rebutted by Krier (1998). At the very least, it could be argued that an emphasis on unity and grandeur in a public setting makes sense only in the case of a city of extreme public importance. In other words, the monumentalism and grandeur of the Washington Plan of 1902 was legitimately an expression of the ideals of the Republic – Greek, Roman or early American. The city plan was appropriately used to connect to the heritage of the Founders, including their ideals of the meaning of citizenship. Stylistically, Beaux Arts architecture was not inappropriate because classical architecture reflects national heritage unlike Gothic, Romanesque, or commercial styles (Wilson, 1989). Some have argued that Americans were more attuned to small town life and the American frontier than Ancient Rome, making the chosen style seem all the more pompous and misplaced, but small town form would not necessarily have adequately expressed American ambitions.

There is a direct, positive correlation between the size and grandeur of a plan and the level of critique it engenders. This is because bigger, grander plans appear to be more immutable. What critics must consider, however, is that this is the same characteristic that was most appealing at the time. The immutability that the Plan of Washington 'demanded' was 'a demand to which Congress and the American people seemed eager to accede' (Scott, 1969, p. 55). This was reflected not only in the enthusiastic response to the Plan of Washington, but also in the dissemination of its principles nationwide. But, as this quality of immutability began to wear out, critics, including most planners, saw only overreaching control and a lack of political viability.

Another strategy of urban plan-making that has been controversial in American

urbanism is the notion of functionally separating two important urban domains
– the civic centre and the commercial centre. The concept of grouping public
buildings was popular throughout the City Beautiful and the City Efficient eras. The
consolidation of commercial enterprise was also common, carried to an extreme by
Burnham in the plans for Chicago, San Francisco and Cleveland. It meant that no
areas designated for commercial activity at the neighbourhood level were planned
for. Peter Hall refers to such plans as 'centrocentrist' (Hall, 2002, p. 196). Ironically,
the consolidation of one – the civic centre – was aimed at constraining the other
– commercial excess.

The fundamental problem has to do with separation, a defining characteristic
of anti-urbanism. The critique levelled against Washington, D.C. by Elbert Peets,
and reiterated by Jane Jacobs, stated that the separation of public buildings from
the rest of the city – the construction of a 'court of honour' with a singular purpose
– had the effect of separating the urban realm in a way that was not at all healthy. It
caused the city to lose its ability to function as an 'organism' and suffer a loss that
was both social and aesthetic (Jacobs, 1961, p. 173). For Jacobs, the issue was that
such a proposal contradicted the functional and economic needs of cities. The civic
centre was an attempt, Jacobs contended, to 'decontaminate' the public realm from
the workaday world of cities (Jacobs, 1961, p. 25). By constraining the commercial
enterprise of Washington and constructing a mall that severely separated the city,
its commercial function became disconnected and therefore artificial.

The critique of Thomas Adams' *Regional Plan for New York and its Environs* is
related to this. In an effort to rid the metropolis of congestion, but at the same
time retain centralization, the plan advocated centrally-located Corbusian 'towers
in the park', as well as sub-centres outside of Manhattan that would be 'healthy,
efficient and free from congestion' (Committee of the Regional Plan of New York
and Its Environs, 1929, p. 31). It left no room for the idea that a healthy congestion
of activities is necessary to sustain urban diversity and vitality. The merger of
modernist urbanism with the City Beautiful, presumably facilitated because
both accentuated openness and shortened distances (Kostof, 1991), proved
disastrous for urbanism. Eventually, the grandeur of the ceremonial boulevard
became the traffic engineer's cloverleaf superstructure designed for maximizing
speed.

The plan-maker's approach to merging small-scale incrementalism and urban
plan-making never seemed to gain enough traction. The failed translation was
evident in the 1930s, when planners like Thomas Adams seemed to lose their notion
of the importance of context and appropriateness. He wrote: 'Every building should
have enough open space to give it room to display its form and to obtain for it the
light and shade without which its value as a work of art is impaired' (Adams, 1935,
p. 190). It is exactly this regard for buildings as 'works of art' that conflicts with

the urbanistic requirements of considering context, appropriateness, and the effect of buildings and their placement in the public realm. Urban plan-makers talked readily about the organic nature of cities, the appropriateness of form relative to location, the relation between the formal and informal, proportion and scales in plan-making, and other complexities about city making. But they failed to translate their holistic, complex understanding of cities into a system that could be readily absorbed.

The urban plan-makers possessed the right instincts about city making, but they were too optimistic and reliant on the design skills of individual, benevolent planners. They believed in the primacy of professional expertise, and that 'the city planner must be guided by his own judgment rather than by any formulae' (Adams, 1935, p. 24). This meant that they failed to translate their skills to the level of everyday regulation of the built world. In fact, they actively defied such an approach. Thomas Adams deplored the subordination of design and creativity to legal restrictions, and thought that this was the chief weakness of planning (Simpson, 1985). In effect, urban plan-makers promoted a theory of systematized planning (Birch, 1980b), but they failed to make this system applicable to beauty, art, and good urban form. In the U.S., good design languished underneath the force of a zoning code of law that paid little attention to the quality of urban form.

Insistence on the importance of the designer and distrust of the ability of codes to accomplish the principles of good urbanism made sense as long as the principles could be upheld. The problem was that the implications of zoning beyond separation and opening up the city were only crudely considered by the urban plan-makers. Where they tended to rely on properly trained designers to accomplish good physical form, the codes would be left to dictate intrinsically sterile and even destructive city arrangement. Increasing, *de facto* reliance on codes devoid of good urbanistic principles was clear already in the 1930s. Clarence Perry reacted to it and lambasted the inflexibility and weakness of zoning and its ability to invest a residential district with 'attractiveness' (Perry, 1939, p. 114). When it became clear that 'aesthetics' had a legitimate place in zoning under a 1954 U.S. Supreme Court ruling, Berman v. Parker, the translation to procuring good urbanism seemed remote.

The dilemma that was emerging was that urbanism by way of plan-making was occurring by way of the default planning system (zoning) which, as it was conceived in most places, was incapable of producing good urbanism. But it was not limited to zoning. The entire plan-making enterprise was eroding into a set of data gathering and map-making exercises. In 1943, Eliel Saarinen wrote a lengthy review of current methods of planning and summarized it as 'an aureola of insipidity' (Saarinen, 1943, p. 354), largely because it was overly reliant on the 'scientific method'. Saarinen might have been reacting to the work of planners like

Harland Bartholomew, whose main criteria for the siting of highways was to keep vehicular traffic 'free from conflict' with separated grade thoroughfares running through the downtown. His system of basing street width on anticipated traffic-carrying capacity was, Bartholomew boasted, 'universally-used'. The practice of allowing commercial development along major thoroughfares in order to finance street widening was further evidence of a debased approach to plan-making largely out of touch with the urbanistic goals espoused by earlier plan-makers (Lovelace, 1992, pp. 39 and 92).

Urban plan-makers never actually accomplished the goal of integrating beauty and science, and the result was a backlash against plan-making as it had been defined by City Beautiful and City Efficient era planners. Saarinen ridiculed the idea of a 'practical' planning, stating that emphasis on the practical eventually led to disorder because of a failure to grasp 'organic integrity'. From another perspective, the scientific side of plan-making was attacked on the grounds that it was simply impossible to account for all factors involved. In that case, as Martin Meyerson argued in 1956, planners must be content to leave planning as a goal rather than a substantive reality.

Yet the basic process that came to define plan-making – anticipate the future, convert growth into needs for uses and facilities, make an optimum arrangement for future uses and facilities – missed the critically important third dimension and therefore the ability to conceptualize the city in complete, 'organic' terms, exactly as Saarinen suggested. As plan-makers struggled to make themselves effective, they began to think of plan-making in terms of single components – parks, streets, highways. This was, as Harland Bartholomew put it, 'a divide and conquer system' (Lovelace, 1992, p. 37) in which the city was separated into components for easier analysis, plan-making, and, hopefully, manipulation. Being scientific and efficient meant simplifying, and simplifying meant differentiating. The results were similarly disassembling: 'A street cut through here, a parkway built there, were the noticeable results of almost all such [plans]' (Wilson, 1983, p. 98). Almost every accomplishment in Nolen's 1914 summation of planning given at the London Summer School of Town Planning was about the dilution of urbanism. Nolen wrote that

The principal American contributions to town planning, as compared to European countries, are the parks or systems of parks . . . playgrounds . . . street car transportation, making possible the separation of business and residential neighbourhood . . . metropolitan planning . . . wide residential streets . . . [and] large residential lots. (Nolen, 1914)

Opening up the crowded industrial city had some valid humanitarian goals, but the more effective motivation was that it was good for the efficient functioning of business and the preservation of land values. New York City's landmark zoning

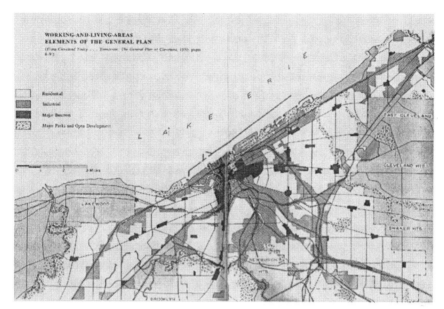

Figure 5.13. The kinds of plans still being produced are similar to this one of Cleveland in 1950, used to illustrate good plan-making in T. J. Kent's bestselling book. (*Source*: T.J. Kent, *The Urban General Plan*, 1964, reissued in 1990)

code of 1916 was intended to secure the property values of merchants along Fifth Avenue and there was no shame in this – on the contrary, the ability of zoning to secure land values was openly promoted (Hubbard and Hubbard, 1929). But the practice was flawed, and zoning became a mechanism for the explicit purpose of creating more tax revenue, regardless of the impact. Slums were designated more intensively 'in the wishful hope that someday someone would buy them up and displace the slums with an apartment or factory' (Lovelace, 1992, p. 92). This had a devastating effect on many inner-city neighbourhoods. Over-zoning for commercial expansion destabilized the residential function of cities (Sies and Silver, 1996).

European plan-makers seemed much less likely to be swept up by efficiency goals, perhaps owing to a deeper understanding and respect for the conditions of urbanity. Where Nolen advocated street widening, Unwin proclaimed that 'the less area given over to streets, the more chance one has of planning a nice town' (Kostof, 1991, p. 77). Other European planners, like Camillo Sitte and Joseph Stubben, influential city plan-makers in the late nineteenth century and early twentieth centuries, were known for their ability to transcend the 'architect-engineer dichotomy' (Mullin, 1976–1977, p. 7). Otto Wagner's plans for Vienna in the 1890s similarly rejected the engineering approach to planning. In England, Unwin and Parker were always thinking about balance – that no one factor should be allowed to outweigh or dominate another completely. Failure to maintain balance would result in 'not a design at all, but a mere compilation'. Most importantly, Europeans seemed to have greater success with applying these ideals within a legal framework. When German planners talked about city extensions as a legal notion, for example, they spoke in terms of appropriateness. Joseph Stubben believed that a plan should 'consider less how the population of the future will be distributed than the question for what kind of structures can a certain piece of ground best be used, according to its location and other qualities' (Stubben in Marsh, 1909, p. 41). He was much more attuned to the issue of land use mix, and discussed the need for retailers to 'connect their places of business with their dwellings,' and that careful planning could situate homes in proximity to businesses and factories. Most importantly, there was a sensitivity to the need to create a use and building type mix that would ensure a mix of social classes. Stubben wrote, 'the mixing of the wealthy and the poor should be promoted . . . [social] grouping . . . should never . . . be strictly exclusive' (Stubben in Marsh, 1909, pp. 41–42). American plan-makers were initially attuned to this, but they lost their sensitivity to its translation in plan-making terms.

By the time of the landmark 1926 zoning case, Village of Euclid vs. Ambler Realty Co., the segregationist orientation of leading plan-makers was firmly established. Harland Bartholomew had been arguing in 1922 that a new zoning ordinance for Washington, D.C. should not increase the area zoned for apartments in locations where residential property values could be damaged. The U.S. Supreme Court legalized this kind of rationale in Euclid v. Ambler. Justice Sutherland stated: 'the apartment house is a mere parasite, constructed in order to take advantage of the open spaces and attractive surroundings created by the residential character of the district. Moreover, the coming of one apartment house [brings] disturbing noises . . . depriving children of the privilege of quiet and open spaces for play, enjoyed by those in more favored localities'. This decision was lauded by plan-makers. By 1935, Thomas Adams was proposing four classes of residential zones in the hope of reducing the 'injury' that one type could cause on another (Adams, 1935, p. 302).

Perhaps all of the failures – the separations, the specializations – arose out of a profound frustration with a general lack of progress. It is possible to feel the frustration in Nolen's writings. In an address entitled 'The Civic Awakening', Nolen asks why American cities are so lacking in 'convenience, order and beauty':

Why is it? Are we too poor? Are we without knowledge and taste? Have we no trained men to consult, experts in city-making? Are we more selfish than other peoples? Have we less foresight? (Nolen, 1910a, p.1)

Today, at the beginning of the next century, the frustrations of urbanists have changed little.

Notes

1. The firm produced 563 comprehensive plans over the course of 65 years (from 1919 to 1984). See Lovelace, 1992, p. 53.
2. Nolen (undated) Summary of selected projects.
3. A situation which later caused much confusion since it confused legal enforcement with planning aspiration; see Kent, 1964 and Scott, 1969, p. 144.
4. Duany, Plater-Zyberk and Speck (2000) present the argument as to why 'it is utter nonsense' to rely on the private sector to create well-designed communities. Their reasoning is as follows: because private investors discount current investment (based on lost future earnings), money earned years from now is worth only a fraction today. Therefore, extra money invested to create a 'long-lasting building', or, for that matter, any other benefit for the public realm, is not a good business decision (pp. 220–221, footnote).
5. Something Berlage had emphasized in his scheme for Amsterdam; see Kostof, 1991.
6. Reportedly, Leon Krier, the godfather of new urbanism, is a devoted Ayn Rand fan.
7. She agreed with Eliel Saarinen here, quoting the architect as saying 'There must always be an end in view, and the end must not be final' (Jacobs, 1961, p. 383).
8. For example, the Dayton's *Daily Journal*, 1901 cited in a footnote in Peterson, 1976, p. 424.

Chapter Six

Planned Communities

What differentiates the culture of the planned community from other cultures of urbanism is its exclusive focus on the complete, well-designed, and self-contained unit of human settlement. Planned communities of all sorts – ranging from neighbourhood units to towns and complete cities – are united by a common, optimistic purpose. All are asking, and attempting to answer, the same question: can the ideal human settlement be planned coherently and all at once, as a separate, distinct entity? Advocates of the planned community working in the late nineteenth and early to mid-twentieth centuries thought so. Many believed that planning for complete communities was necessary to ensure the quality of the environment. It was the only way to control the whole range of factors influencing planning outcomes.

The builder of the American planned community needed to move well beyond Plato's *Republic* or Thomas More's *Utopia*. Planner C.B. Purdom gave a seemingly simple answer to the question of human settlement in 1921, stating that new towns 'should be planned to make convenient, healthy, and beautiful places to live and work in'. But, Purdom went on, 'We want something more than an obvious reply, we want an illustration in detail of what is meant' (Purdom, 1921, p. 11). It was the laying out of urbanism completely that was the essential role fulfilled by the planned community, and that has proved to be the principal source of both its innovation and its downfall.

Planned communities, as defined here, are not innately anti-urban. In fact, in defining American urbanism, they play an essential function – articulating a level of urban intensity that remains especially appealing to the American population. Yet the biggest problem for the planned community has been its relationship to the existing city, a problem not initially recognized. Olmsted, Sr., was able to think of the metropolitan area as both city and peripheral settlement, conceiving of both as part, at least theoretically, of the whole metropolitan package (Rybczynski, 1999).

This allowance has mostly eroded, and the planned community is commonly interpreted now as evidence of giving up on the city – a celebration of the rural and a denunciation of the truly urban. Undeniably, the planned community seemed to have fewer problems when defining its relation to nature, and some have said that the most important legacy of planned communities in the form of garden cities is their ability to 'frame a discourse about "nature"' (Luccarelli, 1995, p. 207). This paradigm lies at the heart of the critique that the planned community is anti-urban, although Walter Creese effectively countered this in his classic study *The Search for Environment* (1992). Proponents of planned communities have not really been interested in ruralized suburbs devoid of urbanity. John Ruskin, one of the patrons of the Garden City movement, wanted 'no festering and wretched suburb anywhere, but clean and busy street within' (Ruskin, 1865). There was much more of a careful balance between the urban and the rural required. Two of the most prominent figures in the history of the planned community, Ebenezer Howard and Raymond Unwin, were acutely aware of the difficulty. Unwin stated: 'It is not an easy matter to combine the charm of town and country; the attempt has often led rather to the destruction of the beauty of both' (Unwin, 1909, p. 164).

Planned communities have an ostensibly appealing set of qualities: self-contained, usually picturesque, holistically conceived and implemented, often with an acute appreciation of the details of urban form. They varied in their social intent:

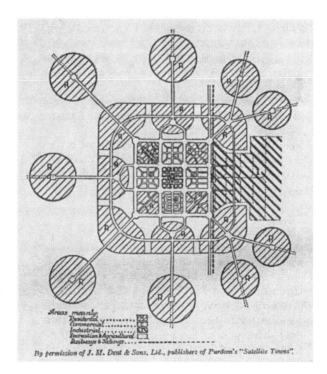

Figure 6.1. Planning by discrete unit. This scheme of 'satellite towns' by Raymond Unwin and reprinted by Nolen showed distinct areas separated by open spaces. (*Source*: John Nolen, *New Towns for Old*, 1927b)

early planned communities like Riverside, Illinois, a railroad commuter suburb, were driven, despite Olmsted's view of it, by bucolic tendencies and a desire to escape the industrial and immigrant-thronged city. Later ideas about the planned community were concerted efforts to create better living conditions for all classes, especially the working class. Despite these efforts, it is difficult to escape the fact that the planned community is often missing two fundamental qualities of urbanism – whatever their initial intent, they are generally lacking in social mix; and, because they are internally focused, they tend to have poor linkages to the existing city. Again, these failings do not make all aspects of the planned community anti-urban, but they do signify that the planned community is not a complete solution, but merely one particular aspect of defining American urbanism.

Not all pre-World War II planned communities are noteworthy (although, compared to today's development types, the vast majority may seem so). According to planning historian John Reps, company towns, industrial villages, and the huge number of towns 'puffed into life by American railroads' added almost nothing to our knowledge about the proper planning of communities (Reps, 1965, p. 414). Even suburban development organized around public transit was, in general, not in the form of coherent, nodal communities consciously planned. Warner's study showed that the streetcar suburbs surrounding Boston in the late nineteenth century were essentially street layouts, not communities and neighbourhoods organized to promote public life. The tendency for commercial development was strip oriented and centreless, and institutions like schools were often located according to land price rather than accessibility. Residents were forced to construct their own community life from a set of spatially disaggregated social functions. On the other hand, peripheral communities of the kind that developed outside of Boston between 1830 and 1870 were fully mixed in population and services. These were not residential suburbs, but budding cities possessing their own industrial potential, motivated by a desire to 're-create the conditions of Boston' (Warner, 1987, p. 19).

What is of interest, then, are the planned communities that stand out, and although they represent a small percentage of the total amount of building activity over the century, there are many. The majority are generally thought of as suburbs rather than complete towns. The condition for inclusion here is that, first, the community must have *some* qualities of urbanism or the potential to foster urbanism; and second, the development must have been purposefully designed, not improvised. These conditions mean that most suburban development will be excluded, since most of it was improvised rather than designed – even starting in the eighteenth century (see, Fishman, 1987) – and most shows little concern for the principles of diversity, connectivity, mix, public realm, and the other parameters of urbanism.

Whether or not the planned community exhibited qualities supportive of American urbanism is a matter of degree. The discussion presented here highlights those planned communities that seemed to exhibit the most *potential* for urbanism, if they did not contain it outright. This means that the relevance of the type of settlements built by the community builders in the mid-twentieth century – those analyzed by Weiss (1987), for example – will vary widely. Many of those communities included provisions for maintaining uniformity in social terms by establishing uniformity of design – unvarying building lines, standard lot sizes, and tight architectural control – and thus it is difficult to think of these developments as contributing to the definition of American urbanism. What is important to recognize is that there were differences between large-scale private residential subdividing and the building of complete planned communities with a view to larger ecological, social and humanitarian purposes. Either end of the spectrum could be defined as 'community building', and both could have strong, if not exclusive, profit motivations, but they did not all have the same degree of potential for urbanism.

This is not a distinction that is usually made. In Weiss' analysis, community building is distinguished on the basis of being large-scale and long-term, having singular control by one developer, employing deed restrictions, successfully enticing public agencies and private utilities to work cooperatively for the benefit of the community and the developer, and integration of all levels of the development process – brokerage, financing, insurance and construction (Weiss, 1987, p. 46). My distinction is focused on the degree to which the planned community was able to exhibit the qualities of urbanism. And, because of my focus on urban form and pattern, I allow a much greater parsing between the different brands of community building put forward. For reasons that will be discussed, the Country Club District of J.C. Nichols can not be equated with other automobile-dependent postwar suburbs, despite the similarities in purpose.

Some of the personalities discussed in this chapter have already been encountered as activists, planners or architects in either the incrementalist or urban plan-making cultures. Thomas Adams, for example, was not only a well-known garden city planner in Britain, but was also head of the culminating plan-making event of the City Efficient era, the *Regional Plan of New York and its Environs*. Henrietta Barnett, who helped build the planned community Hampstead Garden suburb, was also a settlement house reformer who engaged in incrementalist reform. There are also specific planning ideas that link incrementalist, plan-making and planned community cultures, most notably the neighbourhood paradigm, which is pervasive in all three.

Just as there are strong linkages between the incrementalists and the urban plan-makers, there are also strong linkages between the urban plan-makers and the community planners. When urban plan-makers made their plans for existing cities, they sometimes thought in terms of completing a settlement – creating a 'new town in town', not unlike the way Bedford Park in London, essentially a network of streets, created a complete planned community within its urban context (Stern and Massengale, 1981). Yet the difference can be made clear. Incrementalists and urban plan-makers – the high urban intensity end of the urbanist grid – did not seek an alternative kind of city. They took the established patterns of settlement as more or less givens. These patterns could be modified and added to, but not re-drawn from scratch. Designers of the planned community thought in terms of establishing a new pattern of urbanism. They were largely utopians, and their schemes were mostly focused on the complete formation of new human habitats from the ground up, taking the form of a complete neighbourhood, suburb, village, town or city.

Planned community culture was also intricately tied to regionalism, although, as I will discuss in the next chapter, the two cultures evolved quite differently. There was a fundamental difference between the idea of placing settlements in the region, and designing cities internally. The two objectives are complimentary but there is a significant distinction in terms of scale and orientation. The regionalists' vision was broader and their ideas about natural context were pre-eminent. The community planners complemented the larger framework that the regionalists provided, but their focus on the internal design of cities led them down a different path. Sometimes this meant that they did not hesitate to alter the landscape to suit the needs of their designs, for example by exaggerating the features of their sites. This was something natural regionalists in the vein of Ian McHarg would have been less likely to do.

The implications of designing complete communities on a clean slate – *tabula rasa* – are significant. Planned communities do not operate within the same rules and processes of urbanism that generate, spontaneously, traditional urban form. This means that the elements comprising the planned community can be conceived of simultaneously. There may be a progression in implementation, but the plan itself is conceived in total at one point in time. In so doing, the hope is that more or less 'pure' ideas about optimal city form will have a greater chance of being realized. Concepts like boundaries, edges, centres, separation vs. interconnection, cohesiveness and internal immersiveness seem less relevant to urbanist cultures that deal with the existing urban realm, because the existing city is pre-established and therefore constraining. If a planned community is being established, the problems of organizing the elements of urbanism in a way that meets specific objectives becomes, at least theoretically, controllable, and therefore attainable.

The great advantage that planned community advocates had, of course, was their ability to think holistically and organically. They had the luxury of being able to consider the interrelations of parts and the interconnectedness that was required in a way that was much less intrinsic to other planning cultures. They could think about the human domain as the arrangement of the whole of life, not just one component of it. Urban plan-makers were often found focusing narrowly on one element of urbanism, for example on transportation systems. This inevitably meant that planners honed in on the need for wheeling traffic through town rather than on how it might affect a range of other dimensions of urban life. The planned community had the advantage of considering all elements in synchronized fashion.

This is why advocates of the planned community at times seem so heroic. Unwin expressed an understanding of the complexity of urban form and the interrelatedness of elements that has impressed more than one generation of planners. But when urban plan-makers attempted to apply Unwin's notions to the existing city their ideas seemed by comparison crude and narrow. It was the ability to think holistically in planned community development that permitted a sophisticated conceptualization about urbanism, and that opened the way for Unwin to declare his concern for the 'pattern of life' (Creese, 1967, p. 22) more than half a century before Christopher Alexander wrote about patterns as an approach to urban design.

Planned Communities – A Typology

To the American city planner, the idea of conceiving of a human settlement holistically generally conjures up the image of the garden city. Indeed we are now into the fifth generation of garden city development (Birch, 2002). Many planners consider Ebenezer Howard to be the pivotal figure in the development of the profession. Sussman (1976) compares garden city planning as a breakthrough in city-building analogous to the impact of Copernicus on astronomy, and Peter Hall (2002, p. 88) calls Howard 'the most important single character' in the intellectual history of twentieth-century urban planning. Coincident with this, there have been an inordinate number of histories on the garden cities movement.

But the focus on holistic settlements and what they mean for American urbanism requires a broader perspective than garden cities, important as they are. In the historical development of American urbanism, new town development began long before garden cities arrived on the scene. The history of planned communities in America can be said to begin with the first colonial settlements, such as Williamsburg and Jamestown. In the 200+ year history of the U.S., there has been a wealth of planned settlements, conceived of as complete cities, towns, villages or neighbourhoods. Despite this interest, the vast majority of urbanism in the U.S. was not thought of in terms of the complete planned community. After the 1920s especially, subdivisions consisting of single-uses on vast tracts of land, or street layouts for the accommodation of the automobile were the primary methods of 'community' expansion.

The typology of planned communities has been broken down in different ways by different authors. Often there is a distinction made between the utopian settlements of the nineteenth century, industrial villages, railroad towns and later streetcar suburbs, and finally the automobile suburbs of the 1920s. One useful typology of the suburban planned community – a locational distinction that applies to most of the new planned communities discussed here – was developed by Stern and Massengale (1981). It divides planned suburbs into six categories: railroad suburbs (e.g., Riverside and Lake Forest, Illinois); streetcar and subway suburbs (e.g., Forest Hills Gardens and Shaker Heights); industrial villages (e.g., Pullman and Letchworth); resort suburbs (e.g., Coral Gables); automobile suburbs (e.g., Country Club District and Mariemont); and recent suburbs. My concern is not exclusively suburban, so the typology below is somewhat modified, consisting of five types: colonial towns and frontier settlements; railroad and streetcar suburbs; utopian communities and company towns; automobile suburbs, and garden cities, villages and suburbs.

Although the focus is on American development, some attention is given to England since it was particularly influential here. My purpose is to provide a brief overview of the different types of planned communities – broadly defined as holistic settlements – that were a part of the American experience. This is a broad survey; it is obviously not a complete history of any of these ideas, only an outline of the main developments and the ideologies behind them. As throughout, I focus on those concepts that can, in some way, be tied to the lineage of American urbanism.

Colonial Towns and Frontier Settlements

John Reps (1965) wrote the definitive study of the development of colonial towns and frontier settlements in America, *The Making of Urban America*. One indication of the degree of importance of these settlements is how they have continued to hold interest for subsequent city building. Frontier towns and villages became the models that many of the earliest planners in the U.S. looked to. 'How-to' manuals on urban planning often began with chapters on the history of town development that included the American colonial town. John Nolen (1927b), for example, opened his book *New Towns for Old*, with a discussion of the glories of the New England town, which he admired for its 'diversity'.

Williamsburg, established in 1699, is admired as an example of colonial town planning at its best: a high degree of order and formality oriented on an axial plan; attention to the third dimension; and the achievement of something intimate and serene, not portentous. The New England small town is more admired for its integration of town and country. The basic pattern of land development was a small village surrounded by agricultural land known as the 'common fields'. Communal ownership of land ensured that the needs of the community were placed ahead of individual needs, but it also ensured that the town remained intact and bounded, a compact village design completely distinct from the surrounding countryside. This was not a condition that arrived fully formed all at once – it was years in the making, sometimes fifty or even one hundred years – an indication of the strong code of conduct at work in moulding development form. Internally, the New England village was organized around a village green that was fronted by buildings of civic and religious importance. The greens could have a wide variety of shapes and were relatively small. Few were square or rectangular (Arendt, 1999).

One of the most important characteristics of the new town in America was the predominance of the central square. Spanish colonial town planning required them, William Penn established them for Philadelphia, James Oglethorpe for Savannah, and hundreds of courthouse squares embodied the physical expression of the central role to be played by community life. The documentation of the wide variety of courthouse square arrangements – the Harrisonburg square, the Shelbyville

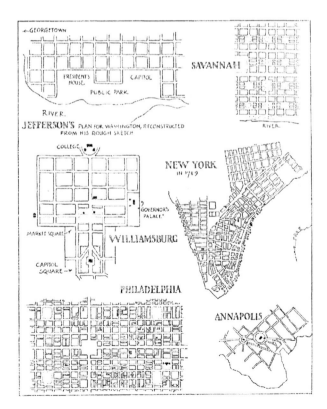

Figure 6.2. A few planned colonial towns published in an essay by Elbert Peets. (*Source:* Elbert Peets, 1927)

square, the Lancaster square, to mention a few – testifies to the attention paid to civic space. As the primary organizational feature of the new town, the square had strong symbolic importance. A study of hundreds of courthouse squares in Texas revealed its dominance, articulated in numerous subtly different ways, but always the commercial and civic focus of the planned settlement (Veselka, 2000).

By the late period of Colonial America, the 'rectilinear urban habits' of Americans were well-established (Kostof, 1991), and thus the application of a grid across the unsettled territories of the U.S. in 1785 by Thomas Jefferson can be seen as a logical extension of the grid culture of U.S. town planning. But while the colonial grid had a strongly socialized notion of land value, in which land became valuable only after a building was placed on it, the unimproved grid that became the basis of nineteenth-century expansion was focused on land speculation and consumption (Marcuse, 1987). It was one difference between planned and unplanned settlement.

Railroad and Streetcar Suburbs

How the concept of a 'suburb' contributes to American urbanism is a complex matter. If Fishman's definition of a suburb is used – that the suburb, the 'bourgeois utopia', was an exclusive middle-class development that excluded industry and lower-class residents (Fishman, 1987) – then it is, on the face of things, not particularly useful for defining American urbanism in a positive way. It defies too many of the core values of urbanism – diversity and connectivity in particular. There is no avoiding the fact that most suburbs were residential enclaves, set apart ideologically and physically from industrial villages or towns meant to decentralize the congested city. They were satellites dependent on the central city and they purposefully shunned the integration of places of employment for the working classes. They were, in a word, exclusive.

Ostensibly, then, American urbanism should reject suburbs on the grounds that they are too often homogeneous socially and economically. However, this would be a mistake for the simple reason that suburbs designed as complete planned communities hold valuable lessons. Suburbs were (and are) the predominant American version of organized decentralization and should be studied for the rich legacy of design principles they hold. One approach to bringing suburbs into a discussion of urbanism then is to focus primarily on their structural components. As in the case of urban plan-making, the ability to draw connections rests on the ability to disassociate from the social rhetoric. The connection between suburban development and American urbanism will rest on issues having to do with human functionality and design coherence.

From this perspective, it is the degree to which peripheral human settlement was internally integrated that is of relevance. How 'internally integrated' is defined, and how it varies, constitutes the bulk of the discussion here. If such developments were designed as complete communities, rather than as expedient groupings of housing units – single-family detached or otherwise – there would be reason to explore them and assess their relevance to American urbanism. It is not just about excluding sprawl. The proliferation of row houses in places like Back Bay in Boston and Society Hill in Philadelphia were suburban geographically, but do not constitute the kind of holistic growth by planned community to be included in this discussion.

It is not my intent to recount the historical lineage of suburban development. A large literature on suburbia and its meaning can be cited to get a better sense of its history and variation, notably Kenneth T. Jackson's *Crabgrass Frontier: The Suburbanization of the United States* (1985), Mark Baldassare's *Trouble in Paradise: The Suburban Transformation in America* (1988), and Robert Fishman's *Bourgeois Utopias* (1987). These studies are particularly focused on the social and political ramifications of suburban exclusivity, rather than the significance of their design and the implications of their pattern and form for defining American urbanism.

There are two main types of suburban planned communities that are relevant: transit based suburbs and automobile based suburbs. In the first group, it is logical to begin with the communities that were connected to railroads in the mid-nineteenth century. Although Kenneth Jackson's history of suburban development begins with a commuter suburb linked by Ferry boat, Brooklyn Heights, and there were several Staten Island suburbs developed in the early 1800s, the main course of American transit-based suburban development first arose in the form of railroad communities. The population of these suburbs was not insignificant. Chicago was described in 1873 as a city 'more given to suburbs than any other city in the world', where 'the number of suburbs of all sorts contiguous to Chicago is nearly a hundred'. These were serviced by the more than 100 trains that entered and departed the city daily (Jackson, 1985, p. 93).

An admirable quality of railroad suburbs was that they were intrinsically compact – residents needed and wanted to live within a fifteen minute walking radius (or 'pedestrian shed') of the rail station. Since railroad commuting was expensive and time consuming, communities developed 'like beads on a string': discontinuous, separated by green space, and relatively distant from the city centre (Jackson, 1985, p. 101). Development was, in a sense, coerced into a compact form that allowed accessibility to the rail node. This created the 'railroad village' – limited in size, compact in form, walkable, and within easy reach of the surrounding countryside (Fishman, 1987, p. 136). And, because suburban residents commuted to the city daily to satisfy needs that could not be satisfied by a village centre, the outward expansion strengthened rather than depleted the city. As Fishman put it, 'For a brief moment, the railroad tracks held city and suburb in precarious equilibrium' (Fishman, 1987, p. 137).

There is no doubt that railroad suburbs were mostly exclusive places, but there was also some degree of social mix. Alongside the dominant, elite class, there were also significant numbers of lower-income people, the 'supporting minions', who lived in railroad communities and found jobs servicing the elite. Many of them lived in small dwellings near the railroad station or town centre. This fact meant that the nineteenth-century railroad suburb was actually more heterogeneous than the typical suburb of the late twentieth century (Jackson, 1985).

Despite this, class segregation was a strong element of transit based development. Warner's study of streetcar suburbs (1870 to 1900) showed how much class segregation was part of the system of urban expansion (Warner, 1962). By 1900, the streetcar transportation system in Boston had produced a divided city. Where previously 'streets of the well-to-do lay hard by workers' barracks and tenements of the poor', now the affluent were moving out. Low-income groups did reach the streetcar suburbs, 'by sheer enlargement of their numbers', but, in many cases 'they could occupy them only by destroying much of what the suburb had achieved' (Warner, 1962, pp. 19, 161). In other words, the hidden cost for low-income renters who infiltrated the streetcar suburbs was a worsening of their environmental conditions. Needless to say, the infiltration of low-income tenants was not generally planned, it happened by dividing up buildings into multiple units.

But they were sometimes exemplary, focused, designs – one reason why the railroad suburb of the late nineteenth century has been referred to as the 'classic stage of suburbia' (Fishman, 1987, p. 134). Lake Forest, Illinois, platted in 1857 and designed by landscape architect Almerin Hotchkiss, is a good example. It was a planned picturesque model but its organization around a railroad stop gave it a particular configuration – a central station, a town square, and a surrounding commercial centre. It was a city in a park for wealthy commuters, but its form was not only beautiful, it was efficient and functional.

Railroad suburbs were often associated with the 'planned picturesque'. The picturesque aspect had roots in the landscape paintings of the Northern European Renaissance, English gardens, and Chinese and Japanese landscape gardening (Barnett, 1986). In England, John Nash was among the first to apply the principles of the picturesque to urban design, notably his design for Regent's Park in London, commissioned in 1811 by George IV. In America, picturesque suburbs in the nineteenth century bore some resemblance to model industrial villages in England. There was also a close connection with Andrew Jackson Downing, who was encountered in chapter 4 in the context of promoting village improvement. By the end of the nineteenth century, almost every major city had an outlying subdivision consisting of a curvilinear, picturesque layout. Some were mechanical repetitions of romantic features; others, in the hands of an expert designer like Olmsted, were skilfully planned (Reps, 1965). The more ruralized developments, like Glendale,

Ohio and Llewellyn Park, New Jersey, consisting of organic street patterns and large lots, have little connection to American urbanism.

Riverside, Illinois, begun in 1869 and designed by Frederick Law Olmsted, Sr., may have a stronger connection to American urbanism than the earlier groupings of country estates in suburban parks. Olmsted, together with Calvert Vaux, laid out sixteen suburbs in his career, but Riverside was his most famous. It was to be a rural antidote to the congested city, but it is not at all a typical American sprawling suburb. This was a relatively cohesive community (in physical planning terms) linked by railroad to the urban core of Chicago. Riverside's self-containment was balanced to some degree by its direct link to the industrial city. But, as in all affluent transit suburbs of the time, this was a paradox. Its seemingly perfect merging of nature and city – its internal tranquillity – was wholly dependent on the mayhem of the industrial city it was trying to escape.

There were two indications of urbanity at Riverside – inclusion of a commercial component, and the ample provision of public space. Olmsted wrote that suburbs should not 'sacrifice urban conveniences' like 'butchers, bakers, & theatres', but integrate them within rural conditions (Olmsted, 1870, p. 294). At Riverside, this careful balance was achieved by means of a quaint village-like commercial district adjacent to the train station – not part of the original plan but added early on – a model repeated in many of the earliest planned railroad suburbs. In addition, the emphasis on public space reflected Olmsted's insistence on promoting what he called the 'life of the community' (Fishman, 1987, p. 130). Public areas (including streets and roads) constituted one-third of Riverside's total area (Rybczynski, 1999), not including the generous front lawns that were too public to be part of private family life. Front lawns, by creating the 'illusion' of a park, belonged to the community (Fishman, 1987).

By the late nineteenth century, as the rail system expanded to include streetcars and subways, suburban living came within reach of the middle class. The trolley or electric streetcar, rapidly adopted by American cities from the late 1880s, was particularly important because it opened up the city for people of modest means. It also strengthened the central business district, since trolley lines invariably converged at a central point and radiated outward from there. The great department stores of the late nineteenth and early twentieth century are testaments to the increasing importance of this centrality.

Streetcar suburbs of the era are well-known. Roland Park in Baltimore, laid out initially by George Kessler, typified the ideal of a suburban enclave of houses meant to instil the feeling of being in the country, while still conveniently linked by rail to downtown. Another well-known example of the transit-linked planned community was Shaker Heights in Cleveland, Ohio. Started in 1916 by the Van Sweringen brothers, it became an affluent district with strong design control. In

1929, the brothers developed a Georgian-style shopping centre attached to the rail station. Shaker Heights is interesting because of its extreme attention to detail, and the explicit way in which the Van Sweringen brothers attempted to strengthen a moral ethic through their control of every detail of the physical environment.

Automobile Suburbs

By the 1920s, suburbs were growing at a much faster rate than central cities. Again, the degree to which this suburban development contributes to a definition of American urbanism rests on the extent to which it was planned with some consideration of the conditions of urbanism, rather than being developed as unplanned, speculative, single-use extensions. The situation was mostly the latter. The 1920s era automobile suburbs were basically tighter versions of present-day sprawl. The so-called 'infill suburbs', which became working-class, close-in suburbs around every major urban area during the 1920s and 1930s, had few amenities, were not pedestrian-oriented, and, with zoning sanctioned by the U.S. Supreme Court, were single-use and homogenous. As a result, most of the automobile suburbs that began to proliferate in the 1920s are not likely to be useful to the refinement of a definition of American urbanism.

While the unplanned automobile suburb characterized the vast majority of development occurring in the 1920s and beyond, there were some examples of planned automobile suburbs that were qualitatively different. A highly regarded example is Mariemont outside of Cincinnati, Ohio, planned by John Nolen and developed by Mary Emery in 1923. It was significant as a philanthropic venture, designed specifically for the industrial worker as an alternative to industrial squalor. It was one of the first suburban developments consciously to accommodate the automobile by providing parking areas and garages, but that did not detract from it. It was a mixed use, mixed income community of rentals and owner-occupied housing, with a central community green, integrated community facilities, and a centrally located commercial district. Most units were grouped into duplexes or rows of attached units, and the development benefited from the involvement of numerous well-known and skilled designers. It was not a co-partnership in the manner of the English garden city – Mary Emery recognized that Americans were far too individualistic for that – but it did nevertheless have a strong communitarian basis through its emphasis on civic amenities.

By the early 1920s, many automobile suburbs were much more exclusive, heavily marketed by developers who were mostly interested in profit-making or fame. As I have argued, such developments may be useful for defining American urbanism, in that they offer lessons about successful planning and design. Examples of beautifully designed and planned automobile-oriented suburban areas include

Figure 6.3. Mixed uses at Mariemont. Apartments and shops in the Dale Park neighborhood center. (*Source*: John Nolen, *New Towns for Old*, 1927*b*)

Highland Park outside of Dallas, and Coral Gables outside of Miami. Coral Gables was laid out in 1921 by developer George Merrick, who wanted to create an artistic, aesthetically cohesive suburb of Miami. This meant that every detail was attended to, from the careful zoning restrictions to the design of lamp posts. There were residential areas and country clubs, tennis courts, bridle paths, parks, and places for business and industry. Like the other suburbs of this genre, it was to be a relatively complete town.

Another highly regarded automobile suburb is Jesse Clyde Nichols' 1922 Country Club District outside of Kansas City. It was laid out with all the right planning principles – an integrated commercial area, interconnected streets, no unnecessary removal of trees, and no needless disregard for topography. Most importantly, there was a mixture of housing types that included 6,000 homes and 160 multiple-family buildings ranging from walk-ups to 10- and 12-storey apartment flats (Jackson, 1985). In addition, civic spaces were carefully planned for and distributed throughout the development, giving the place a park-like quality inspired by the usual motivation of wanting to provide plenty of space, light and air for the community. Unfortunately, covenants with racial restrictions were initially tolerated in Country Club District, a not uncommon phenomenon that puts a serious blemish on many noteworthy examples of the American planned community.

Utopian Communities and Company Towns

The lineage of new, model communities in the U.S. has to include the nineteenth-century phenomenon of utopian communities. One of the most interesting facets of utopian community building is its cyclical regularity. Barkun (1984) has documented four periods of intense utopian building in the U.S. – the 1840s, the 1890s, the Great Depression, and the 1960s. Berry documented the correlation of utopian community building with economic downturns or 'long-wave' crises. Utopian communities are, in his view, 'critical reactions to the moving target of capitalism' (Berry, 1992, p. xv).

The fact that 250 of them were constructed in the U.S. in the 100 years between 1820 and 1920 (Schultz, 1989), meaning that they did not remain utopian, testifies to their significance. Utopian settlement was promoted through literature. Edward Bellamy's *Looking Backward, 2000–1887*, published in 1888, was the most noticeable work, but there were many others. Historian David Schuyler counted 100 utopian and dystopian novels in Great Britain and another 150 in the U.S. written in the 1880s and 1890s (Schuyler, 2002). These books consisted of visionary proposals for a peaceful world that produced harmony between nature and humankind.

Along with literary figures like Mark Twain, Dean Howells, and Edward Bellamy, utopians constructed a new type of American urban culture. That culture is significant for defining American urbanism because of the way it explicitly connected the quality of the physical environment with quality of life. Over the course of the nineteenth century, American utopians developed a sense of the city as a 'total environment' capable of producing 'better culture' (Schultz, 1989, p. xiv).

According to Kostof (1991), however, most utopian towns were mundane in terms of town design. In fact the degree of importance attached to the physical plan and form of the town varied. Many were formed as religious commonwealths and are much more significant for their social experimentation and moral agenda than their lessons in urban design and town planning. At one end of the ideological spectrum, communities in the nineteenth century were established to challenge the prevailing capitalist system, and the towns created were laid out as communistic social settlements. This meant, in many cases, simple grids with 'loose assemblages of buildings' (Kostof, 1991, p. 168). An example is New Harmony, Indiana, a utopian community started in 1814 by one communal sect, the Harmony Society, and later settled by a second group under the leadership of philanthropist Robert Owen. It is, and always was, a very small town. There is one traffic light, and from this intersection it is possible to see the entire settlement. Yet it was the physical reflection of small town urbanity, like 'a small section cut out of a city,' as one contemporary put it (Schultz, 1989, p. 10). Like other small utopian settlements, its beauty lies in its elegant simplicity.

There were some short-lived attempts to implement the 'phalansteries' of Charles Fourier, collections of attached buildings similar to those found at Versailles and populated by mixes of races, classes, sexes and ages (Kostof, 1991). But the Mormons had the most success in applying their town planning ideas on a larger scale. Their designs were equally ideological, but simpler. They implemented a grid arrangement of strict geometric proportions, derived from descriptions of cities in the Bible (in Numbers 35 and Leviticus 25). Streets were extremely wide (132 feet), lined with half-acre lots and houses set back 25 feet. Certain centrally located blocks were designated for churches and public buildings. The simple egalitarianism of these 'Cities of Zion' (Reps, 1965, p. 264) was directed at shunning the sinful ways of American society, and preparing for a new social and religious order. It is somewhat ironic that the form they chose was identical to the one seen as most befitting of commercialism.

One utopian ideal that should be reviewed because of its later influence on Ebenezer Howard is James Silk Buckingham's model town of Victoria, described and illustrated in his 1849 book *National Evils and Practical Remedies*. Buckingham was influenced by Robert Owen, although, interestingly, his model was rooted in capitalism, not socialism (Kostof, 1991). This meant that the economic laws of land price and accessibility applied, and the wealthy were situated where they would have the greatest access to economic and cultural goods, i.e., at the centre of town. The layout called for concentric rows that were square, not round, with rows of buildings that gradually diminished in size toward the periphery. Buckingham was a politician and a philanthropist and his idea was to provide a decent living environment for the 'unfortunate' (Eaton, 2002). Thus lower-income housing was situated close to green open space, whereby the poor could have better access to nature.

Buckingham's model town lies somewhere between the socialist model of utopian settlement and the phenomenon of the industrial village. As a second category of the ideal city, model industrial towns were blatantly focused on the promotion of capital accumulation, however beneficial they might have been for workers. There were company towns constructed to help workers (and thus companies) almost as soon as industrialization began. In this way town planning became secularized to emphasize the cooperation of workers for the good of the company rather than the good of the religious community. Despite their fame (or infamy), well planned company towns were rare. Most industrialists were far more interested in the beauty of their factories than of their workers' living environments. Industry-based housing developments have been described as 'improvisational, squalid settlements' (Kostof, 1991, p. 168) that coexisted uneasily with the gleaming factories and estates of their owners.

The exceptions to this are of interest. In Europe, model villages first started to appear in the wool manufacturing centres of Yorkshire. Creese labels these early industrial era settlements as 'The Bradford-Halifax School', so named for the concentrations of villages in a triangular region near Leeds in north central England. The first was Copley, begun in 1844, but the more famous and much larger town was Saltaire, started by Sir Titus Salt about six years later and intended for a population of 4,356. Despite Salt's paternalism, the town has been heralded for its use of the medieval tradition of districts, its high density, and its effective integration of building style and grid layout (Creese, 1992). The social contract of the industrial town of Saltaire is represented by the close proximity of church and factory, and the strict controls Salt placed on his tenants.

Later in Europe, industrial towns were modelled after garden cities. These included the Krupps family town established outside Essen, Margarethenhöhe, and the garden city at Hellerau, outside Dresden. In a way that was not the usual *modus operandi* of the nineteenth-century industrial capitalist, a few patricians made the effort of constructing a holistic environment that they considered to be wholesome, morally uplifting, and a better place for workers to live. In return, such places were believed to be conducive to increased worker productivity. Nelson P. Lewis, the engineer-planner encountered at the forefront of early twentieth-century plan-making, reported that the towns were run at a financial loss that was offset by an increase in worker efficiency, a direct result of the improvement in living conditions (Lewis, 1916). Thus the industrialists' goal of providing better living conditions must be seen for what it was – a business decision.

Two other European examples were particularly well-known in the U.S.: Port Sunlight, near Liverpool, started in 1892 and developed by the soap manufacturer W.H. Lever; and Bournville, near Birmingham, started in 1895 and developed by the chocolate manufacturers, the Cadbury brothers. From the standpoint of conceptualizing American urbanism, these towns and villages are important as examples of industrial decentralization. Both were greatly admired by later American city planners. Their disadvantage, of course, was the singularity of their purpose. In the U.S., company towns like Tyrone, New Mexico, a copper-mining settlement, rose and fell based entirely on the strength of one industry.

Of interest are the numerous design innovations experimented with in these early model industrial villages. Port Sunlight was 'highly influential' in making popular the picturesque, with its irregular street plan and neo-vernacular architecture (Kostof, 1991, p. 73). It was also an early instance of the 'superblock' arrangement in which houses faced an interior greenspace rather than the street, popularized in the Radburn scheme 36 years later. Port Sunlight included housing for a range of incomes that, through its design, minimized the distinction between single-family and multiple-family dwelling types. The towns included housing on both sides of the streets that served to 'characterize and punctuate' space rather than simply delimit it (Creese, 1992, p. 122). Bournville was also successful in maintaining social diversity by limiting how many of the company's employees could make their

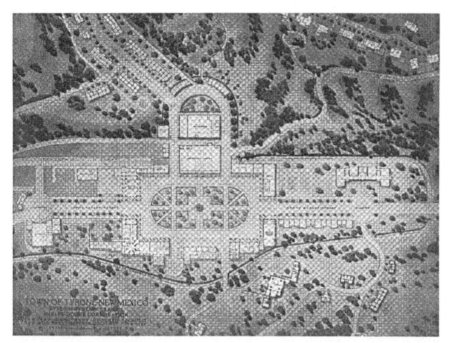

Figure 6.4. Bertram G. Goodhue's 1915 plan for Tyrone, New Mexico. (*Source*: Thomas Adams, 1935, *Outline of Town and City Planning*, 1935)

residence there. George Cadbury believed it should be limited to one-half of the town, to avoid the closed-in feeling of other industrial villages (Eaton, 2002).

A well-known early example of the company town was Lowell, Massachusetts, planned in 1822 as a neat arrangement of factory buildings and modest houses. But the most famous company town in the U.S. was unquestionably Pullman, built 10 miles south of downtown Chicago in 1881 by George Pullman, founder of the Pullman Palace Car Works. Initially, the town seemed to be a model of corporate philanthropy: housing, clean factories, stores, and recreational facilities together forming a model industrial environment for the good of the workers, their productivity, and, of course, company profits. But following the depression of 1893, Pullman laid off employees, cut wages, and failed to reduce rents or cut the cost of services. Jane Addams weighed in on the situation and concluded that personal benevolence – the Pullman model – was inferior to her settlement house model which was based on 'cooperative effort' directed at social justice. She likened the tragedy of Pullman to the fate of King Lear (Addams, 1912).

Strictly as a town planning model, Pullman is interesting because of the attention paid to the third dimension: the design of its buildings was given as much consideration as the layout of streets and spaces. It was a simple grid plan, but the architect, Solon Berman, created a sense of enclosure by lining the gridded streets with multi-storey row houses. Pullman also included well-designed civic spaces, including a market square. Of course, the provision of these spaces was tempered by the fact that they were all company owned, a condition that made it seem less like a real town and more like an exercise in pure social control. Gans (1967a, p. 183) described Pullman as a 'beautiful and efficient reformatory . . . for people who had done nothing wrong'.

Subsequent company towns were somewhat less paternalistic than Pullman, although they were also susceptible to worker unrest that undermined whatever impression of social harmony was trying to be obtained. Kohler, Wisconsin, founded in 1913 and designed by Werner Hegemann and Elbert Peets of *Civic Art* fame, was an improvement over Pullman in that the town was incorporated and governed by its residents, not the company. By the 1920s, there were company towns being built to satisfy the industrial workers of the factories burgeoning in response to Fordist production techniques. Ford himself was involved in creating 'village industries' meant to unite factory worker and agricultural labourer (Mullin, 1982). Many of these were built with the automobile in mind, signifying not only the capitalist's desire to create an automobile-dependent society, but a greater recognition of the American worker's need for independence and individuality (Stilgoe, 1988). By 1930, there were over two million people living in company towns that spanned the entire U.S. (Crawford, 1996).

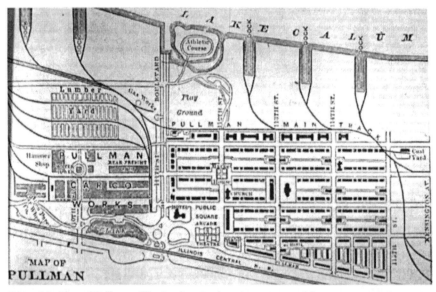

Figure 6.5. Plan of Pullman, Illinois, showing housing, commercial areas, community center, and factories. (*Source: Harper's Monthly Magazine*, 1885)

Garden Cities and Garden Suburbs

Although there is strong overlap among many of the planned community types listed thus far, garden cities can be separated out along one important dimension: they had an overt social purpose that revolved around the need to improve living conditions for the working class and the poor. The kind of planned community that emerged in the 1910s and 1920s that was explicitly modelled on Ebenezer Howard's garden cities, and took the form of garden villages and suburbs, might later have become affluent, but the intention to integrate housing types and provide for a range of community needs accessible to all residents made garden cities, villages and suburbs distinct from the more speculative developments of the same period.

Garden city type developments existed prior to Howard. Before he published his famous book in 1898, *To-Morrow: a peaceful path to real reform*, others had proposed ways to better integrate human development and nature, a sort of 'back to the land' movement for the nineteenth century (see Lewis, 1916, p. 300). Nelson Lewis claimed that garden cities predated Howard by an entire generation, and cited the workingmen's colonies developed by the Krupps family outside of Essen starting in 1856 as the logical precursors.

The lineage of garden cities based directly on Howard begins with the three 'true' garden cities: Letchworth, Welwyn Garden City and Wythenshawe (Hall, 2002). Beyond these there were garden city-like developments that could be labelled garden villages or garden suburbs. Numerous European developments and spin-offs from the garden city ideal, notably the English garden cities proposed in Patrick Abercrombie's post World War II Greater London Plan, had influence in the U.S. Unfortunately, despite a number of interesting translations of garden city principles by philanthropic organizations like the Russell Sage Foundation, the garden city paradigm was significantly downgraded and parts of it used to legitimize all manner of suburban extension.

The garden city ideal was thus translated into a variety of forms and contexts. Initially, the aesthetic principles were based on Ruskin, as articulated in his 1865 treatise, *Sesame and Lilies*, then augmented with the socialist ideals of William Morris, and later translated by Raymond Unwin and Barry Parker into a number of garden city-like developments. Ruskin-Morris principles were a merger of socialism and design, a spirit of cooperative craftsmanship in keeping with Morris' contention that beauty comes from within and works outward. Regardless of architectural style, garden cities were inspired by the same set of goals – the need to create a healthy alternative to the industrial city that could also provide a full range of daily life needs, ready access to nature, and 'a full measure of social life' (see Lang, 1996, p. 123).

Many of the precursors of Ebenezer Howard's garden cities have already been

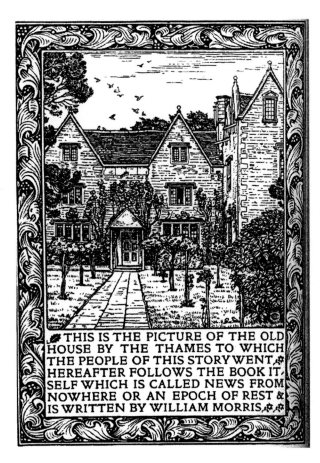

THIS IS THE PICTURE OF THE OLD HOUSE BY THE THAMES TO WHICH THE PEOPLE OF THIS STORY WENT, HEREAFTER FOLLOWS THE BOOK ITSELF WHICH IS CALLED NEWS FROM NOWHERE OR AN EPOCH OF REST & IS WRITTEN BY WILLIAM MORRIS.

Figure 6.6. Frontispiece from one of the influential writings of William Morris, *News from Nowhere*, first published as a serial in the Socialist magazine *Commonweal* in 1890.

discussed, for example, Port Sunlight and Bournville. Both developments were extremely influential in garden city design, and, as testament to this, were the locations of the first two garden city conferences held in 1901 and 1902 respectively. Other influences included the picturesque landscape design of Frederick Law Olmsted – it is believed that Howard visited the town of Riverside outside of Chicago – and the Australian city of Adelaide laid out by Colonel William Light in 1836. The latter was laid out on a grid pattern with a central square and parks and smaller squares for public functions distributed throughout.

It is difficult to disassociate suburban development, particularly commuter suburbs, from garden cities if one takes a generic view of what garden cities are. Certainly Riverside and Llewellyn Park, categorized as romantic suburbs, were attempting to merge the best of town and country. But the kind of merger envisioned by Howard was structurally very different, since it was predicated on co-partnership – housing cooperatives in which there was to be no private ownership of land. Additionally, garden cities in the Howardian sense integrated industry along with housing, commercial and recreational functions, and thus were not meant to be dependent on the central urban core as most American suburbs were. A more inclusive definition, which many garden city advocates were not adverse to, was also used. In the 1913 book *Garden City Movement Up-to-Date*, the distinction was made as follows: garden cities were self-contained towns; garden suburbs provided a way for the growth of existing cities to be along 'healthy lines'; and garden villages, such as Bournville and Port Sunlight, were 'garden cities in miniature, but depend upon some neighbouring city for water, light and drainage' (Culpin, 1913, p. 6).

Development modelled explicitly on Howard's garden city paradigm began almost immediately after the publication of his book, in the early 1900s. In 1903, the First Garden City Company purchased 3800 acres near London to build a self-contained town complete with industrial, commercial and residential functions. Letchworth, laid out by Barry Parker and Raymond Unwin, was followed by two others: Welwyn and Wythenshawe. In the U.S., the Garden City Association of America was formed in 1906 by Howard, church leaders and businessmen intent on carrying the garden city message forward, but they did not produce any viable projects.

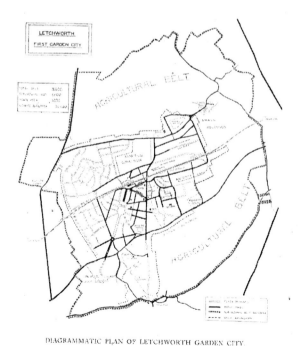

Figure 6.7. Diagrammatic plan of Letchworth Garden City, 'showing the relation of the Town Area to the Agriculture Belt' and illustrating the main features proposed by Ebenezer Howard, according to this 1913 publication. (*Source*: Edwart G. Culpin, *The Garden City Movement Up-To-Date*, 1913)

DIAGRAMMATIC PLAN OF LETCHWORTH GARDEN CITY

This plan of Letchworth Garden City, showing the relation of the Town Area to the Agricultural Belt, illustrates the main features of Mr. Ebenezer Howard's proposals.

The first garden city development in the U.S. was the Russell Sage Foundation's philanthropic quest to build a model garden suburb for the working classes at Forest Hills Gardens, located in Queens a short distance from Manhattan and conveniently connected by rail. The 142-acre development designed by Frederick Law Olmsted, Jr. and Grosvenor Atterbury is deemed particularly significant because it was here that Clarence Perry, while a resident, conceived of his unique articulation of the neighbourhood unit. Forest Hills Gardens had, in fact, a neighbourhood structure to it and Perry believed good design could contribute to the development of a 'neighbourhood spirit' (Perry, 1929). Housing units were arranged in small groups rather than blocks, a strategy meant to emphasize the difference that 'scientific principles' of town planning could have on rectifying the drudgery of the endless Manhattan grid. The impact of this extended beyond Perry. The neighbourhood plans sponsored by the City Club of Chicago in 1913 were also directly influenced by it, particularly the first and second prize designs (Stern and Massengale, 1981).

Street layouts and building designs at Forest Hills Gardens were innovative. Olmsted laid out the streets in such a way that, although gridded, they were kept quiet and slightly curvilinear – in direct contrast to Manhattan. The intent of its backer, the Sage Foundation Homes Company, was to promote a better standard of residential design that merged, as with all garden cities, the benefits of town (in this case New York City) and country. There was a concerted effort to mix housing types and therefore classes, and the designers successfully placed high-density apartment buildings on the same streets as single-family houses. However, critics note that, despite a desire to provide for people of middle income, the reach did not extend to day labourers.

True garden cities were more radical. They were intended to prevent land speculation by ensuring that increases in land value went to the community as a whole, not the individual – a concept picked up by CIAM, which advocated the same radicalism. Garden city advocates struggled with maintaining the purity of the idea. As one contemporary put it: 'a garden city or suburb is not simply a pleasant town or suburb with a few gardens within it' (Lewis, 1916, p. 302). It was instead meant to counter 'purely commercial enterprises' along a completely new model of urbanism. As one proponent put it 'The garden city stands . . . as the preventative, not as the palliative' (Culpin, 1913, p. 6). This goal was not achieved. In Europe, where it would seem to have a better chance of success, any radicalism exhibited by John Ruskin, William Morris or Ebenezer Howard was kept in check by the 'bureaucratic tendencies' of Fabian Socialism (Lang, 1999, p. 123).

Garden suburbs settled for the accomplishment of other social goals. Hampstead Garden Suburb, developed in 1907 by Henrietta Barnett, the wife of Samuel Barnett of Toynbee Hall settlement house, was successful at deliberately mixing housing types – and thereby deliberately mixing social classes. It also provided housing specifically for the aged and the infirm. In this is reflected the social goals of Toynbee Hall and later Hull House – the idea of bringing upper-class residents into the inner city to mix socially with people of different income levels and social needs. The ultimate goal was to build tolerance: 'to break down the barriers between classes, or at least to bring about a more kindly feeling between them' (Lewis, 1916, p. 303).

In their review of the Anglo-American suburb, Stern and Massengale (1981) describe Hampstead Garden Suburb as 'the jewel of the suburban crown', a 'complex and subtle' composition that demonstrated the legitimacy of the suburban development in England. But others have interpreted it as confusing. The layout is considered too informal, with curving streets and culs-de-sac. There is also an Edwin Lutyens component reminiscent of the City Beautiful. A vast central square is described by Peter Hall as 'dead' space that seems to be 'a dummy run for the approach to the Viceroy's Palace at New Delhi' (Hall, 2002, p. 108). These same Grand Manner qualities are present at Letchworth, and have been the basis of that community's critique as well.

In any event, the garden city model was having a clear impact on all types of planned developments in the U.S. in the decades immediately following Howard's treatise. In England, there were fifty-eight garden city-like developments underway by 1913 (Culpin, 1913). In the U.S. it was during the First World War that housing projects were beginning to show the garden city influence, coinciding with what Mumford termed the start of 'modern planning'. Because of a housing shortage in industrial towns, the U.S. government under Woodrow Wilson created a programme for building workers' housing near munitions and shipbuilding factories.

The goal was to support the war effort, but one development, Yorkship Village (later renamed Fairview) near Camden, New Jersey, has been described as 'a product of the best and brightest minds in the progressive housing, architecture, planning, and housing reform movement' (Lang, 1996, p. 143). The design inspiration was the garden city as articulated by Parker and Unwin, who were known for their ability to translate social ideals into planned communities. Yorkship Village was designed by Frederick L. Ackerman who thought of his garden village plans for wartime housing as the 'more rational and more humble' counterparts to the Columbian Exposition of 1893. Rather than magnificence, the goal was simply 'better conditions of living' (Ackerman, 1918, p. 86).

Housing advocates, who were influential at the time, sought an improvement in the living environments of industrial workers. In England, where housing projects influenced by garden city ideals and intended for industrial workers flourished in the 1910s and 1920s, this took the form initially of suburban limited-dividend housing developments like Hampstead Garden Suburb. The estates were essentially picturesque row houses in carefully planned arrangements that produced a very different environment from conventional working-class housing. They succeeded at positioning high-density housing in such a way that, instead of the old terraced housing and long rows of identical dwellings, had a village-like feel (Lang, 1996). Government sponsorship was critical. The London County Council (LCC), whose work was directly influenced by Howard and Unwin, built a series of transit-linked housing estates for the working classes between 1900 and 1914, such as Totterdown Fields (1903–1909) and Norbury (1906–1910).

These developments had an effect on American planners, largely through the dissemination of garden city material in the main journal of the American Institute of Architects. Under sponsorship of editor Charles Whitaker, Frederick L. Ackerman made an excursion to England in 1917 to photograph and document new garden city developments, and these were subsequently published in the *AIA Journal*. Through lobbying by both Whitaker and Ackerman, garden city planning subsequently made its way into U.S. federal housing policy. Two federal agencies, the Emergency Fleet Corporation and the U.S. Housing Corporation, were involved with the construction of thousands of units of wartime housing in more than 150 developments and towns.

Direct involvement in the construction of planned communities was abruptly ended in 1919, largely because U.S. government involvement was deemed too

Figure 6.8. Mixed commercial and residential uses at Yorkship Square, Yorkship Village. (*Photograph*: Sandy Sorlien)

socialist. A handful of high quality garden city-like communities were constructed, totalling 25,000 housing units (Jackson, 1985), but the federal government complained that they were of too high a quality (Scott, 1969). Since private housing development was not paying this kind of attention to community-building, it is not surprising that the federal government was unhappy with the way these quality, planned communities made the rest of private housing look (Lang, 1996). For example, in Bridgeport, Connecticut and Wilmington, Delaware, housing was provided within walking distance of industrial sites and neighbourhood services. The designs were modified picturesque, with irregular street layouts, Sittesque enclosure and attention to the street vista. There were public spaces, a central village green with commercial areas and community facilities that together formed a quality living environment that few industrial workers could dream of at the time. The planners paid attention to mixing income levels by providing a range of housing types, from clustered row houses and apartment buildings to single-family housing. At Yorkship Village, the housing was arranged in 243 different groups consisting of 27 housing types in 70 combinations (Stern and Massengale, 1981). The neighbourhood unit concept conceived by settlement housing leaders like Jacob Riis, Jane Addams and Mary Simkhovitch, and later articulated more explicitly by William Drummond and then Clarence Perry, was also present in Yorkship Village.

The next phase in planned community culture with direct links to garden cities was the work undertaken by the Regional Planning Association of America. Their new community ventures, many of them planned and designed by Clarence Stein and Henry Wright, produced some of the most well-known planned communities in the U.S. Their first was Sunnyside Gardens in Queens. In 1924, Clarence Stein, a self-described 'disciple' of Ebenezer Howard and Raymond Unwin, suggested to Alexander M. Bing, a wealthy developer, that he fund the building of a garden city there. Four years later they created Radburn, less a garden city than Sunnyside Gardens but significantly more influential. In either case, the garden city ideal was severely compromised because, according to Stein, 'the purchase of the property could not be financed quickly enough to prevent the land being subdivided and thrown into the speculative market' (Stein, 1951, p. 21).

Yet these American versions of garden city ideals were innovative and instructive. At Sunnyside, Stein and Wright developed 'the theoretical basis of land and community planning' that they subsequently applied to Radburn, N.J., Chatham Village outside Pittsburgh, the Greenbelt Towns, and Baldwin Hills in Los Angeles. Sunnyside Gardens was developed by a limited dividend company organized by Bing in 1924, and consisted of 1200 housing units on 56 acres, constructed between 1924 and 1928. The site was convenient for workers, linked by rapid transit to Manhattan, and ultimately successful at proving what Bing and other garden city advocates wanted to prove – that development according to sound planning principles could be not only economically viable but could also provide residents with open, green spaces without public subsidy. They drew from Raymond Unwin and his famous 'Nothing Gained by Overcrowding' doctrine that showed that open spaces – called 'green commons' – could be preserved at block centres with no additional cost per lot. They were also able to show that garden city principles could be adapted to a dense urban grid.

Again Sunnyside Gardens succeeded at the deliberate mixing of housing unit types for reasons of social integration. There, the integration was achieved by making the block rather than the individual lot the unit of development. Within this framework, single-family housing sat next to two-family residences and apartment buildings. A possible source for this innovation was Port Sunlight, which used an array of eclectic styles to build rows of houses that could barely be delimited one from another, transforming rows of cottages into streets of mansions (Creese, 1967). Planned community designers knew that the merger of housing types required the right streetscape – cohesive, with a close relationship between building and street. Stein's approach at Sunnyside Gardens in the 1920s was to create combinations of rows of single-family, two-family and multi-family dwellings, which, he claimed in his book *Toward New Towns for America*, did not cause 'social difficulties' (Stein, 1951. p. 35). The social integration goals at Radburn were the same.

It is significant that Stein perceived no demonstrable problem of social incompatibility. He wrote, 'In spite of the speculative operators' fear of such indiscriminate grouping, and the zoners' preoccupation in keeping dwellings of similar types together, we found this did not cause sales resistance'. Their success with overriding the tendency of zoning to require strict segregation was due to the fact that the land was zoned industrial rather than residential. Therefore, said Stein, 'we were free to design for community and aesthetic objectives' (Stein, 1951, p. 30).

Figure 6.9. A comparison of the planned communities system of streets and a conventional system, one requiring policing, the other providing safe, inner block paths. (*Source*: Clarence Stein, *Toward New Towns for America*, 1951)

Radburn, which was intended to be a 'complete garden city' for 25,000, was unluckily started just prior to the stock market crash of 1929. Its principal backer, Alexander Bing's City Housing Corporation, was financially ruined shortly after the crash. In the attempt to follow Howard's ideas more closely, Radburn was supposed to be surrounded by a greenbelt and to include industry – a town meant for both living and working as Howard intended. These basic garden city ideas had to be dropped, and Stein concluded that new towns required active government involvement, since a private corporation has 'only a gambling chance' of succeeding (Stein, 1951, p. 67).

Aside from the financial innovation needed to make the building of a garden city in the American context work, Radburn was an attempt to work out the problem of the automobile. In so doing, its main design significance was the development of 'The Radburn Idea' as Stein called it: the superblock (Stein, 1951, p. 38). There were previous examples. Clarence Stein noted that superblocks were built by the Dutch in Nieue Amsterdam (New York) as early as 1660, and that the cul-de-sac was prevalent in early American colonial villages. The superblock could be found in Cambridge and Longwood, Massachusetts even in the early nineteenth century. The success of culs-de-sac was demonstrated at New Earswick in England, where they were used to encourage build-out on irregularly shaped lots. Culs-de-sac were also sensitively handled at Hampstead Garden Suburb.

Separation of different means of communication (i.e., separation of pedestrian and automobile traffic) had already been worked out by Olmsted in Central Park in the mid-nineteenth century. According to Dal Co, the 'real model for Radburn' was Olmsted's Plan of Central Park, since it was there that the separation of traffic was introduced in the American consciousness (Dal Co, 1979, p. 241). At Radburn, the solution to the unsafe environment created by the automobile was a separation of the pedestrian and automobile, creating superblocks of houses turned inward, away from the street. Variations on this idea are longstanding. For example, limited vehicular access to service lanes behind rows of houses, with parks and sidewalks between house fronts, was seen in Louisville, Kentucky in the nineteenth century (Arendt, 1999). Other translations of the basic idea include Stein and Wright's Chatham Village near Pittsburgh, laid out in 1931.

Following a 95 per cent drop in residential construction in the early 1930s, the federal government's attempt to restart the homebuilding industry by promoting so-called Keynesian suburbs fell far short of the planned community principles of earlier decades. Encouraged through zoning and facilitated by the freedom of the automobile, development at the periphery marched to the tune of separation and segregation. In the rare instances of planned community building, developments of the 1930s and 1940s took on a very different character from the pre-Depression era projects. FDR's Greenbelt Town Program lasted only 3 years (1935–1938), and has been described as 'one of the most curious chapters of American urban history' (Kostof, 1991, p. 80). The programme was overtly intended to apply Howard's garden city principles, creating low-cost housing and local economic cooperatives. But by that time the translation had taken on a completely different feel from that envisioned by Unwin and Parker, with little attention given to principles of social and land-use diversity, walkability, protection from the automobile, and attention to the civic realm.

The three Greenbelt towns that were constructed, Greenbelt, Maryland (which was an adaptation of Radburn's superblock structure), Greenhills, Ohio, and Greendale, Wisconsin, all have the look and feel of a more conventional suburban development. In addition to these projects, Stein's plan for Hillside Homes, a self-contained arrangement of five-storey apartment buildings around open courtyards, was an early Public Works Administration project that won the admiration of Catherine Bauer. Though it integrated commercial and recreational activities, its modernist-style housing blocks created a feeling of 'towers in a park' efficiency and urban disconnection characteristic of later urban renewal and high-rise public housing schemes.

Figure 6.10. Plan of Radburn, New Jersey, showing houses facing inward onto parks that connect throughout the development. (*Source:* Clarence Stein, *Toward New Towns for America,* 1951)

Baldwin Hills Village, developed in 1941, is another adaptation of Stein's 'Radburn Idea', this time applied in Los Angeles. Here the break with traditional urban diversity is complete – superblock, complete separation of pedestrian and auto, and 'park as community heart and backbone', all of which was crystallized into a 'functional unity' (Stein, 1951, p. 169). From Baldwin Hills Village, there sprang numerous developments that could more generally be viewed as suburban development with a nod to garden cities. They were severely watered down, and the single-use, monolithic suburban developments that they amounted to were a far cry from Howard's, Unwin's, or even Stein's ideas about community development.

This brief overview of garden city-inspired development reflects a gradual deterioration of garden city principles. By mid-century, development in the U.S. was less about the planned community and more about unplanned suburban sprawl. At the same time, planned community developments that did continue following World War II seemed further and further removed, as a physical planning matter, from the pre-War garden city models. Two new towns of the 1960s – Reston, Virginia and Columbia, Maryland – were experiments in planned community design that seemed particularly detached. They consisted of development in small units (neighbourhoods), an emphasis on leisure amenities, and the inclusion of pedestrian paths linking residential areas and village facilities (Merlin, 1971).

Both Reston and Columbia had strong social objectives, motivated by a desire to build socially diverse, non-segregated societies. Columbia was started by James Rouse in 1967 as an 'open community' with all the right intentions. It was to house a diverse population in terms of race, income and age. It was also to be a community fully mixed in use, providing places to work, live, shop and recreate within easy proximity. In short, these developments had all the same components of the idealized planned community of the pre-World War II era, but the environment that was created turned out to be significantly different from the planned communities of the 1910s and 1920s. This can be attributed to principles of design. The later communities were products of the design, style and spatial logic of modernism. They are characterized by separation and hierarchy rather than a more fine-grained urbanism. Their buildings were designed in a dressed down style that looked as if they were all built by the same architect at the same time. And the commercial components were automobile based, so much so that they were transformed into auto-oriented strip malls by the 1990s. Jane Jacobs thought of them as antithetical to the nature of cities: 'very nice towns if you were docile and had no plans of your own', she commented (Jacobs, 1966, p. 101).

Connections

The fundamental goals of the planned community are amazingly consistent across a number of time periods and even ideologies. Fishman has compared the urban plans of Ebenezer Howard, Frank Lloyd Wright and Le Corbusier and found that they shared three goals – the need to offer an alternative to the nineteenth-century city, the belief in modern technology, and the sense that communitarianism – the 'brotherhood of man' – was attainable and close at hand (Fishman, 1977, p. 10). A similar comparison of utopian ideals was made by Wilson who found essentially the same commonality among Lewis Mumford, Frank Lloyd Wright and the Resettlement Adminstration (Wilson, 1983). Translated into the physical goals of the planned community, this has meant that the need for communal facilities, civic spirit, social integration, proximity to nature, recreational facilities, public transportation, and easily accessible daily life needs have all been part and parcel of the planned community ethos.

Yet not every expression of the goal of civic spirit and the need for community facilities turned out to be a model of good urbanism. The physical manifestations presented vastly different environmental experiences. Catherine Bauer's planned community concept included mixed income, mixed use communities in the form of compact settlements, but the modernist form she advocated would not be likely to be considered a positive force in American urbanism. Industrial decentralization in post-war America brought plenty of talk about the need for the well-planned community, including a whole slew of 'scientifically analyzed' and rationally allocated components of the dispersing metropolis. But the effects could not have been more different. It may be true that mega-cities like Los Angeles were growing by 'dispersed and discrete clusters' and even nodal communities that considered the relationship between residence and workplace, but that hardly guaranteed a noteworthy contribution to American urbanism (Hise, 1996, p. 261).

James Rouse also exemplified the common planned community ideals of civic spirit and functional communitarianism. Rouse regretted that 'there is little or no physical definition of community', but instead 'an irrational scattering of the institutions . . . with the result that people live in a kind of negative, impersonal, depersonalized massiveness' (Christensen, 1977, p. 299). This statement could have been made by Jane Addams, Raymond Unwin, or even Jane Jacobs. But while the frustrations and goals were the same, the physical manifestation of identical principles has taken very different forms. Reston, Virginia has virtually identical principles to New Urbanism, yet the look, feel and experience of it is not something New Urbanists would seek to emulate. Why is that so? What makes planned communities qualitatively different? The discussion that follows, first under 'Connections' and then 'Conflicts', attempts to sort this larger, difficult question out.

Many planned communities were established in response to the conditions of existing cities that were found to be unacceptable and either too difficult or too intrinsically flawed to change. In Europe, initial responses to the industrial city took the form of long, impersonal straight streets replacing the more intricate, enclosed urbanism of the medieval city. There were compelling reasons of public hygiene and traffic flow, but the impersonality of the changes was oppressive to many. It is one reason why the messages of Sitte, Howard and others who promoted the intimacy of the complete planned community were taken seriously.

Later, suburbanization suffered the same problems of monotony and impersonality. Virtually all garden city advocates disliked the suburbs as much as they deplored the congested industrial city. Even before the automobile had significant effect, Parker and Unwin were denouncing the idea that housing should stand 'alone in the middle of its own little plot' (Creese, 1992, p. 190). Once the automobile opened up suburban land conversion at a previously unknown rate and scale in the 1920s, investors cavorted with public utility operators to encourage expedient forms of suburbanization – developments that lacked coherence, diversity and a public realm. The financial gain of the subdivision was dependent on large land holdings that, for the most part, were not organized as communities. In the U.S., this situation was overwhelming, but the idea of the planned community as antidote never died.

Beyond the idea of communal objectives (interpreted as social control and thus problematic), what is the basis for the continued relevance of the planned community in American urbanism? One basis could be the innovation of their designs. Intimately scaled buildings, seamlessly integrated housing types, ways of handling traffic, public spaces with charm and pedestrian focus – all can be regarded as valuable lessons in civic design appropriate for American urbanism. And the success of design principles implemented in the planned community can be easily assessed. Compared to interventions in existing cities where a myriad of factors are already at work, planned communities are more transparent when it comes to understanding what has been effective and what has not, what conditions seem to correlate with success and non-success, what design principles seem to produce the best human environments.

Treatment of the automobile was particularly important in this respect. An early lesson was provided by Olmsted who had insisted that, in the suburban planned community, 'all that favours movement should be subordinated' (Rybczynski, 1999, p. 292), a sentiment echoed by contemporary urbanists who have emphasized the importance of 'slow urbanism' (Moule, 2002). Many planned communities from the 1920s onwards shared the goal of accommodating the automobile but not allowing it to dominate at the expense of urban quality. Thus the way in which parking lots were integrated in Country Club District, or garages incorporated in Chatham Village, offer very valuable models of automobile accommodation that keep its disruptive tendencies in check.

The fact that design quality did not translate into a rejection of high density is also significant. Some suburban planned communities were able to achieve extraordinarily high densities – Saltaire housed 90 people per acre – but still put residents in close proximity to the surrounding countryside. One could argue that it is only in the context of the planned community that such a relationship could be worked out.

The planned community will only be valued, however, if there can be an acceptance of the legitimacy of peripheral development. It will be necessary to think in terms of decentralized urbanism rather than suburban escapism. This is not the natural inclination. Ever since Sinclair Lewis' *Babbitt* (1922), a commentary on the middle-class suburb and its social expectations, the intellectual *avant-garde* has ridiculed suburbs for being sterile, trivial and elitist. Overcoming this will require a keener appreciation of the examples where planned communities were able to achieve socially justifiable objectives, or where the quality of the planning and design is worth studying, or where it was possible to achieve social integration, good design, access to daily life needs and housing for the working classes in one settlement.

Some would view the mere attention to design inherent in the planned community as important to emulate – in a world of market-driven approaches to urbanism, the conscious sitting, arrangement, and planned form of all elements of human habitation can seem inspiring. It has been argued that it was the self-consciousness of suburban design – what Fishman calls 'suburban style' – that made the suburban idea take off, not Jeffersonian 'antiurbanism that had somehow lain dormant in the American urban soul' (Fishman, 1987, p. 121). Applied holistically and made consistent with urbanism, the appeal is potent.

Attention to design extended far. The focus on detail found in a planned community like Shaker Heights, where the Van Sweringen brothers controlled everything from roof lines to pavement colours, and where dark coloured mortar could not be used without written consent (Stilgoe, 1988, p. 245), can, from one perspective, be viewed as something positive. It is a recognition of the impact individual decisions can have on the whole community. When compared to the magnitude of inattention Americans have been putting up with in their own landscapes, the attention to detail seems gratifying. The unfortunate downside is that strong attention to design quality correlates with affluence. This essential dilemma – between design quality and affordability – lies at the heart of much of the criticism of planned communities.

It is also possible to assess the planned community in design terms by looking at the doctrine of appropriateness, which the planned community was often good at responding to. Mumford called it 'the element of charm', and used it to distinguish good design from bad (Fishman, 2002, p. 65). A review of Hampstead Garden

Suburb published in *Town and Country Planning* (Rasmussen, 1957) reflected on the principle of appropriateness and the ability of Unwin to recognize it. The example given was of the seeming divergence between enclosure and open space – between, in essence, town and country. Unwin successfully included both. A similar success had to do with the hierarchy of street types Unwin and Park advocated, ranging in width, pavement type and purpose, depending on varying contexts within the community.

One of the most controversial aspects of the planned community is the notion of self-containment – the organization of human settlement into discrete units. Even if the planned community is constructed over a period of time, the incrementalism that may exist is subsumed by an overarching, holistic conceptualization of form. This implies not only internal coherence but external delineation.

From the perspective of the planned community advocate, self-containment is simply a condition of thinking organically. Unwin, in his quest for harmonic relationships among urban elements, likened city design to William Morris wallpaper (Creese, 1967), but there was a distinct advantage to thinking in these terms that was not limited to neat harmonies that looked good on paper. The mark of a good town design, Arendt (1999) states, has to do with the clarity, comprehensibility, and functionality of the design. Thinking holistically meant that any one element of urbanism was less likely to dominate – not the streets, not the buildings, not the recreational spaces. Specialization could undermine the principle asset of the planned community, i.e., its ability to approach the city as a system of integrated conditions that require balance.

The search for organic integration stimulated a certain innovativeness in planned community design. The critique that the planned community was packaged and lacked innovation cannot be universally applied, for it was in the context of holistic community planning that the search for new ideas about what the best human settlement forms and patterns could be took place. Groupings of dwelling units, mix of housing type, the relation between two- and three-dimensional design, the incorporation of neighbourhood greens, the handling of cars, the creation of new types of streets – all of these were explored fully by planned community advocates. Holism motivated the emphasis on street pictures and changing viewpoints, in turn forcing the designer to think in terms of context – building placement, typology, relation to other buildings and to the street.

Somewhat ironically, it was the quality of being self-contained that gave the planned community the quality of being urban, since self-containment implied the need for internal diversity. The underlying logic of many planned communities, in contrast to unplanned settlement, was one of creating diversity through design. But it was a controlled diversity. This was brought out in a recent analysis of Forest Hills Gardens, which detailed how the laying out of all the elements of community

– paving, sidewalks, landscape, utilities – preceded the marketing for individual houses. This practice not only positioned the public realm ahead of the private, but helped to establish a 'comprehensive aesthetic' that elevated standards for quality and character and allowed diversity in design which may have had some effect on social diversity (Klaus, 2002, p. 165).

This control was necessary because promoters of the planned community lacked faith in the ability of cities to emerge well on their own, especially when controlled by land markets and government regulation. Any semblance of order or convenience found in an unplanned place was, Unwin (1909, p. 2) believed, due purely to chance. It was not thought possible that, in modern, twentieth-century society, the order and convenience of the planned community could occur spontaneously and naturally. It was the planner's job to rise above mere aggregations of people and produce something, consciously and explicitly, of beauty. Unwin believed that, in

Plan of Buckingham when entire project is completed; a neighborhood unit of 2,000 families almost completely self-contained. "Through-traffic" is shunted around the community. Local services and recreational requirements are provided at points of greatest convenience and safety. 1. Proposed School Site and Playground; 2. Shops; 3. Community Center.

Figure 6.11. Plan of Buckingham, Virginia, outside of Arlington. Designed by Henry Wright and admired by Clarence Perry because it was a 'completely self-contained' neighbourhood unit for 2,000 families that 'shunted' through-traffic. It also included a school site and playground, shops and community centre. (Source: Clarence A. Perry, *Housing for the Machine Age*, 1939)

an earlier time, there existed very different impulses that acted as a 'natural force' to produce towns of beauty 'where additions were made so gradually that each house was adapted to its place, and assimilated into the whole before the next was added' (Unwin, 1909, p. 14). In the twentieth century, Unwin argued that the traditional impulses of city building had been lost, and only the consciously planned community could get them back.

The planned community was an expedient way to achieve quality – a human settlement that is simultaneously beautiful, efficient, ordered, healthful, and able to instil reverence among its inhabitants. For lack of a better phrase, it is the physical manifestation of *pride of place*, a self-consciousness about community building that advocates found difficult to replicate in existing cities. It parallels the sense of pride that the Laws of the Indies attempted to regulate by forbidding the entry of Indians into their new towns until they were 'complete': '. . . so that when the Indians see them they will be filled with wonder and will realize that the Spaniards are settling there permanently and not temporarily' (Reps, 1965, p. 30). The history of the American suburb has been approached as a history of how people came to recognize their communities as distinctive places (Schaffer, 1988), but the planned community consciously sought this recognition from the start. The question is whether community self-consciousness necessarily implies exclusion, or whether it can be viewed as something more positive.

The act of 're-tribalizing' (Ellin, 1996), replicating by finite, complete units, is a very different proposal from growth by extension and spread. Unplanned sprawl is one basis of contrast, but as an ideology, a clearer distinction can be made with the linear city. Metropolitanism was more a result of agglomeration economies than deliberate planning for largeness, but the lineal city of Ciudad Lineal devised by Arturo Soria y Mata in the late nineteenth century was intended to be an infinitely expandable urban form. The lineal city extended along transportation routes in a way that ran counter to the notion of expansion by internally focused, discrete, cohesive units. The incomplete application of this concept in the form of strip malls and arterial based development can not be blamed on Soria's conception, but the distinction can nevertheless be made.

Why not, as Catherine Bauer advocated in 1934, control decentralization in such a way that outward growth is organized into complete, socially and economically diverse communities? This could be accomplished in more than one way. Savannah's system of cell-like expansion by plots of housing and public buildings clustered around a public square can be every bit as admired as Perry's neighbourhood unit paradigm as a method of organized decentralization. Both claim the idea of self-containment, centrality of functions, and the need for spatial definition.

It has been argued that growth by unplanned metropolitan enlargement has a serious downside – dismal environmental conditions, long commutes, stress on community facilities, and various other incivilities that Jane Jacobs, according to Mumford (1968), chose to ignore. The idea has a long history – that once a city reaches a certain size, it is time to colonize a new one, not just keep expanding the old one. Suburban development has evolved under this logic, but not always in the manner of the planned community. Suburban sprawl is more an embodiment of capitalism, while the planned community was often conceived as a rebuttal to it.

For over a century Americans have been experiencing first hand the implications of growing by spread rather than by organized unit. The peripheral, unplanned, subdivision growth that was already occurring in the nineteenth century was easily degraded. And the very qualities that people were attempting to find at the periphery – quiet, closeness to nature – were undermined as the popularity of the idea spread. It was the 'tragedy of the commons', and planned community proponents were inspired to avert it. What they were asserting was that the degradation intrinsic to unplanned spread could only by avoided through the mechanism of the complete planned community.

Containment and organized decentralization implied certain rules about urbanism. In many cases it warranted a nucleus of some sort, since the centre could have symbolic, civic, social, cultural and economic value. For Ruskin, the centre was the public version of the sacred family home. Perry's neighbourhood unit scheme embodied this, as only neighbourhood institutions of public value were to be located at the centre. Unwin's *Town Planning in Practice* devoted a chapter to urban centres, tracing the Greek agora, the Roman forum, and other examples of 'the splendour' of centrally positioned public buildings and meeting places (Unwin, 1909, p. 175). In this there is an affinity with the City Beautiful, although central spaces in the planned community had a very different scale. Unwin recognized that re-creation of spaces like the Roman forum was 'hardly possible,' but used them to emphasize his point that a plan – even at the community scale – needs a centre.

In addition, the containment aspect of a planned community was tied to some notion of surrounding, boundary-defining green space. This was true of company towns like Pullman, where the countryside was the primary tool of containment. It did not have to be belt-like. Henry Vaughan Lanchester's 1908 proposal for green areas wedged between urban spaces was used to confine the lateral spread of development and got a boost when Thomas Mawson reprinted it in his 1911 book *Civic Art*. But the more accepted idea was Howard's permanent green belt of open and agricultural land encircling the city, a notion that was to become part of the British new towns scheme in the 1940s, and growth control in the U.S in the 1980s and 1990s.

The virtues of boundaries were extolled by John Ruskin in *Sesame and Lilies*. As later conceived by Unwin, boundaries which could be formed by boulevards, playing fields, or belts of parkland served two purposes. First, they ensured the careful use 'of every yard of building space' within the boundary. Second, a boundary theoretically puts a stop to sprawl, and Unwin was as aware of this in 1909 as we are today. The way he put it, boundaries prevent 'that irregular fringe of half-developed suburb and half-spoiled country which form a hideous and depressing girdle around modern growing towns' (Unwin, 1909, p. 154). Potentially, a boundary functions as a constraint, engenders a tightening up of development and motivates more careful planning. Perry went so far as to view the 'menace' of the automobile as 'a blessing in disguise' because, by creating boundaries of traffic arterials, it made self-containment in the form of the neighbourhood unit more logical and necessary (Perry, 1929, p. 31).

Externally, containment implied that roads linking self-contained communities should not be allowed to swell with peripheral development, but instead should remain as linkages only. Once established, they should retain their quality as parkways – roads freed from development pressure because that development was to be channelled into the adjacent planned communities. To do otherwise would undermine the integrity and viability of the planned community. This is one of the most pervasive ideas of American urbanism, and is found in the work of Frederick Law Olmsted, the City Beautiful, the European garden cities, and Benton MacKaye, among others.

The contained, bounded settlement has also been thought of as having a particular size, beyond which it loses its organic quality and its ability to control the more destructive impulses of human development. Boundedness is the Aristotelian concept of the city (Fishman, 2002), and it implies that there exists a proper city size. What that size was supposed to be is debatable, but there are some interesting regularities. Leonardo da Vinci, Ebenezer Howard and Jane Jacobs all used a population of 30,000 to define the optimal self-governing district (Mumford, 1968). Tony Garnier's Une Cité Industrielle was designed for a population of 35,000. At a smaller scale, the rule of 10,000 has been used often. James Buckingham's model city of Victoria was built for a population of 10,000, as were Tugwell's Greenbelt towns. Christopher Alexander advocated for communities of 5,000–10,000, beyond which 'individuals have no effective voice' (Alexander et al., 1977, p. 71). Almost 20 years after its groundbreaking, the first garden city, Letchworth, had a population of 10,313, and one observer declared that it had reached the status of 'normal community' (Purdom, 1921, p. 27). Perry's neighbourhood unit was meant for less than this number, but later uses of the neighbourhood unit, such as in the British new towns, were based on a population of 10,000 (Goss, 1961). New Urbanists today use the same number to define the optimal population for a neighbourhood, as does Leon Krier, with his notion of the urban village (Krier, 1998).

The integration of non-residential elements was deliberate and embraced as an important component of the planned community. In some planned communities,

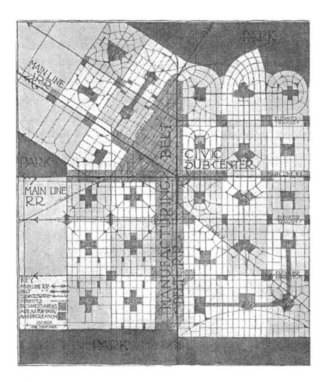

Figure 6.12. An original transit oriented development. William Drummond proposed this neighbourhood unit plan in the 1913 City Club of Chicago competition intended to 'stimulate interest in the more intelligent planning of the outlying portions of large cities'. (*Source*: Alfred B. Yeomans, *City Residential Land Development*, 1916)

commercial areas were less celebrated and more a matter of necessity, for example at Roland Park, where commercial buildings were relegated to one block and given the same building typology and style as the residential units in an effort to lesson their impact on the intended park like character (Stern and Massengale, 1981). Yet even developments that were mostly residential paid attention to the spatial logic of accessibility by positioning the planned community in proximity to industrial sites and existing community facilities, as at Bridgeport, Connecticut. However, the merit of addressing the service needs of decentralized self-contained communities has been downplayed since the facilities and services being provided were exclusively for local residents. Some view the provision of such services as merely facilitating the exclusivity and separation of the upper and middle classes, at least initially. These were not services that contributed to urban complexity in a way that would have pleased Jane Jacobs. Still, a broader view would make note of the connection between facility provision and shared, collective space as a beneficial social goal, even if one is referring to the Central Square of Lake Forest or the shops of Shaker Heights.

Self-containment has also been intertwined with the concept of the neighbourhood unit, which became the logical building block of the planned community. It was essential to Howard, used in Forest Hills Gardens, developed more explicitly by William Drummond in his design for the City Club's 1913 contest

(Johnson, 2002), taken further by Perry in 1923, and applied to Radburn in 1929 by Stein and Wright. Perry's analysis of Forest Hills Gardens in which he identified five factors of good neighbourhoods, is revealing for how closely it connects to the self-contained planned community concept in general: clear boundaries, a connected street system that promotes internal accessibility, land uses that support community functions, a central area with community facilities, and neighbourhood parks and recreation. Within cities, the conceptualization of self-contained units as a basis for urban organization extends way before Perry. Leon Battista Alberti's Renaissance ideas about the provision of recreational spaces for each district of the city can be viewed as a kind of neighbourhood planning statement (Alberti, 1485). Lewis Mumford saw the neighbourhood as an organic, natural outcome of urban growth, naturally occurring in great cities like Venice and Paris. Perry's neighbourhood unit, in other words, was a restatement of a centuries-old way of thinking about

Group Planning

Two houses are combined on adjoining lots. Each has more usable free space.

Six houses are built as a group. All are enhanced in outlook, privacy and open area.

Community Planning

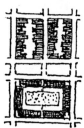

Forty builders fill up two city blocks with a motley mass of ugly and crowded tenements.

The community planner omits a costly street and groups more efficient and more open dwellings around a beautiful central garden.

Town Planning

A town is planned for platting and selling convenience. Ten per cent to 40 per cent is taken for indiscriminate streets.

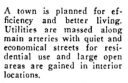

A town is planned for efficiency and better living. Utilities are massed along main arteries with quiet and economical streets for residential use and large open areas are gained in interior locations.

Figure 6.13. Planning at three levels, emphasizing the necessity of orderly plans and grouped housing for maximum efficiency and convenience. (*Sources*: Henry Wright's article in *Survey Graphic*, 1925, entitled 'From Roads to Good Houses', and reprinted in Karl B. Lohmann, *Principles of City Planning*, 1931)

urban arrangement. Perhaps this was a factor in the rapid acceptance of Perry's neighbourhood ideal. As implemented at Radburn and Baldwin Hills Village, it quickly became standard planning dogma, promoted by planning textbooks (Dahir, 1947), government regulations, chambers of commerce, and social service agencies starting in the 1930s (Patricios, 2002).

It is important to note that the planned community was almost never seen to exist in isolation – it was seen as part of a hierarchical system that extended in two directions. Internally, there were neighbourhood units, superblocks and culs-de-sac, as at Radburn, and externally, there were neighbourhoods, villages and communities, as at Columbia, Maryland. Howard's garden city diagram embodied these linkages on a conceptual level – a hierarchy consisting of a central city of 58,000 surrounded by six satellite cities of 32,000. Radburn had its own system, consisting of enclaves, blocks, superblocks, neighbourhoods, towns and regions, all nested and grouped to form the next higher level in the hierarchy (Patricios, 2002). It was this nested hierarchy of the self-contained planned community that connected it to a regionalist planning culture. The regionalists recognized that the more development spread outward in the form of unplanned growth, or, to use Patrick Geddes' phrase, in the form of a 'conurbation', the more the healthy proximity between people and nature was compromised. What was needed was for 'component parts' to be combined in 'coherent containers' (Mumford, 1968). Theoretical justification was not hard to find. Multinucleation was supported by the economic logic of Christaller's central place theory, and by R.D. McKenzie's hierarchical system of smaller cities grouped around larger ones (McKenzie, 1933).

As with planned communities more generally, it is where the self-containment of the neighbourhood overstepped its bounds to include an effect on social control that the self-contained, hierarchical neighbourhood unit became problematic. Critics like Jane Jacobs and Herbert Gans based their critiques of the neighbourhood unit on the notion of social control, which, at various times, was an overt goal of neighbourhood proponents. The problematic nature of these social objectives as they materialized in the redevelopment era was obvious: neat arrangements of living environments according to explicit, mindless ideas about healthy neighbourhood social structure. In fact, neighbourhood units and superblocks applied to public housing during the 1950s and 1960s had little to do with existing social structures (Moore, 1969).

Now, the self-contained planned community is sometimes seen as an anachronistic form of escape not unlike previous forms of suburban development. Self-segregation reflects a deep alienation with 'the urban-industrial world' that the middle-class suburbanite helped to create (Fishman, 1987). But the change from peripheral settlement that contributed to the localization of life to suburban development that disregarded this completely might be seen as a fundamentally different and more radical break. Suburban development in the form of the planned community had an enclave status, but at the very least, it functioned properly for the residents who inhabited it. Within reasonable distance, they could enjoy the main functions of daily life – shopping, schooling and civic and social engagement. Ever since the independently planned shopping centre became viable – demonstrated during the interwar decades by places like Suburban Square in Philadelphia and Hampton Village in St. Louis – shopping and planned residential development became separated (Longstreth, 1997). Conventional suburban development that was not in the form of the planned community therefore excluded daily functions. It worked to spread out, compartmentalize and individualize daily life in a way that was categorically different from what the planned community had been trying to achieve.

The value of the planned community is only appreciated if viewed in light of this contemporary, unplanned suburban growth. When compared to the post-World War II spread of edge cities and 'technoburbs' (Fishman, 1987) – where industry and commerce followed residential growth in a way that was not well planned – then the planned community, even if peripherally located, seemed to have something significant to offer. It was the lack of any viable, pedestrian level commercial function in suburban development that constituted the main difference between orderly decentralized growth in the form of planned communities and single-use, homogeneous, unplanned sprawl. The contemporary reality of sprawl is so far removed from the idea of a compact, diverse and walkable community organized around a coherent centre that even the unplanned streetcar suburb seems exemplary in comparison. Warner (1962) lamented the physical fragmentation of community life in streetcar suburbs in which facilities and services were separated, but in nineteenth-century Boston these elements were still within walking distance. Residents were forced to construct their own communities out of a spatially dispersed set of destinations, but that dispersion seems miniscule compared to today's sprawling and fragmented settlement reality.

Taking this same point of view allows communities like Shaker Heights to be valued as precursors of the transit oriented development, not as socially unjust models of exclusion. It requires a re-interpretation of social justice, such that the provision of a sidewalk and a transit stop take on social value in a way that would never have been imagined in a previous time period. And, if the form of development can be valued in terms of human functionality, it may be possible to overcome the once dominant social goals that we now find objectionable. Whether the planned community can be incorporated in the historical lineage of American urbanism rests on whether the overt social purpose of exclusivity can be extracted.

One problem for the planned community has been its focus on relating physical and social goals. In an earlier time, the overt social agenda of the planned community advocate was a more accepted ideology, although it always stood in

Figure 6.14. Baldwin Hills Village, 'showing the contrast between the development according to the Radburn Idea and the typical speculative development to the north and south'. (*Source*: Clarence Stein, *Toward New Towns for America*, 1951)

stark contrast to the other basis of American settlement – what Sam Bass Warner, Jr. calls 'privatism' or the pursuit of individual wealth (Warner, 1987). In the era of the planned communities of the nineteenth and early twentieth centuries, privatism was tempered by a strong insistence on communal objectives. This was pronounced in the garden city model of development, where the landlord and the community were one and the same.

Where the planned community was simply responding to the associative needs of individuals rather than attempting to engineer socially, the critique that planned communities were mostly about social engineering is tempered. That is, where the ideal of community was a dependent rather than an independent variable, where extant community existed and was looking for a design conducive to it, the planned community could not really claim to be engineering something. There are examples of this. Klaus (2002) compared the early residents of Forest Hills Gardens to those of Celebration, Florida, finding similar faith in the communitarian abilities of the planned community. Both groups of residents saw themselves, at least initially, as pioneers looking for a way to nurture the communitarian spirit. They were, in other words, predisposed.

In one sense, the early planned community advocate should be appreciated for even getting the social implications of human settlement on the table. The broad-minded thinking of Geddes, Mumford and Henry Wright, in which the sociological implications of planned communities was taken into account, is now standard, but was originally considered 'crack-pot' (Churchill, 1994, p. 247). The problem was that planned communities, as with the neighbourhood unit, became proposals for an alternative social structure. In a manner similar to City Beautiful ideology, there were social and moralistic overtones. Yet it is important to note that Howard's notion of the social community was based on collective ownership, not on specific physical forms (Ward, 2002).

Thus the same arguments used to justify disassociating the City Beautiful from its rhetoric apply here. The case was made that Beaux Arts Classicism can be appreciated without needing to endorse absolutism. Similarly, the domestic ideals of mid-nineteenth-century writers who made the suburban ideal popular, like Catherine Beecher (*A Treatise on Domestic Economy*) and Andrew Jackson Downing (*Cottage Residences*), and who glorified the individuality of home and the sanctity of family life, do not need to be adhered to in order to appreciate the utility of the planned communities they helped to inspire. In reality, some motivations behind the planned community will seem valid and even honourable, while others will not. The culture of the planned community has always been one of mixed messages and motivations. For example, residents of streetcar suburbs resisted annexation because, on the one hand, they saw the importance of localized communal association, but on the other they had a desire to remain free of poor immigrants (Warner, 1962). To the extent that the first does not *necessarily* require exclusion, it is possible to see a significant difference between these motivations.

American urbanism must find a way to appreciate and legitimize the design achievements of planned communities in a way that is free of 'bourgeois anxieties'. There can be little other recourse since the anxieties many earlier planned community residents felt amounted to a hatred of people unlike themselves (Fishman, 1987, p. 154). One way to counter this is to work decisively to ensure there is a social mix where none existed before. Social mixing occurred 'naturally' in pre-industrial cities. With the onset of industrialism, provision of a range of housing unit types became a matter of necessity – the company town of Lowell had to include housing for single women while Kohler had to include housing for single men. Garden city-inspired development may have included flats for single tenants, bungalows for the elderly, and cottages for the middle class. In Bournville George Cadbury combined low-density housing and smaller detached housing for workers, and Pullman provided a range of housing types. The bourgeois of early suburban enclaves often provided housing for all incomes if only for the purpose of housing their employees, or later, to house workers in industries that had moved out to the periphery.

But planned communities had the option of providing or not providing, specifically, for social integration. The planned communities selected here often did provide for a diverse social structure by carefully mixing a variety of housing types. The deliberateness of providing for a range of social needs is important to emphasize since there is a general perception that the planned community has always been exclusively for the wealthy. Histories of planned neighbourhoods in particular tend to stress social homogeneity as a prevailing idiom (see Banerjee and Baer, 1984). It is true that entities as entrenched as the Federal Housing Administration attached restrictive covenants to promote social homogeneity in various types of planned developments. But despite the policies of the FHA, the importance of social heterogeneity was in fact recognized, and was actively being promulgated by many planned community advocates.

In dense urban environments like Manhattan, social mixing could be achieved through the provision of quality public spaces, and Olmsted's pride in accomplishing social integration in Central Park was justified. But the planned community could not engender diversity on the basis of density alone – it had to accomplish this objective more deliberately. Company towns paid attention to it for philanthropic and practical reasons, but moving beyond individual commitment to social mixing usually required governmental support. It was through public backing that planned communities like Yorkship Village were at least initially able to retain their affordability. This simple reality and the inability to effectuate it is what has most compromised the planned community ideal.

Conflicts

Whereas some will view the planned community as an embodiment of civic spirit, functionality, beauty, and plain common sense, others will see it as escapist, exclusionary, and controlling. Where one observer will see the planned community as logical and reflective of the best of human endeavour, another will see it as nothing more than an insidious quest to find the most bankable version of that elusive quality known as charm. Where some will see an efficient reliance on past urban forms, others will see repetition and expediency. Instead of branching out and devising new, more responsive city forms, some interpret the application of planned community elements as demonstration of ignorance at the multiplicity of forms available (Lynch, 1966).

The problem the planned community has is rooted in its low intensity, high order nature. Even the City Beautiful at least took the existing city as its starting point. The planned community starts with a *tabula rasa*, which can be seen as an unrealistic attempt to freeze human activity patterns. Any effort that involves the laying out of city form according to abstract principles of geometry can be interpreted as an attempt to oversimplify the true nature of cities.

Perhaps this underlies the reason why the planned community is so prone to misapplication. It was a common complaint of garden city advocates that the term 'garden city' was being co-opted by faux garden city knock-offs. One contemporary complained that whenever there was a need to claim good planning practice the term 'garden' was tacked on. 'This confusion is serious, because the term "garden city" has a precise meaning that is possessed by no other term' wrote Purdom (1921, p. 15). But it has always been difficult for the exquisitely conceived planned community to retain control over its design. The seriousness of this problem lies in the piecemeal extraction of elements, epitomized by suburban design as it evolved after World War II. The design by Olmsted at Riverside, for example, with its curvilinear streets and wide front lawns, did not translate well into an automobile-dominated, large-scale suburban form. Nevertheless, the extraction of this motif was readily misapplied in the suburbanization that came a century later. Largely this was a matter of the vast increase in scale, but it was also a function of attention (or inattention) to detail, massing and layout.

This is not to say that there is something innately wrong with curvilinear form found in suburban development. Interestingly, according to Kostof (1991), organic street patterns were historically associated with communities of mixed classes and incomes, in Antiquity and in the Middle Ages. And organic, curvilinear form was historically not limited to low-density suburban development. Curved features were a significant part of many great cities, including Athens and Rome. What matters is how the elements of connectivity and context were handled, how elements of form were treated in relation to street pattern and curvature. The problem for American urbanism has been a remarkable insensitivity to these contextual considerations.

Radburn is the classic example of inappropriate extraction. Its culs-de-sac and superblocks, posited in one of the first functional street plans in the U.S. in which roads were arranged hierarchically, may only work well in the context of a self-contained community where street patterns are interconnected and part of a complete circulation system. Such a system required paying careful attention to the way in which cul-de-sac access tied into the rest of the development. Integration of elements was everything, and the designers of Radburn saw it as the basis of their innovation. What was new at Radburn was the combination of design proposals to form a 'new unity'. Because of these clear examples of success, the superblock was labelled an 'admirable device' by Mumford (1951, p. 11), one that he believed should have been picked up on even earlier in town planning. But without an integrated system, the use of elements like culs-de-sac produced sub-optimal development. Reston, Virginia's appropriation of Radburn concepts is often given as an example. There, open spaces were too large, densities were too low, and the connectivity of the system failed.

Another example of piecemeal adoption of elements was experienced when the Federal Housing Administration promoted suburban development through manuals like *Planning Profitable Neighborhoods* (1938). The pamphlet ensured the adoption of curvilinear street arrangements, promoted as being low-risk, but did so without the necessary integration of street and pedestrian networks and attention to scale requirements that were essential (Kostof, 1991). The legacy of Radburn is that the practice of adopting innovative design features piecemeal became standard practice (Birch, 1980*a*). Because of the unfortunate misapplication of selected ideas, Radburn is often cited as being a major contributor to suburban sprawl (Van der Ryn and Calthorpe, 1986). Had housing developments appreciated the importance of integrated, holistic design rather than street layouts with uniform setbacks, side yards and lot widths, the banality of the post-war landscape may have been lessened.

Even if it were possible to adopt elements more completely, some critics see a fine line between the 'new unity' of planned community innovation, and anachronism. One reason is that the scientific wisdom of planners working from the perspective of the complete planned community can become outdated even very soon after proposals are made. This was particularly true of the way the automobile affected planned community design. The 'scientific principles' Olmsted, Jr. applied at Forest Hills Gardens quickly became unscientific when the design inadvertently channelled heavy traffic through town (Stilgoe, 1988). Similarly, critics question whether it is possible for the planned community to generate a certain type of urbanism unless the transportation system upon which that urbanism has been based is also copied. According to this view, elements of the planned community are tied to the transportation system that produced them, 'and can no more escape this dynamic than a creek can escape the watershed it is part of' (Marshall, 2000, p. 33). Now, in the face of globalized consumer networks of activity, the planned community and its localized networks seem illusory. Ironically, the ability of such local systems to succeed may in fact be dependent on how externally linked they are. The question is, to what degree does a Starbucks in a planned community – globalized capital in an environment dependent on localized social networks – create a disjuncture of sorts?

This relates to the fact that the commercial component of the planned community has always been difficult to maintain. Riverside, Illinois went bankrupt in part because of its failed commercial aspect. Howard's first garden city, Letchworth, was in grave financial straights from the start, and Howard's detailed schemes of public financing proved unworkable. Howard was unrealistic about the commercial component of his cities. Letchworth developed only one-eighth of the shopping area Howard envisioned, which was really all a community of the size of Letchworth could be expected to support (Barnett, 1986). Later developments like Baldwin Hills Village fell victim to budget cuts, and the public facilities and commercial areas that were considered essential components had to be omitted. Such communities, lacking a commercial component, began to look a lot less like towns and a lot more like dormitory suburbs. In the end, planned communities that have been able to achieve a healthy mix of land uses, including especially a mix of housing unit types, are those in which some form of socialization of land value took place. What this means is that the importance of the planned community for American urbanism extends beyond design to matters of policy structure and financial organization. Early garden city proponents understood this. Their developments were not just plans and design, they were 'creative organizations' (Purdom, 1921, p. 45) that possessed dynamic energy in pursuit of an ideal.

Looking at this criticism through a historical lens it is striking how quickly the design of the planned community could become 'outdated' in light of technological changes. Virtually every planned community type was linked to some technological improvement, first steam-ferry networks, then railroads, then horsecars, then streetcars, then automobiles. Yet the view that technological change automatically renders a previously conceived development type unusable seems extreme. It would be inconceivable to claim that the urban system of Europe, much of it put into place before the Industrial Revolution, is now obsolete because of its association with various outdated technologies. What is required of the planned community may simply be that it pays attention to multiple determinants and requirements of urban form – some technological, some artistic, some social.

There is also the question of adaptability. The finality of the design and spatial-geographical principles of the planned community are seen as unduly rigid. Forest Hills Gardens, according to Stilgoe, is an example of a planned community that was unable to absorb change, and therefore new requirements – parking lots, for example – proved disastrous, marring its 'jewel-like perfection' (Stilgoe, 1988, p. 238). But adaptability is also about the ability of inhabitants to appropriate the urban artefact they inherit. Unfortunately, sometimes this was blocked. There are examples where control in the planned community conflicted with residents' needs, for example when they wanted to hang their laundry in the street at Saltaire but were prohibited by Sir Titus Salt (Creese, 1992). On the other hand, it could be argued that it was the lack of control that undermined residents' needs in the first place, for example when back-to-back housing eliminated space for laundry hanging altogether.

Americans are not very happy with being the objects of social control. Stilgoe argued that the 'corporation-owned, worker-inhabited company town, whatever its physical appearance, grated on the nerves of visitors and inhabitants alike' (Stilgoe, 1988, p. 238). This was due to its 'company town' stigma and its inability to respond to American individualism. There was a distrust of the planned company town in the same way that there was a distrust of big government and socialism, and by the 1920s, the ideal of the American 'do-it-yourselfer' took on the patriotic tone of

American capitalism and free enterprise. Even designers of the planned community were aware of the problem of overt social control. Atterbury, the architect of Forest Hills Gardens, complained that the term 'model' community attached to it a 'sanctimonious atmosphere' that at least he was not intending (Atterbury, 1912, p. 317). Richard Ely's 1885 'social study' of Pullman showed sensitivity to this when it brought out the fact that not one of its 8,000 residents dared to openly give their opinion of the town. Clearly the experience at Pullman emphasized the danger of attempting to squelch the American spirit. Where great industrialists may have thought of the planned company town as a logical extension of corporate control, their experiences with unhappy, discontented workers quickly undermined the idea of the worker engineered for happiness and contentment. The planned community offered the promise of security and harmony, but it shunned the reverse, equally magnetic values of adventure, expansion and desire.

It is curious how seriously the social goals of the planned community have been taken by some planners. One planner writing in the 1940s bragged that only 3.2 per cent of the families of one planned community failed to take part in community life, since 'it was an unusual family that was not observed to grow and expand in community mindedness in such an environment' (Tylor, 1939, p. 182). But there was always a danger that this thinking would backfire. During the New Deal, communitarian goals were criticized as being socialistic. The Greenbelt communities were labelled a 'dangerous communist experiment', and even the socialist tendencies of the cooperative grocery stores they contained were debated (Easterling, 1999, p. 172). Social cohesion goals could be viewed as 'social cleansing' (Schubert, 2000, p. 135). It may be easy to overlook the social naiveté of Progressive Era planners, but Nazi admiration of garden cities and neighbourhood units (Schubert, 2000) has been seized upon by critics as evidence of the insidiousness of claims about social cohesion in the planned community.

It is true that the planned community endorsed social mixing, but that mix was selected from an incomplete socioeconomic strata. Forest Hills Gardens is an interesting case in this regard. It was one of the most tightly controlled planned communities, and its social goals were explicit. A brochure advertising the Gardens declared: 'The Gardens is NOT and never will be a promiscuous neighborhood' (Stilgoe, 1988, p. 228). The owners believed they could obtain this goal by requiring character references for prospective tenants. In spite of an innovative blending of housing unit types, and the fact that the developers were sensitive to the need for income diversity, there was an explicit attempt to create a community that was white, middle-class, Protestant, homogenous, and 'congenial'.

There are two central ironies present in the social control critique of the planned community. First, the planned community was usually conceived of not as limiting to the individual but as a conduit for freedom – freedom from the tyranny of the city, from social pressures, from financial worries, from want of the basic needs of daily life. It was the reason garden city advocates were often hostile to the City Beautiful movement, since Burnham's planning approach was viewed as intolerant of freedom and the rights of the individual (Manieri-Elia, 1979). According to proponents of the planned community, there was greater affinity between the planned community and the freedom envisaged by social utopias popularized in the nineteenth century than between the planned community and the City Beautiful. Social utopias were generally conceived of as embodying not only religious, political and economic freedom, but sometimes also sexual freedom (Meyerson, 1961).

Second, the main alternative – private suburban construction not organized into planned communities – did not engender greater freedom. What was realized instead was that pursuit of private gain often directly conflicted with the communitarian basis of the planned community. Unwin put it this way: 'our towns and our suburbs express by their ugliness the passion for individual gain which so largely dominates their creation' (Unwin, 1909, p. 13). In the U.S., the relinquishing of control to private speculation did not produce a freer interpretation of the American spirit, it only homogenized it. The idea that mass production of housing without benefit of community planning was somehow more in line with American individualism is an incongruity that even detractors of the planned community recognize. The potential antidote, then, was the aesthetically controlled planned town in which individualism was tamed, and cooperation coerced into finding its expression.

The communal goals of the planned community are especially seen as contradictory to the modern, technologically-enhanced world of far-flung social networking. Local communities of propinquity, according to some critics, have become irrelevant, and trying to get them back is another example of anachronistic thinking much like the idea that pre-automobile urban forms are viable as real places. The notion of the 'community of place' is, critics contend, a pre-automobile, pre-internet relic, and in the cold light of non-proximal modes of community, shared space seems superfluous. David Brain has rebutted this by pointing out that the real issue is loss of civility rather than community. While proximally-based community may not be as important, our capacity for public life, our ability to 'maintain a sense of order and trust in impersonal relations', and our 'embedding' of personal communities in a larger framework are all dependent on 'the durable construction of the features of a common world' (Brain, 2005).

Webber's non-place urban realms challenged the social and economic validity of neighbourhood organization, the building block of the planned community (Webber, 1963). Gans' study of Levittown (1967a) and Banerjee and Baer's study of neighbourhood perceptions (1984) reached similar conclusions. Critics maintain that planned communities are an exercise in abstraction, where the essential elements of the complexity of the city are sorted out, abstracted, and frozen for easier manipulation and management. They argue that cities, towns and even neighbourhoods cannot be recreated by extracting certain key variables and reapplying them. There can be no re-creation of urbanity by applying numbers and thresholds. The human settlement process must be conceived of in terms of complex systems of organization and not, as Jacobs termed it, a 'two-variable system of thinking' (Jacobs, 1961, p. 435). Jacobs pointed out that the 'multiplicity of choices and complexities of cross-use' cannot possibly be pinned down by the community planner and distilled into holistically conceived settlements.

Critics have questioned the legitimacy of the fully arrived planned community, articulated all at once. The organized complexity of urban development described by Jane Jacobs is, in contrast to the planned community, believed to be a process of gradual, incremental, emergent complexity, and can be impeded (if not completely undermined) by the attempt to build it single-handedly at one point in time. Despite claims that the element of time will eventually foster a new, naturally evolved urbanism, the planned community requires commitment to policies regarding schools, land use and retail that are fixed (Herbert, 1963).

This is one way in which planned communities are interpreted as being anti-urban, a point which planned community proponents are unwilling to concede. In the anti-urbanism debate about planned communities, garden cities were often regarded as the worst offenders. They could never accommodate the wishes of some people to be 'in the very hub of things' (Lewis, 1916, p. 307). The idea of a communal village, even with an urban face on it, is seen by some as intrinsically ruralist (Harvey, 1997). Almost immediately upon their proposal, garden cities were considered monotonous, dull, and lacking in the sociability requirements that were readily satisfied in cities. When the attempt was made to legitimize garden cities in terms of public health by citing statistics on infant mortality in cities, critics countered that the answer should be to clean up the city, make it compact but healthy, and not proliferate the 'monotonous diffuseness of garden cities' (Lewis, 1916, p. 308).

In Britain, Thomas Sharp was one of the first and most prolific critics of what he believed was an anti-urban ideology underlying the garden cities movement. He found their 'little dwellings crouching separately under trees' to be 'mean and contemptible'. What he advocated, instead, was 'sheer, triumphant, unadulterated urbanity', which he believed garden cities were attempting to undermine (Sharp, 1932, p. 163). Garden city advocates resented the charge that 'in a garden city the garden comes first and the city comes afterward' (Lewis, 1916, p. 308), but their rhetoric could easily be interpreted that way. The Garden City Association of America explicitly pushed for 'a good home in a country community' (Scott, 1969, p. 90).

Planned community culture cannot deny its tradition of denouncing the existing metropolis. Ruskin, for example, once proposed that New York City should be levelled and not rebuilt, and advised that people should 'make the field gain on the street, not the street on the field' (Lang, 1999, pp. 19, 43). In fairness, Ruskin loved cities, but only when they looked like works of art. Industrial, commercial, technological, mercantile cities – all were to be subordinated to art. The city was meant to concentrate 'within its sacred walls the final energies and the lofty pleasures' of man, a 'treasure-house' of the best humankind had to offer in artistic and cultural terms (Lang, 1999, p. 35). Ruskin, therefore, was unwilling to appropriate the messy diversity that inevitably coincides with cities.

The neighbourhood unit is associated with anti-urbanism as well. Creese (1967) pointed out that the neighbourhood idea has roots in rural society, drawing on the agrarian village admired by garden city advocates and articulated in plan and form by Parker and Unwin. Ruskin and Morris based their critique of industrialism on the 'fracturing of the agrarian sense of communal interdependence', which, it was hoped, the neighbourhood unit would re-establish (Miller, 2002, p. 100). Clarence Perry had a definite bias against big cities, and his 1939 book *Housing for the Machine Age* is full of anti-urban rhetoric. In the first few pages he includes a quote which says 'The city has done things to us . . . city people are more nervous and more of them go insane'. Perry then lays out his plan for rectifying 'how ruthlessly the city has disrupted the family nest' by ensuring that new housing is constructed as part of a neighbourhood unit: 'dwellings set in the environment that is required for the proper development of family life' (Perry, 1939, pp. 23–24).

The anti-urban critique is not limited to garden cities and picturesque suburbs. And it extends beyond the suburban focus of Perry. The planned industrial town has been interpreted as anti-urban because of its strained economic structure. The merger of factory and town was seen as an artificial alliance that did not mirror true urbanity. Cities are made up of complex interactions from a diverse set of enterprises, not just a factory, housing, and services for factory workers. What is missing is reciprocity. The industrial town subsumed the social life of the town, combining urban life and economic productivity in such a way that the city was, in a sense, annulled. People, housing and services existed as a direct function of work productivity, not as a function of their own needs for investment or production of capital (Dal Co, 1979). Thus there was no system of growth outside of the factory.

Anti-city feeling in the planned community has always been a matter of degrees, since planned communities were not all of one type. The garden city interpretations of Yorkship Village and Greenbelt, Maryland can be contrasted. Greenbelt was aimed at deconcentration in the form of planned communities, but the focus was explicitly on escaping the city, and then later, to paraphrase Tugwell, tearing down the slums and making them into parks (Arnold, 1971). The difference in intention with wartime industrial housing is significant. In Yorkship Village, for example, the mix of housing types, land uses, the attention to picturesque elements and the distribution of civic space show an affinity for urbanism that deconcentration specialists seemed to lack. This was not true of all planned communities, nor is it necessarily a condition of location. The fact that a new community was sited away from an existing city did not automatically make it anti-urban. Sometimes the location of the planned community was more a function of financial necessity, a matter of needing to build on cheap land, and cheap land was usually more available at the periphery. This was the case for Nichols' Country Club District, built on land that was, at the time, beyond the municipal transportation system.

Why should starting anew be labelled 'unurban' (Krieger, 2002, p. 52)? Lewis Mumford was certainly willing to have an open view of what was urban and what was not. He defined the garden city as the 'antithesis of the suburb', not rural, but instead 'the foundation for an effective urban life' (Mumford, 1968, pp. 39–40). It certainly was not Ebenezer Howard's intention to be anti-urban. He was trying to find the proper balance and proportion between nature and city. Garden city proponents were aware of the need for both urban density and vitality; they were attempting to achieve it minus the negative externalities. C.B. Purdom, writing in 1921, argued that, for the garden city, 'concentration up to a point is the essence of its being' (Purdom, 1921, p. 48).

The architecture of the planned community did not help it detach from its anti-city stigma. Revival of Gothic medieval style associated with many early planned communities was considered 'dishonest' (Lewis, 1916). Invoking the picturesque English landscape meant that there was an emphasis on the creation of scenic effects and thus more attention was being paid to visual landscapes and scenery, to vistas markers and rural imagery, than to the 'authentic' elements of urbanism. A planned community like Forest Hills Gardens, Stilgoe notes, was not just 'pretty as a picture . . . It *was* the picture' (Stilgoe, 1988, p. 232). The bourgeois culture of the suburb with its traditional architectural forms and village plans was particularly hated by the modernists. The response produced an 'adversary culture' (Trilling, 1979) where churches could look like factories and houses like office buildings, in an attempt to find an egalitarian architecture for the proletariat (Stern, 1981).

Planned communities often emphasized curvilinearity and open spaces – two elements that are not generally regarded in the U.S. as being hallmarks of urbanity. In fact, the winding roads of the picturesque suburb were conceived in response to the urban grid. The value of this design idiom is that it can be both landscape-responsive (i.e., context-sensitive) and an effective way to break up the monotony of the gridiron. As already discussed, the problem is more a matter of the way it was interpreted in subsequent suburban design. In the hands of large suburban developers, winding roads that were too long and too winding lost their functionality and conflicted with the urbanistic goal of connectivity.

The planned community has been critiqued for tending to water down urbanity.

Sometimes this goal was explicit, a deliberate attempt to 'ruralize the town and urbanize the country', in the words of the Spanish utopian planner, Arturo Soria y Mata (Eaton, 2002, p. 145). There are examples of skilful balance – the small, urbanized parks incorporated into Forest Hills Gardens, for example – but this balance has always been difficult. The problem of the 'urban compromise,' as David Schuyler calls it – the successful merger of town and county – is how to bring greenery and open space into the city (Jackson, 1985). In such noble planned communities as Letchworth and Hampstead Garden Suburb, the City Beautiful components of their designs have been interpreted as inappropriate injections of green space in inappropriate places (see Hall (2002) and Stern and Massengale (1981), who use the same critique but for different places).

The town-country merger ties into the final, most problematic aspect of the planned community: its social exclusivity. Even when sought, there is a question whether social integration was ever actually achieved. In Radburn, a survey in 1934 found no blue-collar workers anywhere in the development (Schaffer, 1982). Forest Hills Gardens was similarly white, middle-class and Protestant. Although it was intended to be a planned community for residents of modest income, land costs and the high quality of design and building materials quickly priced homes beyond the means of labourers. For American urbanism, there may be an opportunity to transform the integrative designs of the planned community into something more successful in social terms. But again, this is likely to be achieved only with deliberate effort, most likely requiring public involvement.

The way in which low-income groups were eventually accommodated – through the dividing up of buildings into smaller units, or the subdivision of lots, or the inhabitation of accessory units – is essentially the same approach used when the inclusion of lower-income groups is deliberate. The difference was how the community as a whole was coordinated, how the requirements of the public realm were to be maintained, how city services and facilities were to be provided. These collective elements are what drove costs beyond the reach of the poor.

It should not be the case that low-income groups can only infiltrate if, as Warner (1962) described the low-income settlement of nineteenth-century streetcar suburbs, the environment is degraded in the process. Yet this is precisely what Stein and Wright had in mind when they economized their developments after Forest Hills Gardens so that subsequent communities would not suffer the same, gentrified fate (Mumford, 1951). It is a planning truism that the 'bright side' of places that lack planning amenities is that they are a source of affordable housing (Ewing, 1990). For the planned community that had social goals in mind, this is an intrinsic paradox that worked to undermine even the most socially utopian communities. In this sense, the failed utopias of the nineteenth century did not fail because of economic weakness, but rather economic success.

Then as now, the planned community required a long-term commitment to community needs way beyond the short time frame of land investors and real estate developers. This has always made the planned community a tough financial sell as well as an unlikely provider of affordable housing on its own. For one thing, the planned community, whether it was Letchworth, Reston, or Kentlands, required a lot of funding for land and infrastructure up front. As the developer Alexander Bing admitted, the planned community would never succeed if built on 'the sole object of profit making' (Bing, 1925, p. 172).

Chapter Seven

Regionalism

To a greater degree than the three planning cultures reviewed so far, regionalism is already an amalgamated culture. In stern defiance of the plan-making approach that had come to dominate in the 1920s, the regionalism of Patrick Geddes, Lewis Mumford, Clarence Stein and Benton MacKaye was a synthesis of other traditions and ideas that had come before, and it attempted to fashion a new ideal that was simultaneously pragmatic, idealistic, and dedicated to reform. Mumford had described plan-making in *The Culture of Cities* (1938, pp. 389–390) as 'the belated mopping up after the forces of life have spilled over: never catching up with its opportunities, committed to drifting with the current, never tacking to catch a breeze'. The regionalists were to take a different approach to defining human settlement. They were not limited to multi-jurisdictional organization or clustered, multi-nucleated development. The source of their ideology was deeper.

This chapter outlines the low-intensity/low-order section of the grid by reviewing the regionalist approach to American urbanism, with particular focus on the defining work of the Regional Planning Association of America (RPAA). The regionalist perspective in America is rooted in the work of Geddes and the RPAA, which crystallized as the enigmatic movement that was 'partly romantic-poetic myth and aspiration, partly cultural revolt, and partly realistic response to the possibilities and challenges of a new technology' (Lubove, 1963, p. 83). The regionalist movement had two distinguishing features. First, it rejected the large metropolis, and thus had a distinctly different outlook to cities than the urban plan-makers. Second, it was deeply connected to the notion of the ecological region. This latter quality meant it was a forerunner of the environmental planning movement, working its way from Geddes and MacKaye, towards a transformation through the work of McHarg and, finally, aligning itself with present-day environmentalism.

Regionalism is the flip side of the planned community perspective. The two have always been intertwined for one obvious reason: the planned community

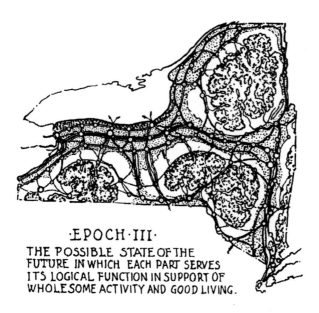

·EPOCH·III·
THE POSSIBLE STATE OF THE
FUTURE IN WHICH EACH PART SERVES
ITS LOGICAL FUNCTION IN SUPPORT OF
WHOLESOME ACTIVITY AND GOOD LIVING.

Figure 7.1. Urban development, according to the regionalists, is most importantly framed by natural land features. (*Source: Report of the New York State Commission of Housing and Regional Planning*, 1926)

was and is almost always discussed in terms of a regional context. From Ruskin on, regional planning has been about patterns of villages, towns and cities set in protected open space. Anyone advocating the development of self-contained units of human settlement knows that these units must be positioned geographically – that it is necessary to think of them in terms of an integrative framework. On this point there is little disagreement, and the idea has been operative since the regionalist perspective applied to city planning came to fruition roughly 100 years ago. From the regionalist point of view, the planned community was the best, most efficient way to accomplish a regional re-distribution of population and industry, all of which had become much too concentrated.

But how far should regionalism go? At one end is the view that true regionalism requires a new framework for civilization. At the other, regionalism is viewed simply as a more efficient and equitable way to manage resources. Against these two competing concepts, regionalism has been at the crossroads of one of the most significant divisions in planning culture. The primary conflict is not only about scale, but about social and economic structure. The tension was present in the famous exchange between Mumford and Adams following the New York Regional Plan Association's 1929 *Regional Plan of New York and its Environs*. Adams encapsulated the critique when he suggested that Mumford wanted to 'untie the traffic snarl in Times Square by rerouting the movement of wheat' (Adams, 1932, p. 207). The division was analyzed in the book *The American Planning Tradition* (2000) edited by Robert Fishman, where the views of Adams and Mumford are contrasted as representing the 'metropolitanists' vs. the 'regionalists'. The former was tied to metropolitan restructuring and governance, and the need to reorganize sprawl as a network of concentrated, walkable centres oriented around transit. The latter was more concerned with fitting urban development into its natural regional context. The conflict was fundamental and was not, as Sussman (1976, p. x) writes, 'a pious point of professional ethics', but rather a fundamental clash over political and social ideologies.

There are other interpretations of this essential division. One focuses on the split in the lineages of Olmsted versus Burnham; the former seen as radical and the latter as pro-business, one cutting across the grain of American society and the other working within it (Simpson, 1976). Johnson (1988) interpreted the division as the difference between progressive reformers and 'meliorist' reformers, one concerned with remaking the structure of society, the other seeking only to remedy its consequences. Yet another manifestation was reflected in the rejection of true garden cities in favour of (or in acquiescence to) garden suburbs. This transformation was seen in Unwin's 'great apostasy' of 1918–19 in which he embraced the satellite suburb as a more realistic alternative to the self-contained garden city (Hall, 2002, p. 182). To Mumford, whether suburb or satellite, both were drops in the bucket. What was needed was to change the shape of the bucket (Mumford, 1927).

But there are also strong connections. The three planning cultures of regionalism, plan-making and planned communities have all been intertwined, leaving out, for the most part, the incrementalist view. One indication of the connection is that its leadership overlapped significantly. Clarence Perry, for example, was a member of the RPAA but was also a key player in the RPA's *Regional Plan of New York and its Environs*. Members of the RPAA were strong supporters of the garden city movement. On a personal level, there was a great deal of interaction, including long correspondences between regionalists and planned community proponents.

In spite of the overlap, there are important reasons for treating regionalism as a separate culture. First, regionalists have always had a perspective that could be characterized as being from the outside looking in. The regionalist emphasis tends to be less about the specifics of internal urban form and more about urban positioning within its natural, regional context. As a result, regionalists tend not to be as closely tied to design, which makes their connection to plan-makers and community planners that much more important. Geddes' background as a biologist turned sociologist and geographer, rather than a designer, meant he was more inclined toward discovery and empiricism than design of the new (Hall, 1975). His concern was more about understanding society and its place in nature as a basis of planning. Second, the planned community and regionalist perspectives, once tightly connected, developed in very different ways, and over time became more separate. Developed in sync, planned communities went one way, regionalism another. Seaside, Florida is a lineal descendant of planned community culture, but the outcome of regionalism is exemplified by the work of McHarg and others who tended to be more focused on natural ecology than the internal configuration of planned communities. This is not to say that regionalists in the McHarg tradition were not involved in the creation of planned communities – McHarg's Woodlands community outside of Houston is one example – only that their focus on the qualities of urbanism was subordinated.[1]

The existence of a 'natural regionalism' has been broken down further. McHarg and Steiner trace two traditions of the 'organic' in American planning: landscape architecture and planning. The first they see evolving from Olmsted, and the second from Geddes, Mumford and MacKaye. A third strain, that of 'naturalist-scientist-conservationist' includes Howard and Eugene Odum, as well as Rachel Carson. All of these traditions, Steiner and McHarg write, come together in the work of McHarg, who stands as the 'heir and propagator' (McHarg and Steiner, 1998, p. 85). But the regionalism described here, the one that forms an important urbanist culture that can be used to define American urbanism, is the regionalism rooted in nineteenth-century concepts and evolving out of the work of the RPAA.

History

Looking at the world from a regional perspective is surprisingly old. As a formal structure, it has been traced back as far as the eighteenth century, when the natural and cultural geography of Europe seemed particularly suited to regional differentiation. A number of definitions evolved, ranging from a focus on human economy and cultural distribution to the identification of natural boundaries. These precepts were formulated much earlier than Geddes and Howard. Hall (2002) points out that the idea of towns of limited population surrounded by agricultural green belts is a recurrent theme found in the writings of Ledoux, Owen, Pemberton, Buckingham, Kropotkin, More, Saint-Simon and Fourier, all of whom were influential before 1900.

The liability of thinking in regionalist terms emerged almost simultaneously. One geographer summed up regionalism as 'trying to put boundaries that do not exist around areas that do not matter' (Kimble, 1951, p. 159). It is the fluidity of regions that has made them problematic as working concepts. Already when the New World was opening up for exploration, the cultural differentiation of Europe was eroding. These changes in regional definition have meant that the concept of regionalism is constantly being redefined. In the past century, it has shifted from European regional geography to what has been termed metropolitan regionalism – the idea that issues like housing, transportation and the environment, and the political governance of each, must be treated as an interconnected, multi-jurisdictional whole. This was a concept embraced by urban plan-makers. Olmsted's concept of linking parks into complete park systems, an approach also advocated by Burnham, was a regionalist, ecologically-motivated concept. Eliot and Baxter's regional parks proposal for Boston at the turn of the nineteenth century also had the essential elements of regionalist thinking – wanting to integrate city and country through a series of parkways and stream systems that flowed from country to city in the greater Boston metropolitan area (Scott, 1969).

This tradition, which focuses on the greater area surrounding a metropolis, is much different than the social reform movement started by Patrick Geddes in the early twentieth century and carried through by the Regional Planning Association of America in the 1920s. The doctrine of 'anarchistic communism based on freed confederations of autonomous regions', as Peter Hall described it, was a much more ambitious project, in geographical, social, and intellectual terms (Hall, 2002, p. 143). It was not simply an efficient new pattern of organized decentralization or an ecological approach to metropolitan parks planning. It was a project for social change involving a consideration of the social, political and economic implications of thinking and planning regionally.

Much has been written about Geddes' brand of regionalism, the relationship between Geddes and Mumford – see especially *Lewis Mumford & Patrick Geddes: The Correspondence* (Novak, 1995) – and the group that formed to implement his ideas. I will not recount this story, but highlight what is necessary in order to understand its relevance to American urbanism. To begin with, regionalism today bears limited resemblance to the Geddes variety. Importantly, however, it carries on the tradition, also consistent with Geddes, of the multi-nucleated settlement system, of the clustered, decentralized metropolitan region, and the idea of conceptualizing urban issues in regional terms.

Geddes is singularly important because of his direct influence on the emerging discipline of urban planning. He first had an impact through his lectures in Boston in 1899, and his writing of *City Development* published in 1904 (Boyer, 1983). His ideas were French in origin, based on the writings of the geographers Elisée Reclus (1830–1905), Paul Vidal de la Blache (1845–1918), and the French sociologist Frederic Le Play (1806–1882). The people that Geddes admired were those who wrote about the interrelationship between society and the natural environment. Paul Vidal de la Blache, the 'father of French human geography', for example, wrote encyclopaedic works on the environmental context of human activity (*Columbia Encyclopedia*, 2001). Geddes admired Le Play for his model of interaction between 'Place, Work and Folk', which Geddes, a botanist, expressed as 'Environment, Function, and Organism'. In his system, 'environment acts, through function, upon the organism: and the organism acts, through function, upon the environment' (Geddes, 1915, p. 200) . He extended this thinking in a number of synthesizing diagrams, some of which seem quite convoluted. What he was seeking was synthetic thought, and

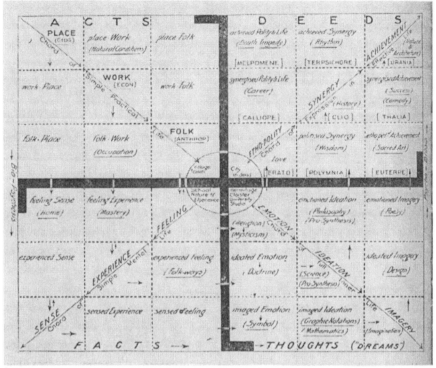

Figure 7.2. One of Geddes' intricate synthesizing diagrams. (*Source*: Patrick Geddes, *Cities in Evolution*, 1915)

synthesis relied on finding some underlying principle of unity in the relationship between human activity and the natural environment.

One of the most important principles guiding Geddes and the other regionalists was the notion of human cooperation. They envisioned a world guided not by Taylorist labour discipline, but by a sense of social justice, mutual aid, and communitarian spirit. In this thinking there was a connection to Reclus, who studied the history of human cooperation in, for example, the Greek *polis* and the medieval city. Given that these reformers were writing at a time when science was paramount, the radicalism of their views must be appreciated. Frederick Taylor's science of industrial management, in which workers were reduced to automatons, was embraced by both Lenin and Henry Ford, but it contrasted sharply with the communitarian individualism of Geddes and his regionalist associates.

This group also rejected the Darwinian idea of survival of the fittest. Tolstoy, for one, interpreted Darwin's 1859 *On the Origin of Species* to mean that Darwin's view of nature was 'might makes right' – that the 'struggle for existence' rendered morality irrelevant or indeterminable. That this was actually the point Darwin was trying to make has been long disputed. The implication for Geddes and other anarchic communitarians was that the Darwinian struggle was interpreted not as might makes right but rather that cooperation and mutual aid bring success, not elimination (Gould, 1997).

The Russian anarchist Peter Kropotkin (1842–1921), another strong influence on Geddes, challenged the Darwinian view that struggle for existence leads to combat. In his book *Mutual Aid: A Factor of Evolution*, published in 1902, Kropotkin argued that struggle leads to cooperation, a condition that Darwin also recognized, but that Darwin's successors, notably Thomas Huxley, squashed (interestingly, Geddes studied zoology under Thomas Huxley in the 1870s while at the Royal School of Mines in London). Evolutionary success, Kropotkin argued, was not about might, but about building on the natural tendency to find mutual support, a fact observed in nature as well as human social organization (Gould, 1997).

From the idea of the communal spirit and the existence of mutual aid as a natural, even Darwinian concept, comes the Kropotkin-Geddes emphasis on human-scaled production systems and decentralization of political governance. These are regionalist principles. To move this agenda forward, Geddes pushed the idea that human settlement should be analyzed in the context of its natural region. Kropotkin was advocating the same – analyzing human society in the context of nature. Views of nature and views of social reform were thus highly interconnected. What emerged was a nineteenth-century 'back to the land' movement that would free society from the oppression of authoritarianism. This was the tie-in to anarchism, the repudiation of established modes of authoritarian control, whether in the form of capitalism, the church, or the state. The mechanism for accomplishing this was to be the communitarian spirit of humankind. At the time, there was plenty of optimism that this was possible, and that the revolution was at hand. Reclus (1891), the son of a minister, believed that religion was finally becoming 'detached, like a garment'.

Replacing this authoritarian oppression would be an egalitarian society that was in close association with nature, and this was the essence of regionalism that Lewis Mumford transferred to the Regional Planning Association of America. Mumford did this via French regionalism. In France, disciples of Rousseau had formed groups in the mid nineteenth century that celebrated local French regional culture. In part they were protesting against centralized government, but what started as a romanticized celebration of local customs grew by 1900 to exert real influence on French regional structure with the establishment of the Fédération Régionaliste Française. This demonstrated to Mumford that a regionally decentralized governance and cultural life was entirely possible (Lubove, 1963). Regionalists of the RPAA believed this would happen through localization of production supported by transportation and social service planning.

In the view of Reclus and Geddes, the industrial city and the problems it was causing for human and natural environments was only being intensified by government and capital. Communism, in the form of a centralized, omnipresent state, was not the solution. There is a connection then to Proudhon, the leading left intellectual of France during the nineteenth century, an inventor of socialism, but someone who advocated decentralization and mutualism – power at the local level. Geddes, Reclus and Kropotkin were part of Proudhon's idealism. What was needed, they believed, was the establishment of harmonious, mutual aid societies, not centralized bureaucracies. Note, therefore, that the anarchic views of Geddes, Reclus and Kropotkin were not about violent overthrow, but instead about the establishment of small communities of consensus. In the reliance on cooperative spirit, government was simply not needed. Instead, positive environmental change was to be accomplished through the action of millions of individuals (Hall, 2002). In this there is some connection to incrementalism.

An egalitarian society needed to be in harmony with nature. This harmony, Geddes believed, must be based on a clear understanding of the cultural landscape – the 'civic survey', as Geddes termed it. The civic survey was more than a survey. It was a 'quasi-mystical' means towards reconstruction of social and political life (Hall, 2002, p. 149). Town planning required 'a synoptic vision of Nature to enable a constructive conservation of its order and beauty' (Geddes, 1915, p. v). In other words, town planning was dependent upon knowledge of the large-scale, regional complexities of the landscape and the human response to that landscape. How people behaved and responded to the conditions of the natural environment was to be understood at different scales, but the regional was paramount. Geddes' views on this were quoted in the opening pages of Mumford's *The Culture of Cities*: the city 'embodies the heritage of a region', as a kind of 'sign manual of its regional life and record' (Mumford, 1938, p. 7).

This was not the type of understanding nurtured in conventional schools and, like Reclus, Geddes believed in the value of a 'rustic' (rather than a 'bookish') schooling experience. Similarly, methodology in town planning became a vital concern. The civic survey was not just data accumulation, it was required to advance a holistic understanding of cities, set in their natural regions, and understood from a 'high' vantage point. Geddes regarded Aristotle as the originator of this idea, as the founder of 'civic studies', in which 'large views in the abstract' depended upon 'large views in the concrete' (Geddes, 1915, p. 6). It is easy to see why Geddes thought Burnham's approach extremely limited. It lacked the 'fuller study of civic', ignoring not only social and cultural life, but the 'spiritual possibilities' of cities as well (Geddes, 1915, p. 189).

One method Geddes used to accomplish deeper understanding of human activity and its relation to nature was the 'Valley Section', a concept diagram that served to integrate multiple conceptions, conditions, and time periods of human settlement. It was a heuristic device that was so compelling to later regionalists in the RPAA that they applied the idea to New York State and mapped a relief model of three regions consisting of plains, plateau and highlands, upon which the regional dispersion of people would occur. The value of these maps was that they could be used as tools for achieving synthetic thought. They would create a holistic understanding in which the 'Folk-Work-Place' scheme of Vidal le Play could be revealed. With his emphasis on past forms of civic life and traditional occupations, Geddes proclaimed the arrival or, more accurately, the rebirth, of a society embedded in its natural regional environment.

By comparison, the Industrial Age, which Geddes called 'Paleotechnic', was crude. The early phase of the industrial city was marked by slums and squalor. What Geddes was hoping for was a new industrial age giving rise to the Neotechnic city, which he believed was already an incipient industrial order that was beginning to replace Paleotechnic disorder. He used imagery like 'houses and gardens' and adjectives like 'wholesome and delightful' to describe this new order. It would be tied to the land, communal, egalitarian, and accomplished by developing a clear understanding of the difference between the 'Inferno' and 'Eutopia' (Geddes, 1915, p. 40).

Geddes had a tendency to ramble, both in speaking and writing, yet his ideas were powerful and he had an immense following. Mumford was especially affected, and much has been written about their long correspondence and relationship (Novak, 1995). In the 1920s, the regionalist ideas spun by Geddes in the earlier part of the century were organized and recast in the form of the RPAA, a New York-based group rarely exceeding a membership of twenty, and whose core members consisted of Mumford, Clarence Stein, Henry Wright, Frederick Lee Ackerman, and Benton MacKaye.

According to Lubove (1963) the origins of the RPAA can be found in the post-World War I housing crisis, which confirmed the necessity of community planning as an antidote to speculative city-building. Stein, Wright, and Ackerman, who have already been encountered in the context of the planned community, were thoroughly involved in postwar planning projects. All three can be characterized as garden city architects, and all had relative success in accomplishing garden city-like development projects. MacKaye's influence marks a different stream, one which set the stage for the evolution of regionalism towards environmentalism.

The group was officially formed in 1923 when it met with Geddes in New York and developed a programme consisting of the following: a plan for regionally-based garden cities; the establishment of a better relationship with British planners; projects to support MacKaye's Appalachian Trail; coordination with the American Institute of Architects' Committee on Community Planning in an effort to instil regionalist thinking; and surveys of important regional areas, such as the Tennessee Valley (Hall, 2002). The core of the AIA's Committee, formed two years earlier, were Stein, Wright and Mumford. The RPAA was thus essentially a splinter group from the AIA that combined forces with, most notably, MacKaye. Through his descriptions of folklands and wilderness trails, MacKaye was the conceptual link between his own conservation movement and the community planning emphasis of the AIA Committee (Thomas, 1994). The quintessential regional planning project – the Appalachian Trail – had been spelled out by MacKaye in the *Journal of the American Institute of Architects* in October, 1921.

Alongside the conservationist perspective infused by MacKaye, the architects of the RPAA were, according to Lubove (1963), primarily concerned with affordable housing. Throughout the 1920s, they focused on ways to promote quality housing and planning and do so at a minimum cost. One of the most important publications in this regard was Henry Wright's 1929 *Some Principles Relating to the Economics of Land Subdivision*, in which Wright worked out the most efficient (i.e., cost saving) means of land development. Later cost-conscious proposals included Wright's *Rehousing Urban America*, published in 1935. Because of this focus, they conducted meticulous analyses of wasteful land use practices, and they insisted on techniques that would save infrastructure costs. One strategy was to promote the block rather than the lot as the primary increment of community planning because it eliminated wasted space. Speculative building practices, they argued, were tied into the increment of the lot – a highly wasteful and cost inflating ritual. This, incidentally, was a strategy carried through by CIAM in the 1930s and beyond.

Intellectually, the group was influenced not only by Geddes and the French regionalists, but by a number of American intellectuals of the era. These included sociologist Charles Horton Cooley for his perspective on the significance of primary social groups, the economist Thorstein Veblen, who was a strong critic of the way in which *laissez-faire* economics and big business were influencing American culture, and the philosopher John Dewey for his theories about knowledge and the processes of inquiry. To these can be added the philosopher Josiah Royce, who advocated 'informed provincialism' in the Jeffersonian tradition, and Frederick Jackson Turner, the famous historian who provided an historical perspective on Royce's view of localism (Thomas, 2000). The conservationism running through the RPAA was inspired by Emerson, Thoreau, and George P. Marsh's *Man and Nature, or Physical Geography as Modified by Human Action*. Published in 1864, it was, according to Mumford, the first scientific study of environmental degradation (Dal Co, 1979).

The definitive statement of the group was the 1925 *Survey Graphic* collection, called the 'Regional Planning Number', which Hall (2002) regards as one of the most important documents in the history of city planning. It was a proclamation where, following on the wisdom of a 'long-bearded Scot', the group of 'builders and rebuilders' pinned their hopes on a new concept, or at least a new articulation of an old concept – the Region (*Survey Graphic*, 1925, p. 129). They believed in technology as a means for accomplishing this new pattern of regional settlement. But they were not technocrats, nor were they advocating technological determinism. MacKaye's definition of planning was that it should be guided by nature. Planners could be successful if they allied themselves with 'the amateur revealer of life's setting', or, in other words, understood human life. Dal Co (1979, pp. 214, 257) characterizes this purity of thought as representing 'the final search for a reconciliation between the world of ethics and the world that was becoming technical', where the reconciliation could be attempted in a way that was 'uncontaminated by the terms of politics'.

This emphasis equated regionalism with the protection of indigenous, regional cultures against nationalist, homogenizing trends. Mumford (1931) quoted Proust from *Remembrance of Things Past* to explain where the indigenous culture came from: 'the rich layer imposed by the native province from which they derived their voices and of which indeed their intonations smacked'. The southern regionalists, under the leadership of Howard W. Odum, pushed the idea that the celebration of local, vernacular culture would be undermined by cities because of their concentrated power and wealth (Odum, 1945). This way of thinking guaranteed that the celebration of provincialism would mean the rejection of the metropolis. In MacKaye's terminology, it was the protection of 'Indigenous America' from 'Metropolitan America'. The latter was an outcome of the consumer-based economy that, perversely, tended to consolidate in the large metropolises of America.

The 'fourth migration', as Mumford called it, was the decentralized movement outward from the city centre that was already occurring, and which the Regionalists wanted to seize upon as an opportunity to produce a more humane settlement pattern. The first migration wanted land, the second industrial growth, the third financial and cultural concentration, and the fourth wanted to expand outward. Metropolitan concentration and congestion was thus becoming obsolete because of a rash of decentralizing inventions – the car, telephone, radio and power sources – a technological revolution. The decentralizing of the metropolis could easily be accomplished by taking advantage of these new technologies. The automobile, the telephone, electricity – all of these inventions could be used not to concentrate population and goods into 'Dinosaur Cities', as Stein called them, but instead to distribute them regionally (Stein, 1925).

This strategy required a new brand of economic thinking, and Stuart Chase (1888–1985) provided it. Chase was a prolific writer interested in many topics, including economic theory, consumer rights, comparative culture, and semantics. He was active in organized labour, and was critical of the advertising and pricing policies of manufacturers. He was particularly active in consumers' rights at a time when the nation was transforming into a mass consumer economy. Later, Chase was very influential in FDR's New Deal programme, and the title 'New Deal' derives from his 1932 book of the same name.

In Chase's view, government needed to play a strong role in economic planning. Private enterprise was not only wasteful, but unable to coordinate 'a million cogwheels' that needed to be 'aligned and oiled'. All of these industries pursuing their own specializations needed coordination in the form of master planning for the economic region – in short, planning for a geographical area large enough to be self-sufficient economically. The interrelations of industries needed to be closely followed and planned for, but this did not mean Marxism. It was instead 'orderly control' of industrial expansion and new investment, for the purpose of limiting the wastefulness of hit-or-miss economic activity that produced the megalopolis as well as environmental degradation (Chase, 1925).

Howard's garden cities fit nicely into this regional scheme for orderly growth although, as Lubove (1963) emphasizes, garden cities were not the only option. In fact MacKaye hardly even mentions garden cities in his great regionalist manifesto, *The New Exploration* (1928). With the holistic basis of the garden city, in which industry was placed alongside town and country to form the perfect, self-contained community, the regionalists understood that the garden city foot the bill for regional dispersion. MacKaye expressed his own version of Howard's regional dispersion diagram in his book, translated in terms of different types of metropolitan 'flows', the best of which channelled growth into 'intertowns'. The diagram looks remarkably like Howard's, but reflects a deeper concern with process, the movement of goods and people, and the interactions and patterns created (Lubove, 1963). But there was something added – conservationism. The American version of regionalism, exemplified by MacKaye in particular, thus

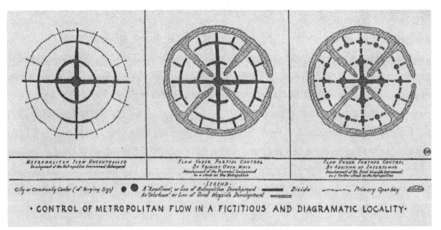

Figure 7.3. The control of metropolitan flow, by Benton MacKaye. On the far right, growth in the centre is controlled by the addition of 'intertowns'. (*Source*: Benton MacKaye, *The New Exploration*, 1928)

expanded Howard, Geddes and Kropotkin and added the necessity for natural resource protection explicitly (Hall, 2002). It was, as Mumford called it, the 'New Conservation'. What was being emphasized by the American regionalists was the need to balance human activity and nature by keeping settlement at the proper scale and level of self-sufficiency – good environmental practice combined with Thoreau's self-reliance and individualism, all coming together in medium-sized, regionally distributed towns (Mumford, 1925).

The conservationist ethic was visualized in regional mapping projects. Henry Wright's portfolio of maps, published in 1926 in the Report of the Commission of Housing and Regional Planning set up by New York State Governor Alfred E. Smith, a report with 'roots in the rich loam of premetropolitan life' was a precursor of McHargian overlay analysis (Sussman, 1976, p. 31). Here were maps of soil deposits, water supplies, rainfall, and economic and agricultural activities, all overlaid to show composite areas favourable to more versus less agricultural production. Composite maps showing areas more suited to reforestation were published to provide a regional framework for future development.

Again, the regionalists bet their money on new technologies. Wright's maps were organized in terms of three 'epochs' – economically independent and regionally distributed towns dependent on water power; growth concentrated in valleys dependent on steam power and rail systems; and the current, third epoch in which new technologies – cars, roads, and electric transmission lines – 'will lend themselves to a more effective utilization of all the economic resources of the state and to the most favourable development of areas especially adapted to industry, agriculture, recreation, water supply, and forest reserve'. Similarly, MacKaye's 'Townless Highway', an idea first published in *Harper's* in 1931, was about leveraging technology – cars – to deconcentrate and consolidate population in clusters that did not spill out from cities in an unplanned manner (Mumford, 1968). It was a more practical proposal than Stein and Wright's – forcefully simple, not unlike the Appalachian Trail. But, unlike the Trail project, and despite its commonsense simplicity, the Townless Highway never caught on.

The RPAA dissolved in the early 1930s at the same time, ironically, as Roosevelt was putting his regionalist plans into play. At their last meeting in 1933 at a week-long conference on regionalism held at the University of Virginia's Institute of Public Affairs, Roosevelt, then Governor of New York, delivered an address on his regionalist agenda. But when, as President, he put this agenda into practice via the Tennessee Valley Authority act, the regionalist vision faltered. In fact the demise of the RPAA has been linked to the 'extraordinary failure' of Roosevelt's attempts at regional planning (Hall, 2000, p. 26). The National Resources Planning Board (NRPB) was Roosevelt's main public relief agency, and through it planning on all levels, including regional, was significantly advanced, at least bureaucratically. It produced 370 major reports at all levels of planning activity, from bridge building to agriculture (Hancock, 1988). In 1933, under the New Deal, eleven regional planning commissions were established, but because they lacked control over implementation, their regional planning accomplishments were small. Ultimately, the New Deal association with members of the RPAA was the source of the latter's demise since it had the effect of muting its creative message (Sussman, 1976).

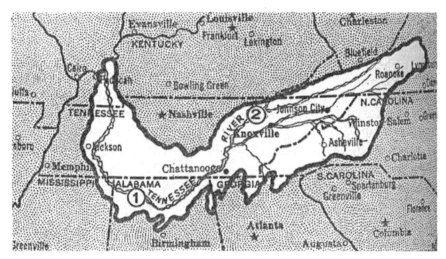

Figure 7.4. The Tennessee Valley Region, showing Muscle Shoals (1) and Cove Creek (2) site of Norris Dam. (*Source*: Thomas Adams, *Outline of Town and City Planning*, 1935)

It was the Tennessee Valley Authority (TVA), established in 1933, that was imbued with implementation authority (Hancock, 1988). Although the TVA is sometimes cited as the hallmark of regional planning in the U.S., it cannot be pointed to as a successful model of regionalism, at least not as the RPAA envisioned. Its main preoccupation was with dam building and promoting industrial and economic activity in the region. As a result, the TVA by 1960 had become one of the country's biggest polluters (Thomas, 2000).

Originally, the regionalists had high hopes for the TVA. Chase (1936, p. 287) considered it to be 'the promise of what all America will some day be'. But critics described it as a state-sponsored extension of monopoly capitalism. A similar interpretation by Thomas (2000) is that the TVA allowed Corporate America to capture the 'middle ground' – the very domain the regionalists were trying to use to implement their vision. The settlement patterns – indeed the regional culture – of thousands of people in the TV area were disrupted. There were vestiges of RPAA's 'organic territorial' structure, but the Tennessee Valley was more about developing resources for human use than creating regional structure (Friedmann and Weaver, 1979). Its experiments in redistributing population in the form of new regionally dispersed towns was also a failure. One town constructed, Norris, Tennessee, was small and largely insignificant, and the displaced population fell between the cracks. Amazingly, there was no organized system of resettlement in the region (Hancock, 1988).

In Europe the ideas of the RPAA fared better. This was clearest in London, which famously executed its Regional Plan under Patrick Abercrombie following World

Figure 7.5. The top photo of an Upland area in Tennessee was, according to Lewis Mumford, 'potentially the scene of a more intensive settlement that will conserve rather than blot out the natural foundations for a good and durable social life'. The bottom image is of the top of the Norris Dam, a TVA project. (*Source*: Lewis Mumford, *The Culture of Cities*, 1938)

War II, consisting of a green framework with eight new towns contained within it. Mumford thought the regional plan for the rebuilding of London exemplary, a mature outcome of Howard's garden cities model. There were other European examples. In Stockholm, Vallingby and thirty other satellite communities were constructed as part of the 'regional city' idea promulgated by the RPAA.

These examples contrasted sharply with the situation in the U.S. There, regional planning was reinvented as 'regional science', a scientific approach that stressed industrial location, economic modelling, and the establishment of growth centres for depressed regions, concepts which did not coincide well with the earlier regionalism of the 1920s and 1930s. The RPAA had sought social, ecological and economic balance, not economic stimulation policies organized around commerce and transportation systems.

The story of post-war urbanism was the rise of the 'centreless city', as Jackson put it, and as Harris and Ullman were able to capture in their 'multiple nuclei model' in the 1940s (Jackson, 1985, p. 265). With its muddled edges and haphazard pattern of land use, the centreless city was the antithesis of what the regionalists were hoping for. They might have agreed with whatever shift away from dependence on the central city occurred, but the realization of Geddesian 'ink-stains and grease-spots' made a mockery of the organized decentralization that was so essential to regionalist thinking. It seemed more akin to Wright's Broadacre City proposal, 'the climax of anti-urbanism', a settlement pattern that was 'everywhere or nowhere' as Wright described it himself (White and White, 1962, p. 209; Grabow, 1977, p. 116).

In addition, the regionalist perspective clashed with post-war city planning that took the form of downtown redevelopment. Whether the renewal was focused on rehousing urban slum dwellers or stimulating downtown economic development, neither of these post-war emphases were consistent with the regionalist view. Catherine Bauer, who had been a member of the RPAA, thought in terms of regionally dispersed, well-planned communities not unlike the Abercrombie model. But as the urban re-housers and the downtown redevelopers joined forces to carry out their urban renewal projects, the regionalist vision became increasingly marginalized. It could not have been otherwise, since developing housing on inflated inner-city land was completely antithetical to regionalism.

Jane Jacobs' attack on urban renewal did not exonerate the regionalist strategy, which she also disliked. Instead, regionalism began to define itself in a variety of different ways, from the economic modelling approach of regional science to systems of governance. By the time these regionalist perspectives came to dominate in the 1970s, the original conceptualization of regionalism by MacKaye, Mumford, and Stein was barely noticeable. For example, the book *Regional Planning*, published in 1983, made no mention of any members of the RPAA whatsoever, despite including a historical overview (Lim, 1983). Instead, the book defined regionalism on the basis of governance structure: supra-state regional planning, city-county consolidations, tiered government structures, councils of government, and special-purpose districts.

Thus, the definition of regionalism has changed dramatically over the past century. Devolving from the regionalism of the RPAA to systems of governance, the presence of regionalism today is sometimes defined as *ad hoc*, composed of a loose coalition of interests (Porter and Wallis, 2003). Not surprisingly, the capacity of government to address issues from a regional perspective is limited. The result has tended to be a focus on economic development rather than regional equity and environmental resource protection. *Ad hoc* groups lack an institutional framework, but even more profoundly, policies are formulated without benefit of a regional identity. Ironically, regionalism is often equated with the lack of local identity and self-determination, exactly the opposite of what the early regionalists were intending.

Connections

For practical reasons, it was regionalism defined as metropolitan coordination that took hold in the American planning consciousness. This occurred in part because that brand of regionalism was well connected to other cultures via Daniel Burnham, Thomas Adams, and John Nolen. Their legacy was a recognition that some elements extend out from a central place and connect at the intra-urban scale. Various types of 'systems', especially natural systems and transportation, were to be planned with this regional interconnection in mind. It started with the recognition, posited initially by Olmsted, that natural systems in a metropolitan region were cross-jurisdictional. For early planners like J. Horace McFarland, long-time president of the American Civic Association, it meant that cities should have more power, transformed into city-states that could self-manage. The unifying urban schemes of the 'Greater San Francisco' movement of 1906 were not dissimilar to New York's system of borough's and Boston's metropolitan planning board set up by Nolen and others (Scott, 1969).

Yet this way of thinking was, according to regionalists aligned with the RPAA, missing the point. Since regionalism as defined by the RPAA asked 'not how wide an area can be brought under the aegis of the metropolis', but instead how population can be distributed, metropolitan regionalism had profoundly dissimilar goals from the RPAA. More radically, the regionalist idea of a reconstituted central metropolis relied on changing the very processes of change, not just technological change within the same underlying system. This included scrapping the existing divisions of government, promoting common ownership of land, and reorienting the entire land development apparatus to reflect human, not capitalistic purpose.

American urbanism has been caught up in the sustained need to work out a perspective that encompasses both centralizing and decentralizing objectives. In addition to the Olmstedian tradition of emphasizing regional connections within the metropolis, there is a need to consider placing human settlement patterns in their natural, regional context. One of the most prolific themes in American urbanism is that a decentralizing population requires a method of organization. This was something emphasized by the ecological planning of McHarg, and in the framework of regionalism, the insistence that deconcentration be organized continues. Mumford put it succinctly in his essay 'A Brief History of Urban Frustration', that the regional scale of the city means that there should not be a single domineering centre, but a 'network of cities of different forms and sizes, set in the midst of publicly protected open spaces permanently dedicated to agriculture and recreation'. The metropolis would be *primus inter pares*, 'the first among equals' (Mumford, 1968, p. 219).

One of the appeals of regionalism and the reason it is an important component of American urbanism is its rejection of rigid rules and planning bureaucracies that seem unable to see the big picture. Just as Mumford stressed the importance of being able to perceive the future, not as 'the glorified extension of the dying present' but as emergent forms and trends, the best of American urbanism has tended to emphasize the importance of future direction (Wilson, 1983, p. 113). But this in turn brings up the central issue of pragmatics, the cause of failing to embrace the regionalism of the RPAA more fully. A key debate is whether the radicalism they proposed can be moulded into something more aligned with American political realities and still retain its integrity and value. Fishman wonders if the 'opening generation' Mumford had hoped for, to usher in the regionalist perspective, has finally, with a new, inclusive and more realistic voice, arrived (Fishman, 2001, p. xxi). Yet there is also the interpretation that, rather than appearing pragmatic when compared to the regionalism of Geddes, Mumford and MacKaye, the new regionalists appear equally quixotic. The goals of regionally distributed affordable housing, tax-sharing on a regional basis, mass transit, and regional growth boundaries may seem the most workable, but to date not even these less radical strategies have been particularly successful.

While American urbanism is not likely to be based on the establishment of new political and economic structures, on one crucial point there is agreement – that the underlying processes that created metropolitan degradation in the first place are themselves subject to change. This has the flavour of John Dewey and the pragmatists, and the regionalists, especially Mumford, made this point repeatedly. Like Dewey, there was a sense that any statement of knowledge only possesses this status provisionally, contingent upon whether it provides a better basis for human action.

This perspective coincided with the idea that new forms of human settlement may be entirely possible. Mumford optimistically hoped that these changing processes would foster an evolution of pattern more in line with human needs. Change would not simply be a matter of redirecting the existent urban trajectory, but would be more fundamental. This is a perspective that has been articulated recently by James Howard Kunstler (1993, 1996), whose books explore the theme that the 'fiasco of suburbia' is based on social and economic systems that are subject to change, and therefore the notion that sprawl as an urban form is somehow inevitable is a false premise.

It is hard to imagine how American urbanism could accommodate the radical change in social and economic structure advocated by the RPAA. There are continued calls for adjustments to land development, planning, and regulation canonized in conventional planning practice, but conventional structures are where urbanism is likely to dwell, at least in the short term. A different kind of connection to regionalism could be the way in which the RPAA operated – as idealists, as debaters, as innovators. It is this sense of vision and idealism that has a place in American urbanism. Regionalism as originally conceived can be thought of as a mode of thinking, a method, a spirit of engagement, a forum. In fact the RPAA rejected entrenched, bureaucratized regionalism in favour of optimism, proaction, and creative visioning. It was meant to be evolutionary, not stagnant. The prime objective was to 're-educate' rather than 'diffuse the existing stereotypes' (Mumford, 1951, p. 17).

Because the city was a 'collective personality' with its own unique character, the requirements of a diversified, versatile planning approach were intrinsic to good urbanism (Mumford, 1968, p. 17). The early regional planners thought that bold visioning required detachment from standardized patterns. Mumford knew that a model like the British New Towns program could, if stereotyped, eliminate 'the very richness and variety of concrete detail that is inherent in the notion of a city'. The trick was, and still is, the ability to differentiate between a fresh and inspired idea and an idea that will sour. This Mumford seemed to know. In the early 1960s he was already writing about the 'grave liabilities' of the office park and the shopping mall.

The question is whether American urbanists can effectively emulate the in-formality and intellectual stimulation of the RPAA. Perhaps this is what con-stant innovation requires, but the transference to urbanism implemented via bureau-cratized planning is obviously a different model. The RPAA deliberately rejected the word 'organization' and instead used 'association', because they wanted to remain 'unstructured and unconcerned' about official policy-making. They wanted to be a flexible group that respected each other's individuality (Lubove, 1963). The attitude MacKaye (1928, p. 227) sought was one 'not of frozen dogma or irritated tension, but of gentle and reposeful power'. That this attitude prevailed is reflected in the fact that the RPAA had no unanimous views about what, for example, the characteristics of the planned community should be in terms of optimal size. Nor was there any agreement on what the size of a region should be. MacKaye thought in terms of continents and Stein in terms of states, but there was no consensus on the definition of a region other than in the most abstract of terms (Sussman, 1976).

In addition to a potential connection to the outlook and approach of the regionalists, American urbanism can draw from their methodologies. This includes the language of 'visualization' and, relatedly, the power of community 'visioning' in the planning process. It is an emphasis on discovery and intimate understanding of human landscape, as laid out by Geddes and MacKaye. It was technical, but it was also instinctively artistic. MacKaye's emphasis on 'visualizing', in which he urged 'the new explorer' to 'speak softly but carry a big map' and Geddes' valley section survey techniques were part of a new tradition of inventory and understanding that moved across scale and time (MacKaye, 1928, p. 227). Almost everything had meaning and was looked at creatively for potential new insights. The early regionalists made use of participant observation, something relatively unknown at the time. They engaged in these innovative practices because, they believed, if this ability was cultivated properly, more could be visualized. Looking deeper at a forest revealed the food cycle; looking deeper at a landscape revealed its water cycle.

They were building on the idea that, in regionalism, vantage-point and perspective is critically important. A high vantage-point made sure that their knowledge was geographically broad, whether it was from the perspective of MacKaye's Appalachian mountaintop or Geddes' Outlook Tower. Only from high up could the natural framework of cities be perceived. What is particularly intriguing is how this perspective did not limit understanding to generalities – there was an emphasis on detail as well, a linking of the macro and the micro that is enviable and difficult. Geddes mapped the landscape meticulously, looking for interrelationships over time and space. The result has been described as a synoptic 'implosion' in which detailed surveys, embedded in a historical trajectory, were supposed to foster a kind of crystal ball reading of the future (Easterling, 1999).

All of this emphasis on survey, inventory and artistic perspective is important to the development of American urbanism because it focuses attention on exploration and discovery of human settlement rather than, exclusively, invention. MacKaye defined planning in precisely these terms: 'planning is discovery and not invention', an idea he promoted as a 'new exploration'. The important implication of this is that it places heavy weight on historical and present conditions, 'the potential now existing in the actual' (MacKaye, 1940, p. 349). The crystal ball reading of the future was there, waiting to be discovered by an artistic but also technical reading of existing conditions. The critique of this is that it can be self-limiting. Regional study, Kimble (1951) argues, is a personal portrait, a work of art, and although illuminating, rather limited in terms of scientific rigour and definitive analysis. It is possible that this criticism stems from the fact that the regional survey of Geddes had a radical social and political purpose.

American urbanism requires a counter-response to the celebration of innovation and novelty at the expense of context and historical tradition, a price that has taken a toll on American cities. This may not have been how the RPAA would have described their actions, especially given their acceptance of technological solutions. But the regionalist emphasis on discovery over invention, on finding new ways to visualize, is closely linked to the idea that innovation must be tempered and must work within an existing language of urbanism. Leon Krier has articulated the idea most cogently. He argues that tradition and progress are not in conflict, that there is no *zeitgeist* that dictates that urbanism must only have the mark of a particular point in time, but can and should instead 'transend the particularities of its age of creation'. There is no disconnect between being original and being traditional, because traditional architecture and urbanism are simply 'an inventory of genetic capacity' (Krier, 1998, pp. 71, 187). This is a clear affirmation of the artistic historicism of Geddes and MacKaye.

The emphasis on regional survey is yet another version of a theme that has pervaded all urbanist cultures – the importance of localism and sense of place. Here the theme has a regionalist twist. The ecological planning of McHarg, the landscape studies of J.B. Jackson, the architectural explorations of Scott Brown and Venturi, and the 'everyday urbanism' of Chase, Crawford and Kaliski all converge on the notion of rooting ideas in particular places with particular traditions. It is the basis of the movement in architecture known as 'critical regionalism', a phrase adopted by contemporary architectural historian Kenneth Frampton to describe an architecture rooted in local conditions, and recently adopted by some New Urbanist architects because of its local emphasis (Kelbaugh, 2002). Understanding the implications of place recalls the doctrine of appropriateness. Mumford knew the doctrine had been violated when he derided planning in the 1960s for producing 'the wrong type of development in the wrong place for the wrong purpose' (Mumford, 1968, p. 173). It was the emphasis on local knowledge that gave the regionalists the sensitivity to make this determination.

Another aspect of regionalism that is valuable for American urbanism has to do with the ability to traverse, and simultaneously consider, planning at the regional and the community level. The early regionalists seemed to be able to penetrate natural systems and the urban core simultaneously. They seemed able to move back and forth, and in fact interconnect with, multiple scales. Not everyone was convinced they could do it. Adams criticized Mumford as unrealistic for wanting to 'saddle' the Regional Plan with both a state-wide plan and a detailed city plan, two responsibilities that Adams believed would be difficult to engage simultaneously (Adams, 1932). But the whole basis of the RPAA was an interconnection between human settlement and regional context, and this meant, at least conceptually, the micro and the macro scale. It was an integration of community planning and conservationism that naturally occurred at the regional scale, but that had connections to the planned community as well. This was not unlike Stein's earlier conception of the 'Regional City', an idea taken up more recently by Calthorpe and Fulton (2001). They stipulate that designing the region operates on similar principles as designing the neighbourhood – 'parallel features' that reinforce each other at different scales.

This multi-scaled approach was one manifestation of the importance of integration and connectedness that ran throughout regionalism. Other examples include Mumford's four 'migrations' which were not just temporally distinct phases, but were conceived as needing to operate simultaneously. Another was the emphasis on studying multiple dimensions of places as an integrative endeavour that was meant to counteract the tendency toward specialization. Geddes' surveys were focused on the interactions of people, place and work precisely as a way to avoid this tendency. MacKaye's argument for three 'elemental environments', the primeval, the rural and the urban, was based on their fundamental connectedness, whereby the loss of any one had serious consequences for the others. In practice, the RPAA regionalists used an integrative, teamwork approach to develop Radburn, bringing multiple interests together to formulate their plan. The strategy of synthesizing disciplinary interests was a forerunner to today's emphasis on participatory planning, and had a significant impact on the positive response Radburn enjoyed within the planning profession (Birch, 1980a).

A final aspect of regionalism that is relevant to American urbanism is the idea of evaluating urban patterns in terms of inefficiency and waste. For example, there is a parallel condition between the wastefulness of the large metropolis, the RPAA focus, and the wastefulness of sprawl, the more recent embodiment of inefficiency and waste. Both are, or have been, dominant development patterns conceptualized as catastrophic and in danger of collapsing the whole urban system. The regionalist distaste for the inefficiency, waste, environmental degradation and social cost attributed to the large metropolis can now be associated with a similar set of costs attributed to sprawl. Both amount to a basis for articulating what American urbanism should oppose.

Conflicts

Despite the strong positive role of regionalism in the development of American urbanism, there are also significant sources of conflict, largely rooted in the divergent notions of what regionalism is supposed to be. To begin with, there are competing definitions of what a region is. This was previously viewed as an indication of flexibility, but it could also be seen as a source of conflict. RPAA regionalists defined the region as 'any geographic area that possesses a certain unity of climate, soil vegetation, industry and culture' (Mumford, 1925, p. 151). Now, a region is more likely to be defined as 'a large and multifaceted metropolitan area encompassing hundreds of places' (Calthorpe and Fulton, 2001, p. 15). This latter definition seems more aligned with Chicago School sociologist R.D. McKenzie, who predicted the demise of indigenous regional cultures in the wake of the emergence of the economic, functional region. No doubt this is coincident with the view that regionalism, as articulated by Geddes, Mumford, and Chase, was too radical and too socialist to be taken seriously. The conflict over regional definition is therefore rooted in the transformation of the regionalist approach to metropolitan regionalism, something quite separate from the brand of regionalism conceived of by Geddes and Mumford.

Another fundamental source of conflict stems from the fact that the regionalists were largely motivated by an outright rejection of large metropolitan areas. To the degree that environmental planning grew out of regionalism, the retention of the anti big-metropolis point of view can be regarded as an undercurrent that, some say, never went away, and that continues to stimulate conflict. Related to this, there is the perception that regionalism – or whatever part of it evolved into environmental planning – ignores the internal workings of large cities. It does this either because of a lack of caring or a lack of understanding, but in either case its focus on natural systems, despite claims towards multi-dimensionality and interconnectedness, excludes the existing city to some degree. On the worst occasions, this may even translate into a tendency to ruralize urban areas, or advocate low-density, rural development patterns that are indistinguishable from sprawl. On the other hand, the predominance of functionally defined regionalism has been criticized for being inconsistent with environmental processes (Spirn, 2000).

Yet it is often said that, despite their constant rhetoric about the evils of the metropolis, the regionalists were not anti-urban. Defenders of the RPAA have even called the claim that they were anti-urbanist the 'hysterical equivalent to political red-baiting' (Sussman, 1976, p. 29). Surprisingly, the regionalists made little effort to change this perception. In the film *The City* narrated by Lewis Mumford and shown at the 1939 World's Fair, the RPAA doctrine was elicited fairly crudely – the big impersonal metropolis was portrayed as bad, while small communities in touch with nature and village-like in social structure were portrayed as good. MacKaye's hometown of Shirley, Massachusetts, alongside Radburn, were presented in the film as models of good American urbanism. Given this kind of presentation, it is not unjustified to question the urbanistic commitment of the regionalists.

We know, however, that the contempt for the large metropolis was much more nuanced than simply being a matter of anti-urbanism. Mumford strongly criticized the new towns of Reston and Columbia because they lacked urbanity, overemphasized green space, and underemphasized compactness (Mumford, 1968). And all regionalists were united in their focus on the idea that the experience of place is the essential starting point of regionalism.

The debate that underlies the contrasting perspectives on how the existing city is to be treated is about whether the underlying processes of change are seen as something that can be dealt with proactively. As discussed above, there was agreement that the processes that created the industrial city in the first place are themselves subject to change, but this was not universally interpreted as reason to hope for the emergence of an entirely new urban pattern. Plan-makers sought to channel goals through paths of least resistance – repair of the existing city in the form of infill, the establishment of nodes of transit-based development, and stemming the haemorrhage of people and services to the surrounding countryside. In this approach, the issue of metropolitan dominance and its changing status becomes somewhat moot. The quest to 'repossess and replan' the whole metropolitan landscape, involving a reformulation of 'the processes of life, growth, [and] reproduction' is obviously a much more involved proposal (Mumford, 1968, p. 83). Nearly everyone has agreed that it is holistic, but this holism is readily cast aside for being, as Jane Jacobs (1961) labelled it, 'far-flung'.

The RPAA regionalists abandoned cities in the sense they could not foresee turning them around or transforming them into settlements in line with human need. What they were searching for, instead, was the 'middle ground', a place halfway between pure provincial culture and the metropolis (Thomas, 2000). Perhaps it was more like the 'middle landscape' conceptualized by Leo Marx as the achievement of balance between humans and nature. Since the existing metropolis could not help accomplish this, it was necessary to turn to 'the healing order of nature' for help rather than the 'organized complexity' of the dense urban core.[2]

For Geddes, the contagion of the early industrial, Paleotechnic city, needed to be reversed. It was already creating unhealthy conurbations of dispersal and conglomeration – something similar to megalopolis, to use Gottman's later term. The city was still necessary, but it needed to be refashioned as something much more virtuous. The debate that has ensued is over the degree to which this reconstituted urbanity is in fact urbanism. In their discussion of 'The Intellectual Versus the City', White and White (1962, pp. 207–208) argued the opposite. They wrote: 'identifying the city's nodules of growth with Italian restaurants, Polish dances, the Metropolitan Museum of Art and the New York Public Library is hardly a matter of cheering at the top of your lungs for the city'. According to this view, what was missing was the messy diversity tolerated and sometimes even relished by the incrementalists.

What, exactly, was to be done with this Paleotechnic city of slums? The abolition of the city outright was advocated by agrarian extremists like Frank Lloyd Wright and Henry Ford, but what the regionalists advocated was not the same. The regionalists claimed that they had tried to rebuild it in conventional ways, but the effort required the 'labor of Sisyphus' (*Survey Graphic*, 1925, p.129). The solution was redistribution, in direct defiance of the tendency for large metropolitan areas to grow ever larger and assume more and more regional control. This required radical thinking, but there was no point trying to make life, as Mumford put it, 'a little more tolerable' in the congested metropolis (Mumford, 1925, p. 151).

In this lies a direct conflict with the Regional City envisaged by contemporary regionalists like Calthorpe and Fulton. They have conceptualized the 'emerging region' as a revitalized central city coexisting with strengthened suburbs and preserved natural areas. This is metropolitan regionalism, and the regionalist disdain for it – i.e., the brand of planning exemplified by the 1929 *Regional Plan of New York and its Environs* – was fundamental to its ideology. The RPAA regionalists considered the Plan to be a descendant of the City Beautiful because it glorified the monumental city – inhumane, detached from nature, and socially regressive. Other efforts at regional coordination started in the 1920s, for example Philadelphia's Tri-State District and Chicago's Regional Planning Association, were viewed similarly.

These regional efforts were largely aimed at bolstering the industrial economy, and did not mesh well with the RPAA view that factories were to be relocated in the country and given spacious surroundings. The small workshops that cluttered the city were to be demolished to make room for 'slum gardens'. Kropotkin, in his book *Fields, Factories and Workshops: or Industry Combined with Agriculture and Brain Work with Manual Work* (1912), had advocated that industries be scattered 'amidst the fields'. The idea that people ought to be producers who produce for themselves, in factories out in the fields, in close proximity to nature and to a socially cohesive, decentralized system of settlement, is in obvious conflict with metropolitan boosterism.

Perhaps what can be said, then, is that a regionalist like Geddes was not anti-city, just anti messy industrial metropolis – 'the slum of commerce'. Although New York City and London were prime examples, the metropolis to be avoided could be of any size. The distinguishing point was that the 'metropolitan world' attempted to standardize human beings and orient them around industry and commerce, in stark contrast to an 'indigenous world' that was organized as a 'quiltwork' of cultures and regional settings. Geographically, the RPAA regionalists saw the problem in two directions – the congested urban core and the peripheral spread. Cities of all types were to be unified, with definite geographic boundaries and 'no petering out in fattening, gelatinous suburban fringes' (MacKaye, 1928, p. 64). At the core, they were to be great and beautiful, like ancient Athens, Rome, or Renaissance Venice. According to MacKaye, the distinction was one of being cosmopolitan vs. metropolitan: the former added to the world's variety, the latter to the world's monotony.

The key to the distinction was whether the city could sustain community. MacKaye sought the cosmopolitan city, which, quite unlike the metropolitan one, was a sort of grown-up village that was able to facilitate communal life in larger terms. The problem with the metropolis was that it was 'a standardized massing of humanity void of social structure'. True urbanism was thus being submerged not only physically by unbounded sprawl, but socially by the lack of common interest. Self-government was being replaced by large, impersonal bureaucracies, a further wearing down of communalism (MacKaye, 1928).

Few would disagree that the industrial city of squalor was something to be addressed. But Geddes and other regionalists deplored the industrial and commercial city even without the slums – the middle-class 'semi-slum', as well as the quarters of the wealthy which Geddes referred to as the 'super-slum' (Geddes, 1915). Mumford agreed, and criticized Friedrich Engels for thinking that dividing up the homes of the wealthy for the working classes and the poor would be an improvement. The standards of the 'pretentious residences' of the wealthy in the industrial city were, Mumford wrote, 'below those which were desirable for human life'. What was needed was not a reappropriation of property, but a 'revolutionary reconstruction of the entire social environment' (Mumford, 1938, p. 168). It was to be interpreted by later regionalists as going a step too far.

How far the urbanist should go to make the necessary changes depended on one's view of the nature of cities. RPAA regionalists were a low-order/low-intensity culture, but their sense of order was not embedded in the concept of emergence like the later incrementalists. For Jacobs, the city was the product of complex, but organized processes, and there was no escaping these. Geddes and the early regionalists believed in planning, and were prepared to fashion a new societal order through it. Geddes summed this up in phrases like, 'to unify is to see relations'. Jacobs might have been inclined to see this as an unhealthy attempt to undermine the complexity and diversity of a natural, urban organicism. The fact that Geddes disliked the 'grandiose designs of Mr. Burnham' every bit as much as Jacobs did, but was still able to appreciate their 'clearness of communication' shows how his belief in the planner's ability pervaded his world view (Geddes, 1915, p. 189). It also explains why the early regionalists were unable to interpret the disarray of big cities as anything other than pejorative. Large cities like New York were suffering from 'breakdowns' in housing, water and sewer systems, and street arrangement (MacKaye, 1928). The population they attracted and then sent to outlying districts, were nothing more than 'backflows' that submerged, in the case of New York, the quaint colonial villages of Harlem, Greenwich and Chelsea.

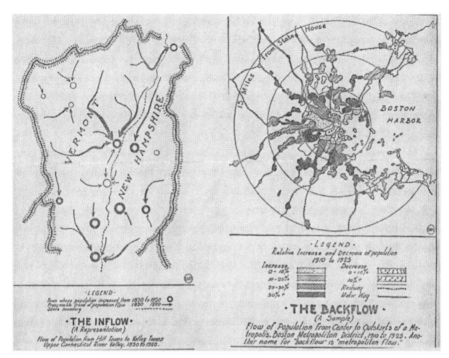

Figure 7.6. The 'flows' conceived by Benton MacKaye. The 'inflow' of people from 'hill towns to valley towns' in the Upper Connecticut River Valley occurred between 1830 and 1920. The 'backflow' was the movement of people from the city centre to the outskirts, here illustrated for the Boston Metropolitan District, 1910 to 1925. (*Source*: Benton MacKaye, *The New Exploration*, 1928)

Unlike the high-order plan-makers, the regionalists were more interested in affecting social relations than in imposing grand schemes for physical order. Some have observed that this made the conservationist ethic of the regionalists conservative – in addition to conserving natural resources, human and social values were to be conserved as well (Guttenberg, 1978). They wanted to preserve nature, but also pre-industrial social arrangements, and the importance of the small social unit came up repeatedly in regionalist writing. For MacKaye, Mumford, Chase and Stein, it was exemplified by the New England colonial village, not really the collective socialism espoused by Kropotkin, Geddes and Howard. In comparison to European notions of communitarianism, the American version seemed particularly sentimental. MacKaye was advocating the systematic development of 'outdoor community life' along the Appalachian Trail in which 'communal farms and recreation camps' would bring forth a heroic sense of volunteerism and willingness to work for a common cause (Thomas, 1994, p. 275).

There is still evidence of this view, and the natural merger between localism and ecology is one way in which regionalism and environmental planning (and, more directly, environmental ecology) are linked. Murray Bookchin has been particularly effective in integrating decentralist, populist idealism with ecology (Marshall, 1992). He is now calling for a libertarian municipalism or 'new politics' that seeks better democratic representation at the local, neighbourhood level – a populist, decentralized and localized approach that has all the overtones of the early regionalist agenda. Today, the anarchic tradition of Kropotkin lives on through the merger of decentralism and ecology.

These notions conjure up the old liabilities of the planned community. The regionalists were complicit in the idea that self-contained human settlements like garden villages and neighbourhood units could be the catalysts for social regeneration. In a glaring way, the implicit moral structure of this project contrasted with the conflicted morality and cultural diversity of the city. The regionalist answer was a physical framework for social interaction, graphically represented on the cover of the *Survey Graphic* 'Regional Plan Number' (1925) which showed a happy family strolling in the countryside near a hydroelectric dam. Social structure was embedded in an environmental consciousness, not unlike the planned community, but viewed from a much wider scale. Here was the neighbourhood concept projected onto the region. Components of neighbourhood, like schools, were associated not only with a surrounding population, but with 'the surrounding world of nature' (Mumford, 1925). This wider perspective seemed to coincide with the fact that regionalists were preoccupied with integrating nature and the machine. This is similar to the phenomenon Dolores Hayden (1976) wrote about in *Seven American Utopias*, where utopians hoped to synthesize idealism that was both pastoral and technological. Industry was to be refashioned better to integrate with the communitarian spirit of settlement form.

In metropolitan America, however, no such synthesis between humankind and nature was possible. This imbalance, which absorbed the regionalists and was explicitly outlined by MacKaye in *The New Exploration* (1928), came to epitomize the antithesis of environmental conservation. The value of the large metropolis in environmental terms was a perspective that was lost on the early regionalists. Some see this legacy as unremitting. Contemporary urbanists perceive a failure on the part of environmentalists now to value urbanism as a cultural product. This is evidenced in the use of the notion of the 'ecological footprint', interpreted as a blanket reprimand on cities for 'stomping' on the environment. This is damaging to urbanism because the environmental perspective has the force of 'science' on its side. This distinct advantage is something of which the early regionalists were fully aware. Geddes' civic survey was a scientifically-derived understanding of the land; it was not knowledge gained by public participation. Geddes' views on this were blunt: 'whether one goes back to the greatest or to the simplest towns, there is little to be learned of civics by asking their inhabitants' (Geddes, 1915, p. 8). He offered a synthetic, creative approach, but he thought that any romantic rejection of the Industrial city, as in the writings of Ruskin and Morris, was ultimately ineffectual and must instead be supported by a scientific rebuttal.

Again we come back to the enduring problem of how to articulate successfully the proper relation between the city and nature, between the urban and the rural. It has always been popular to proclaim, as Lewis Mumford did, that 'urban and rural, city and country, are one thing, not two things' (Mumford, 1956, p. 382). Yet Americans have always had a hard time finding the right balance. Anselm Strauss (1968) identified this as the essential dichotomy of American life and thought, and the division has been described as 'potent'. It does not necessarily suggest anti-urbanism as I have argued, but it does suggest a conflictedness in American and Western European culture, described by Tony Hiss as 'mental baggage' that originated as early as the industrial revolution (Hiss, 1991). According to Harvey, it was the rise of capitalism that spawned a new relationship between people and nature in which the two were separated, and nature began to be seen as a commodity (Harvey, 2000). Progress came to be equated with environmental degradation.

The failure to work out the proper balance between the urban and rural can also be seen in design terms. According to Lawrence (1993), there have always been four primary traditions of nature in the city: tree-lined boulevards, large city parks, residential squares, and the suburban house-and-garden. What is unfortunate about these traditions in the American context is that only two ever really took hold – large city parks and the suburban garden. Not only are these two types the most individually experienced and the least civically-oriented, but their predominance is reflective of the American inability to establish an urbanistic articulation of nature (Kunstler, 2001). Kunstler argues that this was picked up from English culture. Lawrence (1993) explores how the conversion of urban open space from public square to private green in London during the eighteenth century not only represented the ruralized conception of wealth and status, but formed the basis of suburban living later on.

That cities should be contextualized within nature was not disputed. But should nature be contextualized within cities? On this question there continues to be disagreement. A key issue is whether nature in cities is meant to fulfil a civic purpose, or whether nature is fulfilling its own purpose that exists outside the realm of urban civics. The regionalists answered this by postulating that nature forms an encompassing framework, a 'green background' that was to frame development in direct contrast to any pattern framed by human infrastructure (Hall, 2002). Within the city, parks were to provide a spiritual connection to natural beauty. Parks were a matter of living up to the ideals of a republic, the refinement of taste and culture, a vision of what society in American terms could be (Schuyler, 1986). Human healing and restoration were the domain of nature, not the built environment.

Because of their disdain for the industrial metropolis of their day, the regionalists have been implicated in the problem of wanting to green the city, to 'do the city in', as Jane Jacobs would say. Geddes was one of the first to promote the greening of the city. From his Outlook Tower he conducted an 'Open Spaces Survey' of Edinburgh and calculated 10 acres awaiting reclamation as gardens. Thus Geddes' solution was to bring nature into the city. As he put it, 'make the field gain on the street' so that cities would cease spreading like 'ink-stains and grease-spots' (Hall, 2002, p. 154).

The regionalists of the Geddes-Mumford-MacKaye variety had a nuanced understanding of urbanism, but nature was definitely the driving force. The integration of the urban and the rural was not conceptualized as dichotomously as by Olmsted, where urbanity was to be completely shut out from nature, but the philosophy was nevertheless one of urban subordination. Planning was a process of understanding the limits imposed by nature. Some would argue that this subordination reflects a deep ambivalence about the place of cities in America more generally, an indecisiveness that can be witnessed most dramatically in the creation of the American capital (Schuyler, 1986). Washington was a city that made no provision for industry, poor people, or commercial enterprise, and was thus not really a city at all, but a monument. On this there is agreement shared by cultures on the low-order end of the grid – the incrementalists and the regionalists.

The subordination of the urban to the rural meant that the delimitation of the region was to be based on natural rather than political geographies. This was necessary in order to facilitate the local (regional) production of goods and limit economic transaction to intra-regional exchange. This perspective led Benton MacKaye to conceptualize everything in terms of natural systems, likening city planning problems to water engineering and flood control. He made prolific use of natural imagery and analogy. Roadways were to be dams to control sprawl. Open spaces were levees that would control metropolitan infringement. The metropolis, whether large or small, was 'a leaky or ruptured reservoir' (MacKaye, 1928, p. 174). These metaphors fuelled the idea that valued components of cities had naturalistic as opposed to intrinsically urbanistic qualities.

For environmentalists, the richness of environment – essentially its 'complexity' – is derived from the ecological structure of regions. For urbanists, complexity found in the city can be appreciated from a cultural and exchange point of view. By focusing on complexity in natural systems and ignoring urban complexity, ecologically-oriented regionalists have tended to overlook the needs of urbanism, or so it is has been argued (Duany, 2002). Such regionalists lack principles for its internal arrangement, only focusing on prohibiting its extension outright. Their scale is too large, despite the fact that the regional framework of centralized places, open space and infrastructure is meant to inform smaller scale urban design issues in a kind of fractal, nested way. Regionalists like MacKaye seemed to think in highly integrative terms, relying on the region to link specialists – engineer, economist, landscape architect, town planner. But the idea that plans and visualizations could be united on the basis of their attention to the whole (the region) set the stage for the neglect of urbanism. MacKaye's dynamic and visionary approach seemed to leave out the community scale when it came to actual implementation. The *New Exploration* was the visualization of three processes having to do with natural resource conservation, control of commodity-flow and the development of the environment, but there was no working out of the qualities of urbanism.

Paralleling the broader focus of regionalism, environmentalism in planning has been seen as damaging to urbanism by its perpetuation of 'urban discontinuities' – the requirements of maintaining continuous green spaces in such a way that the urban fabric, which requires its own system of connectedness, is violated. It is a system that favours natural connectivity and thereby, according to Andres Duany (2002, p. 254), 'cauterizes the urban pattern'. Regionalists today might reject this characterization, but there is a history to it. It is a manifestation of the view carried forth by Mumford and the RPAA that the only hope for New York City was that it become externally rather than internally focused – that its salvation lay outside of itself. This was the basis of McHargian ecological planning, which directed attention on regional settlement frameworks often to the exclusion of the urban qualities *within* the framework. It is telling that one of the people to whom McHarg dedicates his famous book *Design with Nature* (1969) is Lewis Mumford. Somehow the idea of bringing culture into reciprocal relation with nature, a concern of Mumford's, did not translate in the conservationist version into a concern for the crucial ingredients of good urbanism. The neglect of the specific conditions of urbanity is something Mumford later corrected in the 1960s, but by then the environmental movement was heading in a different direction (Luccarelli, 1995). By the 1960s, regional plans were likely to be 'hydra-headed', consisting of multiple alternatives leading in different directions. The regional plan became entirely open ended, facilitating a kind of 'planned sprawl' that neglected the importance of human-scaled design principles (Thomas, 2000).

We are now left with office parks, shopping centres and housing pods interspersed amid McHarg's preserved natural areas. In the 'utter absence of a corresponding proposition' for urban areas, some maintain that environmentalism-as-regionalism has done nothing to heal a damaged urban realm (Duany, 2002, p. 254). Ecological methods are purported to find the 'optimal fitness' of human uses according to the requirements of the land, and ecological planners state that their methods can be used to address development issues in urban environments (Ndubisi, 2002). What seems to be missing is design – the realization that urban form, context and pattern, and the 'details' of urban environments, play a fundamental role in making places

Figure 7.8. A composite map resulting from McHargian overlay analysis of areas suitable for conservation, recreation and urbanization. The coloured map (shown in grey tones here) indicated land uses showing 'unitary, complementary and competing' values. (*Source*: Ian McHarg, *Design with Nature*, 1969. Reprinted with permission of John Wiley & Sons, Inc.)

humanly viable or not. This is why the environmentalist perspective is critiqued for failing to show how to accomplish goals like 'housing sustainability' in more concrete terms.[3] It is not simply a matter of making cities dense and compact, with lots of green space inserted for fresh air and light. Inattention to the importance of details can quickly spell disaster for quality urbanism.

Nature and the city were kept apart by Olmsted. His parks were ameliorative, not in the sense of beautifying the city, but in offering escape from them. Wilson points out that Olmsted would have thought the idea that parks and boulevards could create a beautiful city completely farfetched: 'The grand old man of landscape architecture . . . never hoped to beautify the entire city through some aesthetic ripple effect. The city was harsh and hard, and parks and boulevards were alternatives to it' (Wilson, 1989, p. 38). Thus what Olmsted had in mind for Central Park was a complete absence of human structure. The park's human elements – a zoo, statues, buildings, flower gardens, cafes – were not what Olmsted had wanted (Fisher, 1994). There was a clear distinction between altering the elements of nature for the purpose of maximizing beauty and a feeling of tranquillity, and altering nature to fit the language and context of urbanity. The latter view did not apply.

The possibility of the conformance of nature to urbanism was not part of McHarg's way of thinking either. In McHarg's 'The Place of Nature in the City of Man', he developed a 'simple working method for open space' that relied on conceptualizing nature in purely biological terms, where the 'city of man' is 'a natural urban environment speaking to man as a natural being and nature as the environment of man' (McHarg, 1964, p. 12). In discussing the superiority of the ecologist over the green belt advocate, McHarg stressed that nature could not be defined within a belt, because nature is not uniform. Clearly, the idea that there could be a contextualized nature subservient to the proper workings of urbanism would have been considered antithetical to an ecological, regional planning in which cities are subordinated to natural processes.

The merger of design and ecology in a way that is more integrative than that experienced conventionally in the fields of environmental design and planning, should, at least theoretically, be a good thing for American urbanism.[4] The emphasis on the interrelationship between human, environment and process as a basis for planning and design is straight out of the RPAA manifesto, even though the members of the latter group did not regularly use the term *ecology*. There will still be scepticism as to whether the regionalist focus on 'the natural and social processes of a specific region' (McHarg and Steiner, 1998, p. 91), can be used as the fundamental basis for planning cities. Ecological planning emphasizes that humans be 'in tune with natural processes', but again the question is, what does this dictum mean for city form specifically, and is there ever a point at which the needs of urbanism trump environmental systems? Failure to answer the first question indicates an answer of 'no' to the second.

Related to this, there is the question of whether localism can properly address questions of urban form. In fact the call for a renewal of localism, articulated by Emerson and Dewey, seized upon by Mumford, and moulded into a planning agenda by the regionalists, has been viewed as an explicit rejection of the American city (White and White, 1962). While it is no doubt a good thing to reject, as the critical regionalists in architecture have done, standardized form and seek instead a sensitivity to local climate, material, building methods and geography (see Kelbaugh, 2002), the idea of focusing on local regional traditions can tend to leave out the urban realm. This is because the emphasis in localism is on folk, rural culture as opposed to urban culture – craft over haute couture.

Urbanists may also wonder how, in the wake of an increasingly homogenized landscape of big box development and chain stores, local urban vernacular tradition can be relied on as a basis for urbanism. In some cases where the onslaught of theme commercialism is dominant, it may be necessary to rely on urbanistic values that are rooted in broader, non-local urbanistic traditions. But this may conflict with the way regionalists and others of the ecological planning school have envisioned things. In the midst of badly damaged urbanism and mass consumer culture, the only local traditions that can be relied on come from the rural and natural – requiring a response *not* rooted in urbanism. Steiner said exactly this when he noted, in reviewing McHarg's emphasis on localism, that 'developing values from a local perspective *based on regional bio-physical processes* differs from importing values from outside the region' (McHarg and Steiner, 1998, p. 89, emphasis added). The antidote to importing ideas from outside the region is to use 'natural ones'.

The political and economic requirements for maintaining localism have passed through several stages. Geddes was aligned with the anarchic communitarianism of Kropotkin, but the regionalism of the RPAA 'personified the idea of an administered society' (Lubove, 1963, p. 63). Their nemesis was the real estate speculator, the banker and the administrator who greased the wheels of speculative practice. The same gatekeepers are criticized today, but because of the entrenched bureaucratic planning apparatus now in place, American urbanists are more cautious about the potential of administratively-based solutions and more open to the idea of market-based ones. However, there has always been widespread belief that urbanism in America cannot succeed without some degree of public involvement. Given the fact that the regionalist brand of reform was never able to impact American financial systems, there is reason to back the approach.

Since the heyday of the RPAA regionalists, thinking has changed in regard to the relationship between market-based economies and urbanism, and what distinguishes good urbanism from bad urbanism has been re-assessed accordingly. It is safe to say that the commercial gridded city is no longer disdained in the same way or with the same fortitude – a reinterpretation that Jane Jacobs helped implement. This is not to say that speculative practice is beloved, just that the circumstances have changed. The regionalists detested the gridded city of the New York Commissioner's Plan of 1811 because of its focus on promoting commercial speculation. Now Manhattan's brand of urbanism is more appreciated. It is interpreted positively for helping to promote urban diversity, via factors identified by Jane Jacobs as connectivity, short block sizes, mixed uses, and variation in building age.

Can regionalism make the shift to market-based solutions? The early regionalists, where they were involved directly in city-building, would have approached the idea of market based solutions through the mechanism of providing 'object lessons', not as a matter of celebrating free market exchange. The regionalists wanted to produce positive models of community planning that exceeded the regulatory approach of Lawrence Veiller's brand of housing reform. They were deeply concerned about affordability, and their focus on costs may have been one reason why some regionalists seemed to neglect human-scaled design issues. When Stein rejected the proposal to clear streets of congestion by building overhead streets, the rejection was based on costs, not on the ill effects such a proposal would have had on the pedestrian environment. The standardization of housing was something notoriously remiss in terms of design. Before long, regionalists had become patrons of the 'aggregated cruciform plan type' – towers in a park (Mumford, 1995, p. 25).

The narrow interpretation of cost as economic efficiency, for example in *Some Principles Relating to the Economics of Land Subdivision* (Wright, 1929), produced problematic conditions like superblocks, low interconnectivity, dendritic street systems and automobile dependence that, ironically, in the long run have added costs. Now, the contemporary view of waste in terms of the 'costs of sprawl' is not the same as the regionalist view of waste. The regionalist concern with 'reducing building costs at every possible point' meant that increasing housing supply overrode other concerns having to do with the civic realm (Lubove, 1963, p. 60). Maintaining a quality urban realm could require capital expenditure incompatible with cost-cutting in the short term. Now there is increasing agreement that a broader interpretation of costs would better serve the longer-term goal of social integration. Whereas the regionalists were primarily addressing the living environments of the poor and middle class in direct fashion, the alternative approach is to affect all income groups concurrently. The goal would be simultaneously to limit sprawl and revitalize depleted urban neighbourhoods by finding ways to mix housing unit types effectively throughout the region.

But the economic perspective of the early regionalists was not confined to cost cutting. The hope of the regionalists was to seize the technological revolution and change its course of direction so that the economic system would be re-organized within economically confined regions. This idea went far beyond the enlistment of regional governance. It required a rechannelling of economic activity away from its global course, toward localized production and distribution systems. Even though the regionalists thought of themselves as being only 'mildly socialist' (Sussman, 1976) – tame in comparison to Florence Kelley and Jane Addams – it was an economic approach clearly not in keeping with basic American parameters. As a result, the relationship between economics and regionalism has changed. Regionalism now does not reject profit motives and industrial specialization. It seeks, instead, coordination of governmental units as a way of reducing social and fiscal inequities. It is a regionalism devoted to revenue sharing and coordinated infrastructure planning, fair-share housing, and a variety of strategies to level the playing field across a metropolitan region (see Orfield, 2002). The RPAA would have snubbed it, but even the RPAA had to admit that Radburn – a satellite suburb of New York – represented a severe compromise in the realization of radical political goals. Not only did Radburn lack a greenbelt, but it was developed on land that was in effect serving as a greenbelt for New York (Easterling, 1999).

Regionalism as a political approach is still critiqued not for being insensitive to localisms – so often the basis of critique in other planning cultures – but instead for making the domain of governance too large. To some critics, this simply reflects the fact that regionalism is too unwieldy, making it unsurprising that only Portland has so far embraced an effective regional planning strategy. Having more and more regional government is viewed as being untenable. Jacobs espoused this view in her critique of regionalism. She saw it as 'escapism from intellectual helplessness', where problems are treated from larger and larger scales rather than addressing the small-scale issues necessary for maintaining urban diversity (Jacobs, 1961, p. 410). A similar critique has emerged in the form of favouring municipal fragmentation as a way of ensuring both local control and local variety (Monkkonen, 1988; see also Anas, 1999). Many small, overlapping governmental units are not only an intrinsic part of our history, but the attempt to overcome the local focus of these entities could be counter-productive.

Another defeat is that, in American urbanism now, there seems to be an unwillingness to expend energy on trying to change the political economy of sprawl – the root cause of big box blight, asphalt landscapes, struggling main streets, and all the other characteristics of the degraded American urban and suburban realm. The early regionalists would not have been afraid to take these issues on. They rejected globalized economies even before globalization had become the dominant paradigm of urban economics. In fact, the disdain for the metropolis, the 'mother of cities', was based on the fact that such cities had an international reach. MacKaye analyzed New York as the 'mouth' of interior regions, similar to Cronon's analysis of Chicago as 'Nature's Metropolis' (Cronon, 1991). What was abhorred was the reach of the metropolis, a kind of precursor to the notion of the 'ecological footprint' in which the impact of the city is measured in terms of the resources it consumes and the wastes it generates (Wackernagel et al., 2002).

Today's regionalism is grounded in the pragmatism of environmental impact statements and a much more technically derived notion of the ecological footprint. Like Geddes' civic survey, it has a scientific basis, but it is less intuitive and, some would say, less sentimental. Perhaps it can be viewed as the logical evolution of a regionalism that started with the need to discern regional particularities and indigenous cultures, but came under the influence of the regionalism of systems analysis. The brand of regionalism that emerged, under the leadership of economists like Walter Isard was, as Thomas notes, the antithesis of early regionalism. Instead of celebrating embedded regional culture, the regionalism of systems analysis was about finding a generalized model that could eliminate 'the multitude of detail that confuses any one specific situation' (Thomas, 2000, p. 52).

That perspective alone has not been particularly relevant to promoting the goals of urbanism. There is a real conflict, still, about whether American urbanism needs to involve itself with finding out what the appropriate economic model of human consumption should be. While there is a committed interest in consumption at the local neighbourhood level, the need to make the grain of retail activity small-scale and pedestrian-oriented has largely come to be seen as detached from the question of production source, but only because of the inability to change that source. The emerging view in much of American urbanism is that the form of the city does not have to be dependent on the source and method of production, nor exclusively on how the distribution of goods and services is carried out. American urbanism is about the materiality of human living, and a refocus on underlying processes to the exclusion of normative ideas about that materiality would seem to contradict that interest. The question is whether matters of street life, human scale, and pedestrian environment can be combined with a concern for globalized economies or economic dependence on the hinterlands. To the early twenty-first century urbanist, the credo of consuming locally, of rejecting the economy of commercial mass consumption is completely sound – but does it constrain the normative ideal? And where would that lead? The early regionalists took the broader view and felt compelled to reject the metropolis – the 'bewildering mass' (MacKaye, 1928, p. 11). Now the dense metropolis is one of the brightest spots American urbanists have.

If American urbanists insist on procuring certain urban forms independent of the means of production and consumption, they expose themselves to the critique of being, somehow, 'inauthentic'. MacKaye's critique of the system was that ends were being distorted to fit pre-determined means; that instead of industry being called upon to help achieve culture, culture was being made to 'echo the intonations of industry'; oil paints were not being made to produce art, but art was being made to advertise oil paints. It all amounted to the 'unnatural tendency of the metropolitan process' (MacKaye, 1928, p. 71).

Marshall's book *How Cities Work* (2001) offers just this kind of interpretation. He criticizes New Urbanism for failing to understand how cities work and attempting to proscribe a form at odds with the underlying processes of urbanism. Marshall does not align himself with the regionalist critique, because, while the regionalists also used the authenticity argument, their criticism came from a different direction. The Marshall authenticity critique is about form following function; the regionalist authenticity critique was about the need to adapt means in order to achieve particular ends. Thus there is variation about whether economies and transportation systems are viewed as givens or adaptable means.

Both perspectives are perplexing when it comes to defining American urbanism. Manipulating a process in order to generate a certain urban form seems as elusive as reproducing a certain form irrespective of process. The idea that urban form must intrinsically match the underlying processes that generate it is a mindset that was translated by the modernists to mean that 'antiquated' urban places with small streets should be wiped clean in order to make way for large-scale rehousing projects and high speed expressways. The obsession with corresponding to the needs 'of our time' and to 'new rates of speed' was used to rationalize destruction. In the rush to be modern, pedestrian routes in the form of streets were the 'heritage of past eras' that could 'no longer fulfil the requirements of modern types of vehicles (automobiles, buses, trucks) or modern traffic volume' (Sert, 1944a, pp. 74, 162).

The question is whether the reproduction of certain urban qualities irrespective of the processes that generated them in the past can be validated by other means. Peter Hall asked a similar question when he wondered, 'in the new urban landscape of technology-led deconcentration, what exactly is the role of the traditional city?' Some will see it as a matter of wanting to save appearances, 'Disney-style parodies of the places they once were' (Hall, 1989). Some will see it as a matter of compromise. Others will see it as wanting to retain workable urban forms and patterns that can be validated by other means, for example, through the principles of complexity, diversity, mix and connectivity.

Notes

1. Duany (2002) has made this point.
2. Compare Mumford (1968, p. 83) to Jane Jacobs (1961).
3. See, for example, a review by Harold Henderson of Frederick Steiner's *Human Ecology: Following Nature's Lead* (New York: Island Press, 2002) in *Planning*, March, 2003, Volume 69, no. 3, p. 38.
4. See Steiner (2002) on the issue of integrating environmental design vs. planning.

Chapter Eight

Successes and Failures

There are two truisms about the fate of urbanist ideals – that urbanists generally failed to solve the problems they were trying to redress, and, that their proposals, implemented in whole or in part, often generated perverse outcomes (Hoch, 1995). Cast in this way, it is difficult to imagine why American urbanists persist. Clearly the American city, in all its various forms, is the product of multiple actions, some benevolent and some not, many of which were not products of any particular urbanist culture but were more likely to be driven by technological change. In any case, if the main summary of our attempts at procuring good urbanism boils down to failure and/or perversity, is it only American idealism and/or vanity that fuels the relentless continuation of these pursuits?

Both the question and the answer are multifaceted, and this chapter attempts to make some sense of these complexities. The broader question I try to address is simply, are the cultures of American urbanism having a good effect; and, are they successful, or have they failed? The most difficult challenge will be to try to separate the assessment of the fate of American urbanism from the fate of planning ideas more generally. The larger category of 'planning' has been implicated in almost all problems associated with the American pattern of settlement. Some argue that the basic ingredients of late twentieth-century Edge City were born out of early twentieth-century Progressive Era planning: an emphasis on transportation over place through the expansion of railway and road; the promotion of enclave development without consideration of social exclusion; the provision of open spaces in the city that fed into modernist conceptions of (anti-) urbanism (Sies and Silver, 1996). As previously noted, the First National Conference on City Planning held in 1909 in Washington, D.C. called for decentralization and dispersal of the congested city in unambiguous, even emphatic terms. Add to this the vast array of planning for specialized facilities like campuses, industrial districts, housing pods and shopping centres, and we have what looks like a failure in the very idea of planning for urbanism. In America, both the ethos and the practical framework of planning cities seem to have been based on fragmentation.[1]

There is another complexity: both success and failure are relative terms and the conditions that underlie them are often difficult to generalize. Some causes of failure in one urbanistic proposal may, in another place and time, be the identical causes of success. One example is the planned community approach to urbanism, where control has been seen as a root cause of both success and failure. Planned communities that were developed under strong philanthropic or institutional control may have been a condition of failure at one time, but at another, a condition of success. One can contrast the experience of the controlled new community and how it was interpreted as stifling individuality (and therefore limited in its success), and the experience of Forest Hills Gardens, in which residents readily committed themselves to the principles of the project in part on the basis of their expressed faith in the controlling authority, the Sage Foundation (Klaus, 2002). One was too controlling, the other was able to use its control as a basis of success. The apparently fine line between paternalism and leadership translated into two different experiences of success in the planned community.

When it comes to the issue of social equity in American urbanism, sometimes success is failure, and sometimes failure is success. For example, as Daniel Solomon argues, the wealthy cause 'paralytic civil strife' when they decide that a particular place, like San Francisco, is a 'cool' place to be. The displacement they generate is a 'serious form of failure, and its cause is success'. On the other hand, failure to achieve good urbanism can correlate with the rise in affordable housing, in which case 'failure' can be viewed as a form of success (Solomon, 2003).

Since my focus is urbanism rather than planning more generally, I do not intend to rehash the already well-developed sources of blame for bad urbanism and sprawl, except where they grew out of urbanistic proposals specifically. In other words, where problems like sprawl – a clear category of 'failure' – are tied to non-urbanistic ideas and planning mechanisms, I am not particularly concerned. The Levitt brothers may have successfully implemented some version of Frank Lloyd Wright's Broadacre City, but Wright's proposal was not about urbanism to begin with, and therefore not directly a problem for American urbanism. But where failure (and success) grew out of ideas that were originally tied to one of the four urbanist cultures, I am more concerned. In these cases, I will try to make an assessment of how urbanism leading out of one or more cultures either succeeded or failed (or had a mixed experience). The distinction is not always very clear, but it describes my approach.

I develop two themes in this assessment, both of which tie back into the initial grid/group structure posed at the beginning. One is that different experiences with success and failure seem to coincide with different ends of the intensity/order spectrum. The other theme is that success and failure in American urbanism are dependent to a large degree on the ability of any given urbanist culture to integrate with other urbanist cultures. The inability to accomplish this integration seems to have occurred along the diagonals: tensions between high-intensity/low-order (incrementalism) and low-intensity/high-order (planned communities), and between high-intensity/high-order (plan-making) and low-intensity/low-order (regionalism).

In my view, this points to a need to promote the integration of urbanist ideas more explicitly and directly. Because, by focusing on where urbanistic ideals have worked and where they have not – ideals that vary by culture – it is possible to see that part of their failing stems from an inability to see beyond themselves. Where they were connected with other cultures, there is evidence of greater success. Thus regionalism, where it extends to the level of the detail of the planned community, is more successful than without it. By the same token, the planned community, where it can embrace the area around it and therefore extend interest to the regional context, is also likely to be more successful. Where incrementalism fails to consider the larger context of civic proposals, like those of the urban plan-makers, it may be prone to glorification of chaotic urbanism that is not, in fact, emerging in a healthy way. Inner-city slums and squatter settlements can be interpreted as 'emergent', but they may need some infusion of urban plan-making or regionalist contextualism to make them more viable. On the other hand, where the City Beautiful and other aspects of urban plan-making culture have failed to consider incremental, small scale and grass roots change, they have often failed to create an urbanism that is better on social equity grounds.

By focusing on these linkages, the effort to dismiss any one American urbanist culture as a categorical failure outright is invalidated. But there are some hard truths to confront, and so far, this book has focused more heavily on urbanist preferences and ideals as opposed to implementation realities. But it was also recognized early on that the separation of ideal from reality is problematic. Both can be studied separately, but they also need to come together in an assessment of outcomes.

Assessments of success and failure in planning more generally (not urbanism specifically) usually consist of one of two types. The first form is largely critical and tends to focus on planning disasters and the perverse effects of a misinformed, small group who mean well but suffer under the laws of unintended consequences. In this category are books like Jane Jacobs' *Death and Life of Great American Cities* (1961),

Peter Hall's *Great Planning Disasters* (1980), and M. Christine Boyer's *Dreaming the Rational City* (1983). The story told in these books is one of elite domination of planning interests. Such books will often relate the story of how the commercial or industrial elite were the true shapers of American settlement, intervening in urbanist idealism for capitalist ends (see, for example, Blackford, 1993; Fairfield, 1993; Schwartz, 1993).

A second form of assessment is much more forgiving, and sees planning as mostly positive. These analyses tend to put great emphasis on the act of planning itself, as if to say that planning is a good thing *ipso facto*. In this category is the classical planning historical text *American City Planning* by Mel Scott (1969), as well as Herbert Smith's *Planning America's Communities: Paradise Found? Paradise Lost?* (1991). Positive assessments of planning that take a more realistic view of planning as a means rather than an end are Paul Grogan and Tony Proscio's *Comeback Cities – A Blueprint for Urban Neighborhood Revival* (2000) and more recently the text *Making Places Special: Stories of Real Places Made Better by Planning* (2002) by Gene Bunnell. Other texts attempt to present a balanced account of the fact that sometimes planning has worked and sometimes it has not. This characterizes Alexander Garvin's *The American City – What Works, What Doesn't* (2002) and *Cities Back from the Edge – New Life for Downtown* (1998) by Roberta Brandes Gatz and Norman Mintz. In these latter two accounts are included stories of planning success matched against the variety of planning ideas that have fared badly.

All of these accounts and many others have tried to take stock of the American planning experience. They have tried, mostly through case studies, to account for the value of planning in general, trying to explain what happened to a given planning idea and why. There is a lot of discussion about the decision-making and participatory processes involved. My evaluation differs from these accounts in two ways. First, I assess only the successes and failures of the four urbanist cultures I have reviewed in this book, not the subject of planning as an enterprise more generally. Second, I am mostly concerned with the assessment of the meaning of urbanist cultures and how the concepts of success and failure, as related to each specific culture, have changed or stabilized these sets of ideas. It is an assessment of the tenacity of planning cultures, informed and verified by the experiences they have encountered.

I therefore address the question: where have the different ideas, the four urbanist cultures, succeeded and failed, and how can this be measured? This starts by addressing the question of what success and failure in urbanism means. It is first necessary to decide whether the sets of ideas that the urbanist cultures put forward were inherently good, inherently bad, or were positioned within some grey area in between. Mostly I work under the assumption that the urbanistic cultures were, and continue to be, positive overall. As argued at the beginning of the book, the cultures I include are limited to those attempting to advance urbanistic principles, not anti-urbanism, which is why modernist urbanism under CIAM was mostly excluded.

This is not to say that each of the cultures has not experienced significant critique on the basis of innate limitations – a form of failure. Assessing the innate goodness or badness of each of the four urbanist cultures has been the main task of this book, and it has not been difficult to find topics to discuss along either dimension. One way to judge failure is by gauging whether a particular idea was problematic on ethical grounds. The most pervasive critique in this regard is that some urbanist proposals neglected the needs of the poor and, sometimes unwittingly, advanced the interests of the wealthy. This is the most important notion of failure in terms of intrinsic quality. None of the urbanist cultures reviewed here purposefully resulted in degraded environmental outcomes, but some of them did, by contrast, purposefully exclude people. On this point the planned community and urban plan-making cultures specifically can be said to have shown innate aspects of 'failure'.

In fact, there is a whole tradition of scholarship devoted to exposing the ways in which urban planning proposals have contributed to the neglect of the poor and the advancement of the wealthy. These works include Fainstein and Fainstein (1987) on urban redevelopment, Foglesong (1986) on the capitalist city, and Goodman (1971) on the ill-effects of planning more generally. According to Friedmann (1987, p. 8), advancement of the interests of the wealthy has always been the main occupation of planning, 'from Auguste Comte to Rexford Tugwell'. More recently, planners have been criticized for engaging in what Dear (1986, p. 380) terms the 'deliberate mutation' of the postmodern city; where the planner's role of technocratic facilitator of private profit hurls planning into a 'new depthlessness'. Some have analyzed how planning goals contribute to class and racial stratification, arguing that planning actions contribute to the oppression of black urban dwellers (Hayden, 2002; Thomas and Ritzdorf, 1997).

These references to planning failure are cited here as a way of positioning my discussion of urbanist successes and failures in a different way, using a different framework. The assessment I use focuses on implementation rather than innate value, although the two are of course interrelated. I am interested in determining whether certain urbanistic ideals found application, or whether they were abandoned or radically altered once realized. Unfortunately, the assessment of planning success and failure in these terms has a largely undeveloped history. We lack a basic understanding of implementation realities, largely because the energy it takes to make the assessment in anything other than broad impressions is absent.

Assessment Framework

There are various possible interpretations when it comes to defining what is meant by success and failure in urbanism. It is possible, for example, to think of four categories of experience, two measures of success and two of failure. These are: 1. Persistence – that the urbanist ideal remained intact/unchanged, irregardless of its implementation (success type *a*); 2. Realization – that the urbanist ideal matured/evolved well in terms of implementation (success type *b*); 3. Abandonment – that the urbanist ideal was abandoned (failure type *a*); or 4. Deterioration – that the urbanist ideal held and matured/evolved badly in terms of implementation (failure type *b*). In the past century of urbanism we can find examples of all four experiences. Each of the four cultures can be evaluated in these terms, and each can be said to have partially experienced each aspect of success and failure. Of course, all of these are a matter of interpretation, and there are grey areas.

However, there does seem to be a particular pattern. Assessing the successes and failures of each urbanist culture using these four categories, there seems to be a correlation with the intensity/order framework used to differentiate urbanist cultures: each half of the grid seems to coincide with one particular measure of success or failure. Persistence more or less characterizes low order; Realization coincides mostly with high intensity; Abandonment characterizes low intensity; and Deterioration is mostly associated with high order. This is graphically represented in figure 8.1.

In other words, it seems that each urbanist culture has had a different set of experiences when it comes to success and failure, and those can be analyzed in terms of their degree of order and urban intensity. This can be summarized as follows. Incrementalism, in my interpretation, has both persisted as an ideal and had some degree of realization. This is easy to interpret: this culture makes low demands, does not entail new systems of order, works with the existing urban realm, and basically does not make anyone very angry. To say that it was and is innocuous is not quite correct, but its low demands corresponding with a low sense of imposed order mean that it has a better chance of success on both counts. Ideologically, it may be viewed as a low impact culture, which is not to say that it cannot exert forceful change, only that such change occurs in small steps and may be less recognizable. Though it is difficult to gauge, it may be the culture that has experienced the most success because small-scale incremental change may meet with the least resistance and be the easiest to implement.

Urban plan-making has had a more mixed history, included both in the success type *b* category (realization), but also in the failure type *b* category (deterioration). On the one hand, projects of a specific, well-defined nature, characteristic of much of urban plan-making culture, were realized. On the other hand, many ideals were prone to faulty implementation, such as the zoning juggernaut that was so clearly counter to whatever urbanistic tendencies this culture consisted of. Large-scale civic centre projects were also realized, but monumentalism came to be associated with the grimmest of urban places – inhumane sterility with little connection to diversity, equity, and good sense of place. Mega-projects like baseball stadiums are now often seen as failures in exactly these terms. Realization of ideals that tend to deteriorate in implementation is possibly the worst combination of outcomes.

The planned community culture can be looked at as having had the most difficulty in its implementation. The idea in pure form – creation of self-contained and complete cities consisting of all the necessary conditions of urbanism – has been largely abandoned in favour of a stripped down and more realistic version consisting only of residential, civic, and, less successfully, consumption components. The production (employment) functions are treated more fluidly. Thus the notion of self-sustaining cities in the region, intimately connected to

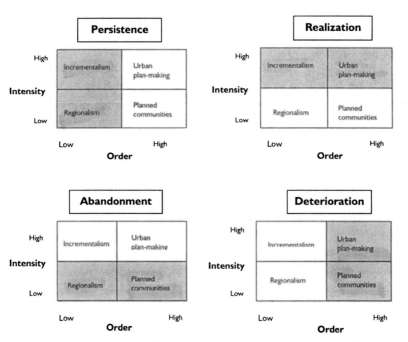

Figure 8.1. Successes and failures of urbanist cultures in terms of the Intensity/Order Grid

their surrounding agricultural land in the manner of Ebenezer Howard, has been abandoned. This has also been viewed as a matter of deterioration. Initial ideals of the planned community are viewed as having devolved into something far off the mark after implementation, generally realizing only design qualities of place and failing to achieve diversity (both social and economic). This does not necessarily mean that the planned community approach to urbanism must be shelved, only that it may need to be – and indeed is being – reconceptualized. One reason to pursue this is that the planned community ideal does persist. What is expected of it may, however, need to be rethought.

Regionalist culture is split in two in the evaluation of success and failure because of the nature of its internal transformation. Early regionalist ideas that were more radical in nature have been largely abandoned (failure type *a*), particularly those put forward by Geddes, Mumford and the RPAA. Yet the appeal of the regionalist idea, in altered form, has persisted (success type *a*). Conceptually, this means that the culture has been, to some degree, pulled apart. The notion of connecting city and nature, of situating urbanism in its regional context, is strongly appealing and in little danger of being abandoned. But what this means in terms of underlying social and economic structural change has gone through significant transformation. The question is what this ideological pulling apart of the regionalist ideal means for urbanism.

Explanations – Success

Assessments of success in planning generally are hampered by (*a*) a lack of definition of success; (*b*) little empirical knowledge about when and where planning has succeeded; and (*c*) the lack of a method for measuring planning success. What analysts are willing to accept as a successful outcome of an implemented plan or policy varies widely. At one end of the spectrum, only literal or face-value implementation (strict linearity) may be accepted as constituting success (Wildavsky, 1973). At the other extreme, mere consultation of a plan may be viewed as an act of successful implementation. In this way the City Beautiful era plans that were never built can be regarded as successful in that they stimulated discussion about the value of planning more generally (Wilson, 1989). Roeseler (1982) offers a variation on this theme, in which he heralds Cincinnati's urban plans as 'successful' because they functioned as creative outlets for the planning genius of Alfred Bettman and Ladislas Segoe (see also, Alexander and Faludi, 1989).

Often planning success is conceived in terms of process. For example, successful procedures are thought to be the ones that are strategically focused, such that

Regionalism (handwritten in left margin)

communities effectively assess and incorporate their market position. Another common theme is that planning procedures are regarded as successful if they elicit communitywide involvement in the decision-making process. In these process-focused accounts, success occurs as planning occurs. Planning is what planners do and thus planning procedures are successful on the basis of their procedural content, not on the basis of what they effectuate. Success may even be defined in terms of plan quality, irregardless of implementation, or on the basis of whether a particular plan preparation procedure was followed.[2]

But even where a particular form of urbanism is implemented intact, there will be disagreement as to the basic success of the element as initially proposed. Thus, some assessment of success or failure will always be a matter of interpretation, and it is possible to get hopelessly lost in a relativistic understanding of success. The grid structure in America is a good example. Some, like Sennett (1990), interpret the gridding of America as a loss of interest and an encouragement of neutral city-making, a denial of urban complexity, and a repression of individual spirit. Others, like Kostof (1993), regard the grid as a framework with lots of potential, the success of which depends on the differences above ground like building height, landscaping, and the rhythm of open spaces.

Another issue is that the multiplicity of factors that bear upon urban development processes makes the establishment of a causal link between plans and outcomes extremely complex. Multicausality is a problem because planners try to manipulate only certain aspects of land development, and trying to assess the impact of planning decisions on economic, social and other urban systems requires overlooking a number of 'contentious steps' in the explanatory chain (Healey, 1986, p. 114).There is also the difficulty of 'counterfactual' evaluation, in which a baseline state is needed to compare what would happen with planning intervention versus without planning intervention (Alexander, 1981). This is not always possible.

With these caveats in mind, which, again, have to do with planning in general rather than urbanism in particular, success in each urbanist culture can be looked at in two ways: as a matter of persistence, and as a matter of realization.

Persistence

One measure of success in American urbanism is the sheer persistence of ideas about human settlement. Ideas, after all, are not 'just ideas', but have powerful, tangible effect. This is why John Reps graciously judges early twentieth-century planners like Burnham and Nolen 'not by how many of their specific proposals were carried out but in the manner by which they planted the seed and cultivated the growth of city planning' (Reps, 1965, p. 497). By a similar token, it was not any particular event or project that stopped the redevelopment bulldozers of the 1960s, but the set of ideas about urbanism that was clearly resonating with many neighbourhood activists.

The tangible effect of persistence is regularly overlooked. M. Christine Boyer's *Dreaming the Rational City: The Myth of American City Planning* (1983) presents a deep appraisal of the rise and fall of the physical planning basis of city planning but the fact that certain ideals persisted is evaluated mostly in terms of nefarious quests for power. The explanations offered as to why the idea of physical planning persisted, but then faltered, rooted in Marxist interpretation, do not seem to explain adequately why the physical planning ideal would rise up again, nor why it would do so at a given point in time. But even when cognizant of the power of persistent ideals, American urbanism has been unable to come to terms with the implications. As a consequence, it has taken a long time for planning as a professional field to reassert its interest in physical planning ideals with the same force of conviction in evidence a century ago.

If we measure success of an urbanist culture by the tenacity of its approach, then what cultures have in fact been successful? It seems to be the case that the lower the sense of normative order, the greater and more widespread the persistence of the ideal. That is, the low-order half of the intensity/order grid has had greater success with persistence than the high-order half, generally speaking (this is not true for all groups of urbanists, as noted below). Thus, the popularity of incrementalism and regionalism is palpably stronger than the popularity of plan-making and planned communities. Jane Jacobs and the regionalists, despite the ironic fact that the two approaches to urbanism are often strongly at odds, are now the most widely accepted brands of urbanism in America.

There are two sides to this. Not only is the left half of the grid – low-order urbanism – non-threatening, but the notion of order is, correspondingly, generally unpopular except with those whose notions of order are being imposed. This is a topic that has come up repeatedly in this book. Order is often equated with extreme forms of control, inharmonious with more modest, individual human activities and needs. Order is associated with determinism, and may be rejected in favour of disorder (randomness). Order is believed to involve hierarchies, foundational principles, and norms, all of which are seen to constrain freedom (Turner, 1995). Given this contemporary perspective, the low-order half of the grid is seen as being more open, realistic, and socially just, thus explaining its higher level of persistence.

Sometimes a persistent idea about urbanism will be revised and transformed in order to fit the contemporary world. This can be said of regionalism, whose persistence may be in part due to its adaptability, consistent with its low-order position on the grid. Of course, the regionalist push for structural change proved untenable almost from the start, and Mumford's small circle of friends in the RPAA never had much chance of altering the means of production and consumption in the radical manner their new system required. But vestiges of regionalist thinking persist. Patrick Geddes did not successfully institute neotechnic regionalism, but his call for 'a synoptic vision of Nature to enable a constructive conservation of its order and beauty in the development of the new health of cities' is still an urgent goal (Geddes, 1915, p. v). Success measured as persistence gains much more ground if the essence, rather than the particulars, is evaluated. From this perspective, the British new towns can be regarded as successes of the RPAA even though they failed to provide a restructured regional development pattern. As Peter Hall (2002, p. 187) has observed, British new towns provide 'a good life, but not a new civilization'.

But a transformed sense of regionalism, entailing broad, integrative planning, the positioning of settlement within its larger regional context, the elevation of environmental principles as a context for compact human settlement, all with a low imposition of order – these are persistent ideals, the recurrent principles of a lasting regionalist agenda. These are the ideals that even adamant critics of New Urbanism rally behind (see, for example, Marshall, 2000). The appeal is in part a matter of the veracity of the regionalist critiques. The observations of the RPAA turned out to be prescient. 'The crumbling ruins of our metropolitan civilization' in the form of congestion, inner-city blight, suburban sprawl and fiscal crisis all became even more pronounced toward the end of the century (Sussman, 1976, p. 44).

The ideals of the high-order half of the grid have been less persistent on a wider scale, but some ideals remain vital. The difference is that the high-order realm resonates with a smaller group. New Urbanists, for example, are able to transmit certain essential principles out of the high-order realm and make them relevant in a contemporary context. They are connected to the idea that the civic realm is important, that the vision of the community in material form is worthy, and that the merger of civic and commercial interests is beneficial. These ideals, in material form, entail a certain degree of normative order.

Urban plan-making in the guise of the City Beautiful has persisted in other ways – not in the sense of Burnham's Plan of Chicago, but in the sense of big plans and mega-projects with both civic and commercial value. The 'public/private' partnerships of contemporary planning that finance stadia, downtown civic centres, and mixed use town centres can all be thought of as persistent extensions of the City Beautiful ideal, albeit in altered form.

The powerful image of a planned community, that idealistic conception of what the coherent, coordinated, socially aware and civically inspired community can be, is also an ideal that persists – although not with the same strength of conviction as the low-order cultures have maintained. This persistence is based on built examples which, however few in number, continue to act as object lessons. There are planned communities that, although not realizations of the complete set of planned community goals, give us a solid reason to persist in pursuing them. As one reviewer remarked about Nolen's Mariemont, 'If Mariemont failed to produce a model workers community, it still provides a model working community', meaning that the community was exemplary in the application of its mixed housing type and mixed use design principles. It still provides 'a shining alternative in a disjointed suburban landscape'.[3]

The fact that there were imitators of the planned community and what it was trying to accomplish is sometimes seen as a measure of the planned community's success. A trustee of Sage Foundation thought of Forest Hills Gardens as successful on these terms, arguing that 'The many imitators and the fame of the Gardens themselves are eloquent testimony' of success (Klaus, 2002, p. 150). Where principles were selected as being worthy of replication, there is evidence of a persistent ideal.

Realization

An account of the successes of physical plans and ideals about urbanism can not rely exclusively on the notion of persistence. Given the physical, material basis of urbanist cultures, an assessment of actual realization is warranted. In this respect, the most common means of measuring success is in the case of an original idea that is implemented basically intact. Using this metric, there have been some successes in all cultures, some more than in others.

In general, successes have been easier to come by for those proposals having to do with existing cities (high intensity) rather than those proposed for a 'clean slate' (low intensity). This is not to say that low-intensity proposals have not been realized. Planned communities built as complete, integrated towns have in some places been qualified successes if the definition of success is realization. The most visible successes have been in Europe, especially the British New Towns. In the U.S., planned communities that incorporated the complete set of principles of good urbanism – connectivity, mix, diversity, sense of place – are more difficult to come by. But even broadening the scope to include such planned communities as Reston and Columbia, the occurrences of the planned community have been exceptions rather than the rule, largely due to the enormous expenditures required up front.

Overall, the success of some planned communities is notable, but small when viewed against the complete inventory of realized urbanistic plans and principles.

Within existing urban places, concrete proposals for specific, small-scale change were realized. It is from this viewpoint that Robert Fishman heralds the achievements of urban plan-makers in the period from 1900 to 1930. It was the ability to create an 'urban vitality' out of the rapid technological improvements of the era which signalled realized success. Planners helped to implement forms 'that expressed the promise of modern urban living' (Fishman, 2000, p. 11). They were able to provide a 'public and collective undergirding' in the form of infrastructure, new building types, and new neighbourhoods. These were the key domains of the incrementalist and urban plan-making cultures, which, it is fair to say, had some success in realizing and accommodating urban change according to the needs of the modern industrial city.

Success measured by the realization of plans and ideas was, in part, predictably a consequence of how well it coincided with the goals of commercial and corporate interests. In the decades at the beginning of the twentieth century, Wilson (1989) argues, plans were realized when businessmen understood that urban plan implementation could help save retail and industrial cores. With the enlisting of the business elite, urbanists were able to convince citizens that the money needed to realize plans was money worth spending.

Success had to do with political adroitness. The ability of the City Efficient to implement its agenda has been seen as a matter of that group's ability to set up local planning commissions controlled by elites, out of the reach of the general public (Fogleson, 1986). Political skill was not necessarily about elite status, however, and could be more a matter of being able to 'bend the governmental ear'. Rosen's study of urban power showed that, in land-use policy, this ability was not limited to the rich and powerful. Any group was capable of 'carrying off some grandstand ploy', and this resulted in a more pluralist notion of power in matters of city-building than is usually allowed. Perhaps success in plan-making can be looked at as a matter of 'political gambit' (Rosen, 1986, p. 332).

It was not only a matter of facilitating the business elite. The degree of realization also coincided with the persuasive power of the idea, in turn a function of specificity and scale. Where projects and ideals were relatively small, unambiguously budgeted and specific in design – the civic adornment and neighbourhood improvements of the incrementalists and the public works components of the urban plan-makers, there was greater realization. City Beautiful projects may be looked at as mere 'showpieces', but they were nonetheless successful at implementation. Burying utility wires, installing street furniture, restricting billboards, creating boulevards, improving the design of public buildings[4] – all of these documented City Beautiful accomplishments were graspable in readily implemented programs.

This also explains why the engineering approach to urbanism was so successful. Frederick Law Olmsted, Jr. lamented in 1909 that success in city making was a matter of municipal engineers rigidly and uncreatively meeting 'the standards and demands of their communities' (Wilson, 1989, p. 289). Altshuler (1983, p. 227) attributed the 'success' of intercity freeway construction to 'clarity of standards' corresponding to a strength of conviction that was 'unclouded'. Engineers possessed the power of the clearly conceived 'blueprint' that laid out specific directives. This is unchanged, and the success of the engineer is still a common occurrence. Then and now the obvious solution is to entice engineers to join in on the goals of urbanism more directly.

The power of specificity is revealed by contrasting the implementation of the ideas of the Regional Plan Association of New York and the Regional Planning Association of America. The former plan-making culture produced an urbanist plan that was both ordered and controlled, specific and project-oriented. Its concrete, small-scale blueprints for change were successfully implemented under the leadership of Robert Moses, most notably via infrastructure projects like highways, bridges and tunnels. The successful implementation of these projects was very much related to their ability to stoke the engines of economic growth, but they also succeeded because they were specific and realizable. Most observers agree that the 1929 plan left a 'considerable imprint' on the New York area, and that 'the infrastructure in place today was created in large measure through the successful completion of many of the proposals contained in the plan' (Johnson, 1988, p. 186).

The contemporaneous proposal of the RPAA called for the re-organization of underlying economic, social and political processes. Its plans were not only less immediate, they depended on inter-agency co-operation. Rebuilding blighted inner cities and creating new cities in regional contexts were not exactly projects that could be immediately realized by one agency. It is true that the RPAA had Roosevelt's ear at one time, and no other approach to urbanism has been so able to influence a national planning agenda, but the influence was extremely short lived, and many of its effects (for example, the TVA) were less about urbanism and more about industrial development. Mumford may have thought of the *Plan of New York and its Environs* as a 'badly conceived pudding' (Sussman, 1976, p. 106), but it was concrete enough to be realized by the existing authority. What Mumford must have known is that, where the goals of urbanism were more concrete, as in Abercrombie's plan for the London region, there was likely to be success in implementation. The London plan had a decidedly 'fixed, unitary quality' with a clear urban spatial future in mind. It made the London region, according to Peter Hall (2002, p. 187), 'one of the few places in the world where it is possible to see the Howard-Geddes-Mumford vision of the world made actual'. But there was an important caveat: it did not challenge the ruling British authority.

A strong physical plan is usually a condition of a heightened sense of order. This was certainly Burnham's approach, and a good percentage of his 'no little plans' in Chicago were implemented by 1925, in part because of their powerful imagery of order. This presents a paradox. The more physically specific and grandiose, the more difficult an urbanistic ideal is to get implemented; but on the other hand, the more likely its chance when compared to non-physical, process-oriented urbanistic proposals. Strong plans may simply have a better ability to present a counterforce to the host of other influences vying to make their mark on urbanism.

This obviously cut both ways – anti-urbanistic plans could find ease of implementation along the same lines as urbanistic ones. Urban renewal plans of the postwar period, which can hardly be called models of good urbanism, shared the urban plan-making characteristic of specificity. City Beautiful era plans may have been realized by virtue of their directness and imagery, but sometimes this 'success' was unfortunate, for example when one of Burnham's diagonal streets cut through a German working-class neighbourhood in a manner not unlike Haussman.[5]

Explanations – Failure

Failure is an accepted part of planning culture. Between Jane Jacobs' notion of planning ineptitude, Wildavsky's famous dictum 'If planning is everything, maybe it's nothing', and James Howard Kunstler's keen critique of planning incompetence, planners are somewhat used to the notion of failure (Wildavsky, 1973; Kunstler, 1993). For Wildavsky, planning, which he defined as control of the future, was destined to fail given that the future is uncertain. By this logic, the act of putting forward a proposal for urbanism in the first place is, by its very nature, a source of failure.

But, assuming (as I am here) that the urbanistic goals organized as four distinct cultures each had something of value to offer, in what ways did they fail, and what were the causes of failure? Three broad categories of failure have been proposed for city planning generally: 1. political complexities and lack of societal consensus; 2. uncertainty and lack of available knowledge; and 3. lack of support in terms of level of funding and level of community support. All of these explanations are rooted in the decision-making environment. Planners have pointed to the 'structure of influence' concept as a way of expressing the pitfalls of attempting to implement ideals. In structuralist terms, there are too many other forces at work, and too many forces beyond local planning control for planning to hope to achieve its stated aims. Others have noted the tendency for planning to fail in the face of uncertainty, at times producing disastrous consequences. Then there is the observation that postmodern spatial mobility of capital has made local determinants of urbanism more ephemeral.[6]

All of these ideas will come into play in the attempt to explain why ideas about urbanism have failed. Two categories of failure are explored: either the ideals of an urbanist culture fell out of favour and thus were not implemented; or, initial ideals were altered in unfortunate ways during the course of implementation.

Abandonment

The two cultures on the bottom half of the intensity/order grid, those of low involvement with the existing city, have had the most experience with abandonment of initial urbanist principles. Some may interpret the neglect of the lower intensity realm of urbanism as a missed opportunity. This is undoubtedly how constituencies within each culture viewed the issue. RPAA members portrayed themselves as 'mistreated heroes' (Easterling, 1999, p. 46). Mistreatment was a matter of inattention.

The regionalism of the RPAA and the idea of the complete planned community in the manner laid out by Ebenezer Howard have both been abandoned in their original form. This could also be said of aspects of early plan-making culture, although the abandonment of the ideological underpinnings of regionalism and planned community culture has been more pronounced. Both were victims of over-extension. They were ambitious undertakings requiring substantial public investment or at least, collective energy on a mass scale. This ambition was a result of their being postulated on a clean slate, making them less conceptually constrained from the outset.

Abandonment is associated with any urbanist culture that relied on strong political and ideological structure. The regionalists of the RPAA variety are a notable case. Garden city proponents as well based their city-building on a particular political and economic paradigm. The deeper ideological and philosophical underpinnings of both the regionalist and the planned community cultures was largely abandoned because of the inability of American political culture to accept the socialist implications and requirements of their proposals. In the low-intensity half of the grid, the rearrangement of the physical structure of urbanism as a matter of idealism and ideology was simply too dependent on broader public participation

– meaning government. The 'clean slate' upon which urbanistic ideals were attempted engendered a level of public involvement that even the City Beautiful era plan-makers could not attempt. This characterizes in a nutshell the experience of the complete planned community in the U.S. The socialization it required, for example, meant the federal experiment with greenbelt towns was dropped quickly and never picked up again. But even where the complete town was a matter of private enterprise, the idea did not fare much better. The requirements on the part of industry were too substantial – industry had to subsidize the town at a level most capitalists were unwilling to sustain.

The notion of planning for industrial decentralization as a way of providing a local jobs base dependent on that community, in the manner of Ebenezer Howard or even Rexford Tugwell, is another example of abandonment. Even with massive federal expenditure, as in the case of the greenbelt communities of the 1930s, a localized jobs base could not be attracted. Today's planned community has mostly abandoned the idea of local industry in favour of providing urban forms and patterns that might accommodate diverse forms of employment (for example, by providing plenty of 'live/work' units). This can be interpreted as an example of adaptation, but it still involves the abandonment of the initial planned community ideal.

Of course, both regionalism and the planned community cultures still exist, but in significantly altered forms. Regionalism is no longer about a restructured economic, political and social system, and there is no longer the view that the central urban core is obsolete. The planned community is no longer about having all the functions of life in one location. Instead of diverse, mixed-use planned communities insulated from the existing city, planned communities are now only partly self-contained, and remain dependent on the metropolis. What has been abandoned, then, is the idea of complete self-containment in the form of a newly constructed city built and planned all at once. However, the planned community culture has retained its idealism about being able to provide a mixed-income, mixed-use form of urbanism. Whatever failures there have been in being able to deliver diversity are therefore not a matter of abandonment of an ideal, but rather a failure of achievement (deterioration).

All cultures have had their share of abandonment of original, key ideals. In plan-making culture, it seems that the further ideals have moved from the urbanistic goals of the pre-war period, the more likely they have been to be retained. Plans became less visionary, less bold, less physical, and less about urbanism. The abandonment of the ideals of the early City Efficient urbanists in favour of suburban-looking planning principles led Gottdiener (1977), referring to Long Island, to observe that the pattern of development produced in post World War II America looked little different than it would have looked if there had been no plans or planners whatsoever: the same pattern of land use resulted. Of course, plans that abandoned basic urbanistic principles and veered toward the *status quo* (unplanned sprawl), would seem to have the least amount of resistance to implementation.

Some will regard the failure of the planned community culture as endemic to it, since each scheme represented 'another spatial utopia separated from economic realities' (Boyer, 1983, p. 197). But another interpretation is that the planned community, by the nature of what it attempts to accomplish in terms of maintaining social and economic diversity planned at one time and within a defined area, requires more assistance. Failure in planning more generally is largely a matter of contending with economic realities, but in the planned community this is pronounced. In new towns and neighbourhood units, failure is a matter of not following through. The experience of government sponsored community building, like Yorkship Village in the U.S, or the new towns programme in Britain, has shown that such programmes require long-term financial commitment (Lang, 1996).

Urbanist ideals were abandoned because they required certain conditions and historical processes that were no longer present. The planned community as a well designed company town in service to the corporation but nevertheless focused on the needs of its residents is one example where the level of order and control was no longer justifiable.

Deterioration

There are those who argue that planning should not be judged by the quality of its unrealized ideals but by what actually gets built because of them (Hancock, 1996). This becomes a political test – an assessment of the ability of urbanists to make their case, bend the government's ear, convince an ambiguous public, or find the necessary financial and bureaucratic savvy to get their ideas put into place, on the ground. By these criteria, the assessment of urbanist culture will be dominated by the view that it has had significant but perverse impacts. The intensely creative urbanist proposals coming out of the Progressive Era have, dishearteningly, been seen mostly as generators of unfortunate outcomes. The regional city of the RPAA has been interpreted by Garreau (1991) as the precursor of Edge City. Radburn is believed to be the ancestor of 'cluster zoning, planned unit development, and large-scale community building' (Parsons, 1994, p. 463), none of which have been strategies that have shown themselves to be good generators of quality urbanism. In these and other examples, ideals about urbanism have been realized in debased form. Overall, it is the right half of the intensity/order grid, the quality of high order, that is the most vulnerable to the problem of deterioration.

Under this category of failure, which I label 'deterioration', a great deal of planning activity – and by association, most urbanist culture as well – has unfolded. It is unfortunate that, of the four generators of suburbia – roads, zoning, government-guaranteed mortgages, and the baby boom – planning can be implicated in three of them. Were it not for the unfortunate outcomes, this would seem to point to a profession with extreme potential for success.

Even honing in on urbanism more specifically rather than planning more generally, the downgrading and perversion – deterioration – of initial, well intentioned urbanistic principles is by far the largest category of success and failure to be discussed. The most visible aspect of this involves a watering down of ideals, a declension of initial urbanistic principles, usually through a process of partial implementation. Deterioration was a matter of partial implementation wherever a particular idea required too much fundamental alteration of the *status quo*. Thus the idea of implementing MacKaye's 'Townless Highway' was fine as a limited access, efficient motorway, but the 'townless' part, which was the most important aspect of his idea but which required stronger measures, was not.

One of the first and most pervasive signs of deterioration of initial principles came when the urban plan-maker's sense of order was translated into a regulatory structure. Just as the early plan-makers had feared would happen, planning for urbanism degenerated into 'a negative regulatory machine, designed to stifle all initiative, all creativity' (Hall, 2002, p. 11). This failing is obvious, and has been the focus of critique for planning in general, sparking widespread interest in the perverse effects of implementing mechanisms. But it is part of a larger problem. Planning has always had a difficult time translating principles into practice effectively. The problem is not limited to zoning. Even Catherine Bauer's well intentioned efforts to create the Federal Housing Administration in 1934 had the perverse effect of redlining the inner city, and later, guaranteeing that new, large-scale suburban developments would be homogenous.

Urbanists have struggled to find the right implementing mechanisms and regulatory codes to make urbanist ideals succeed. We can now see the perverse effects of the wrong kinds of codes clearly, and numerous studies have brought these ill-effects out. From an economic point of view, Dowall (1984) evaluated the effects of land-use regulation and showed their negative impact on housing costs, market readjustments, and spillover effects. Other studies have shown the shear ineffectiveness of land-use zoning in controlling development. The negative consequences of growth management ordinances have been investigated in terms of their spatial impacts and their effect on the real-estate market. Zoning and subdivision regulations have been shown to be counter-productive to the goals of urbanism.[7]

Many of these studies are simply verifying what seems obvious – that initial urbanist ideas were obscured rather than strengthened by their regulatory translation. This failing cannot readily be pinned on urbanists; it is a complex story of accommodation and bureaucratic adaptation. Edward Relph (1987, pp. 74–75) sees it as a case of turning ideals into models, 'simplified for the purpose of textbooks or classrooms or developers, adjusted to the less radical planning tools of zoning and neighborhood units, modified by bureaucracies, adapted to political exigencies, and otherwise thoroughly watered down for ease of application and administration'. This unfortunate translation is epitomized by the products of Hoover's 1931 Conference on Home Building and Home Ownership in which its reports, for example *City Planning and Zoning* and *Subdivision Layout*, endorsed the neighbourhood unit in a form that had by this time been stripped of the best that Unwin, Parker, or even Perry had been able to offer. The idealism of the planned community, or even the neighbourhood unit, gave way to the blatant promotion of property values, racial exclusion, automobile reliance, and middle-class conformity.   It was sometimes a relatively gradual deterioration. The neighbourhood unit concept, for example, can be seen veering from urbanistic principles in its changing pattern and form from one decade to the next. As the concepts of modernist urbanism crept in, and as the needs of the automobile overshadowed the importance of human contact, street-level diversity, and place quality, the neighbourhood unit transformed into something that is hard to admire. One creation was the hybrid 'Perry-Bartholomew' neighbourhood idea, so called from the merger of Perry's ideas with those of Harland Bartholomew. This automobile-dependent, homogeneous, single-use suburban model was implemented widely (Harland Bartholomew, 1932). It eventually landed in places like Plano, Texas, and came to epitomize the worst kind of anti-urbanism produced this century.

The Federal Housing Administration (FHA) did the same with Radburn concepts, taking pieces of the Radburn ideal, extending them in inappropriate and piecemeal ways, and stimulating a deterioration of the planned community ideal. In addition to the fact that zoning disallowed two essential components of urbanism, mixed uses and mixed housing types, the FHA promoted culs-de-sac without a complete treatment of circulation, restrictive covenants without consideration of racial, ethnic and income diversity needs, and large-scale development without understanding of the importance of small-scale diversity (Birch, 1980*a*). On all these fronts, the

FHA enhanced the deterioration of the ideals that were originally an important part of planned community culture.

Two ideas acquired from the culture of planned communities were particularly prone to abuse: the holistic notion of the self-contained enclave, and the idea that there is a relationship between physical form, social cohesion and collective spirit. The first instance is somewhat easier to assess. The unintended consequences of enclave thinking resulted in a lack of integration with surrounding urbanism (physical exclusion); a lack of integration socially (social exclusion); and the tendency to arrange community planning in terms of hierarchies and categories. Note that these first two consequences were meant to be avoided, except in the case of deliberate social exclusion, in which case the attribution to American urbanism is ambiguous anyway. Many of the planned communities included in chapter 6, that is, those that were more about advancing urbanism than in advancing suburban exclusion, wanted to create diverse communities, at least economically.

At the level of the holistically planned enclave, hierarchy and segregation may not have had ill effects. The notion of having a section of the community for retailing and another for recreation, and yet another for industrial activity, may not have been problematic given the integrative nature of the plan. Unfortunately, this kind of arrangement was transplanted on a massive scale in development that was in no way conceived of as holistic in the sense of Radburn. We now have industrial parks and shopping malls, both of which can be interpreted as having evolved out of the hierarchical way of thinking about things.[8]

Failure to consider the whole package of the planned community was a problem of postwar redevelopment. The larger context of housing, including political and social requirements but also elements of form, urban fabric, diversity and the other essential elements of urbanism, was not sufficiently considered. Public housing was a room in an apartment block. Greater attention to the full requirements of an enclave, enforcing more holistic thinking about housing, would have been a good thing.

In light of this, it is somewhat ironic that the lack of social diversity in planned communities – even when they were intended to be urbanistically diverse – was one of the most important instances of their failure. While planned communities failed in terms of including low-income residents, low-income housing failed because of its lack of thinking about a more complete conception of community.

Failure to accommodate social diversity in the planned community is not difficult to see or understand: social diversity goals were wiped out under the weight of market success, and the inability to hold on to collective and other creative means of financing. Forest Hills Gardens, Mumford (1968, p. 173) lamented, failed in its ability to provide workers' housing because of the cost, which 'proved so expensive that the new housing estate was turned into a superior suburb for the well-to-do'. Sunnyside houses, Stein and Wright's hope for the new, cost-efficient planned community, turned out to be more expensive than speculative housing (Lubove, 1963). Often when we see quality high-order urbanism in the form of a planned community or a planned intervention in the existing city, we are more likely to see gentrification of even the smallest apartments. Profit-making and rising property value can be used as measures of success in some cases, but not in the case of building a diverse urbanism. Where this happened, there was deterioration of an ideal.

Another irony is that the deterioration of the high-order plan-making and planned community cultures was related to the inability of the two approaches to integrate better. In otherwise exemplary planned communities like Riverside, Illinois, Mariemont, Ohio and Radburn, New Jersey, the enclaves themselves are exemplary internally, but outside, there is unplanned sprawl and a mostly anti-urbanistic pattern of development. The reason is simply that the plan-making for surrounding areas either did not go far enough, was not implemented, or ignored qualities of place. The contrast with the exquisite planning of the communities they surround accentuates this failure. In some cases, the connections, both physical and political, between the planned community and its surrounding areas might have been blocked by residents on both sides, fearful of being degraded by various externalities.

Sometimes failure attributed to the deterioration of an initial ideal was a matter of the wrong principle being applied in the wrong place. The superblock is one example. This element of the planned community might have made sense in contexts with a less intense urbanism, but applied within a dense urban fabric the superblock was disruptive, disorienting, and gave the development a decidedly 'project' feel. It may have made sense to limit connectivity and redirect traffic to perimeter streets in some situations, but not in the middle of Manhattan, and the severing of public housing into discrete towers within superblocks had legendary, unfortunate consequences.[9]

Notes

1. This is the view of Jon A. Peterson, expressed in a review of Fishman's *The American Planning Tradition*. Published on H-NET Urban History Discussion List, July 3, 2001.
2. For market position see Bryson and Einsweiler, 1987; for communitywide involvement see Smith, 1991; Berke and French, 1994 discuss plan quality; Innes, 1992 discusses the significance of plan preparation procedure.

3. Bruce Stephenson's review of *John Nolen and Mariemont: Building a New Town in Ohio* by Millard F. Rogers, Jr. Published on H-NET Urban History Discussion List, October 5, 2002.
4. See Wilson, 1989, for a fuller list of City Beautiful accomplishments.
5. Ogden Avenue was the only diagonal street constructed per Burnham's Plan of Chicago.
6. See Banfield, 1961 and Bolan, 1967 for structure of influence; structuralist effects see Abu-Lughod, 1991, Harvey, 1973, Markusen et al, 1986; planning disasters resulting from uncertainty see Hall, 1980; postmodern effect see Beauregard, 1989.
7. See Dowall, 1984 on the effects of land-use regulation; see Booth, 1989; McMillen & McDonald, 1990; Natoli, 1971, on the ineffectiveness of land use zoning; for spatial impacts, see Babcock, 1980; for the effect on the real-estate market, see Pogodzinski and Sass, 1991; for counter-urban effects, see Talen & Knaap, 2003; see Pendall, 1999 for the effect on low densities.
8. Ward (2002) suggests that 'industrial estates' and 'collective retailing spaces' are a legacy of Howard's Garden City paradigm.
9. Here one has to disagree with Wilson (1983) who argues that superblocks made sense in the city and that a street grid was an irrational village pattern that RPNY, intelligently, was trying to correct.

Chapter Nine

Conclusion:
the Survival of New Urbanism

Ideas about urbanism in America overlap, complement, or conflict. They overlap in their adherence to the essential qualities of urbanism – diversity, connectivity, public space, equity, place. The articulations of urbanist principles at different levels of intensity, and with different ideas about order, present alternative cultures of urbanism.

Depending on the approach, the principles of urbanism are attended to in different ways. Each culture has its own expression of diversity, for example. In low-order culture, diversity may be more a matter of recognition and tolerance. For high-order, it is a matter of using planning and design to facilitate diversity within some system of order. In high-intensity cultures, there might have been less need to pay attention to the connectivity and mix requirements of urbanism, or at least this was the case initially. In low-intensity culture, the requirements tended to be thought of more deliberately. For every aspect of what it takes to create good urbanism, there is a corresponding proposal fashioned according to the specific orientation of each culture.

There are specific types of overlap. Regionalism is connected to incrementalism in that both tried to accomplish change through the actions of individuals (in the case of regionalism, strong government was also required). Plan-making and planned communities overlap in their belief in the power of the visual image and the clarity of the plan. Conflicts were most likely to occur on the diagonals of the conceptual grid. Plan-makers and regionalists struggle over the issue of structural vs. practical change, and incrementalists and planned community proponents debate the notions of diversity and order. This is represented in figure 9.1.

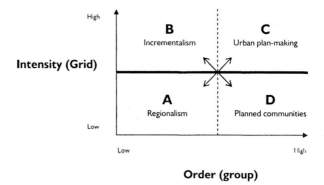

Figure 9.1. The main sources of urbanist culture conflict: order vs. diversity and structure vs. pragmatic change.

From the review of successes and failures, the case could be made that all cultures, if they are to address their deficiencies, need to give something up, add something, or submit to being reconceptualized. This has already happened, although rather than being recognized as evolutionary, it is more often deemed as evidence of incompleteness and failure. For example, planned communities had to evolve to become something that does not seek every facet of living (e.g. industry) within walking distance, and few communities are surrounded by a greenbelt. Regionalism had to give up its requirement for complete and radical change to existing, highly entrenched political and economic systems. Incrementalism remained safe within the confines of small adjustments, but its response to social inequity became weaker. Plan-makers had to give up their master plans and focus instead on process and methods of public engagement.

Against these transformations, cultures need to ensure they are not deteriorating into anti-urbanism. Planned communities have to guard against exclusivity; regionalism against intra-urban neglect; incrementalism against the dismissal of civic purpose; plan-makers against an over-reliance on efficiency and scientific method. The way to accomplish this, as I have argued, is to look to other cultures: high-intensity to low-intensity, high-order to low-order, and, *vice versa*. That this recognition will strengthen each culture individually becomes the primary reason for integrating cultures in the first place.

That there are things 'missing' from each culture does not necessarily mean that each culture will need to absorb elements currently external to them. It means instead that each culture has to look to other cultures for completeness. Each by itself is an incomplete notion of American urbansim. The question I posed in this book was whether these cultures could be reconciled by bringing them into an organized, but pluralist framework of American urbanism. Are ideals about

American urbanism, expressed in four different ways, merely a matter of historical artefact, or could there be some underlying logic to their existence?

The fact that New Urbanism was organized with only minimal recognition of the urbanist cultures that preceded it shows that this logic may in fact exist. In assessing New Urbanism, planned community culture may look dominant, but in fact it is always overlain with elements of the other cultures. There is always a discussion of regionalism in terms not unlike MacKaye, of the importance of small-scale diversity and incremental change precisely as Jacobs wanted things, and of the critical importance of the civic realm in the manner of Hegemann and Peets. The City Beautiful may look hopelessly outdated, but in fact the central idea – that of the importance of public vision and the heightened, physical expression of civic pride – has not gone away.

In the profession of city planning, the lack of conscious connection of so many overlapping causes and historical trajectories is unfortunate. Many in the American city planning fraternity have dismissed the past ideals of urbanism and forged ahead with a clean slate of concepts, technological devices, and more nuanced public participation methods. What is missing is a sense that urbanist idealism has moved forward, that there is a body of work that is beginning to gel and could potentially enable a more powerful effect on settlement form. Instead, there is a sense that no clear notions of good and bad urbanism exist, that the past experiences of city planners amount to nothing more than an interesting backdrop. There is little sense of, to use Lewis Mumford's phrase, a 'usable past'.

I think that many people in the city design professions are unwilling to accept the idea that progress in urbanism is possible. This outlook makes them uncomfortable with the optimism of New Urbanism. They do not see it within the realm of possibilities that certain ideas put forth over the past century could be moving in a certain positive direction. This dismissal can be interpreted as a generalized failure to see any possibility of the development of an American urbanism consisting of overlapping and complementary streams.

It is not difficult to see where this attitude comes from. There have been many mis-steps, and these were brought out in my analysis. Incrementalism began with problems of moral heavy-handedness and ends with a type of relativism that seems unrelated to the other approaches to urbanism; plan-makers and planned community advocates suffered from crude notions of order; regionalists lacked connection to existing cities and the processes that created them. Yet recognition of their liabilities should not result in their dismissal. On the contrary, understanding their limitations should open the way to their continued refinement and strengthening by promoting inter-connections.

In light of the inter-relationships that exist it is legitimate to ask why there is so much violation of urbanistic principles. Is American urbanism really so ineffective, so lacking in actual power? Or, more hopefully, is it simply the failure to see the possibility of a combined and complimentary effort? Failure to produce a more consolidated approach against the problems of sprawl, inner-city and environmental degradation, and a host of other injustices requires a more united front from the planning, environmental and design communities. These are issues that fall under their collective jurisdiction.

City planners and urban designers are now an inclusive group devoted to public process and making sure that all voices are heard. In light of the planning profession's preoccupation with being disinterested, standing back and objectively letting people know how alternative courses of action score on a range of measurable indicators, it is not difficult to form an impression that planners cannot tell good urbanism from bad. No doubt many are not willing to concede that such a distinction can be made. This attitude is clearly at odds with American urbanism as I have defined it, and as it has evolved and culminated in New Urbanism.

The inability to pull something together out of the rich history of American urbanism has been damaging to a profession like city planning which would seem to gain the most from accomplishing it. Partly it is a matter of having thrown the baby out with the bathwater. Civic improvements are disdained as trite or inconsequential, the City Beautiful as oppressive, the City Efficient as narrowly technocratic. These may be fair criticisms in part, but they are too blanketed. Each of these efforts to find the right approach to urbanism contained some good, and some not good. The tendency of American planners to discard them like old shoes has created a situation in which the definition of American urbanism, for them, remains unrefined.

This is partly a result of the loss of connection to the material aspects of urbanism. The transformation of planning from its traditional focus on the physical order of the city to an enterprise concerned with administration, facilitation, and process is certainly something most planners support. In contrast, the connection between the urbanists at the beginning of the twentieth century and the New Urbanists at the end has to do with the mutual emphasis on *physical* planning. Both groups recognized that, while there are many processes involved in procuring physical goals for the city, the physical world and how it is arranged holds meaning because it provides the critical supporting framework for a range of social, cultural and economic functions. Correspondingly, there is a lot of importance attached to the particulars of spatial arrangement and material form.

It is important to understand the degree to which American city planning in general has diverged from physical ideals and suffered a loss of connection to the historical cultures of urbanism. In 1967, the American Institute of Planners amended its charter and deleted all references to physical planning, a reversal of its previous policy to limit membership to those interested in the physical development of cities. Now, there is some evidence of a renewed emphasis on reinstating physical design matters in the profession.[1] This is likely to require, at some point, reconnection with the cultures of urbanism I have described.

One of the recurrent themes of this book has been the failure to maintain a set of ideals during the implementation of those ideals 'on the ground'. Ideas get watered down, subjected to financial realities, and inappropriately applied. This was the main theme of Peter Hall's history of urban planning, in which he showed how the transference of ideas between times and places could, and usually did, spell disaster (Hall, 2002). New Urbanists are trying a different course by attempting to be more flexible and nurturing of ideas – to move them along both theoretically and practically. But they are also open to the possibility that ideas and programmes are failing not because they are flawed intrinsically, but because they are under-developed. Seeing this requires a keen understanding of when and where a given approach should be applied. I think this understanding is something New Urbanists are trying hard to work through.

My analysis leaves open the possibility that many ideas about urban reform have the possibility of coalescing into a new outlook towards urbanism in America. The difficulty is that this outlook requires a certain degree of acceptance of proposals for urban order, and of the utility of normative planning. This runs counter to the main thrust of planning scholarship, which tends to focus on explanation and prediction of city form, not the purposeful guiding of it. There is constant pursuit of collective and analytical approaches to planning, but also a denial of utopian ideals and spatial models in favour of temporal, non-spatial ideals. Aside from New Urbanism, American planning in general is weak on physical, utopian models, but exploding with ideas about how to facilitate communication and analyze urban phenomena. This reflects the elevation of conversations and processes over the substance of vision and order.

The aversion to vision and order is understandable if one focuses only on the issue of overt control that occurred historically. Yet, the problem of over-control was mostly a matter of singularity of vision. What if plural notions of good urbanism could be combined in order to accommodate a plurality of approaches, and thereby mitigate the problem of control? For example, would it be possible to accommodate the idea that streets are social spaces (incrementalists), or the idea that streets are visual, aesthetic elements (the City Beautiful), or that streets promote order, efficiency, and functionality (plan-makers) – depending on the given situation, as a matter of multi-dimensional thinking?

According to the New Urbanists, the same sequence over the response to disorder that occurred in the nineteenth century is occurring now, except that the chaos of urban disorder is sprawl rather than the industrial megalopolis. But the normative response is fashioned from similar urbanist ideals, this time in less monolithic and more context-sensitive terms. This time around, it is possible that rather than letting administrative process and programmatic function wash out the strength of the normative proposal, the proposal will be better integrated with the administrative and legalistic response, thereby blocking the watering down (and misconstruing) of ideals. This time it may be possible to employ multiple strategies that, a century ago, seemed incompatible: code reform, new communities, and an appreciation of urban complexity.

The analysis of planning cultures revealed the importance of maintaining flexibility and the ability to change, grow, and evolve. The inability to do so made a given approach irrelevant. Thus the fate of many of the planning blueprints of the plan-makers was not dissimilar from the fate of CIAM and its inability to continue a discourse because of its position as the only, unchanging and infallible approach. In direct contrast, creating good urbanism in America may be a matter of flexibility, cross-culture recognition, and adaptation. Small-scale ideas may need to adapt to larger-scale scaled ones, low-intensity to high-intensity, high-order to low-order, and *vice versa*. This also means that the implementation devices that a given culture relies on may need to change.

Integrating more than one approach to urbanism also requires ideological tolerance, and New Urbanists have at least attempted to exist apart from any particular political party, religion, cosmology, or other ideological position. It is a strategic recognition that 'urban ideologies', as Fishman (1977) recounts them, have gone down in history as untenable and failed. The city planning of totalitarian dictators like Stalin and Mussolini or even the General Motors 'autopia' of the 1939 World's Fair can be distinguished as ideologies in the sense of Karl Mannheim (1936), ideas intended to advance the interests of one particular class. Sometimes these ideologies are difficult to shed, as in the case of the planned community, but as I argued in Chapter 6, this should not preclude the usefulness of urbanist innovations.

Whether shedding past ideologies is accomplishable or not, there is the constant, urgent need to stick to basic principles of urbanism. There can be flexibility of approach within this, but the goals of urbanism have to be held constant. Failure of an urbanistic ideal like diversity should motivate urbanists from any perspective to work harder to find ways to achieve it within their own particular approach. This requires a connection to recurrent ideals that should be gathering strength rather than diminishing in stature (and requiring reinvention). A proposal historically conceived may not be outdated, but instead may need refinement; instead of abandonment, it may need reworking. This way of thinking essentially means that if we stick to our guns, learn from the past, hold on to certain values, we can refine our success at urbanism. It could also mean that the demise of some urbanistic ideals was premature, and what was needed rather than abandonment was a renewed focus.

There has been an ongoing process of adaptation in the history of American urbanism, changes formed on the basis of where the culture fits in the order/intensity grid. One interpretation of the current status of the four urbanist cultures is shown in figure 9.2. Incrementalism has retained its core focus on small-scale, bottom-up change and is still highly regarded as an approach. It consists of the efforts of neighbourhood activists, everyday urbanists, Alexander and Jacobs followers, and anyone concerned with being as removed from top-down master planning schemes as possible. Plan-making culture is mostly a matter of municipal planning, consisting of bureaucratized planning, the regulations it imposes, the plans of various sorts it continually creates, and the public-private partnerships it seeks in order to secure funding for large-scale civic projects. Planned communities are mostly about private enterprise or public-private partnerships that seek to provide mixed-use development in various forms: residential developments with embedded retail and services, town centres, or transit-oriented developments, for example. Regionalism as originally defined could be broadly cast as simply environmentalism, a category that includes a range of related ways of thinking

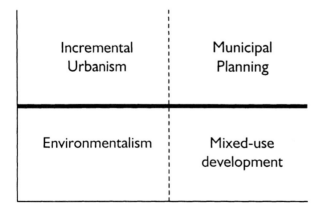

Figure 9.2. The current state of urbanist cultures.

about how to translate human settlement in terms of its natural regional context. Included here would be environmental planning and ecological design.

There is significant overlap but there is also division. Municipal planners support mixed-use development and think of themselves as environmentally minded. Environmentally-oriented planners support compact urban patterns in the form of mixed-use developments of various kinds, and likewise, mixed-use developers see themselves as promoting of environmental objectives. But both mixed-use promoters and environmentalists (in general) are likely to view municipal regulation in the form of zoning and subdivision regulation – a main substance of municipal planning – as grossly insufficient for and even obstructive of good urbanism. In addition, environmentalists may also regard mixed-use development as too land consumptive and not environmentally sound. Incrementalists have few connections with any of the other cultures, and in particular distrust municipal planning as being too insensitive to the needs of poor and minority populations. They have little tolerance for mixed-use development in the form of town centres and planned communities that they see as being mostly for the more affluent.

New Urbanists see that all four cultures have value and need to be incorporated in the promotion of urbanism in America. The regulatory aspects of municipal planning are something to change, but their widespread acceptance and strength is also something to capitalize on – i.e., change in a way that promotes urbanism and its endorsement of diversity rather than promoting of anti-urbanism and its endorsement of separation. They value the broader objectives of environmental planning, and they are at the forefront of promoting mixed-use development within a regional context. All of these are valued at the same time that small-scale urban diversity, incrementalism, is the most revered approach of all.

The Integration Hypothesis

I have argued that the weaknesses of each culture could be addressed to some degree by a better integration of approaches – exactly what the New Urbanists are attempting. This section relates the idea of integrating cultures to the theoretical framework I posed at the beginning.

An analogy between cultural theory and urbanist culture has been used to help contrast, differentiate and compare four different perspectives on urbanism. In the attempt to think more broadly about the relationships among these cultures, there is another important use of Grid/Group theory that can be considered: the idea of pluralism as the basis for an improved approach to urbanism in America. Cultural theorists that use the typology created by grid and group dimensions have postulated that the linkages between the four dimensions are not only necessary but are the basis of each culture's internal vitality and coherence. Each culture is dependent on all other cultures. Despite their conflicting perspectives, there is a need for interconnectedness in order for each culture to be sustained as viable.

This idea can be transferred to the four urbanist cultures as well, and I have argued that urbanism needs to be thought of in these integrative terms. But why should this be the case? On the surface, it seems common sense to say that urbanism in America must be implemented according to varying contexts and norms, corresponding to varying intensities and levels of order. While recognizing that they have at times been complementary and at other times combative, why should urbanism in America require the integration of more than one approach? Is pluralism necessary for maintaining the viability and legitimacy of each cultural type?

It is possible to return to cultural theory for some clues. The analogy with Grid/Group can obviously only be carried so far since the main topic of interest with Douglas' theoretical construct was sociality, a phenomenon with its own unique set of interactions and conflicts. But there are some potentially useful analogies. In a chapter entitled 'Instability of the Parts, Coherence of the Whole' in the book *Cultural Theory* (1990), Thompson, Ellis and Wildavsky discuss the way in which the idea of mutual co-dependence among cultures is necessary for the maintenance of each culture. Further, the 'cohesive clumps' that humans have organized themselves into are in a constant state of 'permanent dynamic imbalance'. There is an ebb and flow to cultural dynamics, where cultures are continually changing their positions and their shape in a way that is neither unilinear nor unidirectional. In the human system, individuals within self-formed cultures move away from one cultural type whenever the failures of that particular culture, or way of life, start to mount. When that happens, individuals within one group start to form alliances with groups outside of it. They sever their allegiance to one group and form bonds with another, and in this way cultures rise and fall in stature.

Cultures 'fail' when they are unable to connect to, or reach out toward, other cultures. For example, hierarchical culture (strong grid, strong group) fails when it does not accommodate the need for individualism and egalitarianism, and its authority goes unchallenged. But cultures can also be prompted to 'reach out for cultural allies who can compensate for their weaknesses'. What is ultimately realized is that each way of life needs the other, not as a matter of consensus, but as a matter of definition and utility: 'adherents of each way of life need the rival ways, either to ally with, define themselves in opposition against, or exploit'. Where there is an attempt to be unicultural, to deny dependent relations, and to define only one way of life, there is failure. Most importantly, the whole remains as such because each way of life needs every other way of life (Thompson, Ellis and Wildavsky, 1990, pp. 88, 96).

Why this should be true is not difficult to conceptualize. Where a society has multiple ways to respond to a given situation – events or shifts in which there are interferences with a particular culture's way of life – the society as a whole will have its best chance of survival. The analogy with urbanism is that, where American society has been able to balance competing urbanist proposals, it stands the best chance of contributing to urbanism. Where balance among cultures occurs, there is less vulnerability to new events and unforeseen changes because there are more options to draw from. There will be less blundering, less tendency to apply the wrong solution in the wrong place. It is a matter of being able to draw from the strengths of each culture, which is not possible where only monolithic cultures are presented as options. Where cultures refuse to see the value in each cultural bias, they 'lose the wisdom attached to that bias, and thus inevitably pile up trouble for themselves' (Thompson, Ellis and Wildavsky, 1990, p. 96). The best systems – in this case, systems of human settlement – are the ones that are open to a diversity of approaches to creating urbanism.

The argument could be made that it is not really true that we need all four cultures to create good urbanism in America. We can never return to a City Beautiful notion of urbanism, for example. However, the case could also be made that all four cultures of urbanism are currently operational in some form, whether we want them to be or not. Mega projects – large civic structures with public significance – are still a part of urbanism in America and probably always will be. And, just like the City Beautiful, it is when proponents fail to understand the requirements of other dimensions of urbanism that they are the least successful overall.

My main hypothesis is that the success or failure of any given culture is linked to its ability to think about its relationship to other cultures, the ability to avoid the 'either/or' propositions of urbanism. The American urbanist experience can be conceptualized as a situation in which planning cultures have tended to be severed, where one culture has doggedly held on to its way of doing things and refused to venture into other approaches to urbanism. This is more pronounced in the U.S than anywhere else. The joining together of the three cultures of plan-making, the planned community, and regionalism occurred in Britain, but the situation in the U.S. has tended to be more divisive (Hall, 2000).

The divisions widened over the course of the twentieth century. Earlier planners were much more integrative, in part a result of common roots. One example is the loss of connection between incrementalist and planned community cultures, which were once more mutually supportive, as seen for example in the connection between the settlement house movement and garden cities development. There was also a loss of connection between the regionalists and planned community advocates. By mid-century, urbanists had largely abandoned the prospect of the planned community in the region. The planned community was subsequently watered down and suburbanized, and failed to keep either condition – the ecological region or the planned urban community – uncompromised and intact.

This is not to say that urbanists of different cultural types have not been aware of the need to be more ecumenical, to look to the possibility of forging alliances that span seemingly disparate ideologies, political philosophies, and religious contexts. Lewis Mumford (1968), for example, advocated both ordered plans for entirely new areas and small-scale opportunities that could work incrementally over the years. The New Urbanists, as I have argued, have been trying for over a decade to promote their integrative notion of urbanism, one that tries to negotiate order that is both incremental and visionary, that is code implemented but allows individual expression, that is sequential but also subjected to master planning. The hope of New Urbanism is that codes and plans (urban plan-making) can be implemented in such a way that they encourage rather than stifle diversity (incrementalism). There is a recognition that focusing on one particular strategy is inadequate.

The integration of urbanist cultures improves the ability to generalize, and urbanists have long recognized the importance of integrative, generalist thinking over and above specialist thinking. Mumford wrote 'the housing problem, the industries problem, the transportation problem, and the land problem cannot be solved one at a time by isolated experts, thinking and acting in a civic vacuum' (Sussman, 1976, p. 13). This has been a recurrent cry in planning – the need to think, plan and act in a way that considers the interconnections of things. But it has also been a largely unachievable goal.

The failure to think integratively, to build on the idea of a pluralist conception of American urbanism, to develop an approach that draws from multiple perspectives about achieving urbanism in America, can be encapsulated in two overriding issues: the linkage of order and diversity, and the linkage of structural and pragmatic change. Each will be discussed in turn.

Order vs. Diversity

The right side of the intensity/order framework was conceptualized as 'high order', or as an approach to urbanism that entails the making of ordered plans. The tension between order and what is seen as its antithesis, diversity, represents one of the most notable divisions in the history of American conceptualizations of urbanism.

The essential problem has been a failure on one culture's part to acknowledge the legitimacy and necessity of the other. This is not about order of the FHA or Euclidean zoning variety, but order as a legitimate element of urbanism.

The idea of ordering the city has become objectionable, and it is now fashionable in city planning to denounce any attempt purposefully to order the city. Planners have become conditioned to believe that attempts at ordering the city, whether based on ideas about nature, value, art, beauty, or social organization, are mostly untenable. The quest to order the city physically is not only foolhardy, but it is a quest to thwart the democratic process, subvert minority interests, overpower the less educated, and inflict social control. As a result, planners get nervous when the discussion of city planning turns to notions of beauty, art, optimal urban form – all of which are related to the notion of order. Their sense is that such notions are entirely subjective, or, at the very least, should either be proven with hard data beforehand or publicly determined through consensus-building processes.

It could be argued that the twentieth-century American urbanist's experience with order has been largely negative and disappointing. Either the attempt at order has resulted in destruction of low-income housing, or it has serviced elite interests at the expense of poor people. There have also been problems with piecemeal implementation. Even more common is the situation in which the original, well-intentioned purpose of order has gone badly. Where, for example, the idea of organizing the city into neighbourhood units transforms into a rationale for isolating the poor, or the attempt to order a chaotic land-use pattern becomes a highly segregated and ultimately dysfunctional single use zoning scheme. The disdain for order, in light of this experience, seems justified.

Another basis of critique is that the imposition of order on the city can not be justified pragmatically. Order is an abstract notion and does not reflect, or integrate with, the true nature of cities. The attempt to impose physical order is utopian but not in a good sense; it is utopian in the sense of being an incongruous idea, a delusion of urbanists that it is even possible to give the city an order. Cities are complex and fine-grained and elude imposed order at every turn.

The person most associated with this critique is Jane Jacobs, and in her essay 'Visual order: its limitations and possibilities', she lays out her argument. She summarizes, 'to approach a city, or even a city neighborhood, as if it were a larger architectural problem, capable of being given order by converting it into a disciplined work of art, is to make the mistake of attempting to substitute art for life' (Jacobs, 1961, p. 373). Jacobs is arguing that the order of life is a very different kind of order from the order of art, and that this confusion has been the problem with planning from the beginning. The agenda of both garden city and City Beautiful schemes – in fact any attempt at imposed town or neighbourhood order – is futile.

This division has been discussed in different contexts throughout. Architecturally, it surfaced as a tension between vernacular and classical architecture. In urbanism, it was evidenced in particular in the disdain of later incrementalists like Jane Jacobs for ordered visions of either the plan-making or the planned community cultures. The tension between incrementalists and the planned community seemed highest, and this tension remains so. This is particularly intriguing since the roots of these two cultures are so connected, both coming out the voluntaristic, communally-minded progressive spirit. But by the post-war period of urban renewal, systems of order had digressed to extremes. What Jacobs and others saw in plan-making and planned communities was the extreme elevation of order over diversity.

Yet complete reversion to diversity without any attention to order may not be the answer for American urbanism. One postulation of success in urbanism is the ability to consider both ordered urbanism and the need for small-scale incrementalism at the same time. It may be useful to cultivate an organic appreciation of intricacy and smallness, as well as an ordered sense of urbanism that allows smallness and diversity to come through and be recognized. Formalism based on conscious plan-making can, sometimes, be seen as a necessary and positive framework for incrementalism. This is not the same as the merging of the picturesque and the formal that was seen in Unwin and Parker's plans, and that allowed them to rise above the contentious debate between the American City Beautiful and the European picturesque rationalized by Sitte.[2] But it does encompass the debate over the degree of planned versus spontaneous organicism, the city of the Grand Manner versus the intricate medieval city, often interpreted as the difference between top-down and bottom-up urbanism, between rigid control and organic, spontaneous diversity.[3]

In the American context, these distinctions have not been very helpful. The failure to recognize the interconnectedness of both ways of approaching urbanism has led us down some dead ends. One reason may be that American society lacks the emergent qualities that other cultures might have in order to make sense of individualized efforts. For example, in Islamic culture, the absence of rules about order in urbanism did not produce an unhealthy, disorganized complexity but rather sustained an organized complexity that was manageable. This, Spiro Kostof (1991) argues, was a result of the strong cultural morays that Islamic society maintained, and that therefore instituted certain overriding principles of urban form that everyone adhered to. There was a shared vision about what urbanism was supposed to look and function like. The absence of top-down governmental control was subsumed by an overarching, ingrained sense of urban-building behaviour.

In the absence of this conformity, and in the presence of the pluralistic nature of urbanism in America, it is arguable that some larger, more formal parameters of urbanism are required.

But in addition, it could be argued that small-scale organic urbanism is dependent on large-scale plan-making, and *vice versa*. Certain strategies of urbanism are scale-dependent, for example a regional light-rail system with designated areas for transit-oriented development is not created through thousands of small local acts. What New Urbanists have in mind is an integration of urbanism that would be the conceptual meeting place of the City Beautiful and the 'voluntary vernacular' described by Spain (2001). It would find commonality between Burnham's 'big plans' and the 'army of builders' needed in the creation of redemptive places. Spain likens the City Beautiful and the voluntary vernacular to the foreground and the background, respectively, of urban physical improvement. Burnham's big plans contributed to beautification of the city in large-scale ways, but the grand plans lacked attention to details. These 'details' included the basic social services needed to sustain a diverse urbanism.

The inability to get it right, to merge large-scale public projects successfully with the incremental processes of urban diversity, has been a continued source of urbanistic failure. How is it possible to build diversity from singular plans conceived at one point in time? The failings of urban renewal, as large urban projects with little connection or acknowledgement of the fundamental diversity of urbanism, can be seen in related terms. The sense of order of the planned community is equally unable to accommodate incremental and small-scale diversity when it is manifested as a peripheral, exclusive suburban enclave. Under these two manifestations of order – urban renewal and suburbanization – it is little wonder that Jane Jacobs and other incrementalists repudiated the idea of order in either format.

Rejection of order might also be interpreted as the rejection of collective notions of shared space in urban places. As a practical matter, collective urban spaces, by definition, virtually require some form of ordering. Most public monuments and spaces did not just happen to occur, they required forethought. This is in some ways a simple affirmation of the importance of planning for the elements of urbanism in the first place, the importance of a human cultural activity that purposefully considers settlement needs in advance. But it also contrasts with the idea that individual, incremental decisions can always self-organize into something that resembles collective space.

While urbanist cultures have recognized that both order and complexity are needed, the problem has been in giving one or the other dimension enough import. This may be a matter of recognizing when one or the other needs to take precedence in a given place and time. For a new planned community, order may be needed at the level of the plan and the implementing code, while small-scale incrementalism may be needed to fill in and fill out the ordered framework. For the revitalization of an already complex and diverse urban place like the inner city, order may be a matter of clarification. This latter tactic was Jane Jacobs' strategy, who said that the task of the urbanist (planner) was to look for ways to clarify underlying order within an existing pattern of diversity.

Structural vs. Pragmatic Change

How far do plans, visions, and proposals for a better American urbanism have to go before they can be said to have succeeded? Is it, as Lewis Mumford believed, that plans would be useless unless positioned within the context of institutional and social change? How deep, in other words, do proposals for urbanism have to go?

The tension between change that gets at the underlying structure of social and economic processes and change that considers only the relatively pragmatic goals of urbanism in physical form is the second major dimension of inter-cultural conflict. What can often be seen in the evolution of urbanist ideals is a gradual wearing away of initial social, economic and political idealism undergirding a particular urbanistic proposal. For example, the anarchist roots of regionalism are now barely perceptible, but the content of the urbanism is still focused on compact, non-sprawling urban form organized within a regional landscape. And while planned communities in America did not show a penchant for communal ownership of property, a social and political ideal, the physical form of the garden city as first conceived by Unwin and Parker is still admired and emulated. The question then is whether the disassociation between physical form and underlying principles like anarchism and social communalism is what ultimately leads to failure.

Some urbanists believe they are moulding a new reality, and that the weakness of the physical planners is their complacency – an approach that, relatively speaking, is merely a superficial adjustment. The contrast was epitomized by the tension between the RPAA and the RPA (discussed throughout this book but particularly in chapters 5 and 7), an obvious case of two cultures colliding. The first question to ask is whether it is necessary, or even possible, to integrate the urbanism of Burnham and Adams (and the commercial focus they had), with the urbanism of Geddes, Mumford and MacKaye, and the more sweeping and radical urbanism they advanced. At the very least, it will require a reinterpretation of what it means to be 'radical' in promoting urbanistic change. American urbanism as a multi-dimensional concept seems unlikely to stake its claim on anti-corporatism, but neither is it about working within the established trajectory of conventional urban development. It is not striking out against the existing political and institutional institutions of urban change, but neither is it surrendering to the forces of urban degeneration.

Resolving the tension between practical change and change to the underlying system is not likely to be easily negotiated. It will involve questioning the stability of the processes that have led to our current predicament. For the more radical urbanist, phenomena like 'just-in-time' inventorying, globalized capital, and large volume retailing based on razor-thin profit margins are not in themselves unchanging. These economic processes have caused great change in the urban landscape, but that is not interpreted as a sign of some innate immutability. In critiquing urban studies that emphasize technological change, Lewis Mumford (1968, p. 113) denounced their underlying assumption that 'the very processes of change now under observation are themselves seen as unchanging; that is, that they may be neither retarded, halted, nor redirected nor brought within a more complex pattern that would reflect more central human needs'.

Had this way of thinking been better received, the RPA might not have made the concessions it made. In the end, the approach to urbanism advocated by plan-makers like Adams amounted to the weakening of ideals – suburbanization of the areas surrounding the core as an ineffective strategy to relieve congestion at the centre. The urbanistic vision became 'purely pragmatic', as one biographer noted, seen clearly in their 'Diagrammatic Scheme for Regional Highway Routes'. Adams' quip that 'there is nothing to be gained by conceiving the impossible' reflected the ultimate triumph of a plan-making culture devoid of serious consideration of the urbanist cultures on the bottom half of the intensity/order grid (Thomas, 1994, pp. 266–267).

One way to assess whether structural changes are required is to analyze why urbanism without these changes failed. Is it possible to detect whether the implementation failed because the structural basis – the political, economic, and social requirements for change – were not altered or alterable? We could consider, as a start, a list of impediments to the implementation of urbanism more generally. The following list is adapted from a statement by Andres Duany[5] on the impediments to walkable, compact and mixed-use communities: environmental regulations like mandatory greenways that thwart urban connectivity; zoning that precludes mixed use and mandates poor spatial definition through mechanisms like setbacks and parking requirements; a public that generally likes to avoid network connectivity, mixed use, density and affordable housing; secondary mortgage markets that only accept standard suburban typologies; marketing that caters to anti-urban biases through its promotion of gated communities and privatized civic amenities; an architectural establishment that accentuates frontage articulation, quantity over quality, and the internalization of urban amenities; civil engineering standards that ignore context, over-engineer infrastructure, and discount transit.

It could be argued that all of these blockages could be changed, and will only be changed, under a different political and socio-economic regime. It could be argued that a different economic reality is needed to change secondary mortgage market requirements, that a different environmental and architectural ethos is needed, that catering to the automobile is an outgrowth of hard political realities that have to do with favouring private consumption and corporate wealth above all else. But it could also be argued that the innate appeal of an emerging American urbanism will ultimately find the power to turn things around.

Notes

1. See, for example, the essays in Rodwin and Sanyal, 2000.
2. In England, it has been argued that Hampstead Garden Suburb fails in its merger of Sittesque informality and heavy-handed, City Beautiful formalism, resulting in parts that are 'curiously dead'; see Hall, 2002, p. 108.
3. See also Kelbaugh, 2002 on this point, especially chapter 3.
4. Michael Mehaffy, personal communication, October, 2001. Mehaffey references the writings of Whitehead and Wittgenstein in his discussion of the progression of human consciousness.
5. Communication sent by Andres Duany and posted on the 'Practice of New Urbanism' (Pro-Urb) listserve on October 4, 2002.

Bibliography

Abbott, C., Howe, D. and Adler, S. (1994) Planning the Oregon Way: A Twenty-Year Evaluation. Corvallis, OR: Oregon State University Press.

Abbott, Carl (1993) Five strategies for downtown: Policy discourse and planning since 1943. *Journal of Public History*, **5**, pp. 5–27.

Abu-Lughod, J.L. (1991) *Changing Cities*. New York: Harper Collins.

Abrams, Charles (1952) Something gained by overcrowding. *American Institute of Planners Journal*, **18**, pp. 95–96.

Ackerman, Frederick L. (1918) Houses and ships. *American City*, **19**, pp. 85–86.

Adams, Thomas (1932) A communication: in defense of the Regional Plan. *New Republic*, **71**, July 6, pp. 207–210.

Adams, Thomas (1935) *Outline of Town and City Planning: A Review of Past Efforts and Modern Aims*. New York: Russell Sage Foundation.

Addams, J. (1893) The subjective necessity for social settlements, in Adams, Henry C. (ed.) (1893) *Philanthropy and Social Progress*. New York: Thomas Y. Cromwell. Republished as chapter six of Jane Addams (1910) *Twenty Years at Hull House*. New York: Macmillan. Also available in *the informal education archives*: http://www.infed.org/archives/e-texts/addams.htm.

Addams, Jane (1895) *Hull House Maps and Papers*. New York: Thomas Y. Crowell & Co.

Addams, Jane (1909) *The Spirit of Youth and the City Streets*. New York: Macmillan. BoondocksNet Edition, 2001. http://boondocksnet.com/editions/youth/ (July 6, 2001).

Addams, Jane (1912) A modern Lear. *Survey*, **XXIX**, November 2, pp. 131–137.

Addams, Jane and Woods, Robert *et al.* (1893) *Philanthropy and Social Progress*. Boston: Thomas Y. Crowell.

Alberti, Leon Battista (1452, 1485) *De re aedificatoria*. Printed by Nicolaus Laurentinii, Alemanus, Florence.

Alexander, Christopher (1965) A city is not a tree. *Architectural Forum*, **122**, April, pp. 58–62; May, pp. 58–61.

Alexander, Christopher (1979) *The Timeless Way of Building*. New York: Oxford University Press.

Alexander, C., Ishikawa, S., Silverstein, M., Jacobson, M., Fiksdahl-King, I. and Angel, S. (1977) *A Pattern Language*. New York: Oxford University Press.

Alexander, C., Neis, H., Anninou, A. and King, I. (1987) *A New Theory of Urban Design*. New York: Oxford University Press.

Alexander, E.R. (1981) If planning isn't everything, maybe its something. *Town Planning Review*, **52**, pp. 131–142.

Alexander, E. R. and Faludi, A. (1989) Planning and plan implementation: Notes on evaluation criteria. *Environment and Planning B: Planning and Design*, **16**, pp. 127–140.

Alland, Alexander (1972) *Jacob Riis: Photographer and Citizen*. New York: Millerton.

Altshuler, Alan A. (1983) The intercity freeway, Krueckeberg, Donald A. (ed.) *Introduction to Planning History in the United States*. New Brunswick, NJ: The Center for Urban Policy Research, pp. 190–234.

Altshuler, Alan A., Luberoff, David E. and the Lincoln Institute of Land Policy (2003) *Mega-Projects: The Changing Politics of Urban Public Investment*. Washington, D.C.: The Brookings Institution.

Anas, Alex (1999) The costs and benefits of fragmented metropolitan governance and the new regionalist policies. *Planning and Markets*, 2(1). Online journal: http://www-pam.usc.edu/.

Appelbaum, Stanley (1980) *The Chicago World's Fair of 1893: A Photographic Record*. New York: Dover Publications.

Arendt, Randall (1999) *Crossroads, Hamlet, Village, Town: Design Characteristics of Traditional Neighborhoods, Old and New*. Chicago: American Planning Association.

Arnold, Joseph L. (1971) *The New Deal in the Suburbs: a History of the Greenbelt Town Program 1935–1954*. Columbus, Ohio: Ohio State University Press.

Asad, T. (1979) Anthropology and the analysis of ideology. *Man*, 14, pp. 607–627.

Atkins, R., Jr. (1991) *Egalitarian Community: Ethnography and Exegesis*. Tuscaloosa: University of Alabama.

Atterbury, Grosvenor (1912) Forest Hills Gardens, Long Island. *Brickbuilder*, 21, December, pp. 317–318.

Babcock, R.F. (1980) The spatial impact of land use and environmental controls, in Solomon, A.P. (ed.) *The Prospective City*. Cambridge, MA: MIT Press, pp. 264–287.

Baldassare, Mark (1988) *Trouble in Paradise: The Suburban Transformation in America*. New York: Columbia University.

Banerjee, Tridib and Baer, William C. (1984) *Beyond the Neighborhood Unit: Residential Environments and Public Policy*. New York: Plenum Press.

Banfield, E.C. (1961) *Political Influence*. New York: Free Press.

Banham, Reyner (1967) *Theory and Design in the First Machine Age*. London: The Architectural Press.

Banik-Schweitzer, Renate (1999) Urban visions, plans, and projects, 1890–1937, in Blau, Eve and Platzer, Monika (eds.) *Shaping the Great City: Modern Architecture in Central Europe, 1890–1937*. Munich: Prestel, pp. 58–72.

Barkun, Michael (1984) Communal societies as cyclical phenomena. *Communal Societies*, 4, pp. 35–48.

Barnett, Jonathan (1986) *The Elusive City: Five Centuries of Design, Ambition and Miscalculation*. New York: Harper & Row.

Barnett, Jonathan (2003) *Redesigning Cities: Principles, Practice, Implementation*. Chicago: American Planning Association.

Bartholomew, Harland (1932) *Urban Land Uses*. Cambridge, MA: Harvard University Press.

Barzun, Jacques (2000) *From Dawn to Decadence: 1500 to the Present: 500 Years of Western Cultural Life*. New York: Harper Collins.

Bauer, Catherine (1934) *Modern Housing*. Boston: Houghton Mifflin.

Bauer, Catherine (1943–1944) Cities in flux. *American Scholar*, XIII, pp. 70–84.

Bauman, John F. (1983) Visions of a post-war city: a perspective on urban planning in Philadelphia and the nation, 1942–1945, in Krueckeberg, Donald A. (ed.) *Introduction to Planning History in the United States*. New Brunswick, NJ: The Center for Urban Policy Research, pp. 170–189.

Beard, Charles A. (1914) *Contemporary American History, 1877–1913*. New York: The Macmillan Company.

Beard, Mary Ritter (1915) *Woman's Work in Municipalities*. New York: D. Appleton.

Beauregard, R.A. (1989) Between modernity and postmodernity: the ambiguous position of U.S. planning. *Environment and Planning D: Society and Space*, 7, pp. 381–395.

Beauregard, Robert A. (2002) New Urbanism: ambiguous certainties. *Journal of Architectural and Planning Research*, 19(3), pp. 181–194.

Beecher, Catharine E. (1842) *A Treatise on Domestic Economy, For the Use of Young Ladies at Home and at School*, rev. ed. Boston: T.H. Webb

Berke, Philip R. and French, Steven (1994) The influences of state planning mandates on local plan quality. *Journal of Planning Education and Research*, 13(4), pp. 237–250.

Bernstein, Basil (1971–1973) *Class, Codes and Control*. London: Routledge & Kegan Paul.

Berry, Brian (1992) *America's Utopian Experiments: Communal Havens for Long-Wave Crises*. Hanover, NH: University Press of New England.

Bing, Alexander M. (1925) New towns for old: can we have garden cities in America? *Survey Graphic*, 7, May, pp. 172–173, 190.

Birch, Eugenie Ladner (1980*a*) Radburn and the American planning movement: the persistence of an idea. *Journal of the American Planning Association*, 46, pp. 424–439.

Birch, Eugenie Ladner (1980*b*) Advancing the art and science of planning: Planners and their organizations, 1909–1980. *Journal of the American Planning Association*. 46, pp. 22–49.

Birch, Eugenie Ladner (1994) From civic worker to city planner: women and planning, 1890–1980, in Krueckeberg, Donald A. (ed.) *The American Planner: Biographies and Recollections*. New Brunswick, NJ: Center for Urban Policy Research, pp. 396–427.

Birch, Eugenie Ladner (2002) Five generations of the garden city: tracing Howard's legacy in twentieth-century residential planning, in Parsons, Kermit C. and Schuyler, David (eds.) *From Garden City to Green City*. Baltimore: Johns Hopkins University Press, pp. 171–200.

Blackford, Mansel G. (1993) *The Lost Dream: Businessmen and City Planning on the Pacific Coast, 1890–1920*. Columbus: Ohio State University Press.

Bluestone, Daniel (1993) *Constructing Chicago*. New Haven, CT: Yale University Press.

Boardman, Philip (1944) *Patrick Geddes, Maker of the Future*. Chapel Hill, NC: University of North Carolina Press.

Boholm, A. (1996) Risk perception and social anthropology: critique of cultural theory. *Ethnos*, 61(1–2), pp. 64–84.

Bolan, R.S. (1967) Emerging view of planning. *American Institute of Planners Journal*, 33, pp. 233–244.

Booth, C. (1902–1903) *Life and Labour of the People in London*. 17 volumes in 3 series. London: Macmillan.

Booth, P. (1989) How effective is zoning in the control of development? *Environment and Planning B: Planning and Design*, 16, pp. 401–415.

Boyer, M. Christine (1983) *Dreaming the Rational City: the Myth of American City Planning*. Cambridge, MA: MIT Press.

Brain, David (2005) From good neighborhoods to the sustainable city: social science and the social agenda of the new urbanism. *International Regional Science Review*, 28, pp. 217–238.

Bressi, Todd W. (ed.) (2002) *The Seaside Debates: A Critique of the New Urbanism*. New York: Rizzoli.

Broadbent, Geoffrey (1990) *Emerging Concepts in Urban Space Design*. London: Van Nostrand Reinhold.

Bryson, J.M. and Einsweiler, R. C. (1987) Strategic planning. *Journal of the American Planning Association*, 53, pp. 6–8.

Buckingham, J.S. (1849) *National Evils and Practical Remedies, with the Plan of a Model Town . . . Accompanied by an Examination of some important Moral and Political Problems*. London: Peter Jackson.

Buls, Charles (1893) *L'Esthetique des Villes*. Brussels: Bruyland-Christople.

Bunnell, Gene (2002) *Making Places Special: Stories of Real Places Made Better by Planning*. Chicago: Planners Press.

Burgess, Ernest W. (1925) The growth of the city: an introduction to a research project, in Park, Robert E., Burgess, Ernest W. and McKenzie, Roderick D. (eds.) *The City*. Chicago: University of Chicago Press, pp.47–62.

Burnham, Daniel H. (1902) White City and capital city. *Century Magazine*, 63, February, pp. 619–620.

Burnham, Daniel H. (1910) A City of the Future under a Democratic Government. Paper presented at RIBA, Town Planning Conference, London, 10–15 October, 1910. Published in *Transactions of the Town Planning Conference*, 1911. London: RIBA, pp. 369–378.

Burnham, Daniel H. and Bennett, Edward H. (1909) *Plan of Chicago*. Republished 1970. New York: Da Capo Press.

Calthorpe, Peter (1993) *The Next American Metropolis: Ecology, Community, and the American Dream*. New York: Princeton Architectural Press.

Calthorpe, Peter and Fulton, William (2001) *The Regional City: Planning for the End of Sprawl*. Washington, D.C.: Island Press.

Caulkins, D. Douglas (1995) High technology entrepreneurs in the peripheral regions of the United Kingdom, in Byron, R. (ed.) *Economic Futures on the North Atlantic Margin: Selected Contributions to the Twelfth International Seminar on Marginal Regions*. Aldershot: Avebury, pp. 285–297

Caulkins, D. Douglas (1997) Is small still beautiful? Low growth firms and regional development in Scotland's Silicon Glen, in Andelson, J. (ed.) *Anthropology Matters: Essays in Honor of Ralph Luebben*. Grinnell, IA: Grinnell College, pp. 53–63.

Caulkins, D. Douglas (1999) Is Mary Douglas's grid/group analysis useful for cross-cultural research? *Cross-Cultural Research*, 33(1), pp. 108–128.

Century, The (1887) Municipal patriotism. *The Century*, 35(2), pp. 325–326.

Chambers, John Whiteclay (1992) *The Tyranny of Change: America in the Progressive Era 1890–1920*. New Brunswick, NJ: Rutgers University Press.

Chapin, E. H. (1854) *Humanity in the City*. New York: De Witt and Daveport.

Chase, John, Crawford, Margaret and Kaliski, John (1999) *Everyday Urbanism*. New York: Monacelli Press.

Chase, Stuart. 1925. *The Tragedy of Waste*. New York: Macmillan Company.

Chase, Stuart (1932) *A New Deal*. New York: Macmillan Company.

Chase, Stuart (1936) *Rich Land, Poor Land*. New York: Whittlesey House.

Christensen, C.A. (1977) The American Garden City: Concepts and Assumptions. Unpublished Ph.D. dissertation, University of Minnesota.

Chudacoff, Howard P. and Smith, Judith E. (2000) *The Evolution of American Urban Society*, 5th ed. Upper Saddle River, NJ: Prentice Hall.

Churchill, Henry S. (1954) Planning in a Free Society. *American Institute of Planners Journal*, 20, pp 189–192.

Churchill, Henry S. (1994) Henry Wright: 1878–1936, in Krueckeberg, Donald A. (ed.) *The American Planner: Biographies and Recollections*, 2nd ed. New Brunswick, NJ: Center for Urban Policy Research, pp. 243–264.

City Planning (1910) Hearing Before the Committee on the District of Columbia United States Senate on the Subject of City Planning. 61st Congress, 2nd Session, Senate Document No. 422. Washington: Government Printing Office, pp. 74–75.

Clark, John and Martin, Camille (1996) *Liberty, Equality, Geography: The Socialist Tought of Elisée Reclus*. Littleton, CO: Aigis Publications.

Columbia Encyclopedia, 6th edition (2001) Paul Vidal de la Blache. http://www.bartleby.com/65/vi/Vidaldel.html

Committee of the Regional Plan of New York and Its Environs (1929) *Regional Plan of New York and Its Environs*. Vol. II. *The Building of the City*. New York: RPNY.

Congress for the New Urbanism (2000) *Charter of the New Urbanism* (edited by Leccese, Michael and McCormick, Kathleen). New York: McGraw-Hill.

Cooley, Charles Horton (1902) *Human Nature and the Social Order*. New York: Scribner's.

Cooley, Charles Horton (1909) *Social Organization*. New York: Charles Scribner's Sons, chapter 3: Primary groups, pp. 23–31.

Corbett, Michael and Corbett, Judy (1999) *Sustainable Development: Learning from Village Homes*. Washington, D.C.: Island Press.

Crawford, Margaret (1996) *Building the Workingman's Paradise: The Design of American Company Towns*. New York: Verso Books.

Creese, Walter L. (1967) *The Legacy of Raymond Unwin: A Human Pattern for Planning*. Cambridge, MA: The MIT Press.

Creese, Walter L. (1992) *The Search for Environment*. Baltimore: Johns Hopkins University Press.

Cronon, William (1991) *Nature's Metropolis: Chicago and the Great West*. New York: W.W. Norton.

Cullen, Gordon (1961) *The Concise Townscape*. New York: Van Nostrand Reinhold.

Culpin, Edwart G. (1913) *The Garden City Movement Up-To-Date*. London: The Garden Cities and Town Planning Association.

Dahir, J. (1947) *The Neighborhood Unit Plan*. New York: Russell Sage Foundation.

Dake, K. (1991) Orienting dispositions in the perception of risk: an analysis of contemporary worldviews and cultural biases. *Journal of Cross-Cultural Psychology*, 22, pp. 61–82.

Dal Co, Francesco (1979) From parks to the region: progressive ideology and the reform of the American city, in Ciucci, Giorgio, Dal Co, Francesco, Manieri-Elia, Mario and Tafuri, Manfredo (eds.) *The American City: From the Civil War to the New Deal*. Cambridge, MA: The MIT Press.

Darwin, Charles (1859) *On the Origin of Species*. London: John Murray.

Davis, Allen F. (1967) *Spearheads for Reform: The Social Settlements and the Progressive Movement,1890–1914*. New York: Oxford University Press.

Davis, Allen F. (1983) Playgrounds, housing, and city planning, in Krueckeberg, Donald A.

(ed.) *Introduction to Planning History in the United States*. New Brunswick, NJ: The Center for Urban Policy Research, pp. 73–87.

Davis, Allen F. (1991) Settlement houses, in Foner, Eric and Garraty, John A. (eds.) *The Readers's Companion to American History*. http://www.myhistory.org/historytopics/articles/settlement_houses.html

Dear, Michael (1986) Postmodernism and planning. *Environment and Planning D: Society and Space*, **4**, pp. 367–384.

Dewey, John and Tufts, James (1908) *Ethics*. New York: Henry Holt.

Douglas, Mary (1966) *Purity and Danger. An Analysis of Concepts of Purity and Taboo*. London: Routlege and Kegan Paul.

Douglas, Mary (1978) *Cultural Bias*. London: Royal Anthropological Institute.

Douglas, Mary and Ney, S. (1998) *Missing Persons. A Critique of Personhood in the Social Sciences*. Berkeley: University of California Press.

Douglas, Mary and Wildavsky, A. (1982) *Risk and Culture: An Essay on the Selection of Technological and Environmental Dangers*. Berkeley, CA: University of California Press.

Dovey, Kimberly (1990) The pattern language and its enemies. *Design Studies*, Vol. **II**(1), pp. 3–9.

Dowall, D.E. (1984) *The Suburban Squeeze*. Berkeley, CA: University of California Press.

Downing, Andrew Jackson (1842, 1981) *Cottage Residences*. New York: Dover Publications.

Draper, Joan E. (1996) The art and science of park planning in the United States: Chicago's small parks, 1902 to 1905, in Sies, Mary Corbin and Silver, Christopher (eds.) *Planning the Twentieth-Century American City*. Baltimore: Johns Hopkins University Press, pp. 98–119.

Duany, Andres (2002) An introduction to the special issue: the transect. *Journal of Urban Design*, 7(3), pp. 251–260.

Duany, Andres, Plater-Zyberk, Elizabeth and Speck, Jeff (2000) *Suburban Nation: The Rise of Sprawl and the Decline of the American Dream*. New York: North Point Press.

Dubois, W.E.B. (1899) *The Philadelphia Negro*. New York: Lippincott.

Durack, Ruth (2001) Village vices: the contradiction of new urbanism and sustainability. *Places*, 14(2), pp. 64–69.

Easterling, Keller (1999) *Organization Space: Landscapes, Highways, and Houses in America*. Cambridge, MA: MIT Press.

Eaton, Ruth (2002) *Ideal Cities: Utopianism and the (Un)Built Environment*. London: Thames & Hudson.

Egleston, Nathaniel Hillyer (1878) *Villages and Village Life: Hints for Their Improvement*. New York: Harper.

Ellin, Nan (1996) *Postmodern Urbanism*. New York: Princeton Architectural Press.

Ellis, R. and Wildavsky, A. (1990) A cultural analysis of the role of abolitionists in the coming of the Civil War. *Comparative Studies in Society and History*, **31**, pp. 89–116.

Elsheshtawy, Yasser (1997) Urban complexity: towards the measurement of the physical complexity of street-scapes. *Journal of Architectural and Planning Research*, 14(4), pp. 301–316.

Ely, Richard T. (1885) Pullman: a social study. *Harper's Monthly*, **70**, February.

Etzioni, Amitai (2004) *The Common Good*. Oxford, UK: Polity Press.

Evans, Harold (2000) *The American Century*. New York: Alfred A. Knopf.

Ewing, Reid (1990) The evolution of new community planning concepts. *Urban Land*. June, pp. 13–17.

Fainstein, N.I. and Fainstein, S.S. (1987) Economic restructuring and the politics of land use planning in New York City. *Journal of the American Planning Association*, 53(2), pp. 237–248.

Fairbanks, Robert B. (1996) Planning, public works, and politics: the Trinity River reclamation project in Dallas, in Sies, Mary Corbin and Silver, Christopher (eds.) *Planning the Twentieth-Century American City*. Baltimore: Johns Hopkins University Press, pp. 187–212.

Fairfield, John D. (1993) *The Mysteries of the Great City: The Politics of Urban Design, 1877-1937*. Columbus, Ohio: Ohio State University Press.

Federal Housing Authority (1938) *Planning Profitable Neighborhoods*. Washington D.C.: Government Printing Office.

Feld, Marjorie N. (1997) Lillian Wald, in Hyman, Paula and Moore, Deborah Dash (eds.) *Jewish Women in America: An Historical Encyclopedia*. New York: Routledge. http://www.mayan.org/voices/history/wvbook/11book_wald.html

Fisher, Irving D. (1994) Frederick Law Olmsted: the artist as social agent, in Krueckeberg,

Donald A. (ed.) *The American Planner: Biographies and Recollections*. New Brunswick, NJ: Center for Urban Policy Research, pp. 37–60.

Fishman, Robert (1977) *Urban Utopias in the Twentieth Century: Ebenezer Howard, Frank Lloyd Wright, and Le Corbusier*. New York: Basic Books.

Fishman, Robert (1987) *Bourgeois Utopias: The Rise and Fall of Suburbia*. New York: Basic Books.

Fishman, Robert (ed.) (2000) *The American Planning Tradition*. Washington, D.C.: The Woodrow Wilson Center Press.

Fishman, Robert (2001) Foreword, in Calthorpe, Peter and Fulton, William, *The Regional City*. Washington D.C.: Island Press, pp. xv–xxi.

Fishman, Robert (2002) The bounded city, in Parsons, Kermit C. and Schuyler, David (eds.) *From Garden City to Green City*. Baltimore: Johns Hopkins University Press, pp. 58–66.

Florida, Richard (2002) *The Rise of the Creative Class*. New York: Basic Books.

Foglesong, Richard E. (1986) *Planning the Capitalist City*. Princeton, NJ: Princeton University Press.

Ford, George B. (1913) The city scientific. *Engineering Record*, **67**, May 17, pp. 551–52.

Ford, George B. (1917) *City Planning Progress in the United States*. Washington, D.C.: The Journal of the American Institute of Architects.

Frampton, Kenneth (2000) Foreword, in Mumford, Eric, *The CIAM Discourse on Urbanism, 1928–1960*. Cambridge: MIT Press.

Friedmann, J. (1987) *Planning in the Public Domain*. Princeton, NJ: Princeton University Press.

Friedmann, John (1989) Planning in the public domain: discourse and praxis. *Journal of Planning Education and Research*, 8(2), pp. 128–130.

Friedmann, John (1998) Planning theory revisited. *European Planning Studies*, 6(3), pp. 245–253.

Friedmann, John and Weaver, Clyde (1979) *Territory and Function: The Evolution of Regional Planning*. London: Edward Arnold.

Funigiello, Philip J. (1972) City planning in World War II: the experience of the National Resources Planning Board. *Social Science Quarterly*, 53(1), pp. 91–104.

Gans, Herbert (1967a) *The Levittowners*. New York: Pantheon Books, Inc.

Gans, Herbert (1967b) Commentary on Stanley Buder's 'The model town of Pullman: town planning and social control in the gilded age'. *Journal of the American Institute of Planners*, **33**, p. 2–4.

Garreau, J. (1991) *Edge City: Life on the New Frontier*. New York: Doubleday.

Garvin, Alexander (2002) *The American City – What Works, What Doesn't*, 2nd ed. New York: McGraw

Geddes, Patrick (1915) *Cities in Evolution*. London: Williams & Norgate.

Gibberd, F. (1953) *Town Design*. Washington, D.C.: Thomson International.

Giedion, Siegfried (1941) *Space, Time and Architecture: The Growth of a New Tradition*. Cambridge, MA: Harvard University Press.

Goodman, Percival and Paul (1947, 1990) *Communitas: Means of Livelihood and Ways of Life*. New York: Columbia University Press.

Goodman, R. (1971) *After the Planners*. New York: Simon & Schuster.

Goss, A. (1961) Neighbourhood units in British new towns. *Town Planning Review*, **32**, pp. 66–82.

Gottdiener, M. (1977) *Planned Sprawl: Private and Public Interests in Suburbia*. Beverly Hills: Sage.

Gould, Stephen Jay (1997) Kropotkin was no crackpot. *Natural History*, July.

Grabow, Stephen (1977) Frank Lloyd Wright and the American city: the Broadacre debate. *Journal of the American Institute of Planners*, **43**(2), April.

Grabow, S. (1983) *Christopher Alexander: The Search for New Paradigm in Architecture*. Boston: Oriel Press.

Gratz, Roberta Brandes, and Norman Mintz (2000) *Cities Back from the Edge: New Life for Downtown*. New York: Wiley.

Grendstad, G. and Selle, P. (1997) Culture theory, postmaterialism and environmental attitudes, in Ellis, R. and Thompson, M. (eds.) *Culture Matters: Essays in Honor of Aaron Wildavsky*. Boulder, CO: Westview.

Grogan, Paul S. and Proscio, Tony (2000) *Comeback Cities: A Blueprint for Urban Neighborhood Revival*. Boulder, CO: Westview.

Guttenberg, Albert Z. (1978) City encounter and 'desert' encounter: two sources of American regional planning thought. *Journal of the American Institute of Planners*, **4**, pp. 399–411.

Hall, Peter (1975) *Urban & Regional Planning*. Harmondsworth: Penguin Books.

Hall, Peter (1980) *Great Planning Disasters*. Berkeley, CA: University of California Press.

Hall, Peter (1989) The turbulent eighth decade: Challenges to American city planning. *Journal of the American Planning Association*, **55**(3), pp. 275–282.

Hall, Peter (1995) Bringing Abercrombie back from the shades. *Town Planning Review*, **66**(3), pp. 227–241.

Hall, Peter (1996) 1946–1996 – from new town to sustainable social city. *Town & Country Planning*, **65**, pp. 295–297.

Hall, Peter (2000) The centenary if modern planning, in Freestone, Robert (ed.) *Urban Planning in a Modern World*. London: E & FN Spon, pp. 20–39.

Hall, Peter (2002) *Cities of Tomorrow: An Intellectual History of Urban Planning and Design in the Twentieth Century*, 3rd ed. Oxford: Blackwell.

Hancock, John (1988) The New Deal and American planning: the 1930s, in Schaffer, Daniel (ed.) *Two Centuries of American Planning*. London: Mansell, pp. 197–230.

Hancock, John (1994) John Nolen: the background of a pioneer planner, in Krueckeberg, Donald A. (ed.) *The American Planner: Biographies and Recollections*, 2nd Ed. New Brunswick, NJ: Center for Urban Policy Research, pp. 61–84.

Hancock, John (1996) Smokestacks and geraniums: planning and politics in San Diego, in Sies, Mary Corbin and Silver, Christopher (eds.) *Planning the Twentieth Century American City*. Baltimore: Johns Hopkins University Press, chapter 7.

Harvey, David (1973) *Social Justice and the City*. London: Edward Arnold.

Harvey, David (1989) *The Condition of Postmodernity*. Oxford: Blackwell.

Harvey, David (1997) The New Urbanism and the communitarian trap. *Harvard Design Magazine*, Winter/Spring, pp. 68–69.

Harvey, David (2000) *Spaces of Hope*. Berkeley, CA: University of California Press.

Hayden, Dolores (1976) *Seven American Utopias: The Architecture of Communitarian Socialism, 1790–1975*. Cambridge, Mass: MIT Press.

Hayden, Dolores. 1997. *The Power of Place: Urban Landscapes as Public History*, 2nd ed. Cambridge: MIT Press.

Hayden, Dolores. 2002. *Redesigning the American Dream: Gender, Housing, and Family Life*, 2nd ed. New York: Norton.

Hays, Samuel P. (1995) *The Response to Industrialism, 1885–1914*. Chicago: University of Chicago Press.

Hayward, Steven (2000) The Irony of Smart Growth Speech to the Center of the American Experiment Luncheon Debate with Ted Mondale, Chairman, Twin Cities Met Council, January 18. http://www.pacificresearch.org/pub/sab/enviro/irony.html#Steven Hayward

Healey, P. (1986) Emerging directions for research on local land-use planning. *Environment and Planning B: Planning and Design*, **13**, pp. 102–120.

Hegemann, Werner and Peets, Elbert (1922) *The American Vitruvius: An Architects' Handbook of Civic Art*. New York: The Architectural Book Publishing Co.

Herbert, G. (1963) The neighborhood unit principle and organic theory. *Sociological Review*, **11**, pp. 165–213.

Heskin, Allan David. 1980. Crisis and response: A historical perspective on advocacy planning. *Journal of the American Planning Association*, **46**(1), pp. 50–63.

Hill, David R. (1993) A case for teleological urban form history and ideas: Lewis Mumford, F.L. Wright, Jane Jacobs and Victor Gruen. *Planning Perspectives*, **8**, 53–71.

Hines, Thomas S. (1991) The Imperial Mall: The City Beautiful Movement and the Washington Plan of 1901–02, in *The Mall in Washington, 1791–1991*. Washington: National Gallery of Art.

Hise, Greg (1996) Homebuilding and industrial decentralization in Los Angeles: the roots of the post-World War II urban region, in Sies, Mary Corbin and Silver, Christopher (eds.) *Planning the Twentieth-Century American City*. Baltimore: Johns Hopkins University Press, pp. 240–261.

Hiss, Tony (1991) *The Experience of Place*. New York: Alfred A. Knopf.

Hoch, Charles (1995) 'The turbulent eighth decade' reviewed, in Stein, Jay M. (ed.) *Classic Readings in Urban Planning: An Introduction*. New York: McGraw-Hill, pp. 25–27.

Hoch, Charles J., Dalton, Linda C. and So, Frank S. (eds.) (2000) *The Practice of Local Government Planning*, 3rd ed. Washington, D.C.: International City/County Management Association.

Holbhook, Agnes Sinclair (1895) Map notes and comments, in Addams, Jane, *Hull House Maps and Papers*. New York: Thomas Y. Crowell & Co., pp. 3–23.

Hood, C. (1996) Control over bureaucracy: Culture theory and institutional variety. *Journal of Public Policy*, **15**, pp. 207–230.

Howard, Ebenezer (1898) *To-Morrow; A Peaceful Path to Real Reform*. London: Swann Sonnenschein.

Howe, Frederic C. (1905, 1967) *The City: The Hope of Democracy*. Seattle, WA: University of Washington Press.

Howe, Frederic C. (1912) The city as a socializing agency: the physical basis of the city: the city plan. *American Journal of Sociology*, **17**, pp. 590–601.

Howe, Frederick C. (1915) *The Modern City and Its Problems*. New York: Charles Scribners' Sons

Hubbard, T.K. and H.V. Hubbard (1929) *Our Cities, Today and Tomorrow: A Study of Planning and Zoning Progress in the United States*. Cambridge, MA: Harvard University Press.

Hudnut, Joseph (1942) Preface, in Sert, Jose Luis, *Can Our Cities Survive? An ABC of Urban Problems, Their Analysis, Their Solutions*. Cambridge: Harvard University Press.

Huet, Bernard (1984) The City as Dwelling Space: Alternatives to the Charter of Athens. *Lotus*, **41**, p. 9.

Hull-House Maps and Papers, by residents of Hull-House (1895) New York: Thomas Y. Crowell & Co.

Ingraham, Catherine (1986) Land of no discovery. *Inland Architect*, **30**(3), pp. 45–53

Innes, Judith E. (1992) Group processes and the social construction of growth management. *Journal of the American Planning Association*, **58**, pp. 440–453.

Isaacs, R. (1948) Are urban neighborhoods possible? *Journal of Housing*, **5**, pp. 177–180.

Jackson, John Brinckeroff (1984) *Discovering the Vernacular Landscape*. New Haven: Yale University Press.

Jackson, John Brinckeroff (1994) *A Sense of Place, A Sense of Time*. New Haven: Yale University Press.

Jackson, Kenneth T. (1985) *Crabgrass Frontier: The Suburbanization of the United States*. New York: Oxford University Press.

Jacobs, Allan (2002) General commentary, in Bressi, Todd W. (ed.) *The Seaside Debates: A Critique of the New Urbanism*. New York: Rizzoli International, pp. 136–152.

Jacobs, Allan and Appleyard, Donald (1987) Toward an urban design manifesto. *American Planning Association Journal*, **53**(1), p. 115.

Jacobs, Jane (1961) *The Death and Life of Great American Cities*. New York: Vintage Books.

Jacobs, Jane (1966) Where city planners come down to earth. *Business Week*, August 20, pp. 101–104.

Jane Addams' Hull-House Museum (1997) List of Hull-House Firsts. The University of Illinois at Chicago. http://www.uic.edu/jaddams/hull/firsts.html

Jane Addams' Hull-House Museum (2002) Bringing Art to Life: Women and the Arts at Hull-House. http://www.uic.edu/jaddams/hull/artlifeexhibit/overview.html

Jencks, Charles (1987) *Modern Movements in Architecture*. New York: Penguin Books.

Johnson, B.B. (1987) The environmentalist movement and grid/group analysis: a modest critique, in Johnson, B.B. and Covello, V.T. (eds.) *The Social and Cultural Construction of Risk: Essays on Risk Selection and Perception*. Dordrecht, Holland: D. Reidel, pp. 147–175.

Johnson, David A. (1988) Regional planning for the great American metropolis: New York between the world wars, in Schaffer, Daniel (ed.) *Two Centuries of American Planning*. London: Mansell, pp. 167–196.

Johnson, David A. (1996) *Planning the Great Metropolis: The 1929 Regional Plan of New York and Its Environs*. London: E & FN Spon.

Johnson, Donald Leslie (2002) Origin of the neighborhood unit. *Planning Perspectives*, **17**, pp. 227–245.

Kantor, Harvey S. (1994) Charles Dyer Norton and the origins of the Regional Plan of New York, in Krueckeberg, Donald A. (ed.) *The American Planner: Biographies and Recollections*, 2nd ed. New Brunswick, NJ: Center for Urban Policy Research, pp. 163–182.

Kelbaugh, Douglas S. (2002) *Repairing the American Metropolis*. Seattle, WA: University of Washington Press.

Kemper, Theodore D. and Collins, Randall (1990) Dimensions of microinteraction. *American Journal of Sociology*, **96**(1), pp. 32–68.

Kent, T. J., Jr. (1964, 1990) *The Urban General Plan*. Chicago: Planners Press.

Kimball, T. (1922) A review of city planning in the United States, 1920–1921. *National Municipal Review*, January.

Kimble, George H.T. (1951) The inadequacy of the regional concept, in Stamp, I.D. and Wooldridge, S.W. (eds.) *London Essays in Geography*. London: Longmans Green.

Klaus, Susan L. (2002) *A Modern Arcadia: Frederick Law Olmsted Jr. & the Plan for Forest Hills Gardens*. Amherst, MA: University of Massachusetts Press.

Knox, Paul L. (1991) The restless urban landscape: economic and sociocultural change and the transformation of Metropolitan Washington, D.C. *Annals of the Association of American Geographers*, 81(2), pp. 181–209.

Kolb, David (2000) The age of the list, Algreen-Ussing, Gregers, Bek, Lise, Frandsen, Steen Bo and Hansen, Jens Schjerup (eds.) *Urban Space and Urban Conservation as an Aesthetic Problem*. Rome: L'Erma di Bretschneider, pp. 27–35.

Kolson, Kenneth (2001) *Big Plans: The Allure and Folly of Urban Design*. Baltimore: Johns Hopkins University Press.

Koolhaas, Rem (1997) What ever happened to urbanism? in Koolhass, Rem and Mau, Bruce, *Small, Medium, Large, Extra Large: The Office for Metropolitan Architecture*. New York: Monacelli Press.

Kostof, Spiro (1991) *The City Shaped*. London: Thames & Hudson, Ltd.

Kostof, Spiro (1992) *The City Assembled*. London: Thames & Hudson, Ltd.

Kostof, Spiro (1993) The design of cities. *Places*, 5(4), pp. 85–88.

Kracauer, Siegfried (1975) The mass ornament. *New German Critique*, 5, Spring, pp. 67–76.

Krieger, Alex (2002) Arguing the 'against' position: new urbanism as a means of building and rebuilding our cities, in Bressi, Todd W. (ed.) *The Seaside Debates: A Critique of the New Urbanism*. New York: Rizzoli, pp. 51–58.

Krier, Leon (1982) The new traditional town: Two plans by Leon Krier for Bremen and Berlin-Tegel. *Lotus*, 36, pp. 101–107.

Krier, Leon (1998) *Architecture: Choice or Fate*. London: Andreas Papadakis.

Kropotkin, Peter (1912) *Fields, Factories and Workshops: or Industry Combined with Agriculture and Brain Work with Manual Work*. London: Thomas Nelson and Sons.

Krueckeberg, Donald A. (1983) The culture of planning, in Krueckeberg, Donald A. (ed.) *Introduction to Planning History in the United States*. New Brunswick, NJ: The Center for Urban Policy Research, Rutgers University.

Krueckeberg, Donald A. (1994) The American planner: a new introduction, in Krueckeberg, Donald A. (ed.) *The American Planner: Biographies and Recollections*, 2nd ed. New Brunswick, NJ: Center for Urban Policy Research, pp. 1–35.

Krumholz, Norman (2001) Connecting Sprawl, Smart Growth, and Social Equity. Paper presented at the Fair Growth Symposium, American Planning Association 2001 National Planning Conference, New Orleans, LA.

Kunstler, James Howard (1993) *The Geography of Nowhere: The Rise and Decline of America's Man-Made Landscape*. New York: Simon and Schuster

Kunstler, James Howard (1996) *Home from Nowhere: Remaking our Everyday World for the Twenty-first Century*. New York: Simon & Schuster.

Kunstler, James Howard (2001) *The City in Mind: Notes on the Urban Condition*. New York: The Free Press.

LaFarge, Albert (ed.) (2000) *The Essential William H. Whyte*. New York: Fordham University Press.

Lamb, Frederick S. (1897) Municipal art. *Municipal Affairs*, 1, 674–676, 678–679, 682–686, 688.

Lanchester, Henry Vaughan (1908) Park systems for great cities. *The Builder*, 95, pp. 343–348.

Lang, Jon (2000) Learning from twentieth century urban design paradigms: lessons for the early twenty-first century. In Freestone, Robert (ed.) *Urban Planning in a Changing World*. London: E & FN Spon, pp. 78–97.

Lang, Michael H. (1996) The design of Yorkship Garden Village: product of the progressive planning, architecture, and housing reform movements, in Sies, Mary Corbin and Silver, Christopher (eds.) *Planning the Twentieth-Century American City*. Baltimore: Johns Hopkins University Press, pp. 120–144.

Lang, Michael H. (1999) *Designing Utopia: John Ruskin's Urban Vision for Britain and America*. Montreal: Black Rose Books.

Larco, Nico (2003) What is urban? *Places, A Forum of Environmental Design*, 15(2), pp. 42–47.

Lasch, Christopher (1965) *The Social Thought of Jane Addams*. Indianapolis: Bobbs-Merrill.

Lawrence, Henry W. (1993) The greening of the square of London: Transformation of urban landscapes and ideals. *Annals of the Association of American Geographers*, **83**(1), pp. 90–118.

Le Corbusier (1948) *Concerning Town Planning*. New Haven: Yale University Press.

Lees, Andrew (1984) The metropolis and the intellectual, in Sutcliffe, Anthony (ed.) *Metropolis 1890–1940*. London: Mansell, pp. 67–94.

LeGates, Richard and Stout, Frederic (1998) *Early Urban Planning 1870–1940*. New York: Routledge.

Levin, Melvin R. (1987) *Planning in Government*. Chicago: Planner's Press.

Lewis, Nelson P. (1916) *The Planning of the Modern City*. New York: John Wiley & Sons (Reissued in 1943 by Harold MacLean Lewis as *Planning the Modern City*).

Lewis, Sinclair (1922) *Babbitt*. New York: Harcourt, Brace and Company.

Ley, David (1987) Styles of the times: liberal and neo-conservative landscapes in inner Vancouver, 1968–86. *Journal of Historical Geography*, **13**(1), pp. 40–56.

Lillibridge, Robert M. (1949) Historic American communities: their role and potential – Part I. *Journal of the American Institute of Planners*, Vol. 19, p. 131–138.

Lim, G.C. (ed.) (1983) *Regional Planning: Evolution, Crisis and Prospects*. Totawa, NJ: Allanheld, Osman and Co.

Lindblom, Charles E. (1959) The science of 'muddling through'. *Public Administration Review*, **19**, Spring, pp. 79–88.

Lindner, Rolf (1996) *The Reportage of Urban Culture: Robert Park and the Chicago School*. Cambridge: Cambridge University Press.

Lofland, Lyn (1998) *The Public Realm: Exploring the City's Quintessential Social Territory*. New York: Aldine De Gruyter.

Lohmann, Karl B. (1931) *Principles of City Planning*. New York: McGraw-Hill.

Longstreth, Richard (1997) The diffusion of the community shopping center concept during the interwar decades. *Journal of the Society of Architectural Historians*, **56**,(3), pp. 268–293.

Lovelace, Eldridge (1992) *Harland Bartholomew: His Contributions to American Urban Planning*. Urbana, IL: University of Illinois.

Low, Thomas E. (2001) Threads of Community in the South: The Past, Present, and Future of New Urbanism. Unpublished paper.

Lubove, Roy (1963) *Community Planning in the 1920's*. Pittsburgh: University of Pittsburgh Press.

Luccarelli, Mark (1995) *Lewis Mumford and the Ecological Region: The Politics of Planning*. New York: Guilford Press.

Lynch, Kevin 1966. Quality in design, in Holland, Lawrence B. (ed.) *Who Designs America?* New York: Doubleday.

Lynch, Kevin (1981) *Good City Form*. Cambridge, MA: MIT Press.

Lyndon, Donlyn and Halprin, Lawrence (1989) Design as a value system. *Places*, **6**(1), pp. 60–67.

MacKaye, B. (1921) An Appalachian Trail: a Project in regional planning. *Journal of the American Institute of Architects*, October.

MacKaye, Benton (1925) The new exploration. *The Survey*, **54**, pp. 153–157, 192.

MacKaye, Benton (1928) *The New Exploration: A Philosophy of Regional Planning*. New York: Harcourt, Brace and Co.

MacKaye, Benton (1940) Regional planning and ecology. *Ecological Monographs*, **10**(3), pp. 349–353.

Mannheim, Karl (1936) *Ideology and Utopia* (Translated by Louis Wirth and Edward Shils). London: Routledge & Kegan auPl.

Manieri-Elia, Mario (1979) Toward an 'Imperial City': Daniel H. Burnham and the City Beautiful Movement, in Cuicci, Giorgio *et. al.* (eds.) *The American City: From the Civil War to the New Deal*. Cambridge, MA: MIT Press, pp. 1–142.

Marcuse, Peter (1987) The grid as city plan: New York City and laissez-faire planning in the nineteenth century. *Planning Perspectives*, **2**, pp. 287–310.

Markusen, A.R., Hall, P. and A. Glasmeier, A. (1986) *High Tech America: The What, How, Where, and Why of the Sunrise Industries*. Boston, MA: Allen and Unwin.

Mars, G. (1982) *Cheat at Work: An Anthropology of Workplace Crime*. Sydney, Australia: Allen and Unwin.

Mars, G. and Nicod, M. (1984) *The World of Waiters*. Sydney: Allen and Unwin.

Marsh, Benjamin (1909) *An Introduction to City Planning, Democracy's Challenge to the American City*. Privately published.

Marsh, Benjamin (1974) *An Introduction to City Planning*. New York: Arno Press (Reprint of 1909 edition published by the author).

Marsh, George P. (1864) *Man and Nature; or, Physical Geography as Modified by Human Action*. New York: Charles Scribner.

Marshall, Alex (2001) *How Cities Work: Suburbs, Sprawl, and the Roads Not Taken*. Austin: University of Texas Press.

Marshall, Peter (1992) *Demanding the Impossible*. London: Harper Collins.

Martin, L. and March, L. (1952) High rise housing. *Journal of Housing*, February.

Mawson, Thomas H. (1911) *Civic Art: Studies in Town Planning, Parks, Boulevards and Open Spaces* London: B.T. Batsford.

McHarg, Ian (1964) The place of nature in the city of man. *The Annals of the American Academy of Political Science* (Urban Revival: Goals and Standards), **325**, March, pp. 1–12.

McHarg, Ian (1969) *Design with Nature*. Garden City, NY: Natural History Press.

McHarg, Ian L. (1998) An ecological method for landscape architecture, in McHarg, Ian L. and Steiner, Frederick R. (eds.) *To Heal the Earth: Selected Writings of Ian McHarg*. Washington, D.C.: Island Press, pp. 212–218.

McHarg, Ian L. and Steiner, Frederick R. (eds.) (1998) *To Heal the Earth: Selected Writings of Ian McHarg*. Washington, D.C.: Island Press.

McKenzie. R.D. (1933) *The Metropolitan Community*. New York: McGraw Hill.

McMillen, D. P. and McDonald, J.F. (1990) A two-limit tobit model of suburban land-use zoning. *Land Economics*, **66**, pp. 272–282.

Melvin, Patricia Mooney (1987) *The Organic City: Urban Definition & Community Organization 1880–1920*. Lexington, KY: The University Press of Kentucky.

Merlin, Pierre (1971) *New Towns*. London: Methuen.

Meyerson, Martin (1956) Building the middle-range bridge for comprehensive planning. *Journal of the American Institute of Planners*, **22**(2), pp. 58–64.

Meyerson, Martin (1961) Utopian traditions and the planning of cities. *Daedalus*, **90**(1), pp. 180–193.

Miller, Donald L. (2000) *The New City/Planned Order and Messy Vitality. A Biography of America.* Allston, MA: WGBH Educational Foundation.

Miller, Mervyn (2002) The origins of the garden city residential neighborhood, in Parsons, Kermit C. and Schuyler, David (eds.) *From Garden City to Green City*. Baltimore: Johns Hopkins University Press, pp. 99–130.

Mills, C. Wright (1951) *White Collar*. New York: Oxford University Press.

Mills, C. Wright (1959) The big city: private troubles and public issues, in Horowitz, Irving Louis (ed.) *Power, Politics, and People*. New York: Oxford University Press.

Monkkonen, Eric (1988) *America Becomes Urban: The Development of U.S. Cities and Towns, 1780–1980*. Berkeley: University of California Press.

Montgomery, John (1998) Making a city: urbanity, vitality and urban design. *Journal of Urban Design*, **3**(1), pp. 93–116.

Moody, Walter D. (1916) *Wacker's Manual of the Plan of Chicago*, 2nd ed. Chicago: Chicago Plan Commission.

Moore, William Jr. (1969) *The Vertical Ghetto*. New York: Random House.

Morris, A.E.J. (1979) The early cities, in *History of Urban Form Before the Industrial Revolutions*. London: George Goodwin, pp. 1–18.

Morrison, Ernest (1995) *J. Horace McFarland – A Thorn for Beauty*. Harrisburg, PA: Pennsylvania Historical and Museum Commission (PHMC).

Moule, Elizabeth (2002) The Charter of the New Urbanism in Bressi, Todd W. (ed.) *The Seaside Debates: A Critique of the New Urbanism*. New York: Rizzoli, pp. 21–26.

Mullin, John Robert (1982) Henry Ford and field and factory: an analysis of the Ford sponsored Village Industries experiment in Michigan, 1918–1941. *Journal of the American Planning Association*, **48**, pp. 419–431.

Mullin, John Robert (1976–1977) American perceptions of German city planning at the turn of the century. *Urbanism Past and Present*, **2**, pp. 5–15.

Mumford, Eric (1995) The 'tower in a park' in America: theory and practice, 1920–1960. *Planning Perspectives*, **10**, 17–41.

Mumford, Eric (2000) *The CIAM Discourse on Urbanism, 1928–1960*. Cambridge: MIT Press.

Mumford, Lewis (1919) The Heritage of the Cities Movement in America; an historical survey. *American Institute of Architects Journal*, **7**, pp. 349–354.

Mumford, Lewis (1924) *Sticks and Stones: A Study of American Architecture and Civilization*. New York: Harcourt Press.

Mumford, Lewis (1925) Regions – to live in. *Survey Graphic*, **7**, May, pp. 151–152.

Mumford, Lewis (1927) The fate of the garden cities. *Journal of the American Institute of Architects*, **15**, pp. 37–49

Mumford, Lewis (1931) Regional Planning. July 8, Address to Round Table on Regionalism, Institute of Public Affairs, University of Virginia, Avery Library, Columbia University. Reprinted in Sussman, Carl (1976) *Planning the Fourth Migration: The Neglected Vision of the Regional Planning Association of America*. Cambridge: MIT Press, pp. 221–267.

Mumford, Lewis (1937) What is a city? *Architectural Record*, November. Reprinted in LeGates, Richard T. and Stout, Frederic (eds.) (1996) *The City Reader*, 2nd ed. London: Routledge, pp. 93–96.

Mumford, Lewis (1938) *The Culture of Cities*. New York: Harcourt, Brace and Co.

Mumford, Lewis (1951) Introduction, in Stein, Clarence, *Toward New Towns for America*. Liverpool: University Press of Liverpool, pp. 11–20.

Mumford, Lewis (1956) The natural history of urbanization, in Thomas, William L.Ed., *Man's Role in Changing the Face of the Earth*. Chicago: University of Chicago Press, pp. 382–400.

Mumford, Lewis (1968) *The Urban Prospect*. New York: Harcourt Brace Jovanovich.

Municipal Journal and Engineer (1906) Demands for the city beautiful. *Municipal Journal and Engineer*, **1**, September 5, p. 243.

Muschamp, H. (1983) *Man about Town: Frank Lloyd Wright in New York City*. Cambridge, MA: MIT Press.

Nassauer, J.I. (1997) Cultural sustainability: aligning aesthetics and ecology, in Nassauer, J.I. (ed.) *Placing Nature: Culture and Landscape Ecology*. Washington, D.C.: Island Press.

National Conference on City Planning (NCCP) (1909) *Proceedings of the Frist National Conference on City Planning*. Facsimile edition. Chicago: American Society of Planning Officials.

National Urban Coalition (1999) National Science and Technology Week report, April. http://www.nsf.gov/od/lpa/nstw/99/nucbrief.htm

Natoli, S.J. (1971) Zoning and the development of urban land use patterns. *Economic Geography*, **47**, pp. 169–184.

Neal, Peter (ed.) (2003) *Urban Villages and the Making of Communities*. London: Spon Press.

Ndubisi, Forster (2002) *Ecological Planning: A Historical and Comparative Synthesis*. Baltimore: Johns Hopkins University Press.

Newman, Oscar (1972) *Defensible Space*. New York:. Macmillan.

Nobel, Philip (2001) Far corner: some new ways of thinking about pragmatism in architecture. *Metropolis*. July. Any more details?

Nolen, John and Olmsted, F.L. (1906) The normal requirements of American towns and cities in respect to public open spaces. *Charities and the Commons [Survey]* **XVI**, June 30.

Nolen, John (1908) The Philosophy of City Planning. From the Rare and Manuscript Collections, Carl A. Kroch Library, Cornell University, Ithaca, NY.

Nolen, John (1909a) City Planning and the Civic Spirit. Lecture presented at the annual meeting of the American Civic Association, held at Cincinnati, November 16, 1909. From the Rare and Manuscript Collections, Carl A. Kroch Library, Cornell University, Ithaca, NY.

Nolen, John (1909b) What is needed in American Planning? *City Planning*. Hearing Before the Committee on the District of Columbia United States Senate on the Subject of City Planning. 61st Congress, 2nd Session, Senate Document No. 422. Washington: Government Printing Office (1910), pp. 74–75.

Nolen, John (1910a) The Civic Awakening. Lecture presented at Northhampton, Massachusetts, January 25, 1910. From the Rare and Manuscript Collections, Carl A. Kroch Library, Cornell University, Ithaca, NY.

Nolen, John (1910b) Comprehensive Planning for Small Towns and Villages. Address delivered in Washington, D.C., December 15, 1910 at the Annual Meeting of the American Civic Association. From the Rare and Manuscript Collections, Carl A. Kroch Library, Cornell University, Ithaca, NY.

Nolen, John (1912) *Replanning Small Cities*. New York: Huebsch.

Nolen, John (1914) Modern town planning in America. Abstract of a paper read before the London Summer School of Town Planning, August 14. From the Rare and Manuscript Collections, Carl A. Kroch Library, Cornell University, Ithaca, NY.

Nolen, John (1916) The Effect of Land Subdivision upon Housing and Public Health. Paper presented at Second Pan American Scientific Congress, December 27, 1915 to January 8, 1916, Pan American Union, Washington, D.C. From the Rare and Manuscript Collections, Carl A. Kroch Library, Cornell University, Ithaca, NY.

Nolen, John (1927a) Twenty years of city planning progress in the United States. *National Conference on City Planning, Washington, D.C.* Philadelphia: Published for the Conference by Wm. F. Fell Co., 1926–1932, pp. 1–20. From the Rare and Manuscript Collections, Carl A. Kroch Library, Cornell University, Ithaca, NY.

Nolen, John (1927b) *New Towns for Old: Achievements in Civic Improvement in some American Small Towns and Neighborhoods.* Boston: Marshall Jones Co.

Nolen, John (1929) *City Planning: A Series of Papers Presenting the Essential Elements of a City Plan.* New York: D. Appleton and Co.

Nolen, John (Undated (a)) The Planning of Residential Neighborhoods. Abstract of address by John Nolen, City Planner. From the Rare and Manuscript Collections, Carl A. Kroch Library, Cornell University, Ithaca, NY.

Nolen, John (Undated (b)) Review of *The City of Tomorrow and its Planning*, Charles-Edouard Jeanneret Le Corbusier. Translated from the 9th edition of *Urbanisme*, with an introduction by Frederick Etchells. New York: Payson and Clarke, Ltd. From the Rare and Manuscript Collections, Carl A. Kroch Library, Cornell University, Ithaca, NY.

Nolen, Joh. (Undated (c)) Public Opinion and City Planning Progress. From the Rare and Manuscript Collections, Carl A. Kroch Library, Cornell University, Ithaca, NY.

Nolen, John (Undated (d)) Summary of Selected Projects. From the Rare and Manuscript Collections, Carl A. Kroch Library, Cornell University, Ithaca, NY.

Norberg-Schultz, Christian (1990) *Meaning in Western Architecture.* New York: Rizzoli.

Northrup, Birdsey G. (1895) The work of Village Improvement Societies. *Forum*, **19**, March, pp. 95–105.

Novak, Frank G. Jr. (ed.) (1995) *Lewis Mumford and Patrick Geddes: the Correspondence.* San Francisco: William Stout.

Nozick, Robert (1974) *Anarchy, State and Utopia.* Oxford: Basil Blackwell.

Odum, Howard W. (ed.) (1945) *In Search of the Regional Balance of America.* Chapel Hill: University of North Carolina Press.

Olmsted, Frederick C. (1870) Public parks and the enlargement of towns. Reprinted in Sutton, S.B. (ed.) (1971) *Civilizing American Cities. A Selection of Frederick Law Olmsted's Writings on City Landscapes.* Cambridge, MA: MIT Press.

Olmsted, John C. (1894) The relation of the city engineer to public parks. *Journal of the Association of Engineering Societies*, **13**, October, pp. 594–595.

Oppermann, Paul (1946) Editorial. *Journal of American Institute of Planners.* **12**(1), pp. 3–4.

Orfield, Myron (2002) *American Metropolitics: The New Suburban Reality.* Washington, D.C.: Brookings Institution Press.

Park, Robert E. (1915) The city: suggestions for the investigation of human behavior in the city environment. *American Journal of Sociology*, **20**(5), pp. 577–612.

Parker, Barry and Unwin, Raymond (1901) *The Art of Building a Home.* London: Longmans Greens.

Parsons, Kermit (1994) Collaborative genius: the Regional Planning Association of America. *Journal of the American Planning Association*, **60**(4), pp. 462–474.

Patricios, Nicholas N. (2002) Urban design principles of the original neighbourhood concepts. *Urban Morphology*, **6**(1), pp. 21–32.

Peets, Elbert (1927) Famous town planners II – Camillo Sitte. *The Town Planning Review*, December, pp. 249–259. Reprinted in Peets, Elbert and Spreiregen, Paul D. (eds.) (1968) *On the Art of Design Cities: Selected Essays of Elbert Peets.* Cambridge, MA: MIT Press, pp. 143–150.

Peets, Elbert and Spreiregen, Paul D. (eds.) (1968) *On the Art of Design Cities: Selected Essays of Elbert Peets.* Cambridge, MA: MIT Press.

Pendall, R. (1999) Do land use controls cause sprawl? *Environment and Planning B: Planning and Design*, **26**(4), pp. 555–571.

Perkins, G. Holmes (1951) The art in city planning. *Journal of the American Institute of Planners*, **17**, p. 110.

Perry, Clarence (1929) *The Neighborhood Unit: A Scheme of Arrangement for the Family-Life Community.* Regional Study of New York and its Environs, Vol. VII, Neighborhood and Community Planning, Monograph One. New York: Regional Plan of New York and its Environs, pp. 2–140

Perry, Clarence (1939) *Housing for the Machine Age.* New York: Russell Sage Foundation.

Peterson, Jon A. (1976) The City Beautiful movement: forgotten origins and lost meanings. *Journal of Urban History*, **2**, August, pp. 415–434.

Peterson, Jon A. (1996) Frederick Law Olmsted Sr. and Frederick Law Olmsted Jr.: the visionary and the professional, in Sies, Mary Corbin, and Silver, Christopher (eds.) *Planning the Twentieth Century American City.* Baltimore: Johns Hopkins University Press, pp. 37–54

Pinkney, Tony (1993) Modernism and postmodernism, in Outhwaite, William and Bottomore, Tom (eds.) *The Blackwell Dictionary of Twentieth-Century Social Thought.* Oxford: Blackwell, pp. 388–391.

Pogodzinski, J.M. and Sass, T.R. (1991) Measuring the effects of municipal zoning regulations: a survey. *Urban Studies*, **28**, pp. 597–621.

Porter, Douglas R. and Wallis, Allan D. (2003) *Exploring Ad Hoc Regionalism.* Washington, D.C.: Lincoln Institute of Land Policy.

Purdom, C. B. (ed.) (1921) *Town Theory and Practice.* London: Benn.

Pyatok, Michael (2002) The narrow base of the New Urbanists. *Planners Network*, **151**, Spring, pp. 1, 4–5.

Rasmussen, Steen Eiler (1957) A great planning achievement. *Town and Country Planning*, July.

Rayner, S. (1991) A cultural perspective on the structure and implementation of global environmental agreements. *Evaluation Review*, **15**, pp. 75–102.

Read-Miller, Cynthia (1988) *Main Street U.S.A. in Early Photographs.* New York: Dover Publications.

Reclus, Elisée (1891) *Evolution and Revolution*, 7th ed. London: W. Reeves.

Reiner, Thomas A. (1963) *The Place of the Ideal Community in Urban Planning.* Philadelphia, PA: University of Pennsylvania Press.

Relph, E. (1987) *The Modern Urban Landscape.* Baltimore: Johns Hopkins University Press.

Reps, John W. (1965) *The Making of Urban America: A History of City Planning in the United States.* Princeton, NJ: Princeton University Press.

Riis, Jacob A. (1890) *How the Other Half Lives.* New York: Charles Scribner's Sons.

Riis, Jacob A. (1901) The Making of An American. New York: Macmillan. http://www.richm ondhillhistory.org/jriis.html

Robinson, Charles Mulford (1899) Improvement in city life: aesthetic progress. *Atlantic Monthly*, **83**, June, pp. 171–185.

Robinson, Charles Mulford (1901) *The Improvement of Towns and Cities or The Practical Basis of Civic Aesthetics.* New York: G.P. Putnam's Sons.

Robinson, Charles Mulford (1903) *Modern Civic Art, or the City Made Beautiful.* New York: G. P. Putnam's Sons.

Robinson, Charles Mulford (1906a) The remaking of our cities: A summing up of the movement for making cities beautiful while they become busy and big – a chain of great civic improvements which mark a new era of urban development. *The World's Work*, **12**, October, pp. 8046–8050.

Robinson, Charles Mulford (1906b) Planning for city beauty. *Municipal Journal and Engineer*, **21**, September 5, pp. 230–231.

Rodwin, Lloyd, and Sanyal, Bishwapriya (2000) *The Profession of City Planning: Changes, Images, and Challenges 1950–2000.* New Brunswick, NJ: Center for Urban Policy Research.

Roeseler, W.G. (1982) *Successful American Urban Plans.* Lexington, MA: Lexington Books.

Rosen, Christine Meisner (1986) *The Limits of Power: Great Fires and the Process of City Growth in America.* Cambridge: Cambridge University Press.

Rossi, Aldo (1984) *The Architecture of the City.* Cambridge: MIT Press.

Rowe, Colin and Koetter, Fred (1978) *Collage City.* Cambridge, MA: MIT Press.

Rudwick, Martin (1982) Cognitive styles in geology, in Douglas, Mary (ed.) *Essays in the Sociology of Perception.* London: Routledge & Kegan Paul, pp. 219–242.

Ruskin, John (1865) *Sesame and Lilies.* London: Smith, Elder & Co.

Rybczynski, Witold (1995) *City Life.* New York: Simon & Schuster.

Rybczynski, Witold (1999) *A Clearing in the Distance: Frederick Law Olmsted and America in the Nineteenth Century*. New York: HarperFlamingo.

Rybczynski, Witold (2000) Where have all the planners gone? in Rodwin, Lloyd and Sanyal, Bishwapriya (eds.) *The Profession of City Planning: Changes, Images, and Challenges 1950–2000*. New Brunswick, NJ: Center for Urban Policy Research, pp. 210–216.

Saarinen, Eliel (1943) *The City: Its Growth, Its Decay, Its Future*. New York: Reinhold Publishing Co.

Salingaros, Nikos A. (1998) Theory of the urban web. *Journal of Urban Design*, 3, pp. 53–71.

Schaffer, Daniel (1982) *Garden Cities for America: the Radburn Experience*. Philadelphia: Temple University Press.

Schaffer, Daniel (ed.) (1988) *Two Centuries of American Planning*. London: Mansell.

Schlereth, Thomas J. (1994) Burnham's plan and Moody's Manual: city planning as progressive reform, in Krueckeberg, Donald A. (ed.) *The American Planner: Biographies and Recollections*, 2nd ed. New Brunswick, NJ: Center for Urban Policy Research, pp. 133–162.

Schubert, Dirk (2000) The neighbourhood paradigm: from garden cities to gated communities, in Freestone, Robert (ed.) *Urban Planning in a Changing World: The Twentieth Century Experience*. London: E&FN Spon, pp. 118–138.

Schultz, Stanley K. (1989) *Constructing Urban Culture: American Cities and City Planning, 1800–1920*. Philadelphia: Temple University Press.

Schuyler, David (1986) *The New Urban Landscape: The Redefinition of City Form in Nineteenth-Century America*. Baltimore: Johns Hopkins University Press.

Schuyler, David (2002) Introduction, in Parsons, Kermit C. and Schuyler, David (eds.) *From Garden City to Green City*. Baltimore: Johns Hopkins University Press, pp. 1–13.

Schuyler, Montgomery (1902) The art of city-making. *Architectural Record*, 12(5).

Schwartz, Joel (1993) *The New York Approach: Robert Moses, Urban Liberals, and Redevelopment of the Inner City*. Columbus, Ohio: Ohio State University Press.

Schwarz, M. and Thompson, M. (1990) *Divided We Stand: Redefining Politics, Technology and Social Choice*. Philadelphia: University of Pennsylvania Press.

Scott, Anne Firor (1991) *Natural Allies: Women's Associations in American History*. Urbana: University of Illinois Press.

Scott, Mel (1969) *American City Planning Since 1890*. Berkeley, CA: University of California Press.

Scruton, Roger and Jeffreys, Sophie (2001) The Future is Classical. www.opendemocracy.net.

Scudder, Vida Dutton (1912) *Socialism and Character*. Boston: Houghton Mifflin.

Sennett, Richard (1970) *The Uses of Disorder: Personal Identity and City Life*. New York: Alfred A. Knopf.

Sennett, Richard. 1990. American Cities: the Grid Plan and the Protestant Ethic. *International Social Science Journal*, 125, pp. 269–87.

Sert, Jose Luis (1944a) *Can Our Cities Survive? An ABC of Urban Problems, Their Analysis, Their Solutions*. Cambridge: Harvard University Press.

Sert, Jose Luis (1944b) The human scale in city planning, in Zucker, Paul (ed.) *New Architecture and City Planning*. New York: Philosophical Library.

Sharp, Thomas (1932) *Town and Countryside: Some Aspects of Urban and Regional Development*. London: Oxford University Press.

Sies, Mary Corbin, and Silver, Christopher (eds.) (1996) *Planning the Twentieth Century American City*. Baltimore: Johns Hopkins University Press.

Silver, Christopher (1985) Neighborhood planning in historical perspective. *Journal of the American Planning Association*, 51(2), pp. 161–174.

Silver, Christopher (1991) Revitalizing the urban South: neighborhood preservation and planning since the 1920s. *Journal of the American Planning Association*, 57(1), pp. 69–84.

Simkhovitch, Mary Kingsbury (1949) Housing, in *Here is God's Plenty: Reflections on American Social Advance*. New York: Harper and Brothers. Reprinted in Krueckeberg, Donald A. (ed.) (1994) *The American Planner: Biographies and Recollections*. New Brunswick, NJ: Center for Urban Policy Research, pp. 85–112.

Simpson, Michael (1976) Two traditions of American planning: Olmsted and Burnham. *Town Planning Review*, 47, pp. 174–179.

Simpson, Michael (1985) *Thomas Adams and the Modern Planning Movement: Britain, Canada and the United States, 1900–1940*. London: Mansell.

Sitte, Camillo (1965) *City Planning According to Artistic Principles*. Translated from the German by George R. Collins and Christiane Crasemann Collins. New York: Random House (originally published in 1889).

Smith, Carl (1995) *Urban Disorder and the Shape of Belief: The Great Chicago Fire, the Haymarket Bomb, and the Model Town of Pullman*. Chicago: University of Chicago Press.

Smith, Herbert H. (1991) *Planning America's Communities: Paradise Found? Paradise Lost?* Chicago: American Planning Association.

Smithson, Alison (1982) *The Emergence of Team X out of CIAM: Documents*. London: Team X.

Solomon, Daniel (2003) *Global City Blues*. Washington, D.C.: Island Press.

Spain, Daphne (2001) *How Women Saved the City*. Minneapolis: University of Minnesota Press.

Spirn, Anne Whiston (2000) Reclaiming common ground: water, neighborhoods, and public places, in Fishman, Robert (ed.) *The American Planning Tradition*. Washington, D.C.: The Woodrow Wilson Center Press, pp. 297–313.

Spreiregen, Paul D. (ed.) (1968) *On the Art of Designing Cities: Selected Essays of Elbert Peets*. Cambridge, MA: MIT Press.

Starr, Ellen Gates (1895) Art and Labor. From Jane Addams, *Hull-House Maps and Papers*. New York: Thomas Y. Crowell & Co., pp. 165–179.

State of New York (1926) *Report of the Commission of Housing and Regional Planning to Governor Alfred E. Smith*. Albany: J.B. Lyon Co.

Stein, Clarence (1925) Dinosaur cities. *Survey Graphic*, 7, May, pp. 134–138.

Stein, Clarence (1951) *Toward New Towns for America*. Liverpool: University Press of Liverpool.

Steiner, Frederick (2000) *The Living Landscape: An Ecological Approach to Landscape Planning*. New York: McGraw-Hill.

Steiner, Frederick R. (2002) Foreword, in Ndubisi, Forster, *Ecological Planning: A Historical and Comparative Synthesis*. Baltimore: Johns Hopkins University Press, pp. ix–xi.

Stelter, Gilbert A. (2000) Rethinking the significance of the city beautiful idea, in Freestone, Robert (ed), *Urban Planning in a Changing World*. London: E & FN Spon, pp. 98–117.

Stephenson, Bruce (2002) Review of Rogers, Millard F., Jr. (2001) *John Nolen and Mariemont: Building a New Town in Ohio*, Baltimore: John Hopkins University Press. H-Urban.

Stern, Robert A.M. 1981. La ville bourgeoise, in Stern, Robert A.M. and Massengale, John M. (eds.) *The Anglo-American Suburb*. London: Architectural Design, pp. 4–12.

Stern, Robert A.M. and Massengale, John M. (1981) *The Anglo-American Suburb*. London: Architectural Design.

Stilgoe, John R. (1988) *Borderland: Origins of the American Suburb, 1820–1939*. New Haven: Yale University Press.

Strauss, Anselm L. (1968) *The American City: A Sourcebook of Urban Imagery*. Chicago: Aldine Publishing Co.

Sudjic, Deyan (1992) *The 100 Mile City*. New York: Harcourt Brace & Co.

Survey Graphic (1925) Regional Plan Number. *Survey Graphic*, **LIV**, May 1.

Sussman, Carl (1976) *Planning the Fourth Migration: The Neglected Vision of the Regional Planning Association of America*. Cambridge: MIT Press.

Talen, Emily and Knaap, Gerrit (2003) Legalizing smart growth: an empirical study of land use regulation in Illinois. *Journal of Planning Education and Research*, 22(3), pp. 345–359.

Thomas, John L. (1994) Lewis Mumford, Benton MacKaye, and the Regional Vision. In Krueckeberg, Donald A. (ed.) *The American Planner: Biographies and Recollections*. New Brunswick, NJ: Center for Urban Policy Research, pp. 265–309.

Thomas, John L. (2000) Holding the middle ground, in Fishman, Robert (ed.) *The American Planning Tradition*. Washington, D.C.: The Woodrow Wilson Center Press, pp. 33–64.

Thomas, June Manning and Ritzdorf, Marsha (eds.) (1997) *Urban Planning and the African American Community: In the Shadows*. Thousand Oaks, CA: Sage.

Thompson, Michael, Richard Ellis and Wildavsky, Aaron (1990) *Cultural Theory*. New York: Westview Press.

Trancik, Roger (1986) *Finding Lost Space*. New York: Van Nostrand Reinhold.

Trilling, Lionel (1979) *Beyond Culture: Essays on Literature and Learning*. New York: Harcourt Brace Jovanovich.

Tunnard, Christopher (1951) Cities by design. *Journal of the American Institute of Planners*, **17**, pp. 142–150

Tunnard, Christopher (1953) *The City of Man*. New York: Charles Scribner's Sons.

Turner, Frederick Jackson. 1961. *Frontier and Section*. Englewood Cliffs, NJ: Prentice Hall.

Turner, Frederick (1995) *The Culture of Hope: A New Birth of the Classical Spirit*. New York: Free Press.

Turner, Frederick (1997) Chaos and social science, in Eve, Raymond A., Horsfall, Sara and Lee, Mary E. (eds.) *Chaos, Complexity, and Sociology: Myths, Models and Theories*. Thousand Oaks, CA: Sage Publications, Inc.

Turner, Paul V. (1977) *The Education of Le Corbusier*. New York: Garland.

Tylor, W. Russell (1939) The neighbourhood unit principle in town planning. *Town Planning Review*, 18(3), pp. 174–186.

U. S. Senate Committee on the District of Columbia (1902) *Report of the Senate Committee on District of Columbia on the Improvement of the Park System of the District of Columbia* Senate Report No. 166, 57th Congress, 1st Session. Washington D.C.: Government Printing Office. http://www.library.cornell.edu/Reps/DOCS/parkcomm.htm

U.S. Supreme Court (1926) Village of Euclid, Ohio v. Ambler Realty Co. 272 U.S. 365. Available at http://www.findlaw.com/casecode/supreme.html.

Unwin, Raymond (1909) *Town Planning in Practice: An Introduction to the Art of Designing Cities and Suburbs*. London: T. Fisher Unwin.

Van der Ryn, Sim, and Calthorpe, Peter (1986) *Sustainable Communities*. San Francisco: Sierra Club Books.

Van Nest Black, Russell (1933) *Planning for the Small American City*. Chicago: Public Administration Service.

Veiller, Lawrence (1916) Districting by municipal regulation. *Proceedings of the Eighth National Conference on City Planning, Cleveland, June 5–7, 1916*. New York: National Conference on City Planning, pp. 147–158.

Venturi, Robert, Scott Brown, Denise and Izenour, Stephen (1972) *Learning from Las Vegas*. Cambridge: MIT Press.

Veselka, Robert E. (2000) *The Courthouse Square in Texas*. Austin: University of Texas Press.

Vincent, John Heyl (1886) *The Chautauqua Movement*. Boston: Chautauqua Press.

Wackernagel, Mathis *et al.* (2002) Tracking the ecological overshoot of the human economy. *Proceedings of the National Academy of Sciences*, 99(14), pp. 9266–9271.

Ward, Edward J. (1915) *The Social Center*. New York: D. Appleton.

Ward, Stephen V. (2002) The Howard legacy, in Parsons, Kermit C. and Schuyler, David (eds.) *From Garden City to Green City*. Baltimore: Johns Hopkins University Press, pp. 222–244.

Warner (Jr.), Sam Bass (1962) *Streetcar Suburbs: The Process of Growth in Boston, 1870–1900*. Cambridge: Harvard University Press,

Warner, Sam Bass, Jr. (1987) *The Private City: Philadelphia in Three Periods of Growth*. Philadelphia: University of Pennsylvania Press.

Webber, M.M. (1963) Order in diversity: community without propinquity, in Wingo, L. (ed.) *Cities and Space: The Future Use of Urban Land*. Baltimore: Johns Hopkins University Press.

Weiss, Marc (1987) *The Rise of the Community Builders: The American Real Estate Industry and Urban Land Planning*. New York: Columbia University Press.

White, Morton and White, Lucia (1962) *The Intellectual Versus the City: From Thomas Jefferson to Frank Lloyd Wright*. Cambridge, MA: Harvard University Press.

Whitehead, A.N. (1929) *Process and Reality*. New York: Harper

Whyte, William (ed.) (1958a) *The Exploding Metropolis*. Garden City, NY: Doubleday Anchor.

Whyte, William (1958b) Urban sprawl. *Fortume*, January.

Whyte, William H. (1988) *City: Rediscovering the Center*. New York: Doubleday.

Wildavsky, A. (1973) If planning is everything, maybe its nothing. *Policy Sciences*, 4, pp. 127–153.

Wilson, Richard Guy (1979) Architecture, landscape and city planning, in Brooklyn Museum (ed.) *The American Renaissance, 1876–1917*. New York: Pantheon Books.

Wilson, William H. (1983) Moles and skylarks, in Krueckeberg, Donald A. (ed.) *Introduction to Planning History in the United States*. New Brunswick, NJ: The Center for Urban Policy Research, pp. 88–121.

Wilson, William H. (1989) *The City Beautiful Movement*. Baltimore: Johns Hopkins University Press.

Wilson, William H. (1994) Planning and urban form in the twentieth-century United States: A review article. *Town Planning Review*, 65(3), pp. 305–311.

Wirka, Susan Marie (1996) The city social movement: progressive women reformers and early social planning, Sies, Mary Corbin and Silver, Christopher (eds.) *Planning the Twentieth-Century American City*. Baltimore: Johns Hopkins University Press, pp. 55–75.

Wirth, Louis (1938) Urbanism as a way of life. *American Journal of Sociology*, 44, pp. 1–24.

Woods, Robert (ed.) (1898) *The City Wilderness*. Boston: Houghton Mifflin.

Wright, Frank Lloyd (1932) *The Disappearing City*. New York: William Farquhar Payson.

Wright, Henry (1929) Some Principles Relating to the Economics of Land Subdivision. Published by the American City Planning Institute, 12 p. Preprint No. 1, November.

Wright, Henry (1935) *Rehousing Urban America*. New York: Columbia University Press.

Yeomans, Alfred B. (1916) *City Residential Land Development: Studies in Planning*. Chicago: University of Chicago Press.

Zueblin, Charles (1903) The civic renascence: 'The White City' and after. *Chautauquan*, 38, December, pp. 373–384.

Zukin, Sharon (1995) *The Cultures of Cities*. Oxford: Blackwell.

Index

9 780415 701334